THATCH

Thatching in England 1790–1940

ENGLISH HERITAGE

ENGLISH HERITAGE RESEARCH TRANSACTIONS
RESEARCH AND CASE STUDIES IN ARCHITECTURAL CONSERVATION

THATCH
Thatching in England 1790–1940

James Moir & John Letts

Volume **5**
November 1999

First published by James & James (Science Publishers) Ltd, 35–37 William Road, London NW1 3ER, UK

A catalogue record for this book is available from the British Library
ISBN 1 873936 95 8
ISSN 1461 8613

Authors: James Moir and John Letts
Volume editor: Nicholas Molyneux
Series editor: David Mason
Consultant editor: Kate Macdonald

Printed in the UK by Alden Group Ltd

Front cover
Thatchers working on the roof, Falmer Tithe Barn, Falmer, Sussex (English Heritage).

Contents

Acknowledgements   *vii*
Foreword   *ix*
Preface   *xi*

PART I DEMAND AND DECLINE   1
Chapter 1 Introduction   3
Chapter 2 Urban thatch   9
Chapter 3 Rural thatch: the northern and
  Midland counties   13
  Stone slates   15
  Pantiles   16
  Tiles   16
  Imported slate   17
Chapter 4 Rural thatch: the south   18
  The south west   18
  The south east   18
  The south   18
    Phase 1: 1790–*c* 1840   19
    Phase 2: *c* 1840–90   21
    Phase 3: 1890–1940   21
Chapter 5 Thatch and new-build   24
    Phase 1: 1790–1840   24
    Phase 2: 1840–90   28
    Phase 3: 1890–1940   29
Chapter 6 Conclusion   37

**PART II THATCHING MATERIALS AND
THEIR SUPPLY**   39
Chapter 7 Materials and habitats   41
  Introduction   41
  Woodland and coppice   41
    Wood shavings   41
  Grassland and pasture   42
  Dry wasteland   42
    Coastal foreshore and sand dune   42
  Wet wasteland   45
    Moorland and bog   46
    Coastal salt marsh   46
    Fen and fringing reed swamp   46
    Managed fen   48
  The water reed industry from 1890 to 1940   53
    Growers   53
    Harvest   54
    Purchasing reed   55
  Cultivated crops   57
    Flax   57
    Cereal straw   58
    The industrial revolution and   58
      Parliamentary enclosure (1790–1840)
    Agricultural improvement   58

The late nineteenth-century agricultural   60
  depression (1840–90)
  The cultivation of land races   60
  Agricultural improvement   61
  Botanical changes in straw   62
The mechanization of cereal harvesting and   68
  threshing
    Reaping   69
    Stubble thatch   70
    Mowing   72
    Hand threshing and combing   73
    Drawing crushed straw (long straw)   79
    The threshing machine   81
    The mechanized production of reed straw   83
    The straw trusser   85
    The specialist straw producer   86
Chapter 8 Fixings   87
  Spars and sways   87
  Rope and cordage   88
  Turf and clay   89

PART III THATCHING TECHNIQUES   91
Chapter 9 Performance and technical change   93
  Locality   93
  Performance criteria   93
    Pitch   94
    Material quality and longevity   96
    Orientation   98
    Maintenance   99
  Heathland and 'solid' thatch   101
    Broom *(Cytisus scoparius)*   101
    Heather *(Calluna vulgaris)*   101
    Bracken *(Pteridium aquilinum)*   102
    Gorse *(Ulex europaeus)*   103
    Solid thatch   103
  Thatching with water reed   104
    Water reed *(Phragmites australis)*   104
    Written evidence   108
    Archaeological evidence   108
    Fleeking   108
    External thatch   110
    Spar coating with reed   110
    The traditional Norfolk ridge   111
  Reed-thatching tools   112
    Measuring water reed   112
    Conclusions   113
  Flax *(Linum usitatissimum)*   113
  Thatching with straw   113
    Reed straw   113
    Crushed straw   120

The archaeology of ancient thatch   128
   Recording thatch *in situ*   128
   Dating   129
   Analysis and interpretation   130
   Straw thatching in England: the *in situ*   131
   evidence

PART IV THATCHERS   **139**
Chapter 10 Phase 1: 1790–1840   141
Chapter 11 Phase 2: 1840–1890   143
Chapter 12 Phase 3: 1890–1940   145
   Estate and house thatchers   145
   Smallholders   146
   Rick-thatching and DIY   147
    Ricks   147
    Transmission of tradition   148

The impoverishment of tradition   153
   The water reed firms   153
   Estate/house thatchers   153
   Smallholders   155
   Conclusion   156
The Rural Industries Bureau and the   156
   discovery of thatchers
   Phase 1: 1909–20   156
   Phase 2: 1921–26   157
   Phase 3: *c* 1925–32   157
   Phase 4: 1933–39   157
Chapter 13 Conclusion   158

Appendix A Buildings excavated and sampled   163
Appendix B Additional buildings visited   200
Glossary   210
Bibliography   211

Acknowledgements

This enquiry into the history of thatching would not have been possible without the generous cooperation of a long list of home owners, thatchers, straw growers, conservation officers, building historians, agricultural historians, botanists, archivists, librarians and researchers from many other fields who brought interesting roofs and historical and technical information to our attention. It would be impossible to thank all of these people individually, and we apologize in advance to those whose names have been left off the list in error or for lack of space.

We are very grateful to the staff of the Public Record Office (London), the London Guildhall Library, the North West Sound Archive (Lancashire), the Rural History Centre (University of Reading), county record offices, local studies libraries and museums with rural life collections who responded to requests for documentary sources on thatching. The Bedfordshire Record Office was particularly helpful and instrumental in facilitating access to the unique unpublished work of Thomas Bagshawe. The authors are particularly grateful to Nicholas and Richard Bagshawe for access to their father's collection of papers. Keith Scholey provided invaluable assistance with the analysis of the Bedfordshire material. Dr Jo Cox provided access to unpublished data on thatching in Devon and the post-1940 period.

Thatchers throughout England provided access to roofs for sampling purposes, with particular help being provided by Rod Miller (Dorset), John Cousins (Suffolk), Keith Quantrill (Bedfordshire), Chris White (Buckinghamshire), Roger Scanlan (Northamptonshire), Malcolm and Arthur Dodson (Huntingdonshire), Nick Mackay (Buckinghamshire), Jack Lewis (Somerset) Paul Norman (Somerset), Arthur Hannabus (Devon), Kit Davis (Oxfordshire), Bob and Alistair West (Berkshire), Jeff Thame (Devon), Brian Hummerstone (Devon), Chris Bovey (Devon), Tim Cox (Suffolk), David Farman (Norfolk), David Tresize (Devon), Nicolas Mustiere (Brittany), Allan Fuchs (Dorset), Alfred Howard (Devon), Steven Letch (Suffolk), Chris Stanford (Cambridgeshire) and David Barton (Oxfordshire).

Straw growers such as Ian White (Devon), Richard Wright (Somerset) and Mick Godfrey (Berkshire) provided valuable insights on production methods and cereal varieties. Mick, in particular, provided essential background knowledge, field space and a practical approach during two years of preliminary field trials of several hundred old wheat varieties at his farm in Berkshire. Dr Sylvia Haslam (Cambridgeshire) and Charles Cater (Norfolk) provided similar insights on the botanical and commercial basis of the water reed industry in the Norfolk Broads, while Dr Joe Kirby provided both published and unpublished data on his research on the decay processes which occur in thatched roofs. Nedd German, Dr Andre Pydyn (Oxford) and Dr Nigel Gilmour assisted with some of the sampling. Building historians, conservation officers and planners such as Michel Kerrou (Northamptonshire County Council), Pam Slocombe and April Waterman (Wiltshire County Council), John Lowe (Dorset County Council) and various members of the Vernacular Architecture Group provided contacts and background information on buildings, archival sources and local policy.

This report has benefited immensely from comparative data generated over the past two years by a research project on the history of thatching in Ireland funded jointly by the Environment and Heritage Service of the Department of the Environment (Northern Ireland) and the Department of Arts, Culture and the Gaehltact (Republic of Ireland). Similarly, this report draws extensively on research undertaken on medieval smoke-blackened thatch in southern England published jointly by the Ancient Monuments Laboratory (English Heritage) and the University of Reading (1999).

The history of thatching can be understood only if it is examined using an interdisciplinary approach rooted in practical common sense and experience, a fact understood to a unique degree by the late Peter Brockett. Peter was an undisputed expert in the craft, a patient instructor and a good friend who visited his last thatched roof in 1996. He brought numerous issues and unusual roofs to our attention, and provided introductions to thatchers and straw growers throughout England. Although this report has benefited immensely from his input, it will forever suffer deficiencies due to the fact that he was never able to comment on its final version.

Dr James Moir
Chiltern Open Air Museum
Newland Park
Gorelands Lane
Chalfont St. Giles
Buckinghamshire HP8 4AD

John B Letts
Department of Agricultural
Botany
Plant Science Laboratories
The University of Reading
Whiteknights, PO Box 221
Reading, RG6 6AS

The two *Thatching in England* volumes were commissioned by Nicholas Molyneux and David Brock, English Heritage Inspectors of Historic Buildings, on behalf of English Heritage. Chris Wood of English Heritage's Building Conservation & Research team coordinated the work of the authors and the editor.

All sources for Figures and data for Tables are given in brackets in their captions. Please refer to the Bibliography for textual souces. All sources, originators and/or copyright holders are given where known. Every effort has been made to trace copyright holders, but English Heritage would be glad to receive any information updating the present list.

Foreword

This volume, and the next in the series, *Thatching in England 1940–1990*, hold the results of two research projects commissioned by English Heritage in 1993 to establish the history of thatch and thatching in England.

The stimulus for the work of James Moir and John Letts, presented in this volume, resulted from concern surrounding the future of thatching as an industry, trade, craft or art in England. These concerns also form part of the continuing story elucidated by Jo Cox's research, published in the 1940–90 volume (vol 6). The combination of pressures upon thatchers from the conservation profession, most notably in those areas where there were conservation conflicts between the use of water reed and wheat straw, as well as the use of combed wheat reed versus long straw, was also significant. Another impetus for the research was created by John Letts's work on medieval smoke-blackened thatch (funded in part by English Heritage's Ancient Monuments Laboratory), which showed that some surviving roofs contained an important archaeobotanical resource. This revelation was of high significance for European archaeobotanical work. This work has been published separately, jointly sponsored by English Heritage and the University of Reading (Letts 1999).

As a result English Heritage decided to commission research into the more recent history of thatch. Whereas the initial study of smoke-blackened thatch was intended primarily as a study in archaeobotany, because of the great interest of the physical survival of early plant material, the roots of the two *Thatching in England* volumes lay in a practical desire to understand a history which has been unusually clouded by myth and controversy. In few occupations can there be so much consciousness of tradition, but so little firm information about past techniques and materials. The study was therefore to be one in which a narrative would be paramount, but the account should also rely, wherever possible, on archaeological evidence. It was undertaken in two parts, breaking the story at 1940, so as to cover the agricultural changes in the first study (1790–1940) and the period of living memory (1940–90) in the second. Initial findings were presented at a conference which English Heritage arranged jointly with the Department for Continuing Education at the University of Oxford in May 1995.

The work has revealed, alongside the emerging evidence from smoke-blackened thatch, that there was a much more complex picture than had previously been recognised, and that the apparently ephemeral material of thatch has not only left extensive traces in the archives, but also survives in substantial quantities, though not so much for water reed thatch, on roofs from the medieval period onwards.

Another revelation has been the rediscovery of the remarkable oral history and associated recording work

undertaken in Bedfordshire in the 1940s by Thomas Bagshawe, which gives a unique snapshot of a county's thatching tradition. This could easily be reproduced as a local study today, and as can be seen from Bagshawe's work it could produce very valuable information on the state of the industry at a given moment. The absence of comparable material for other counties points up the fact that the research reported here cannot by any means be regarded as the last word on the matter.

There is an obvious chronological gap, between this work and Letts' (1999), in which there is much material to be studied. In research terms, Moir's innovative work with insurance records provides a very interesting methodological step forward, clearly demonstrating that there is a major untapped source here for broad-brush building history which would repay a great deal of further study. The researchers have only been able to scratch the surface of some of the sources, so further studies on a national and regional scale would be very valuable.

Longevity has long been one of the major themes of writers on thatch, and it is clear from this and the next volume that this would merit research. Letts has shown the extent to which this question relates to the length of the straw, but we know that the factors are so varied and complex as to almost defy quantification. Examples from the three main modern thatching techniques have survived for more than fifty years, and roofs with smoke-blackened thatch have lasted for at least 400 years, so this can be hardly be thought of as a short-lived material, particularly when the comparative longevity of non-traditional modern roofing techniques are considered.

A lacuna in the research is the result of the emphasis on water reed and wheat straw, the major surviving materials on roofs. This has led to an inevitable southern focus in part of the work since this is where the vast preponderance of surviving thatched buildings are located in England. However, the research does include all the materials known to have been used for thatching English roofs. There is thus scope for more research in the Midlands and north of England on this almost vanished tradition.

There have been a number of other recent advances in scientific research and practical guidance on thatch and thatching: the Building Research Establishment, in collaboration with the late Peter Brockett (to whom all thatching historians owe a tremendous debt), looking at the issue of accelerated south slope decay; the work of RHM Technology on fire prevention (Angold et al 1998); the work of West Dorset District Council in their flexible applications of the Building Regulations to accommodate new thatched buildings; and the BRE work looking at the ventilation needs of new thatch. There has also been recent research on the historical and archaeological aspects of thatch and thatching in Ireland (by Letts) and the work in Scotland reported in two recent publications (Walker et al 1996; Holden 1998).

The research reported here, and the contacts established with the thatching industry, has formed the major part of the background to the production of English Heritage's Guidance Note (published simultaneously with this volume). This seeks to provide a framework for the preservation of our historic thatch and thatching traditions within the overarching historic building legislation and guidance.

Copies of the original research report on which this volume is based have been deposited in the library of English Heritage at 23 Savile Row, London, UK. These include detailed appendices listing sources identified at county level in the course of the work, which can be made available to local researchers, in conjunction with further advice on useful directions for further research.

Nicholas A D Molyneux
October 1999

Preface

His tears run down his beard
like winter's drops, from eaves of reeds.
The Tempest, Act 5, Scene 1, 16

In recent years a debate has raged between sections of the thatching industry and the building conservation community over changes in the materials and methods used in thatching. These changes, it is suggested, have damaged the heritage value and aesthetic appeal of many listed buildings and local communities which conservationists are duty-bound to safeguard. It is a debate that has hitherto been subject to great confusion, misinterpretation and speculation, and it was to rectify the deficiency in reliable pre-1940 data on the topic that research for this volume was initiated by English Heritage.

With the assistance of thatchers, conservation officers, building historians, straw growers, home owners and experts from a variety of fields, a detailed history of thatching in England from 1790 to 1940 has been compiled which examines the general, albeit tortuous, decline of thatch as a roof covering in the light of the changes that occurred over this period in the supply of thatching materials and the manner in which they were applied. All English County Record Offices, local studies libraries and museums with rural life collections were consulted, and visits made to selected repositories such as the Public Record Office (for information on government agencies), the Guildhall Library in London (for insurance records), the British Library and the Rural History Centre at the University of Reading. The application of an archaeological approach to the study of thatched roofs in conjunction with documentary research was a new development, and the results of this enquiry indicate that ancient accumulations of thatch can provide a wealth of data unavailable from other sources. This evidence must be evaluated using an interdisciplinary approach based on a solid understanding of thatching techniques and agricultural botany as much as architectural history. For this report, more than thirty thatched roofs from the main thatching districts were excavated and another sixty surveyed and evaluated in the light of historical, botanical and ethnographic data.

The results confirm the much-suspected prevalence of straw thatching throughout most of the country during this period. Most of the evidence recovered relates to the use of reed straw, now called combed wheat reed, in the West Country, and to forms of crushed straw akin to modern long straw that were used in southern England outside the West Country. More surprisingly, the evidence also demonstrates widespread use of stubble and unbruised, full-length halm straw in southern England and the Midlands prior to c 1850. Within these distinctive traditions lie hybrid methods and materials that reflect the

nineteenth-century thatchers' abilities to craft various types of straw into a coat of thatch that could keep out the rain. The historical data also confirms the use of water reed as a thatching material in wetland and coastal districts where it was abundant, but little ancient reed thatch survives *in situ* for a variety of reasons. However, the *in situ* and botanical evidence confirms the widespread use of wetland and heathland materials such as fen sedge, gorse and rushes for base coats, main coats and fixings, at least until the mid nineteenth century by which time enclosure, underdrainage and the expansion of arable and pasture lands had largely eliminated alternatives to straw and water reed from the repertoire of available materials. The skills needed to apply these alternatives were lost as generations of potential thatchers left the countryside for the promise of a life in the city, free from the drudgery of drawing straw and spar making.

An inability to distinguish between the various kinds of thatching dogs attempts to unravel both historical and contemporary perceptions. The evidence suggests that considerable interest was shown in improving methods of straw thatching in the early nineteenth century, with particular attention being given to West Country methods and materials. Relatively little attention was paid to water reed, but by early this century support had shifted and it had been widely adopted by architects. This expansion was fuelled by the transformation of local water reed production in Norfolk into a national industry that could rapidly incorporate technical and stylistic change. Thatchers were able to adjust to changes in straw over most of the period under review, but the introduction of the combine harvester and shorter-stemmed hybrid wheat varieties severed the ancient link between farmer and thatcher. As a result, the craft of straw thatching declined to a point of near collapse by 1940; a date well within living memory and the *terminus ante quem* of this enquiry. That it survived is clear judging by the number of thatched roofs that continue to grace the English countryside, but many traditions have been abandoned in the quest for a viable modern profession. It is with this rationale that ancient long straw, stubble, halm and reed straw roofs throughout England are being stripped and rethatched with combed wheat reed and imported water reed.

This research will hopefully provide the basis for a more enlightened debate on the pre-1940 history of the craft, and will encourage thatching and conservation bodies to forge a common strategy for recording and conserving English thatching traditions before many more examples are destroyed.

Part I

Demand and decline

1 Introduction

Since I came home, as I this country view
The towns, the fields, now everything is new;
The old thatched cottages have ta'en their flight,
And new til'd houses now appear in sight;
But when the town of Kilham first I saw
The walls were mostly clay, and thatched with straw.
'The Sailor' by E Anderson, 1811. (Harrison 1989, 149)

Take virtually any published source printed between 1790 and 1940 touching on the subject of thatch and the message is clear: thatch is disappearing, thatch is on its way out, thatch has no future. The authors of the County Agricultural Reports published at the beginning of the period under review were particularly gloomy in their predictions as the following excerpts illustrate:

[Berkshire] Too many of the outhouses and barns are still thatched, a mode of covering not less dangerous than expensive, if the frequency of repairs be taken into account. The practice, however, is gradually discontinuing, and in another age will probably become obsolete. (Mavor 1809, 67)

[Northumberland] Straw used to be the universal covering, but it is now nearly fallen into disuse, and tiles or slates substituted in its stead. (Bailey & Culley 1800, 28)

(See also Young 1807 **1**, 49; Farey 1811 **2**, 14; Rudge 1813, 45; Pitt 1813, 27.)

Compare these statements, referring to Northamptonshire and covering a span of 130 years:

A great many farm-houses, as well as out-buildings, are covered with thatch; this, it is to be hoped, will, by degrees, be changed for the more substantial and safe covering of tile or slate. (Pitt 1809a, 26)

Of all these village industries, that of the 'thatcher' (or thacker) is most likely to disappear from our village life unless people re-awaken to the beauty of a nicely-thatched old stone cottage with perhaps a quick-set hedge enclosing a riot of colour in its flower bed, and perhaps with a lovely background of elms, elders, beeches, or other trees. (Nightingale 1939, iv)

The novelty of the prediction that thatch is doomed has perhaps begun to wear off slightly. There were always a

few sceptics, such as W Thomas of Dorset, who, on the eve of the Second World War, wrote:

When my father started to learn thatching from my grandfather, someone said to him, 'If I were you I wouldn't let my boy learn thatching, as by the time he knows the way to do the job, all thatching will have died out'. That was nearly seventy years ago. I have a son who has just learnt the thatching, but I have not had that remark made to me. (Thomas 1940, 470)

The simple perception that a roofing material which was once universal in this country is now a rare species is still deep-rooted. In most commentators' minds this probably translates into a simple graph showing the number of thatched buildings plummeting in a straight line. It would, of course, be absurd to argue that thatch did not once feature much more widely as a roof covering in a national context (Fig 1). In 1790 there were few parts of England where it could not be found. This includes areas where other roofing materials predominated, because thatch could still be found on ancillary buildings even after it had been displaced from the majority of dwellings. Some heavily populated urban areas could nevertheless still find room for examples, while some smaller market towns certainly could still have a predominantly thatched aspect: 'I estimate Daventry to contain 600 houses ... several thatched houses, even in the principal parts of the town' (Pitt 1809a, 298).

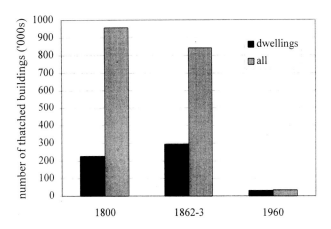

Figure 1 Histogram of numbers of thatched buildings for 1800, 1862-3 and 1960 (after Guildhall Library, London, 1, 2 and 3, and Public Record Office 17).

Not only was thatch a more widespread roofing material in 1790 than is the case today, it could also be found on a wider range of building types. Where once a large proportion of thatched buildings had no domestic function, today the position is reversed, and very few secondary buildings with thatched roofs survive.

In 1790, non-thatched buildings of any kind were rarities in some villages.

> The village [Naseby, Northamptonshire] contains a good many dwelling-houses and other buildings, all of which I observed built with mud and covered with thatch, except the church and two dwellings, one of which seemed the parsonage. The principal inn I saw [the Bell] built and covered with the afore-named materials. The walls of many of the houses apparently shivering under the pressure, and seeming to indicate that a small force or weight additional would convert them and their contents into a ruinous heap. (op cit, 305)

Pitt's comments are of interest because, to him, status tended to be conferred on a building through the nature of the walling material rather than what was used on the roof.

> Geddington is a large village, containing the whole population of the parish of 4 or 5,000 acres. Inferior houses, mud walls, and thatch; many stone-walls and thatch, and a few of the best, stone-walls and slate. (op cit, 309)

At the beginning of our period, therefore, thatch did not necessarily indicate lowly status. Despite the comments of many of the other authors of the County Reports (whose job it was to sell the concept of agricultural improvement), the cognitive map of the majority of the population was still only on the verge of being influenced by the chocolate-box cottage image which dominates the public perception of thatch today.

At the end of the eighteenth century a number of substantial buildings could still be found roofed with thatch. In the limestone belt, a small gentry house like East Haddon Hall retains its thatch to this day (Palmer 1978, 41). In his study of the Banbury region Wood-Jones (1963, 82–4) noted that Hornton Manor, Oxford-shire was covered with thatch and that it was used even on large houses in this central part of the region. The Manor House at Alford, Lincolnshire 'is believed to be the largest manor house in the country with a thatched roof' (G Greenhill pers comm, Fig 2).

Apart from the gentry house, the other dominant institution of eighteenth-century rural society was the church. Thatched churches were evidently viewed as indicators of needy conditions, for Robert Bloomfield, the Suffolk rural poet of the last years of the eighteenth century, refers in his 'Farmer's Boy' to the thatched church of the village: 'The rude inelegance of poverty/Reigns here; else why that roof of straw?' (Harper 1921, 392).

East Anglia is nevertheless still home to many thatched examples. In Norfolk in the first half of the nineteenth century, some '270 churches were thatched as may be seen in the Dawson Turner drawings and Ladbrooke lithographs, but considerable numbers lost this form of covering later in the same century - particularly during the last 30–40 years.' (Deas 1939, 89). In 1939 Deas counted about fifty examples. Jobson (1961, 494, 504) could only find some two dozen out of the 500 churches of ancient foundation in Suffolk which were thatched

Figure 2   Thatched gentry house. The Manor House, Alford, Lincolnshire (Neil Poulson).

and therefore reckoned 'that Norfolk heads the list with about 60 thatched churches and Suffolk comes next. There are only about 10 others for the remainder of England' (see also Harper 1921, 390; Ward 1960, 1508; Ward 1963, 226; Sandon 1977, 18) .

The precise numbers of surviving churches are perhaps less significant than their very limited distribution in the country when compared to the picture in the eighteenth century. According to Mackenzie (1825 **1**, 392) most of the houses of eighteenth-century Wooler, Northumberland, had unspecified forms of thatched roofs, and, prior to a fire in the 1760s, the church had been 'a mean thatched building'. James Allgood arrived as rector in 1705 in the neighbouring parish of Ingram. Writing to his bishop in that year, he remarked that:

> We have taken off the thatch of the church to have it slated but the very walls and timber are so much decayed that it will take a considerable time to repair. (Hay nd)

Other institutional buildings at this time which might be thatched were the parish workhouses, almshouses or other philanthropic housing schemes (Vancouver 1813, 71). Wherever thatch was the dominant roofing material, examples of virtually any kind of institutional building using it as a covering could be found. One intriguing insurance policy for 1862–3 (Guildhall Library 11937[cd527] 1862–3) taken out by Elizabeth Stafford of Doddington, Cambridgeshire, was designed to protect a thatched building 'lately used as a schoolroom now a Surgery'.

In 1790 little correlation can be found between rural building types and the presence or absence of thatch. Thatch remained the predominant roofing material for parsonage houses across much of Norfolk until the end of the eighteenth century. Lucas (1995, 92–3) shows that whereas nearly half the parsonage houses were thatched in 1794, a hundred years later virtually all were roofed with slate or pantiles. The 'barns etc' which belonged to them also followed a similar pattern but on a less dramatic scale and at a slower pace of replacement. Because of the unique status of parsonage buildings, it would of course be misleading to draw any wider conclusions about thatch replacement levels in the county as a whole.

Though many farmhouses created in this period out of the Enclosure movement followed the latest fashion in house design, nevertheless the ones erected when the Mendip Hills were enclosed were 'built with stone, and generally thatched, the inconvenience of which is severely felt, for the moisture of the air, and the powerful effects of the wind, render frequent repairs necessary' (Billingsley 1798, 86–7).

Below farmhouse level, there was a huge inheritance in 1790 of smaller thatched cottages. Some were very primitive as noted by Worgan in his section on cottages in the county report for Cornwall:

> It may be truly said, these are very humble dwellings indeed; of the same materials as the old farmhouses, with only two or three apartments, the upper one immediately under the thatch. I had occasion often, in my dreary walks, during my Survey, to take shelter in some of these miserable dwellings, and found the poor inhabitants busy in placing their bowls, crocks, and pans to catch the waters pouring in at the roof. (Worgan 1811, 26)

At the opposite end of the country, Dickson was equally unenthusiastic about the practice in the Fylde, Lancashire of constructing cottages

> on wattled stud-work with a composition of well-wrought loamy clay and cut straw, or what is locally termed clat and clay. The covering material in these instances is almost invariably thatch prepared from wheaten straw, which is considered as rendering them more warm and comfortable in winter, and more cool in summer, than any other substance that can be conveniently employed. These sorts of cottages have seldom more than a divided ground floor, which with their brown sombre colour, gives them a mean hovel-like appearance far from agreeable, and affords but little accommodation. (Dickson & Stevenson 1815, 104)

But some cottages were also architect-designed for estate landlords using vernacular materials. Pitt, for example, recommended 'the design for a double cottage, given by Mr Holland, and published by the Board is extremely simple; ... and might either be thatched or covered with slate' (1809a, 29).

> In the village of Pottersbury, and other places upon the Duke of Grafton's estate, considerable attention has been paid to the accommodation of the cottagers; the cottages are built of stone-walls and thatch, and let, as I was informed by Mr Roper, at less than forty shillings [£2] per annum each; but comfort to the occupiers and not outward appearance, is the object in view. They are built in an oblong row, forming the side of a street, with conveniences beneath and two or more lodging-rooms to each. (op cit, 30–31)

Beyond dwellings and institutional buildings, it is primarily in the sphere of ancillary, non-domestic structures where it is so easy to underestimate the tremendous variety of applications where thatch was once employed. M Wight's photographs of 1936 (Walton 1975, 43), showing the manufacture of Collyweston slates being carried out under a thatched screen propped up at an angle, is a chance survival illustrating just one example of the kind of temporary structures littering the English countryside in this period. The insurance policy sample for 1800 (see Bibliography, 216) gives a much more detailed picture of the extent of the diversity of thatched structures.

Joseph Brown of St Nicholas, Suffolk, for instance, had a 'stud and thatched' neathouse, clearly of some quality as it was insured for £25. William Bright of Tarrant Hinton, Dorset, actually included a thatched garden wall in the insurance policy he took out on a house he owned in the village. In most cases, such small structures are probably encompassed by the more general terms of 'offices', 'outhouses' or 'sheds'. These might include fuel-, wood- or coalhouses. In parts of Yorkshire, heather was used to cover fuel stocks (Hartley & Ingilby 1968, 166).

The County Reports show a similar picture. In Wiltshire:

> Stones and lime being in general scarce in this district, most of the fence walls, and sometimes the walls of the stables and other out-buildings are built with 'mud' viz the chalky loam of the country mixed with short straw. The expense of these is trifling, seldom exceeding 10s [50p] for a perch long and six feet high. They are usually covered with straw. (Davis 1811, 13; see also Pitt 1809b, 26 and Stevenson 1812, 86)

In towns and villages, craftsmen, shopkeepers and traders kept their wares in or operated from a range of workshops. William Tomlinson's ironmongers shop in Kirkham, Lancashire, was thatched, as was William Thring's bakehouse in Quidhampton, Wiltshire, and Sarah Walker's weaving shop in Lyme, Dorset. Some of these buildings were clearly quite large, and are a reminder that the early industries or proto-industries which flourished, particularly in the south of England in the seventeenth and eighteenth centuries (tanning, cloth working and the like), did not turn their backs on thatch as the later factories of the Industrial Revolution would do in the north. A clothier and carrier of Bow, Devon, worked from a thatched sizing house and stable with an air-drying loft over. Isaac Richards, a sailcloth maker in Odcombe, Somerset, owned a thatched workshop with

Figure 3   Thatched industrial building: a late nineteenth-century Birmingham nailshop, Henry Pope (Birmingham Museums & Art Gallery).

offices adjoining. Thomas Gotch's warehouse in Kettering, Northamptonshire was thatched, as was the shoemaker's workshop in Guisingthorpe, Essex, a tarhouse and 'Workhouse' for twine manufacture in Bridport, Dorset, a slaughterhouse in Wellington, Somerset, and a range of specialist structures in a tanner's yard in Donington, Berkshire, including a bark barn, beamhouse, drying shed, leather house and drying loft. Solomon Fountain's wheelwright's shop at Buckland in Buckinghamshire was thatched, as was Richard Painter's carpenter's shop and saw house at Brightwalton, Berkshire, and Daniel Burton's

Figure 4   Thatched farm with outbuildings (Illustrated London News, 19 February 1867, Museum of English Rural Life).

blacksmith's shop at High Easter, Essex. John Cooper, a bricklayer, also owned a brickworks in Maidenhead, Berkshire, and the brick-drying shed and tile house were described as thatched (Fig 3).

Inns and alehouses often had thatched ancillary buildings listed; these might include a brewhouse or more substantial malting offices. Many farms and larger houses also had their own malthouses. James Taylor's oasthouse at Healstow, Kent was thatched. In the West Country, we find the equivalent cider houses (East Stower, Dorset) and pound houses (Dalwood, Dorset). Thomas and Charles May's cooperage at Basingstoke, Hampshire was thatched.

Agriculturalists were of course more at home with thatch than any other sector of the population. Temporary thatch was applied to ricks and even to stooks or shocks, Thomas Batchelor referring in 1808 to 'the precaution which is adopted in some parts of England, of covering the shocks with other sheaves spread into a kind of thatch' (Batchelor 1808, 374). Thatch was also used extensively for covering crops and other organic materials when stacked or stored in the open.

The more durable farm buildings in the 1800s represented a huge array of thatched structures (Fig 4), from Thomas Poulton's henhouse in St Michael's parish, Hertfordshire, through to James Poynter's large barn 'with two floors' at Upper Deal, Kent. In mixed arable areas in particular, the range of thatched buildings that might be encountered in a typical courtyard layout of the period was impressive. Stonewall Farm, Bosham, Sussex in 1862–3 had a completely thatched steading with a barn on the north side of the courtyard, calfpens and a fowlhouse on the east side, stable and pigpen on the west side, and a cartshed on the south side (Guildhall Library 3).

Barns tended to remain thatched long after other buildings had had their roof coverings replaced. There was some prejudice against using alternative materials. In Surrey, for example, 'the barns and other buildings are generally covered with thatch ... some barns are built with brick and tiled, but are found not to be so good for the grain' (Malcolm et al 1794, 61). In arable districts, the degree to which crops were housed rather than ricked tended to determine the size of the barns and therefore the surface area of thatch required.

Edmund Tapper of Whiteparish, Wiltshire had a 'stavel' barn, of the kind described by Vancouver and particularly popular in the counties of Hampshire and Wiltshire.

> A very excellent practice seems to be fast gaining ground ... of building wheat barns, as well as corn stacks in general, upon stone stands or staddles. The barns thus constructed are usually of beech, elm and fir-boards, with oak, beech or elm plank for thrashing-floors; the other part of the bottom of the barn or mows may be formed of any other old and useless planks or boards. These barns are sometimes covered with tile, but more frequently thatched. (Vancouver 1813, 64)

Joshua Lilley of Bourn, Cambridgeshire, stored his wheat in a simple thatched 'hovel', while John Foster of Hambledon, Hampshire distinguished in his policy between a thatched 'rickhouse' and a 'rick barn'. Ridgway

Newland of Farnham, Surrey had a thatched 'strawhouse'; John Bridge's barn at Winford Eagle, Dorset was described as both 'new' and, early for its time, 'housing a threshing machine'. 'Roundhouses' such as that belonging to Rev John Rowe of Wellington, Somerset, also begin to make an appearance. John Farey gives a description of a threshing machine and horse-engine house at Union Farm, Ashby, Leicestershire in 1811. The machine cost 100 Guineas (£105). 'Of Bricks and Lime and laying ditto 7*l* and a Thatch-roofing to the Horse-walk 15*l*, in all 127*l*' (Farey 1811, **2**, 54). Another architectural novelty of the early nineteenth century was the skeleton barn, thrown up to meet the expansion in wheat production during the Napoleonic Wars. Arthur Young describes and illustrates a thatched example in the Essex County Report (Young 1807 **1**, 306–8, pl 3), similar to the one described in Appendix A (A3 Berkshire).

Between the henhouse and the barn were many other farm structures for housing implements and animals. Horses were accommodated in thatched stables in Braughing, Hertfordshire, and in 'team stables' and 'horse lodges' (Chilston, Kent), 'great stables' and 'nag stables' (Eastrop, Hampshire). As late as 1862, a thatched ox shed was insured at Charlton Abbots, Gloucestershire. Cows were housed in 'beasthouses' (Winstantow, Shropshire), 'cowhouses' (Swanbourne, Buckinghamshire), 'cowpens' (Lower Wallop, Hampshire), 'calfpens' (Bodenham, Wiltshire), 'calves houses' (Stour Provost, Dorset), 'fatting pounds' (Chilston, Kent) 'linhays' (Dalwood, Dorset) and 'skillings' (Whiteparish, Wiltshire). An 1831 report on the state of buildings at Northwood Farm, Pillfoot in the parishes of Hibaldstow and Redbourne, Lincolnshire refers to 'temporary cattle sheds of Thatch and Gorze' (Lincolnshire Record Office 3).

Dairying took place in 'milkhouses' (Christchurch, Hampshire) and 'cheeserooms' (Stour Provost, Dorset). One of the few instances in the County Reports where a flicker of enthusiasm for thatch can be detected comes in the Cheshire Report of 1794.

> The cheese rooms are commonly placed over the cowhouses, and this is done with a view to obtain that moderate and necessary degree of temperature so essential to the ripening of the cheese, to which the heat arising from the cattle underneath, is supposed very much to contribute. The most desirable covering for a cheese room, as contributing to that even temperature so much desired, is thatch, for reasons that must be obvious. (Wedge 1794, 56)

Fourteen years later, Holland also noted in the revised report for the same county:

> The covering of the old buildings is generally of thatch; and here it may be noticed that the dairy-maids usually give the preference to the thatched cow-houses, from their preserving a more uniform temperature than those covered with slates, or tiles. (Holland 1808, 83)

Other farm animals were housed in thatched 'lamb-suckling houses' (Shalford, Surrey), 'sheep-pens' (Bickleigh, Devon) and 'hog-' or 'pigsties' (Bray and

Wantage, Berkshire). A whole range of thatched shelters, some temporary, others more durable, were erected to protect stock in inclement weather. Vancouver wrote of a gentleman from Watermouth, Devon who was

> judiciously distributing his feeding-houses, sheep and bullock-yards, over all the highest parts of his farms, that in future the dung may be conveniently distributed over the whole of the cultivated lands below. In such fields as yet lie at a distance from any of these buildings, temporary sheds are constructed, inclosed with yards, for the sheep to lodge in; these sheds are made to take in pieces for the convenience of removal, and which with care may be repeated for many years. The frame-work is commonly of deal covered with thatched hurdles; the sheep are penned upon a fresh piece of turnips daily, and driven to these sheds at night, where they are well littered. (Vancouver 1808, 87; see also Vancouver 1813, 118–9)

William Garrett, a thatcher of Trent, Dorset, was paid 1/- (5p) on 20 March 1848 for 'thatching of hurdles' (Dorset Record Office 1). In exposed situations, individual hurdles might be interwoven with straw or reed to provide shelter: 'on Romney Marsh the thatch-backed hurdles [were] traditionally used as lambing pens. The reed thatch gives the newly born lambs some protection from the biting winds that often blow across the Marsh at lambing time' (Filmer 1981, 32). Animal foods were stored in thatched 'fodder bins' (Winstantow, Salop), 'fodder houses' (Hambledon, Hampshire) and 'hayhouses' (Dalwood, Dorset) or prepared in a thatched 'chaffhouse' (Stow, Gloucestershire, 1862). The ubiquitous granary was less likely to be thatched, presumably because of vermin problems, though examples do occur (eg Brigstock, Northamptonshire; Bourn, Cambridgeshire). We also find a thatched 'granary over a coach house' at Basingstoke, Hampshire. Other wheeled vehicles were housed in thatched 'carthouses' (Bray, Berkshire) 'carthovels' (Hockcliffe, Bedfordshire), 'cart lodges', 'waggon lodges ' (both George Best of Chilston Kent) or 'wainhouses' (Winstantow, Salop).

A more extended list of thatched building types recorded in nineteenth-century documents could be compiled, but even this cursory examination of the evidence illustrates that thatch was plentiful in a wide range of contexts. The severely restricted use of thatch today makes it easy to forget that, in the 1790s, it could be encountered everywhere, on every kind of man-made structure. Though some improvers were just beginning to associate it with lower status buildings, thatch could be found as a roof covering on a multitude of types, ranging from gentry houses to cribs. Moreover, it differed from other roofing materials such as stone slates or peg-tiles in that they had a very limited application beyond their primary function as a roof covering. Straw, however, was used extensively in other contexts, and although a wide range of materials could be used for thatching, English thatch was by and large synonymous with straw thatch.

Table 1 Proportions of roofing materials by building type in England: 1800 (Guildhall Library, London, 1 and 2).

	Thatch	Tile	Slate	Other	Total
Owner-occupied dwelling	98	361	90	20	569
% of total	17.2%	63.4%	15.8%	3.5%	
tenanted dwellings	260	778	182	29	1249
% of total	20.8%	62.3%	14.6%	2.3%	
farm buildings: barns	353	65	8	13	439
% of total	80.4%	14.8%	1.8%	3.0%	
other farm buildings	480	175	16	28	699
% of total	68.7%	25.0%	2.3%	4.0%	
miscellaneous buildings	319	698	240	86	1343
% of total	23.7%	52.0%	17.9%	6.4%	
Totals	1510	2077	536	176	4299
% of total	35.1%	48.3%	12.5%	4.1%	

Straw was to be found everywhere, so thatch was to be found everywhere, on all types of structure. This is not, however, the same as saying that thatch was the predominant roofing material to be found in this country at the end of the eighteenth century.

The insurance policy sample for 1800 distinguishes between thatch, tile and slate. In some cases mixed materials are found on buildings insured as a single range. These are included in the 'Other' category. Table 1 clearly shows that even in 1800, thatch was not the dominant roofing material in the country when analysed according to the whole range of building types. Tiles (either peg- or pantiles) were to be found on nearly half the structures in the country, thatch on just over a third, while only one in every eight building in England was covered with slate. There were, of course, significant regional differences in the distribution pattern. Clay-peg tiles were abundant in the Chilterns and in the south-eastern counties of Kent, Surrey, Sussex and Essex. Pantiles had begun to appear on the north-eastern side of the country and in the Bridgewater area in the south west. There were pockets of stone slate in various parts of the south, while in the north it played a much more significant role. The policies do not distinguish between local and imported slate, but it is clear from other sources that at this time Welsh slate was still a rarity in most parts of the country.

The picture in 1790 is thus clear: thatch was found on a tremendous range of different building types throughout England. Unlike the various types of stone slates, which had great variety of texture and form, were more localized in their distribution, and also tended to have status connotations, thatch was common everywhere, as yet in its non-pejorative sense. Significant changes had already occurred during the eighteenth century, in particular the decline of thatch in an urban context. More detailed analysis of insurance policies also indicates that in the nineteenth century, a nose-dive graph illustrating a continuing simple decline in the number of thatched buildings does not tally with the evidence. The following four chapters examine thatch in these differing contexts, as an urban roofing material, on a regional basis and finally as a 'modern' roof covering employed on new-build structures.

2   Urban thatch

Convincing arguments have been put forward to suggest a link between the decline in the incidence of fire damage in many parts of England, which fell off steeply about 1800, and the shift towards the use of brick and tile instead of mud, timber and thatch (Jones 1968, 140–9; Jones & Falkus 1990, 121–7). This rebuilding was responsible for the predominantly Georgian aspect of many market squares, particularly in the southern half of the country. Jones's data for four southern counties are presented in Table 2.

It is obvious that the spread of fire through a densely populated, predominantly thatched town would have been difficult to contain 'especially when the wynde aryseth and bloweth the flakes from howse to howse over the whole cittie' (Porter 1986, 310). It is also clear that such fires could trigger dramatic visual changes to the townscape.

It matters little that thatch was not always the guilty party. It does not in itself cause fires: the practice of dangerous trades such as smithing, pottery making, dyeing, tanning, tallow chandling and malting, or simply the failure to maintain a domestic chimney were the culprits here. Nor was thatch the only combustible medium found in towns that could fuel a major fire. Refuse or stacks of loose hay and straw, as vital in the town for fodder and litter purposes as they were on the farm, might be just as responsible.

But even if thatch was not always the actual cause, it was the fear of fire as a result of its combustibility which undoubtedly had a key influence on several developments in the eighteenth century. These in turn all contributed to the further abandonment of thatched roofs in urban environments. First, increasingly powerful insurance companies applied discriminatory premiums against thatched properties. The Sun Insurance Company in their 1727 policy proposals introduced a classification which lasted as a practice, both for themselves and

other offices, to the middle of the nineteenth century. The premiums were arranged according to the value of the sum insured and then differentiated according to whether they were 'Common Insurances', 'Hazardous Insurances' or 'Doubly Hazardous Insurances'. Under the head of 'Common Insurances' came buildings covered with a slate, tile or lead roof, under that of 'Hazardous' came 'timber and plaster buildings', while 'Doubly Hazardous' consisted of, among others, all thatched buildings. Thus an annual premium of 5/- (25p) was payable on a thatched building worth £300 compared to only 2/- (10p) on a slated building insured for the same sum (Raynes 1964, 202).

Despite steady improvements in fire-fighting equipment, the limitations of manual pumps and unpressurized water supplies meant that throughout the period fire-fighting equipment was unable to cope effectively with major conflagrations. This in turn may have encouraged landlords to rebuild with or change to more durable roofing materials.

Finally, the legislative framework was tightened. Most towns passed regulations concerning fire hazards, imposing fines for such misdemeanours as carrying naked lights into thatched outbuildings. Larger towns attempted to ban thatch as a roofing material. Coventry, Salisbury and Worcester had all prohibited the use of thatch in the fifteenth century (Porter 1986, 310; see also Bailey 1856, 130; Thacker 1932, 59; Robertson 1938, 29, 31–2; Stedman 1960, 126, 138, 227–8, 268; and Sandon 1977, 92).

After the 1731 conflagration at Blandford Forum, Dorset, an Act of Parliament (5 George II cap 16, 1731–2) provided for the demolition of fire-damaged houses and specified that new houses should be covered with lead, slate or tile instead of thatch. Similar stipulations were made in the Acts of Parliament relating to Wareham (1762) and Bridport (1786), both in Dorset, following major fires. Some of the many municipal Improvement Acts passed in the early nineteenth century undoubtedly also helped to regularize the situation (as at Devizes, Wiltshire in 1825). This was a trend which continued into the present century, and 'but for the restrictions of local by-laws, framed to lessen the danger of fire, many more new buildings in many counties would be thatched' (Diplock 1929, 620).

In the final analysis, however, none of these influences had a significant impact in discouraging the use of thatch on a national scale.

In Norwich, despite repeated attempts in the previous two centuries to eradicate thatch

Table 2 Major fires 1690–1849 (Berkshire, Dorset, Hampshire and Wiltshire). A major fire is deemed to be one that destroyed more than 10 houses (Jones 1968, 140–9).

1650–59	12	1750–59	12
1660–69	9	1760–69	8
1670–79	1	1770–79	5
1680–89	8	1780–89	3
1690–99	3	1790–99	2
1700–09	3	1800–09	1
1710–19	8	1810–19	1
1720–29	8	1820–29	0
1730–39	7	1830–39	0
1740–49	6	1840–49	1

Figure 5 Urban thatch: Ye Olde Thatche, Eccles Cross, Lancashire (Accrington Local Studies Library).

almost one fifth of a sample of houses which were insured with the Sun Fire Office during 1728–31 had thatched roofs ... The change to tile evidently proceeded slowly, for the presence of thatched roofing in Norwich was still being commented upon in the early nineteenth century. (Porter 1986, 311)

Legislation was never tackled on a systematic basis, and borough bye-laws were applied in an *ad hoc* manner until well into the twentieth century.

Jones and Falkus (1990, 126) themselves accept that all these factors can only help to explain the decline of urban thatch on a very limited basis. Indeed, the very nature of the statistical evidence they use, the actual numbers of major fires in towns across the country, means that they must dispense with any woolly explanations which can accommodate a much less specific fear of fire as a contributory factor. What they try to show is that there is a correlation between the use of brick and tile in towns and the decline of major fires. Instead of simply plotting the recorded number of major urban conflagrations in the late seventeenth and early eighteenth century, they chart the inverse percentage and label this as the 'inferred spread of brick and tile'. They point out that there are 'drawbacks to the method: a town built of flammable materials does not necessarily burn down, nor is one built of comparatively nonflammable materials necessarily exempt'. They admit that 'strategically placed tile roofs sometimes reduced fire losses without much use of brick' (Jones & Falkus 1990, 127). At Beaminster, Dorset, Hine comments 'on the destruction of the poorer quality houses by the fire of 1781' (1914, 128) whereas 'the stone houses, built after a previous fire in 1684, escaped in this

later conflagration' (1914, 123; see Hutchins 1861–73, 341; Gardiner 1949, 235).

What is not mentioned, however, are cases where combustible walling materials, in association with more durable roofing materials, might have been a major contributory factor in causing fires to spread relatively easily. The Great Fire of London was possibly so destructive because the buildings were timber-framed, not because they were thatched. Strategically-placed buildings of whatever walling material but with tile roofs might also have acted as effective barriers between clusters of thatched buildings. Thus, a town might retain thatch on the greater proportion of its buildings after a major fire even if all destroyed buildings were rebuilt using tiles.

It seems highly probable that the role of fire in the decline of thatch has been grossly exaggerated. Whereas Jones and Falkus' graph indicates a total obliteration of urban thatch in the 1790s, there is abundant evidence to illustrate its survival well into the nineteenth century.

Photographs from early this century show 'Ye Olde Thatche' surviving at Eccles Cross, Lancashire (Fig 5), a low single-storey shop built gable end to the road and sandwiched between two late-Victorian shops each of two full storeys. In Broad Street, Wolverhampton, a similar thatched building was photographed in 1870 with a large industrial chimney looming in the background (Fig 6). The sheer incongruity of these buildings in the streetscape tends to invest them with an air of imminent destruction, but these late survivors are noteworthy as they clearly belie the ingrained notions of industrial landscapes littered only with dark satanic mills.

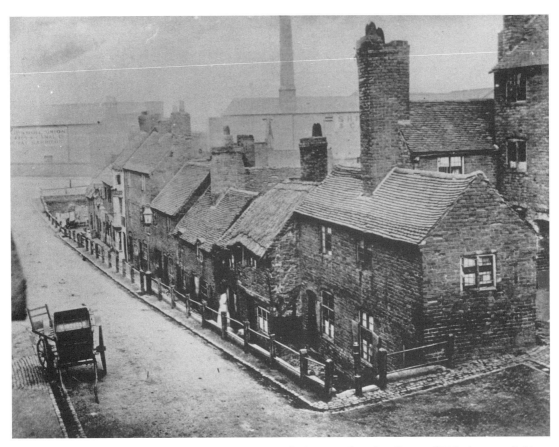

Figure 6 Thatched house in urban landscape, Broad Street, Wolverhampton (from the collection of Wolverhampton Archives and Local Studies).

Indeed, economic expansion per se did not inevitably destroy thatch. The growth of suburbs in the seventeenth and eighteenth centuries no doubt added to the stock of urban thatched buildings, particularly as legal bans on thatch often did not extend beyond ancient city walls. While market squares of country towns might assume a standard Georgian brick and tile elegance, flimsier, cheaper housing was still being built on the routes into these towns. Suburban expansion in the late nineteenth and early twentieth centuries would also add a sprinkling of Arts and Crafts residences with thatched roofs.

Many smaller market towns retained a high percentage of thatched dwellings well into the nineteenth century, if not beyond. A valuation of Helmsley in Yorkshire in 1868 records that, of 256 houses in the town, 66 were thatched, 156 tiled and 34 slated (McDonnell 1963, 309–10). In Devon, market towns such as Chulmleigh still retain three-storeyed thatched houses in the centre of the town, so the urban thatched roof still cannot be considered a relic of a past age.

And of course, if the discussion is limited only to dwellings, then the late survival of thatch on a whole range of ancillary urban buildings will be overlooked. Insurance policies can be invaluable here. Edmund Bland, for example, owned a house and brewhouse at Harborough, Leicestershire, which in 1800 were tiled, but the range of stables adjoining was thatched. Thomas Bellamy of Brigstock, Northamptonshire, owned a slated dwelling house, but his 'brewhouse, woodhouse, barn, stable and small tenement adjoining' were all thatched. William Arding, a sailcloth maker of Wantage, Berkshire

had a dwelling house with spinning house adjoining, which were described as being 'part tiled, part thatched'. Many of these smaller thatched buildings survived well into this century.

Another contributor to the stock of urban thatched buildings was the rapid emergence of that new urban phenomena of the nineteenth and early twentieth centuries, the seaside resort. Cowells of Soham found a good deal of water reed work in the resorts, and used photographs of their roofs on the Eastbourne Promenade shelters to advertise their work. The not very appealingly named Ozonia Hotel on Canvey Island sported brick, waney weatherboarding and a jaunty reed-thatched roof which must have tested the skill of the thatcher to the utmost (Fig 7).

Figure 7 Thatch in a seaside resort: the Ozonia Hotel, Canvey Island, Essex (McCave 1987).

Thatched roofs had therefore by no means disappeared from the urban scene at the end of the eighteenth century but their numbers were dwindling fast. This decline had nevertheless been underway for centuries (Jones & Falkus 1990, 124).

England's dramatic urban growth of the later eighteenth century (Wrigley 1988, 13), riding on the back of rising agricultural prosperity, encouraged town dwellers to replace their houses using more durable materials and with three or four storeys instead of two. That the prices of roofing materials appear to have moved closer together during the eighteenth century may also have encouraged a shift towards more durable materials. The raising of buildings by one or two storeys was also likely to have been one very practical reason for a more widespread abandonment of thatch, because its deterioration would have been hastened where these older single storey or low two-storey structures abutted the new, taller buildings. Complete or even partial enclosure by taller structures would also block out light and air, again contributing to more rapid decay.

In the eighteenth century, then, it is this peculiarly English phenomenon of massive urban growth and the economic implications that flow from this, rather than any random scatter of devastating fires, which changed the face of the country's town and market centres. This change had ramifications for thatched buildings way beyond the urban streetscapes. As a result of town remodellings all over the country, a wedge was effectively driven between urban and rural lifestyles, the divide becoming ever more pronounced during the eighteenth century. It thus became increasingly possible to associate thatch with rural innocence and charm. Urban growth on this scale could only take place on the back of impressive advances in food production. Bread was still the staple food of both town and country; thatch was (for the most part) its by-product. Increases in wheat production and changes in breeding techniques clearly impacted on the availability and quality of straw. The eighteenth-century English town may appear an unlikely place to commence an investigation of thatch in the nineteenth and twentieth centuries, but this breaking of the rural-urban link was really only the first in a series of changes that would transform thatch and thatching in the nineteenth and early twentieth centuries.

3   Rural thatch: the northern and Midland counties

It is clear that the demand for thatch in urban areas declined drastically between 1790 and 1940.

> The number of thatched cottages in Kettering can now be counted on the fingers of one hand ... The last of the Kettering 'thackers' died in the old workhouse-lane a few years ago, and anyone needing the services of a thatcher must now perforce go far afield to secure one. (Northamptonshire Local Studies Library 1)

If the urban thatcher had become a rarity by this time, it was almost as difficult to find a thatcher in rural areas of the north by the turn of this century. The 1891 Census records only seven thatchers in Lancashire, three in Northumberland, two in the North Riding of Yorkshire, only one in the West Riding of Yorkshire, and none at all in the East Riding of Yorkshire, Durham, Cumberland or Westmorland. In comparison, there were 1971 slaters recorded in Lancashire alone at that date. Some of the Midlands counties were better off, particularly those in the southern half such as Gloucestershire which could still boast 61 thatchers in 1861, although only five of the 12 counties reported more than ten thatchers (PP 1863). As a result of this meagre presence, one would have assumed that the numbers of thatched buildings in the region in 1900 were few and far between (Fig 8). They are certainly a rarity today, and in 1961 Mitchell (1961a, 784) could find only 34 thatched buildings in the whole of Yorkshire.

It would seem that the wishes of the authors of the County Reports had been granted (Strickland 1812, 40). It is all too easy to assume from their comments that the chunky stone and slated or tiled houses of the north and Midlands had always been a permanent fixture in the landscape. It is much more difficult to accept that many villages in some parts of the region were predominantly thatched until well into the late nineteenth century. Even within living memory, the impression is one of a fair survival.

> Fifty years ago there were over twenty thatched cottages in Old Malton. Today the number is three, with another only partly thatched. There were eight thatched cottages on the Malton side of the village, five in Chapel Lane, two near the School and five on the Pickering side. William Bradley and Tom Freer were thatchers here in living memory ... as I walked down the street I felt it was a pity that this pleasant North Yorkshire village is gradually losing its thatched homes. In a few years they will only be a memory. (Metcalfe 1953, 296–7)

It is clear that thatched buildings had once been a common feature in the northern landscape (Horrox 1953, 515; Mitchell 1961b, 134–5; Hartley & Ingilby 1972, 5; 1986, 52). In 1760 the inhabitants of Stanhope, Durham, 'thatch their houses with a very thick coat of heath and make the roofs steep that the melted snow may not soak into the thatch, and lay loads across the top of it to keep out the water', while at Rothbury, Northumberland, 'the houses are mostly thatched; they cover them with sods for warmth, and thatch with heath, which will last thirty years' (Hodgson 1914, 209, 223). Later still, a survey of Sir Edward Smith's property in Normanton and neighbouring settlements in 1819–23 examined 36 holdings. Roofing materials are described in 27 cases, and of the 53 structures itemized, 33 were thatched, 19 were slated, and only one is described as tiled (Table 3) (Local Studies Library, Wakefield, 1).

Figure 8 Heather thatch at Newshaw, Northumberland (James Moir).

Table 3 Survey of Normanton, Yorkshire, 1819–23 (Wakefield Library 1).

	Thatch	Slate	Tile	Total
House	8	5	0	13
Cowhouse	3	1	0	4
Pigscote	6	2	1	9
Coal Place	2	0	0	2
Stable	2	4	0	6
Elm Shed	1	0	0	1
Cart Shed	4	0	0	4
Shed	1	0	0	1
Shop	1	0	0	1
Barn	4	4	0	8
Henhouse	1	1	0	2
Kiln	0	1	0	1
Privy	0	1	0	1
Total	33	19	1	53

Table 4 Total number of thatched dwellings in England by county: 1800 & 1862/3. (Guildhall Library, London 1, 2 and 3; Public Record Office 17).

1800	[1]	[2]	[3]	[4]	[5]	1862–3	[1]	[2]	[3]	[4]	[5]
SOUTH											
South west											
Cornwall	0	5		34378			9	36		76867	
Devon	59	113		61190			1	30		107491	
Dorset	47	75		22262			7	31		39585	
Somerset	38	53		50176			10	66		92155	
total for South west	144	246	58.5%	168006	98283		27	163	16.6%	316098	52472
South east											
Kent	5	185		52998			0	84		132550	
Middlesex	1	34		118083			1	66		295983	
Surrey	3	96		47586			0	26		136434	
total for South east	9	315	2.9%	218667	6341		1	176	0.6%	564967	3390
South											
Bedfordshire	8	19		12073			1	34		28314	
Berkshire	11	70		21195			3	27		65638	
Buckinghamshire	7	31		20986			3	17		36515	
Cambridgeshire	2	6		16451			9	32		39003	
Essex	12	169		39398			22	66		86010	
Hampshire	23	167		39257			40	171		90792	
Hertfordshire	3	23		18172			5	39		36649	
Huntingdonshire	6	14		6976			13	43		14276	
Norfolk	7	25		49140			0	14		102009	
Northamptonshire	15	41		27401			21	52		50965	
Oxfordshire	6	40		21193			0	24		37570	
Suffolk	17	45		32805			2	37		76719	
Sussex	5	27		25993			4	28		68816	
Wiltshire	59	153		30589			46	82		55654	
total for south	181	830	21.8%	361629	78835		169	666	25.4%	789530	200540
MIDLANDS											
Cheshire	1	27		35621			0	73		104009	
Derbyshire	1	3		33191			0	3		73219	
Gloucestershire	4	28		48172			0	39		98091	
Herefordshire	0	9		17944			0	6		26299	
Leicestershire	0	3		26734			11	86		54778	
Lincolnshire	2	13		42489			0	60		91445	
Nottinghamshire	1	16		26153			0	13		67532	
Rutland	0	0		3361			0	1		4840	
Shropshire	3	18		32111			0	2		82330	
Staffordshire	0	13		47193			0	10		157230	
Warwickshire	3	11		43783			0	26		124089	
Worcestershire	0	46		27820			0	2		67298	
total for Midlands	15	187	8%	384572	30766		11	321	3.4%	951160	33290
NORTH											
Cumberland	0	0		22445			1	12		42892	
Durham	0	32		28366			0	93		89641	
Lancashire	9	90		117664			0	100		46196	
Northumberland	0	4		28052			0	3		58885	
Westmorland	0	9		8212			0	1		12479	
Yorkshire	0	105		174857			0	64		450826	
total for North	9	240	3.75%	379596	14235		1	273	0.4%	1116419	4666
TOTALS	358	1818	19.7%	1512470	228460		209	1599	13.1%	3738174	294358

[1] number of thatched dwellings (from insurance policy samples)
[2] total number of dwellings (from insurance policy samples)
[3] percentage of total number of dwellings thatched, ie [2] as a % of [1]
[4] total number of dwellings, 1801 and 1861 censuses
[5] number of thatched dwellings, extrapolated from the percentage of thatched dwellings, [3], and the total number of dwellings, [4]

In the low-lying, arable areas, thatch appears to have dominated until the mid nineteenth century. According to an 1879–80 survey of the Rufford Hall Estate in Lancashire 'within the last year or two many of the homesteads have been judiciously repaired ... chiefly by re-roofing with slate in lieu of thatch' (Lancashire Record Office 2).

Despite these late survivals there can be no doubt that the loss of thatch in the north and Midlands was on a massive scale. The figures from Tables 4, 5 and 7 (see also Figure 9) suggest that the north experienced, in terms of volume, a greater loss of thatched buildings in the first half of the nineteenth century than at any subsequent period. The 1960 figure under-represents the total for the whole

Table 5 Estimated number of thatched buildings by region: 1800, 1862–3, 1960 (Guildhall Library, London 1, 2 and 3; Public Record Office 17).

	1800	1862–3	1960	% decline 1800–1862–3	% decline 1862–3 – 1960
north	59646	13344	30	77.6	99.8
Midlands	128909	95209	1173	26.1	98.8
south	768691	733308	33459	4.6	95.4
Totals	957246	841861	34662	12	95.9

Table 6 Wage comparisons: 1790 and 1804 (anon 1804, 25).

	Mason 1790	1804	% rise	Thatcher 1790	1804	% rise
south	2s 1d	2s 11d	40	1s 11$^{1/2}$d	2s 8$^{1/2}$d	38
Midlands	1s 101/2d	2s 11d	55	1s 9d	2s 7$^{1/2}$d	50
north	2s 0$^{1/2}$d	3s 2$^{1/2}$d	57.1	1s 7$^{1/2}$d	2s 11d	77.5

region, (the Rural Industries Bureau only bothered to collect statistics from Yorkshire), but this does not alter the fact that thatch has been virtually eradicated from the region since 1862–3. In the Midlands, by contrast, the figures suggest a fairly static picture between 1800 and 1862–3 followed by a really massive decline in the later nineteenth and early twentieth centuries.

Between 1790 and 1804 (Table 6), a period of very high inflation, the wage of a thatcher in the north of the country rose far more steeply than that of his southern counterpart, jettisoning him from the bottom to top wage-earner within his craft. The daily rate in the north increased sharply compared to masons, challenging the traditional reliance on thatch as an inexpensive roof covering. In the stone areas of the north, estate managers would see the added contractual advantages of employing a slater as opposed to a thatcher, because the former could be employed in bad weather on indoor work such as 'flagging' and other masonry work.

Estates greatly influenced the differing chronologies of thatch decline in the north and south. On average, estates in the north were larger, and northern landlords keen on 'improvement' could therefore be instrumental in eliminating thatch from vast areas.

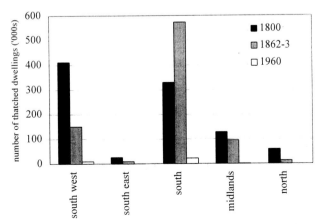

Figure 9 Estimated number of thatched dwellings by region: 1800, 1862-3 and 1960 (after Guildhall Library 1, 2 and 3, and Public Record Office 17)

One notices too that a passion for the picturesque was rather more muted in the north than in the south. The hand of the architect was felt much more strongly in the model villages of the north. None even toyed with the idea of employing thatch as a suitable roof covering (Darley 1978, 32–36).

While some landlords were at the vanguard of the conversion process, pockets of thatch might equally be preserved as a result of an estate owner's whim (Hartley & Ingilby 1968, 166; Mitchell 1961a, 784). Landowners also seem to have been the driving force behind the one or two new-build schemes in the first half of this century. 'Sir Frederick Akroyd, of Birstwith Hall some few years ago rethatched in modern style a house and building adjacent to the "Tang" road leading from Birstwith to Kettlesing village' (Ridsdale 1946, 138).

While the individual preferences of landholders were obviously important, the density of settlement in an area might also be a significant element in influencing the differing rates of attrition in the north and south of the country. If the settlement pattern is one of small hamlets and scattered buildings, then a drop in the number of thatched buildings would have a more deleterious effect than an equivalent loss in a more densely settled area. This was because in an area of scattered settlements, the thatcher would have to work over a much wider area and transport considerations would therefore become relevant.

Local availability of a much more diverse range of roofing materials and the comparative ease with which these could be transported to the site was another important factor accounting for the abandonment of thatch in the north. Indeed, part of the problem with identifying trends in the north and Midlands is that the process is not a simple one of loss of thatch to a single competitor. The range of alternative materials was broader than in the south.

STONE SLATES

Compared to their attitude to thatch, the authors of the County Reports were always enthusiastic when they encountered the use of stone roofing. Bailey and Culley noted in Cumberland that 'through the greatest part of this county, the farm-houses are remarkably well built of stone, the blue-slate roofs, and white dashed walls, give them a look of neatness that is peculiarly pleasing' (1794, 12). Holt commented that recently-built cottages in Lancashire were 'covered with slate' (1795, 19) while 'in most parts towards the north, and in the whole of the eastern side, there are excellent stones, flags, and slates, in great abundance, and to be had at a cheap rate' (Dickson & Stevenson 1815, 101).

Compared to the south of England, the north was well endowed with slate quarries. The exact pace of conversion is not easy to establish because the chronology in the north varied in different contexts. Buildings were replaced or re-roofed for a variety of reasons, on the death of a tenant, through structural failure, for status reasons, or as a result of accident, such as fire.

The building accounts for the Rufford Estate in Lancashire which run from 1852 to 1871 illustrate the process of thatch replacement in some detail, and the scattered references demonstrate that there was no whole-sale demolition of buildings on the estate at any one time. Thatch might disappear as a result of complete rebuilding or discrete replacement. As an instance of the former, in 1854 (week ending 14 October) Mrs Loxham of Mawdsley was having a new shippon built. The bricklayers began by 'Pulling down the Old Thatch Building' (Lancashire Record Office 1/7). In August 1857, the bricklayers were employed at William Hull's farm in Hesketh, and were paid 'for raiseing the walls of the House and Beamfilling one side of Do and building 2 Chimney Tops of the House.' The carpenters were paid 'for Rooffing the New Shippon, Taking of Thatch and timbers and Rearooffing the House for slate ...' (Lancashire Record Office 1/8). In August 1859 payment was made for 'Taking the old roof off a part the Sail Room Cottages Raiseing the walls and roofing them for slate' (Lancashire Record Office 1/8).

In September 1864, Thomas Higham's cottage in Hesketh was renovated in the same manner. 'Takeing off the old roof of the cottage' cost 12s 2d (61p), while 'Raising the wall and slating the cottage' added a further £1 15s 4d (£1.77) to the bill. 'Fixing ceiling joists over Bed Rooms, Repg Bedroom floors' cost a further 12s (60p), and plastering the walls and pointing slates completed the job for 19s 6 ¾d (98p), a total in all of £3 13s 10 ¾d (£3.69). The repairs to the bedroom floors indicate that no upper floor was being gained through the conversion (Lancashire Record Office 1/9).

Only in one case where a cottage required major repairs to the roof structure did thatch go back on (week ending 21 May 1864: Dobsons Cottage, Lancashire Record Office 1/9). On all other examples where retimbering or raising the walls were concerned, and on all new buildings (including farm buildings), slate was used. The material was brought onto the estate by boat; in 1858, two bricklayers and three labourers were each paid for a day 'Discharging Slates at Spark Bridge and getting them up to the Yard' (Lancashire Record Office 1/8). Ridge tiles were brought from Preston.

At Eshton in Yorkshire, work began at a house and blacksmith's shop in 1798: 'Mar 19 Begun to pull of the Thatch and Timber of the House.' (Yorkshire Archaeological Society archives 1). Masonry work clearly involved raising the walls, as the intention was to create an upper storey. A new roof of 'eight ribs' and '40 spars' was fitted, and 5 tons of slate replaced the former thatch. The new bedrooms were reached by a 'Steep Lather'. The whole conversion cost £21 11s 10d (£21.59). All the bills had been paid by 31 March, indicating that the entire job had taken less than 12 days. At the same time as these alterations were being carried out, the barn on these premises was also being reroofed, but in straw.

This example suggests there were perhaps two phases of decline in the north, first, the pragmatic replacement of thatch by slates on domestic buildings so as to create more living space. There was no immediate benefit at this stage of replacing thatch on, for example, older farm buildings. The second stage probably took off with improved agricultural yields and increased stocking levels

in the early nineteenth century. Wherever new farm buildings were being erected, the tendency was to roof with slate.

PANTILES

Stone is not so abundant on the eastern side of England, and it was here, from the mid eighteenth century, that pantiles began to make an appearance. From about 1740 they were being imported from northern ports to Whitby, where a tilery was eventually established (Charlton 1779, 340).

The individual histories of parsonages in North Yorkshire

> give some indication of the inroads which tiles made on thatch ... Of the seventeen ... terriers of 1764, fifteen note thatched roofs, one of them specifically 'thatched with straw', while two, at Old Byland and nearby Scawton, are part slate, part thatch ... The continuing use of thatch, however, is indicated by the terrier of Middleton which recorded in 1764 'the house is rebuilding', and in 1770 the house as 'stone built, thatched'. Thatch seems to have been retained on many parsonages into the 19th century, with rebuilding or renewal gradually taking its toll. (Royal Commission on the Historical Monuments of England 1987, 208)

The conversion to pantiles was therefore a long drawn-out affair. The percentage of thatched roofs retained in rural areas until long after pantiles had become established should not be underestimated. It was not until 1847, for example, that Lord Willoughby discovered pantiles.

> We have just taken off the thatch from John Browns Cottage Edenham and got it covered with Pantiles and the new ridge tiles. His Lordship [Lord Willoughby] is quite pleased with its appearance, and has ordered that Measuns [?] and Son are to do nothing else this Autumn but to put new Pantiles upon all the Cottages that are in the worst order at present, and has pointed out several houses to be done and at the same time to put up stone chimnies where they are now Bricks. (Lincolnshire Record Office 1).

As in the case of slates, pantiles crept more slowly on to the roofs of ancillary and agricultural buildings. 'The barn, stable and cowhouse at Hawsker [Yorkshire], listed in 1777 as the property of Sleights chapelry, were built of stone and thatched; by 1857 they were tiled' (Royal Commission on the Historical Monuments of England 1987, 208).

TILES

Some plain clay tiles were also encountered in the north, although they were not highly regarded. Farey (1811 **2**, 13) complained about the lack of durability of the red tiles of Derbyshire, while in Shropshire

> Any cover is preferable, both in look and duration, to the common clay tiles of this county. Those of Jackfield, indeed, are durable, but all are ugly. (Plymley 1803, 106)

By the early nineteenth century, most counties in the north or Midlands would include plentiful examples of virtually all types of roofing material.

> Thatch coverings to buildings are falling rapidly into disuse; and are succeeded by brick, or stone tiles. The former are either plain or waving ('pantiles'): both are made with knobs, by which they are fastened to the lath, but the latter have the property of securing a flatter roof than the other, and are, therefore, more often used on sheds. The stone tile is brought from the various parts of the Cotswolds ... or raised in the neighbourhood, as in the Forest and lower part of the Vale. This kind of covering requires strong timbers, and is on that account objectionable; yet, being cheaper, and more durable, is much used. (Rudge 1813, 45)

IMPORTED SLATE

The availability of Welsh slate from the early part of the nineteenth century introduced a further complication in the decision-making process. It was pointed out that in a county like Staffordshire

> the materials now very generally used in modern farm-buildings, are bricks for the walls, and the covering tile or slate. This last material is not raised in or near the county, but very conveniently brought in from Wales, Westmoreland, and elsewhere, by means of the navigable canals. It is much used and esteemed, as being neat and durable, and is not, I believe, dearer than tile. (Pitt 1813, 26)

In Shropshire, 'at the present price of straw, the comparative expense of blue slates, which are gotten from the neighbouring counties of Wales, is not excessive' (Plymley 1803, 106).

The manufacture and distribution of alternative roofing materials were the product of a more industrialized society. The north and Midlands had of course progressed further down this path than the south, and so had the requisite economic institutions and transport networks in place to promote investment in new durable building materials. As a result of infrastructure improvements due to industrialization, these could be shifted to most parts of the region using the same integrated system of roads, canals and railways catering for the import and export of raw materials and finished products.

In the north and Midlands, farmers gradually abandoned cereal growing in favour of dairying and livestock production. The reduction in the cereal acreage affected the availability of straw for house-thatching and in some areas dispensed completely with rick-thatching skills. This was not the case in southern England, where industrialization and agricultural change followed a different route and where thatched buildings enjoyed a very different pattern of survival.

4   Rural thatch: the south

Compared to the drastic decline of thatch in the north, the south experienced a very different pattern of thatch replacement in the nineteenth and twentieth centuries. Table 7 demonstrates that when the number of thatched buildings in the south is broken down into sub-regions, the slight overall decline in the region as a whole masks some interesting differences. Compared to the south east and south west where the numbers declined, in the south the number of dwellings appear to have increased from some 78,000 in 1800 to over 200,000 in 1862–3. What accounts for these variations? Table 8 illustrates the relative importance of slate, tile and thatch in the sub-regions, and the relative proportions of roofing materials are quite different in each (Figs 10 and 11).

THE SOUTH WEST

Despite the romantic image of the Devon cob and thatched cottage, local slate had always played an important role in the south west, and in 1793 Cornwall and Devon were still responsible for one fifth of total British slate production (Cox & Thorp 1991, 5). However, the northern coasts of Cornwall and Devon were exposed to the Welsh slate industry from an early date, and improved rail networks opened up the remainder of the south west to this foreign competition during the course of the nineteenth century. To the east of the region, Stonesfield slate occurs at the base of the Great Oolite, while the Purbeck beds had been quarried from Roman times (Walton 1975, 38–40). Large quantities of pantiles were being produced at Bridgewater, Somerset in the early nineteenth century, and these gradually made their way into most parts of the county. Plain clay tiles were of little importance in the region, but had spread into the eastern-most areas of Somerset and Dorset.

THE SOUTH EAST

The south east by contrast was distinctive in that the plain clay tile was by far the most significant roofing material in the region by 1790. Boys noted in Kent that the newer cottages tended to be built 'with bricks and tiles' (1805, 33). In Middlesex 'those farmhouses that have been built within the present century are generally erected with bricks; and, owing to the high price of straw, and the great value of manure, the roofs are now, for the most part, covered with tiles' (Middleton 1798, 40). In rural areas of the south east, high status buildings rarely retained their thatch.

A survey of the Herrings estate in Dallington, Sussex in 1793–4 illustrates that 'of the [twelve] dwellings, all but one (which was partially tiled and partially thatched) had tiled roofs ... Clearly by this date thatching was no longer common on houses, but with the exception of a few eighteenth-century examples, was usual on farm buildings' (Martin & Martin 1978, 34–5).

Stone-slated buildings were common in parts of the south-east. The stone tiles of the Weald had a significant inland presence straddling the county boundaries of Kent and Surrey.

THE SOUTH

Virtually the entire spectrum of roofing materials was employed in this sub-region. Plain clay tiles were to be found all over the area but were particularly prevalent in the areas of good brick clays.

Pantiles were spreading in the eighteenth century into the north-eastern part of the region, almost to the county boundaries of Cambridgeshire and Hertfordshire, eastwards into the northern half of Suffolk and sweeping up

Table 7 Estimated number of thatched buildings by sub-region: 1800, 1862–3 and 1960 (Guildhall Library, London 1, 2 and 3; Public Record Office 17).

	1800	1862-63	1960	% decline 1800 – 1862-3	% decline 1862-3 – 1960
south west	411805	150069	9789	63.5	93.5
south east	26568	9695	556	63.5	94.3
south	330318	573544	23114	(+42.4)	95.9
subtotal	768691	733308	33459	4.6	95.4
Midlands	128909	95209	1173	26.1	98.8
north	59646	13344	30	77.6	99.8
Totals	957246	841861	34662		

Table 8 Proportion of roofing materials by sub-region: 1800 (Guildhall Library, London, 1 and 2).

	Thatch	Tile	Slate	Misc.	Total
south west	361	105	75	15	556
	64.9 %	18.8%	13.5%	2.7%	
south east	91	501	4	17	613
	14.8%	81.7%	0.6%	2.8%	
south	991	1184	32	102	2309
	42.9%	51.3%	1.4%	4.4%	
Midlands	57	196	52	29	334
	17.1%	58.7%	15.6%	8.7%	
north	10	91	373	13	487
	2.1%	18.7%	76.6%	2.7%	
Totals	1510	2077	536	176	4299
	35.1%	48.3%	12.5%	4.1%	

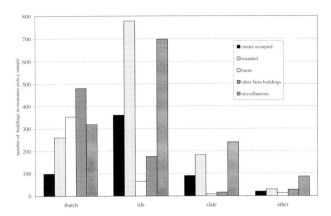

Figure 10 Proportion of roofing materials by building type: 1800 (after Guildhall Library 1 and 2).

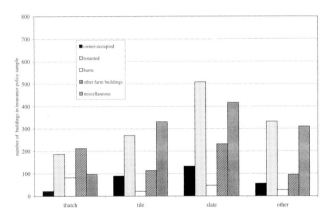

Figure 11 Proportion of roofing materials by building type: 1862–3 (after Guildhall Library 3).

in a north-westerly direction through north Bedford-shire and Northamptonshire. In Norfolk 'the covering is of three kinds, Dutch tiles generally for the houses, and the common pan-tiles for stables and barns, or sea or marsh reed' (Kent 1796, 112). Cotswold stone tiles sweep in an arc running from the south coast up through the western halves of Wiltshire, Berkshire, Oxfordshire and Northamptonshire. Collyweston slate was quar-ried for slates primarily in Northamptonshire (Walton 1975, 38–40).

Stone slates in the Limestone Belt differed from those in the Pennines and in Sussex both in character and size. With the small Cotswold slates, the pitch may be as high as 55E° whereas in the Pennines it is usually between 30E° and 40E° and rarely exceeds 45E° (Walton 1975, 38–40). A roof in the Cotswolds could thus switch from slate to thatch or vice versa without disturbing the roof profile, whereas much more sig-nificant alterations were required before slating a northern roof. While the trend in the Cotswolds was principally from thatch to stone, in some cases old stone roofs were stripped and replaced with thatch (Wood-Jones 1963, 138).

Apart from these more marginal areas of stone slates and pantiles, generally speaking the heartland of the south consisted of the low-lying arable vales where heavy clays predominated. Straw was abundant, and cheaper than plain clay tiles. The area was less accessible to the expanding Welsh slate industry than anywhere else in the southern half of England.

Thatch was not only the dominant roofing material in the region, but the evidence suggests that, in contrast to the south east and south west, the numbers of thatched dwellings actually increased in the first part of the nine-teenth century from 78,000 in 1790 to over 200,000 by 1862–3. The unique experience of the south is best charted by keeping the national context in view.

Phase 1: 1790–*c* 1840

In the first phase, a trend continued in which the country as a whole was being split apart into two radically different regions as a result of industrialization. Of course, architectural styles do not divide neatly between the two regions, yet it is striking how thatch as a material very interestingly becomes a symbol of southern escapism into a rustic, idyllic past, while in the north it is rejected in favour of durable, non-inflammable, no-nonsense slate and tile. The north/south divide is neatly drawn between Shropshire, the cradle of the industrial revolution, and Herefordshire, the cradle of the cult of the picturesque. In the latter county, Price and Knight, both leading lights of the Picturesque Movement, had thatched cottages in the style erected on their respective estates at Foxley and Downton (Lyall 1988, 65).

Several other factors boosted the numbers of thatched buildings in the south, but depressed the growth of rural settlements in the north. For example, the agricultural labour force increased by about one third between 1750 and 1850. Between 1811 and 1851 the increase was from 910,000 to 1,010,000. In the south east, in particular, migration to London was not sufficient to reduce the labour surplus; in the north and Midlands, by contrast, migration was greater because of the wider opportunities of indus-trial employment. As a result a gap opened up between agricultural wages in the north and those in the south.

Employment opportunities were further reduced in the south as a result of a change in the composition of the workforce. The amalgamation of farms on estates and the sale of land by small landowners after Parliamentary enclosure depressed the number of farmers, while the number of farm labourers was increasing both absolutely and as a proportion of the total farm work-force. The ratio of labourers to farmers rose from 1.74:1 in 1700 to 2.5:1 in 1831, and to 2.9:1 by 1851. This ratio was much higher in the arable south than in the pastoral north.

This weighting of numbers towards the labouring classes was compounded by the gradual abandonment of service in the south. Before 1750 between one third and one half of the labour force had consisted of farm servants, young men and women between 14 and 25 years of age who, most significantly, lived in the farmer's house and worked on the farm. The number of farm servants living-in declined in the late eighteenth and early nineteenth centuries as the growth in population provided an abundance of day labourers available at low wages. This created a need to house a greater proportion of the agricultural labouring population, as age at first marriage also fell and the newly-married couples sought to set up house on their own. In the north and west 'in-farm' service lasted much longer; in the north high industrial wages attracted labourers from the farms, so farmers had to offer yearly contracts to ensure they kept them. In the remoter districts it was difficult to get labour without the practice of living-in, while in pastoral areas the constant attention that livestock needed ensured the survival of farm servants on larger farms (Prothero 1923; Coppock 1971; Darby 1976; Grigg 1980; Creasey & Ward 1984; Snell 1985; Langton & Morris 1986; Armstrong 1988; Grigg 1989).

The population increase in rural areas in the early nineteenth century was not confined to the pure farming sector. A host of associated trades and crafts, some purely rural, some of a rural industrial nature, sprang up to service the expanding agricultural and urban markets. The woodland and particularly underwood trades; hurdle, besom-broom, trug-basket and rake-making and so on were in demand, and the commons surviving as woodland pasture became a focus for housebuilding activity. Common land and roadside verges everywhere in the south were really the last remaining frontiers for development, and colonization carried on apace well into the mid nineteenth century (Moir 1990). The cottages were built in the vernacular style using local materials, and in the south this meant that thatch was the most common roofing material.

The variety of opportunities for making a living on the common was often lacking in the ancient village settlements. These, too, expanded in the early nineteenth

century, and probably the worst examples of poor housing are to be located here. The 1893–4 Royal Commission on Labour distinguished three grades of cottage. The worst grade were thoroughly bad cottages with 9' x 9' (2.74m) living rooms, no back kitchen and a single bedroom reached by a ladder. 'One third of the houses in open villages are said to be of this character' (Machin 1994, 11). Many of these were better described as hovels, and mud, turf and thatch featured in their construction. Thomas Keywood's cottage at Mudtown, Walton-on-Thames, Surrey, was one of six single-storied cottages built by the occupants between 1820 and 1832. Internal measurements of 9' 3" (2.82m) by 21' 3" (6.48m) gives 197ft^2 (18.27m^2); above average nineteenth-century accommodation (Harvey 1945, 127–9) (Fig 12).

These factors, a rise in population, increasing wage differentials, a change in the balance between farmer and farm labourer, the abandonment of service and the growth of rural industry, stimulated a rapid expansion in rural housing in the south, the majority of it designed to cater for this poorer end of the market.

This was a very different experience to that of the north and the Midlands. There, industrialization and population increase encouraged migration to the towns where the wages were higher. This expanding urban population still had to be fed. Demand was met by improving arable yields in the south, while in the north, a more pastoral but less labour-intensive economy emerged.

The corollary of this specialization in arable farming in the south was an increasing need for housing all the paraphernalia associated with corn-growing areas, always much more demanding in terms of covered space than in a pastoral region. Mechanization and improved transport networks threw up a need for a whole range of implement and vehicle sheds. Barns and granaries increased their capacity to accommodate the ever

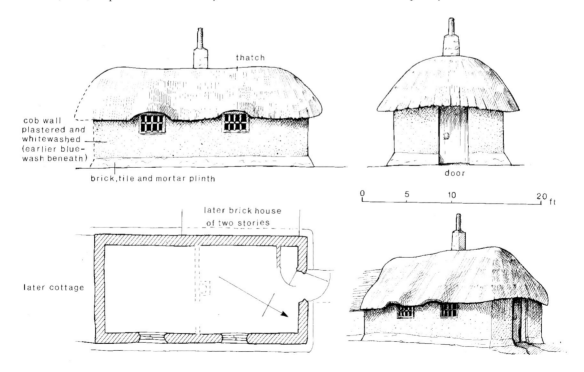

Figure 12 Thomas Keywood's 'squatter' cottage at Mudtown, Walton-on-Thames, Surrey (Judith Dobie, after Harvey 1945, 127).

growing quantities of grain, and the greater horse-power required to service this extra activity necessitated more stable and tack room.

Phase 2: *c* 1840–90

The years stretching from the 1840s through to the mid 1870s were years of relative prosperity in agriculture: high production achieved through intensive cultivation, aided by rising livestock and dairy produce prices, and the application of agricultural science and technology. Increased production levels were sustained by the expansion of urban markets, gradually rising real incomes, and the growth of the railway system. Rural population levels in the south probably peaked in the 1840s with the result that less of the cheaply-built type of housing needed to be provided. Farm building activity tended to mean improvements to existing farmsteads, rather than establishment of new ones. The replacement of roof coverings with more durable materials was just part of an improving movement which began to put the brake on any increase in thatched buildings in the south.

The last quarter of the nineteenth century presents an apparently sudden contrast to this 'golden age' and was quickly christened the period of the Great Depression in British agriculture. Its main characteristics were rising imports of agricultural produce, falling grain prices, a run of generally bad weather in the 1870s and 1880s, disease amongst farm stock, and financial distress amongst landowners and farmers. Between 1870 and 1937 the arable acreage fell by 5 million (2 million hectares), and as arable farming was more labour-intensive than most livestock production, this reduced labour needs from sixteen to nine men per 1,000 acres (405ha).

The census data shows that the total agricultural labour force fell by one third between 1851 and 1901, compared to only 14% between 1901 and 1951 (Grigg 1989, 143–4). Between 1851 and 1951 the number of farmers showed little change and most of the decline in the workforce was due to the fall in the number of hired labourers. In the same period, the average wage in agriculture was half that in manufacturing industry, and less than for most other jobs which were urban-based. Urban and industrial expansion swallowed up farmhouses, hamlets and agricultural land, some 4 million acres (1.6 million hectares) since the 1870s.

Some features of the depression had their origins in the preceding period of prosperity. The balance of consumer demand, for instance, had been shifting away from cereals and towards livestock and dairy produce for much of the century. Import levels of agricultural produce had been steadily increasing ever since the removal in 1846 of the restraints imposed by the Corn Laws. But other features of the depression were new: corn prices, although they had periodically fallen to low levels after 1846, fell permanently in the late 1870s. Allied to the shift in consumer demand away from the cereal sector this development was obviously a recipe for disaster in predominantly grain-growing areas, although livestock farmers could use cheap grain as animal feed. There was a shift in emphasis from wheat to oats, the oat acreage having

overtaken that of wheat by 1881. The acreage of wheat itself fell dramatically, from a high of 3,688,000 acres (1,492,000ha) in 1869 to only 1,375,000 acres (556,000ha) in 1904, also causing a massive reduction in the availability of suitable wheat straw for thatching.

The phase 1840–90 does not at first sight appear to hold together well given these dramatic contrast in farming fortunes at the beginning and end of the period. But from the thatch point of view, the agrarian rise and fall does form a single narrative. The impact of the golden age and the depression was felt most keenly in the arable areas of the south, where the number of thatched buildings had actually risen in the early nineteenth century. The golden age period witnessed the rebuilding of many farmhouses and steadings, while many of those which escaped would be more likely to suffer neglect and deterioration during the depression. During the 1840s, an increasing shortage of labour appears to have developed, implying that little new housing for rural labourers was being built. Empty, crumbling cottages were the legacy of emigration and the drift to the towns during the depression that followed.

Phase 3: 1890–1940

Agricultural change

Migration to the towns and overseas continued to depopulate rural areas into the twentieth century, and on the farm was matched by an unprecedented increase in output due to the success of scientific plant breeding. In production terms, however, the labour requirements for cereal production had reached their basic minimum and were reduced to modern levels only after the widespread adoption of the combine harvester in the 1940s and 1950s. The farming sector embraced mechanization and chemical inputs so as to maximize output, and many of the smaller farms that managed to survive the depression of the 1920s and 1930s were gradually integrated into larger production units on 'industrial' farms. Ancillary buildings on superfluous farmsteads were abandoned, and farm dwellings were sold or rented to townsfolk with access to transportation and the resources to replace thatch with higher-status roofing. The adoption of lower housing densities after the First World War, combined with the depressed state of agriculture and the consequent willingness of owners to sell, led to large losses of land between the two World Wars, at an average rate of over 60,000 acres (24,000ha) a year in the 1930s. Between 1850 and 1939 the agricultural land available per head of population probably fell from nearly 2½ acres (1ha) to under one acre (0.4ha) (Coppock 1971, 13).

Changing patterns of consumption and the improvement in transport networks shifted the emphasis from arable to livestock farming. It has been estimated that, whereas the gross output from livestock was 20% greater than that of crops in 1860–9, it was 168% larger in 1911–13, the output from crops having halved in the interval. The wheat acreage, however, had not altered significantly between 1900 and 1939, remaining close to 1.7 million acres (688,000ha), the extension through a massive effort during the war years being offset by the depression years of the late 1920s and early 1930s (Mitchell & Deane 1962, 78–9).

The knock-on effects in this phase of the agricultural depression of the 1880s and 1890s continued to be felt and were not confined to farmers, for many landlords also suffered a loss of economic and social status. Reductions of rent in the 1880s and 1890s reduced their incomes considerably and as a result some landowners, particularly those with no alternative income (ie from industrial or urban rents and investments), found their rent rolls so drastically reduced that the upkeep of their country houses and sporting estates became a luxury they could no longer afford. Consequently, these estates were either sold or let, the first two decades of the twentieth century witnessing a dramatic change in the pattern of landown-ership. The Local Government Act of 1894 which widened the vote and transferred power from local vestries to urban and district councils, hastened the decline of agriculture by transferring power away from landlords and farmers to the State and the Board of Agriculture. The decline of the rural estate had a dramatic impact on capital and maintenance building programmes and therefore on the role of the estate class of thatcher.

Apart from these tenurial problems, political changes in the period reverberated through the farming commu-nity. The combination of an increasingly industrial economy, waning social and political influence and continuing economic difficulties all contributed to the relegation of agriculture to a secondary consideration at government level. This relegation was mirrored in the comparative or in some cases complete lack of interest shown in this phase to rural regeneration, to the role of country craftsmen, to their need for materials such as good quality thatching straw.

Local authority intervention
The transferring of power onto local statutory authorities played an important role in the treatment of rural housing issues. In relation to thatched buildings, the impact was only really felt in the south of England. This was because, in the north, the major decline had already occurred, as a result of private choice and without any institutional interference.

Local authorities were active in destroying rather than preserving thatched buildings with the powers invested in them through housing and planning legislation. The 1935 *Rural Housing Annual Report* in Northamptonshire traces the slow progress of local authority involvement in housing and provides a useful starting point for studying the regional effects of housing policy on the survival of thatch (Northamptonshire County Council 1935).

Prior to 1890, the absence of any national framework for controlling housing policy meant that the landlord's whims were really paramount. Following the 1890 Act, Rural District Councils were given a fair opportunity by the legislature to remedy the worst evils. But hardly anything was done: in Northamptonshire, the rebuilding of Ashton as a model village in 1908 was the only flicker of light in the general gloom. The effect of the 1909 House and Town Planning Act was considered to be minimal, while that of the First World War had been exaggerated.

> It is sometimes assumed that the post-war housing difficul-ties were caused by the Great War. It is true that cottage-building came to a standstill between 1914 and 1919, and - what was more serious - existing houses were allowed to become dilapidated. But the roots of the trouble lay far deeper. A policy of 'laissez faire' and in some cases wanton destruction during the first half of the nineteenth century, created the rural slums: the subsequent failure of the rural housing authorities to make use of the facilities offered to them - urged upon them - by parliament, brought the slum problem to such a pass that it could be solved only by heroic measures. (op cit 16)

1919 was seen as a new beginning and 'all parties and all classes combined in a genuine enthusiasm to redress the evils of the past' (op cit 18). Between 1921 and 1925, a total of 895 local authority houses were completed in the rural districts of Northamptonshire, while private enter-prise contributed 458. Very soon, however, the situation had reversed, for between 1926 and 1929 only 490 houses were completed by local authorities, and 806 by private enterprise. The latter did not provide new accom-modation for the working classes. This indeed, was the crux of the problem, for of 2,187 houses built between 1919 and 1935 by local authorities in Northamptonshire, only 22.7% could be classified as agricultural.

So with very little new accommodation being pro-vided, the older style properties were suffering accord-ingly, as before 1926 the legislature had given no positive encouragement to owners of rural cottages to keep their property in repair. The Housing (Rural Workers) Act of 1926 was designed to tackle this problem, and it proved to be a very useful measure wherever its powers were fully exploited. The object of the Act was to give substantial help to owners willing to reconstruct or to recondition buildings suitable for occupation by agricul-tural workers or persons in a similar economic position. The Act was operated by the County Council, except where the duties were delegated to District Councils. The Rural Housing Act of 1926 was therefore the first to focus attention on the existing housing stock in rural areas rather than simply provide for new housing. Increasing assessment of the condition of this stock soon led to more embracing legislative powers in the Slum Clearance Acts of 1930 and 1935. While many studies have highlighted the outcome of these Acts in urban areas, the effects on rural housing have been less well investigated.

The *Rural Housing Annual Report* for Northampton-shire, for example, was prepared as a result of the requirements of the Act, and illustrates the point that rural areas, particularly the 'open' villages with tightly-packed, overcrowded back yards, could also be ripe candidates for clearance orders. The *Report* is a salutary antidote to the many slushy portrayals of life in thatched cottages and villages published in the 1930s.

Bozeat: Church Cottages (2): ... In No.2 ... the living-room is low, gloomy and very damp at the back; the parlour is so hopelessly damp that a constant fire is necessary, in order to preserve the furniture. The first bedroom has two windows - very low in front. One can see the pantry below through the gap between the floor and the wall. The second bedroom is uninhabitable. The floor is below ground level. The thatched roof is in bad condition, and the walls are gradually falling out. For demolition. (op cit 109)

As a result of his inspections, the County Medical Officer condemned 5,175 out of a total of 28,192 houses in the County (omitting Corby, Duston and Weston Favell). In Kings Sutton, 74 out of a total of 280 houses were condemned, of which at least 24 were thatched and 15 slated.

In reality, the ability of the local authorities to act on these recommendations was proscribed by technical questions of ownership and enforcement. Nevertheless, the fact that so many cases had to be earmarked was a symptom of the state of neglect at this poorer end of the rural housing scale. The discovery of the countryside by the urban middle-class elite was grafted on to this scene of dereliction, and their movement into it fed off and was in part sustained by a good supply of rural retreats which had been abandoned by their native occupants. But the trend took a long while to gather momentum and the numbers of people emigrating to the countryside in the 1920s and 30s in no way compensated for the contrary exodus from the countryside to the towns. Moreover, those contributing to a measure of rehabilitation were not always scrupulous or sympathetic to the local vernacular, choosing instead to speculate in rather than occupy the objects of their restoration schemes.

Great Doddington: A glaring example of inadequate reconditioning can be found in this village ... an L-shaped group of three dwellings has been 'dealt with'. One house has a new cement floor in its living-rooms, but the dampness remains as before, together with rotten window frames, cracked ceilings, bulging walls, and a leaky roof. ... The other two ... were reconditioned as follows: several courses of brick were inserted to increase the height of the bulging walls. The old thatch has been replaced by asbestos tiles with spouting which does not fulfil its function of taking water from the roof. (op cit 113)

Another group of middle class emigrants turned their backs completely on these ramshackle cottages and chose to impose their own vision of a pastoral idyll on the landscape by building afresh in a style which evoked a rather indeterminate vernacular tradition without sacrificing the standard of living to which they had become accustomed. Thatch blended well with this version of rural lifestyle and is a reminder that new build played a small but significant role in creating a demand for thatching materials in this period.

5   Thatch and new-build

PHASE 1: 1790–1840

The arguments for retaining and preserving thatch were well established in 1790. Even some of the authors of the County Reports begrudgingly admitted that it had its advantages (see Plymley 1803, 112). No general review of the subject fails to trot out the 'warm in winter/cool in summer' cliche. Henry Holland remarked that

> It may be doubted, whether the substitution of slate for thatch, in cottages and small farm-houses, is an advantage. Thatch renders a house warmer in winter, and cooler in summer, than slate. In winter, it prevents the warmth produced by the fires from escaping; and in summer it absorbs few of the sun's rays; at least, it allows but little heat to penetrate through it. A room below thatch may be kept warm with half the fuel which it would be when below slate. (Holland 1808, 86ff).

One of the main arguments for retaining thatch was the comparative lack of performance of other roofing materials (Middleton 1798, 41–2). The aesthetic qualities of thatch were also rarely questioned, even by some of its most vociferous enemies. Pitt, who never ceased complaining about thatch, nevertheless included details of Mr Smith's Cottage at Ashby Wolds, Leicestershire built of brick, 'but the roof covered with thatch, to give a more rural appearance' (Pitt 1809b, 25).

Other advantages of thatch, which were only infrequently stressed, included its easy availability (no mining of stone, digging of clay or firing of kilns) and its comparative lightness, at least where extensive buildup of layers had not been permitted. More obscurely, another easily overlooked advantage of thatch was that it could serve as a hiding-place: 'Their money bags in the thatch/ Was hid with careful thought', wrote Thomas Parker, thatcher and poet of Wombleton, Yorkshire (Hartley & Ingilby 1972, 38).

This last benefit excepted, the arguments in favour of thatch remained pretty constant throughout the period 1790–1940. This consistency in approach cannot be

Table 9 Major fires in Wessex, 1650–1799. A major fire is deemed to be one that destroyed more than 10 houses (Jones 1968, 148).

	Small town	Village
1650–99	50 %	19 %
1700–49	35 %	48 %
1750–99	15 %	33 %
	100 % = 20 fires	100 % = 33

attributed to the anti-thatch lobby, whose objections subtly shifted in emphasis over the same period.

In this first phase (1790–1840), combustibility was put forward as the primary incentive for abandoning thatch. 'Thatched buildings, in hot, dry, or windy, weather are exposed to the danger of conflagration, insomuch that I wonder accidents of this nature are not more frequent.' (Pitt 1809a, 26; Pitt 1813, 27) Although major urban thatch fires reduced in the eighteenth century (Table 9), villages were still prone to major conflagrations which could quickly obliterate large numbers of thatched buildings (Wood-Jones 1963, 247). The chalk and thatched cottages of the 200 people made homeless by the fire of 1850 at Ashwell, Hertfordshire were rebuilt in more durable brick and tile (Davey 1980, 35).

Particularly bad storms or hurricanes clearly created a demand for repairs. In some cases they may actually have caused a change to more 'durable' materials. In 1822, on the Leagram Estate, near Preston, Lancashire:

> there were still 'rattle and daub' houses and outbuildings existing ... A storm of unprecedented violence ... in November 18–, effected a revolution in the roofs of the district. Every thatched barn and building was more or less stripped, and there being no straw to renew them, all repairs were made with the more serviceable material. In Leagram at least thatched cottages disappeared from that date. (Harrison 1989, 98–9)

Tuke (1800, 35) complained that:

> the practice of thatching the roofs of buildings, is far from being economical; this kind of covering being frequently in want of repair, and often not attended to in due time, causes other parts of the building to be injured.

Another objection was that:

> in this mode of covering too, the ground is deprived of a large portion of manure by the quantity of straw thus used. I hope the land-proprietors will gradually introduce a system of building with materials more durable and less combustible than those now in common use (Pitt 1809a, 26).

The value of the straw for horse litter was lost if it was diverted onto the roofs of local buildings, particularly in the counties surrounding London.

Most of the authors of the County Reports viewed thatch as 'primitive', being more appropriate to the colonies than the mother country. Thatch was associated with superstition and witchcraft: undoubtedly it was an ideal material in which to secrete charms, coins or other 'magical' items, and instances arising well into this century can be quoted (Blackburn 1982, 16).

On the other hand, landowners influenced by Picturesque philosophy embraced the idea of the 'primitive' nature of thatch in order to blend in with their grand construction schemes. The landowner's commissioning role was important, for the use of thatch to achieve particular architectural aims was locked exclusively into the rural estate system at this time.

Model villages, of course, had begun to dot the landscape long before the cult of the Picturesque grasped the imagination of landowners. The interesting point is that in the early schemes, the construction of which was left to master-builders rather than architects, local vernacular materials were respected, including thatch where appropriate. Milton Abbas, though formal in its layout, followed the local Dorset vernacular with its forty white-washed cob and thatch cottages (Darley 1978, 20–22, 24–29, 35–36).

Thatch in particular met all the essential Picturesque criteria: 'roughness and irregularity, accident, contrast, a painterly, dynamic balance of light and mass (and, in theory, colour) ... arranging disparate and irregular forms together into a satisfying, casual, irregular whole' (Lyall 1988, 44). This visual quality of thatch comes increasingly to the forefront in the annual exhibition catalogues of the Royal Academy in the early nineteenth century. James 'Antiquity' Smith provided countless etchings of

tumbledown cottages, many around London with 'patched plaster ... various tints and discolorations ... weatherbeaten thatch ... The unrepaired accidents of wind and rain offer far greater allurements to the painter's eye' (op cit 58).

The simultaneous discovery of the cottage by architects, painters and authors is nicely encapsulated in Malton's description of 1798:

> a small house in the country, of odd irregular form, with various, harmonious colouring, the effect of weather, time and accident; the whole environed with smiling verdure, having a contented, cheerful, inviting aspect, and door on the latch, ready to receive the gossip neighbour, or weary, exhausted traveller ... a porch at entrance; irregular breaks in the direction of the walls, one part higher than another; various roofing of different materials (thatch particularly) boldly projecting; fronts partly built of walls of brick, partly weather boarded, and partly brick-noggin dashed; casement window lights. (Lyall 1988, 15)

One of the principal champions of thatch was the founder of the Picturesque movement, Uvedale Price, who 'waxes lyrical on the virtues of thatch' in his *Essay on the Picturesque* (1794). There was nevertheless a subtle shift in the attitude to thatch as the movement matured in keeping with the wider changes that occurred in Picturesque design, in particular the evolution of the primitive cottage into the cottage orné of the early nineteenth century.

The earliest natural cottage style was the Rustic, a natural successor to root-and-branch hermitages and huts

Figure 13 Rethatching the Lodge at Blaise Castle, Henbury, Gloucestershire, 23 May, 1936 (Museum of English Rural Life).

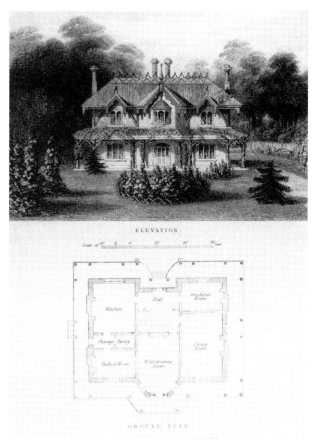

ELEVATION.

GROUND PLAN

Figure 14 A cottage orné in Richard Brown's Domestic Architecture *(1842), 'rather late in the style's history and, since the plan is rigidly symmetrical, decorative rather than Picturesque' (Lyall 1988, 78).*

found in English gardens from 1750 onwards. A Picturesque cottage, Queen Charlotte's Cottage, had been built in Kew Gardens as early as the 1770s (Appendix B: B29). According to designers, such as John Plaw, the most appropriate material for such structures was 'thatch [which] may be of straw, reeds, rushes, etc' (Lyall 1988, 68).

The early Picturesque cottage consists of a symmetrical and minimal core with an overlay of decoration and detail. However, as the pattern books continued to proliferate so the buildings illustrated became more florid. Shadwell Park, Norfolk, for example, has at least five rustic cottages scattered around the estate and two rather larger house-sized cottages with thatched front verandahs and bracketed timber posts (op cit 68).

The rustic cottage eventually developed into the full-blown style of the cottage orné. These appeared singly at first on estates (eg Badminton, Gloucestershire) or in villages (eg Erlestoke, Wiltshire). Nash and Repton began in this vein with a thatched dairy in the grounds at Blaise, near Bristol in 1802, before moving on to the grander scheme of the Hamlet, constructed for J Harford in 1810 (Fig 13). For the first time, cottages in the style were grouped together in a new creation. Unlike the earlier settlements, Blaise did not replace a demolished village. Three of the ten cottages were thatched, the rest stone slated. They exhibited much more complexity than their rustic predecessors, the roofs being of an irregular shape with eyebrow eaves and dormers, testing the thatcher's skills. Blaise thus paved the way for more elaborate schemes and larger cottages, popularized by the royal lodge at Windsor Great Park (1814), which was

Figure 15 Design for a picturesque villa – note heavily patterned ridge (Ricauti 1840, frontispiece).

closer to a villa but mocked small-scale traditional buildings with its thatch and fancy detailing (op cit 77).

Designs were disseminated through the many pattern books. Nathaniel Kent's *Hints to Gentlemen of Landed Property* of 1775 and J Wood's *Plans for Cottages* of 1781 (first published in 1792, see Harris & Savage 1990, 490) are two of the earliest, extolling the virtues of 'cottage' living. They undoubtedly influenced the public's perception of thatch, if only to implant the idea of the cottage orné style in the minds of a wider audience. In this respect, it is irrelevant whether it was the pattern books themselves or the actual architectural compositions resulting from them that continued to inspire (or for that matter dissuade) builders from adopting a style which favoured thatch as the natural roof covering. It was no doubt a combination of the two which had a significant impact on design criteria which are still subjects of debate today.

For example, the pattern books are full of designs which illustrate heavy patterned ridges. A rustic cottage orné by T F Hunt in *Designs for Parsonage Houses, Almshouses etc* (1827), for example, has a heavy ornate ridge. Richard Brown's *Domestic Architecture* (1852) has the most extraordinary design for a ridge, a triangular block cut repeated above in a second tier of pierced straw or wooden triangles finishing in ball finials. Quite how this was to be constructed in practice is not made clear (Fig 14). Ricauti's *Sketches for Rustic Work* (1848) includes a Swiss style lodge with barge-boards spiked with pine-cones and diamond liggers to the ridge and the eaves, the latter covering almost a third of the entire roof surface (Fig 15). All his other designs in this work employ thatch 'being the only covering used for the roofs ... on account of its rustic character' and incorporate these features. Most of Lugar's thatched designs, such as that for Rose Hill Cottage, near Maldon, Essex, show heavy ridges with liggers laced in diamond patterns (Lyall 1988, 23). As Lugar was an Essex architect, it is tempting to suggest that knowledge of local thatching styles influenced his designs. Whether or not this was the case, the association of heavy, ornate ridging with architect-designed compositions, an association which is still in evidence today, can almost certainly trace its origins to the cottage orné period. It is interesting to note that some cottages ornées were subsequently given this heavier treatment. A lithograph published by George Davey in 1826 shows the thatched cottages at Blaise Hamlet with what appears to be a plainer treatment than they have subsequently received.

A second design element of the period was the use of windows to break up a roof surface. W F Pocock's design for a cabane orné in 1807 had a thatched roof with eyebrowed dormer and porch (Pocock 1807, pl 12; Lyall 1988, 75). In 1789, Humphrey Repton designed his first vernacular cottage for a water porter as part of his Holkham Hall landscape proposals (not executed), which had 'a sunken and eyebrowed thatch roof' (Lyall 1988, 34, 62). Dormers in thatched roofs were of course nothing new, but the fascination for windows, particularly of an eyebrow shape, which were entirely in the roof surface was not something borrowed from existing vernacular examples. Plaw's design in 1795 for a primitivist

double cottage, for example, has a two-centred Gothic window in the thatch (op cit 67).

Thirdly, and more generally, both these design features became associated with the use of reed, and water reed in particular. Although flailed straw perhaps presented a more rustic appearance than water reed, for the architect it was the overall charm of thatch as a material rather than a specific style of thatching that was the prime consideration. As a result, architects chose what was perceived to be the most durable material, combed reed or water reed. Ricauti (1848, pls VII and VIII), for example, stressed that 'the best description of reed for the thatch, is that which has had the ears of corn "cut off", instead of being "thrashed out" and the straw considerably damaged by the flail'. The bringing together of all these elements, thatch, polite design, reed, ornate surface patterning, dormers, is a significant feature of the pattern books' contribution to the history of thatch.

This begs the question as to whether pattern books, because they were widely available, actually contributed to the standardization of thatch and thatching styles. It seems unlikely. Although distributed widely, the number of buildings actually constructed which slavishly followed the designs was very small, and many of the recommended thatch finishes were impractical.

In fact, pattern books designs probably enriched the repertoire of those thatchers who were contracted to carry out the work. For the first time, thatchers were being challenged to extend their abilities by taking on large, complex projects, such as John Nash's vast, rambling thatched Royal Lodge at Windsor for the Prince Regent (Lyall 1988, 15, 59). The designs ranged from small thatched shelters to large asymmetrical residences suitable for a 'large and opulent family'. Some of Plaw's *Sketches* (1800) show Gothick detailing to the thatched dormers and arcades which would have introduced thatchers to the two-centred arch for the first time. The semi-circular arched dormer now common in mid-Bedfordshire has spread in a very localized fashion from its polite, Picturesque source at Old Warden. Whether it has now become a vernacular feature of the area is a moot point.

Because the cottage orné style favoured singular rather than collective projects, it did not spawn a breed of specialist craftsman, but rather extended the capabilities of thatchers who would otherwise be engaged on vernacular buildings. Finally, the pattern books may have given a whiff of other vernacular styles. Repton pointed out that his water porter's cottage for the Holkham estate in Norfolk was based on a West Country design for a fisherman's hut, and this probably accounts for its distinctive 'dumpy' roof profile. The cottage was not built, but it stands as a reminder that thatchers were probably not quite as blind, as is so often portrayed, to styles and methods of thatching other than their own.

In the longer term, perhaps the most important influence of the pattern books was to encourage a much wider visual appreciation of 'polite' thatch than would otherwise have been the case. Readers could see that the cottage orné need not be the preserve for aged estate retainers, game- or gatekeepers but also 'afford[ed] the necessary conveniences for persons of refined manners and habits' (Pocock 1807, 8). One example of theory being carried through into practice is Robert Lugar's Rose Hill Cottage at Maldon, Essex, which is a large house made up of masses grouped together casually with tall chimneys breaking through the thatched roofs.

The move from the primitive to the cottage orné style thus encapsulated a significant shift in the public perception of thatch. The frontispiece to the English edition of Laugier's *Essay on Architecture* (1755) shows a Greek Doric temple in the process of being thatched. The illustration underlines the fact that the Picturesque by no means involved a complete rejection of Classical principles. Laugier in fact constructed his whole theory of Classicism based on lessons learnt by Original Man from nature in assembling the first building. Thatch (and rough timber) was thus associated with primitive shelters, and the New World of course tended to provide primitive models which apparently supported such arguments (Lyall 1988, 50–1).

The bonus in terms of social engineering was that the association of ideas, colonial influences, verandahs, primitive huts, thatch, emphasized and reinforced the primitive social state of the peasant inhabitants. There is an apocryphal story that in the mid nineteenth century the peasant tenants of the cottages in the thatch and curly bargeboard Bedfordshire village of Old Warden had to wear red cloaks and pointed hats as they went about their business in the village street. Murray (1895) commented on the red clothing worn by the cottagers there to match the paintwork.

With the adoption of the cottage orné style by a more affluent class of occupant, however, the notion that thatch was a covering suitable only for the poor man's hovel was no longer sacrosanct. In this revisionist light, thatch became the natural covering for country retreats, symbolic of the need to escape from the mounting pressures of modern life. This new conception of thatch took some time to mature. The Picturesque movement was in part responsible for this, a victim really of its own success. For when the inevitable reaction set in, it took the form of a stark rejection of rustic natural materials such as thatch. Aided and abetted by the reformist's zealous quest for air and light in the labourer's home, thatch would disappear almost entirely for a time from the architect's repertoire. By the 1860s many cottages ornés were unsaleable and often in a state of collapse.

PHASE 2: 1840–90

During the second phase architects such as P F Robinson produced a few designs which incorporated thatch, but as antiquarian interest tended to focus on the manorial and lordly end of the spectrum, then the evidence tended to favour the more expensive and durable materials of slate and tile rather than the more rustic alternative (Lyall 1988, 17–19, 26, 39, 80, 90). While large landowners could indulge in whimsical thatched cottages, these were hardly compatible with the work ethic upheld by the majority of the middle classes. Charitable and reforming zeal with an emphasis on moral living tended to favour

sharp architectural lines and cleanliness (as at Talbot Village in Bournemouth): thatch was thought not to be conducive to either of these requirements.

The disregard for thatch in urban, new-build schemes during this period only served to reinforce the rural, pastoral, antiquated image of thatch. Some landowners, such as the Whitbreads and later Lord Ongley at Old Warden in Bedfordshire, adhered to the Picturesque concept of thatch as a covering suitable for peasant cottages.

The rural beauty of thatch which these settlements sought to capture was underscored in the 1880s onwards as the agricultural depression began to take its toll in terms of neglected steadings and decaying farm buildings. The equation that thatch equalled rural charm underlay the work of the artist circles that established themselves at this time in the southern counties, particularly Kent and Surrey and their paintings became early marketing tools in the rediscovery of the countryside by the urban masses.

Perhaps as a legacy of the anti-thatch lobby, the architects associated with the early garden suburbs, starting with Bedford Park, London in 1877, did not tend to advocate thatch as a suitable covering (Darley 1978, 117–121).

Relegated to the second division by the 1830s, thatch for new-build work nearly disappeared from the league table altogether in the period 1840 to 1890, apart from in seaside resorts and on a few quirkily-designed buildings, such as the Bell Inn at Finedon, Northamptonshire, reconstructed in 1872 with a reed thatched roof (anon nd [1], 71).

Some of the old fears about thatch were being voiced more loudly in this period, the dread of fire in rural areas being fuelled for instance by the spread of portable steam and traction engines. Competition from more durable materials, usually slate, was now seen as the main factor causing a decline in thatched buildings.

On the one hand, the problem may have been exacerbated in this second phase due to the vast numbers of buildings covered with thatch that had been left to deteriorate as a result of rural depopulation and the effects of the agricultural depression. On the other, the concept of cleanliness in any case was beginning to influence the design of cottages. Isaac, in his article on the improvement of agricultural dwellings under the heading 'Providing for Decency' commented:

> a suggestion has been made to raise all thatch roofs to the pitch of slate – that is, to raise the walls, substituting tile or slate for the thatch. This is peculiarly necessary where, in order to give a proper subdivision of the rooms, the cubical contents have been diminished. (Isaac 1856, 119)

this was the kind of thinking which advocated drainage schemes, clean water supplies, earth closets and tidy slate or tile roofs as essential contributors to the 'health of the village' (Fig 16).

A very dismissive view was expressed in the *Architects' and Builders' Journal* which held that

> thatching is materially an abomination and morally a snare, and forms the most unhygienic roof covering ever devised by the wit or witlessness of man, and it fosters a fatuous and

Figure 16 Improved farm cottages built in 1848 with a sample of those they replaced, from William Gray's Rural Architecture *(1852) (Woodforde 1969, 52, copyright Routledge Kegan Paul).*

enervating love of picturesqueness. Its only merit is that it easily takes fire, and this conveniently gets rid of the multifarious disease germs of which it is an unrivalled collector and distributor. (quoted in Potter 1914, 43)

Though extreme, the fact that such sentiments were expressed at all was a reflection of the low esteem in which thatch was held in the late nineteenth century, at least in architectural circles.

PHASE 3: 1890–1940

An important development affecting thatch in this period was the production of new roofing materials. In the first two phases, the only real competitors to thatch were slate and tiles, whereas many new roofing materials came onto the market in the late nineteenth and early twentieth centuries. The transfer from organic to industrial materials drew attention to the fact that roof pitches and spans could be extended and the pitch flattened, thus taking roof shapes further away from the very minimum requirements for thatch. Corrugated iron was particularly popular in agricultural circles and changed the face of traditional steadings (Bowley 1960, 117–8) (Fig 17).

The earliest known date of the use of concrete tiles in this country is 1893, and their production had overtaken roofing slates by 1938. Asbestos cement tiles and sheets were introduced into this country in the first decade of this century. They were early regarded as superior to corrugated iron where good insulation was required. Resistance to fire and to corrosion, and the absence of need for painting it, were also recognized as advantages. The war brought an increased demand for a light roofing material for numerous temporary and permanent buildings.

The shortage of traditional building materials after the war encouraged the more widespread use of asbestos cement tiles, slates, and sheet on other buildings (Bowley 1960).

An obscure connection between asbestos and thatch was outlined in *The Architect and Building News*. An extraordinarily fussy method of fireproofing thatch involved first soaking it for 15 to 20 minutes in a solution of sodium aluminate, then rinsing it in clean water, then subjecting it to steaming (the hiring of a small vertical boiler was recommended for this operation), and then finally dipping the thatch 'in powdered asbestos' mixed with water.

From some inobscure reason the asbestos thus applied shows no tendency to scale under the influence of the

Figure 17 Thatch being replaced by corrugated iron, Donhead St Mary, Wiltshire (Museum of English Rural Life).

Table 10 Comparison of roofing materials: 1790 and 1940.

1790	1940
Slate	Slate (+ imports)
Clay tiles	Clay tiles
Pantiles	Pantiles
Thatch	Thatch
Turf	Corrugated iron, etc.
Lead/copper	Asbestos sheeting & slates
	Metal sheeting: steel/copper/zinc/lead
	Glass
	Concrete tiles
	Paper roofs

weather, and neither does it alter the general appearance of the thatch. (anon 1927b, 1066)

Corrugated iron was also often placed over existing layers of thatch, thus preserving the material if not the appearance. Old and new roof coverings were thus not always in direct competition with each other.

In summary, the period between 1790 and 1940 witnessed a massive expansion in the choice of roofing materials (Table 10). Despite on the whole being cheaper, easier to apply and more durable, the availability of a whole new range of roofing materials did not have the effect of obliterating thatch. On the contrary, the spread of these brash-looking, factory-produced coverings into rural areas created a backlash of sentiment:

Figure 18 'Romantic' thatch: a painting from the Kent school (Dick & Allingham 1992, 167, copyright Bracken Books).

Few lovers of our matchless English countryside can have failed to observe with regret the extent to which the thatch of our rural cottages and farms has of late years been replaced by a material, not only unpicturesque, but actively disfiguring - the frankly hideous corrugated iron roof ... Hennock and Ashton, in the Teign Valley, [are] examples of exquisitely picturesque villages, the charm of which has been completely destroyed by unsightly roofs on many of the beautiful old houses they comprise (Kennaway nd, 3).

This kind of reaction was part of a significant reawakening of interest in thatch during 1890–1940, which manifested itself in a variety of ways, not least in the artistic portrayal of country cottages, which constantly reinforced the rusticity of thatch and its romantic image (Fig 18). In 1933, *The National Builder* noted that thatch

has been successfully introduced in some new building estates on the coast and elsewhere, in which the maintenance of a rural character helps the profitable sale of sites ... The trade of thatching is not only prosperously carried on, but employment in it has been increasing during recent years. One significant fact is that Builders' Price Books contain detailed particulars and prices of thatching, and the names of firms or individuals who undertake it. Another, that thatched roofs are being affected by the flair for advertisement. Recently in a bus-route village not far from Royston, Herts, the roof of an old, low house in the chief thoroughfare was golden with new wheat-straw thatch. The house, with shop, was occupied by a confectioner, and the thatcher craftsman had ornamentally lettered with gleaming withy bands the street wings of the roof so that all who approached - particularly those on a bus top - got information that ices were obtainable within. Only a thatched roof could be used for commercial publicity of this nature, and remain pleasing. (anon 1933, 238)

L Mark Kennaway, a solicitor based in Teignmouth, was an 'earnest advocate' (Potter 1914, 44) and on the eve of the First World War wrote a pamphlet *To Lovers of English Rural Scenery* (also quoted above). Although couched in flowery prose, it made a number of practical points, some of which have a curiously contemporary ring:

and in cases where all things must be weighed in the banker's scales, it may be pointed out that, in these days when so many seek residence or change in the country for its charm's sake, the destruction of rural beauty must soon affect the rural purse by diverting the traveller to less disfigured spots. (Kennaway nd, 4)

Kennaway was realistic about what steps should be taken to save the thatched roof. He was dubious about the feasibility of setting up any kind of thatch preservation society. Instead, he offered two possible solutions. He encouraged landlords to take the lead, either directly where buildings were in their own hands or through leases which contained covenants requiring tenants to maintain thatch coverings. Secondly, individual feeling should be 'roused' and 'directed'. 'The influence and support, not only of artists, but of all who prize the harmony of rural landscape, is needed for the preservation of the thatched roof' (op cit 4–5).

As a contribution to this campaign, Kennaway collected letters of support and, since notice of the appeal had appeared in advance in the press, the names of the more prominent correspondents were included at the end of the pamphlet. These included the Secretary to the National Trust, the artists Walter Crane and M A Hughes (describing himself as a 'Peasant Artist'), the author Rev Sabine Baring-Gould, and more unlikely candidates such as Fred Fisher, consulting surgeon at the Dorset County Hospital. Adding a practical dimension to these names was the author and land agent G W Hinton who indicated in his letter of support that the use of thatch on farm buildings was being positively encouraged in some agricultural circles. 'In the first place, I may inform you that there is nothing to equal a thatched roof for rearing any class of stock' (op cit 7).

In 1910, the Board of Agriculture and Fisheries itself published a leaflet entitled *Thatching*. This was specifically aimed at encouraging farmers to train their regular staff in rick-thatching skills:

> The art of thatching can be learnt by any intelligent farm labourer, if he is given a few opportunities for practice and a little instruction ... After harvest the local thatcher is often hard-pressed with work, so that it may be difficult to obtain his services when they are most required. Meanwhile the unthatched ricks are exposed to the weather, and, should a wet season be experienced, the damage may be considerable. All risk of this sort is avoided if the thatching can be done by the regular staff. (Board of Agriculture and Fisheries 1910)

It is not clear quite where the Board gathered its information on thatching techniques, although the leaflet was apparently written by a Scot, and describes two systems of straw thatching. The first method was clearly that of the north-west of England (though the leaflet does not say this), using turves as a base and 'stapple' thatch as the overcoat. The second method described involved sewing the straw to the battens, but there is no suggestion that additional spar coats were ever applied or any mention of fixing materials such as wooden spars and sways. Finally, heather, described as the 'staple medium' for thatching in the north and central counties of Scotland, reeds 'used in a similar manner to straw, being either sewn direct to the roof or inserted through turves' and broom are mentioned as suitable thatching materials.

The leaflet is probably the first 'official statement' on thatching in a national perspective. Its northern regional bias reflects the fact that very little published information on the subject was available. J Cowell, a Cambridgeshire reed thatcher, was clearly incensed by the inaccuracies. At the end of his copy, he scribbled

> whoever wrote this knew *very little about it*: might have been so a Hundred years ago, but would not do today. I never yet saw a roof covered with turf before thatching, and I have been on some queer old buildings. (Cambridgeshire Record Office 1)

The leaflet reflects the shortcomings of much of the literature on thatching: when written by the lay person it can invent and perpetuate so many fallacies. Nevertheless, these first excursions into thatching methods were a sign of a new sensitivity to regional identities and techniques.

Innocent complained that the Board of Agriculture's leaflet was likely 'to destroy those local aspects of the craft which make it so interesting to students of old building construction' (Innocent 1916, 188). Innocent's own *The Development of English Building Construction* published in 1916 was one of the first published works to address the topic of regional variations in thatching methods and materials. The author believed the craft to be on the eve of extinction, due to the evil influences of 'printing and improved communications' and the emergence of the 'capitalist thatcher' (ibid). The capitalist thatcher was one who tended to turn his back on the main stock of thatched buildings of an agricultural nature, and focused instead on the new housing markets.

As early as 1909, *The British Architect* commented on

> a large revival of thatch for the roofing of new buildings. To this Mr Schultz referred in one of his recent lectures at the Carpenters Company's Hall, and we believe he indicated that the demand was often in excess of the supply, especially in regard to the Norfolk reed thatching. He and other able modern architects have used thatch with excellent results, and it appears to us that the building by-laws should recognise it as a proper building material in certain cases ... The examples we publish to-day are of simple buildings, and are illustrative of the charm that goes with thatched roofing, both old and new, but quite elaborate examples of modern thatching are to be found in large houses recently built, more especially in the Eastern counties of Norfolk reeds...The new cottages were built for the Earl of Lovelace, by Mr C F A Voysey, and show how well the feeling and character of the old ones have been preserved. The more elaborate design, by Mr Morris ... shows a good recent example, and we published a delightful tea-house with a thatched roof, by Mr Schultz in our issue for January 22 ... When we remember the value of form and outline and texture which is obtained by thatch, we must feel that it is a craft to be preserved and encouraged. (anon 1909, 145)

In the description of the 'cottage' by Morris, attention was drawn to the fact that

> In those districts where the by-laws are not so stringent, the use of thatch to a modified extent has been revived. Mr C Spooner, in Sussex, Mr Gimson, in Leicestershire, and Mr Detmar Blow, in Norfolk, have all used thatch in an

Figure 19   Architect-designed Arts and Crafts House of cob built by Ernest Gimson near Budleigh Salterton, Devon (Ellis et al 1947, Country life Publications).

individual way, and with charming results. (Morris 1909, 149, fig 19)

The majority of architects associated with the Arts and Crafts Movement experimented at some stage with thatch. The Movement was probably the single most important influence on thatch and new-build in the twentieth century. Nouveau riche landowners, in particular, were active in commissioning buildings which combined thatch and Arts and Crafts detailing. The architect Huckvale designed stone cottages with deep-thatched roofs clustered around the green at Ashton, Northamptonshire for Charles de Rothschild. Debenham's Briantspuddle in Dorset was built in a full-blown Picturesque style (Darley 1978, 243–7). Less eccentric but concocted out of a similar blend of utopian and Arts and Crafts teaching coupled with the rediscovery of vernacular materials and the bourgeois exodus to the countryside, was the Garden City. Letchworth, for instance, contained examples of key architect-designed buildings with thatched roofs, such as Barry Parker's own house and studio of 1907 derived, significantly, from the vernacular architecture of East Anglia.

Apart from during the hiatus of the First World War (common to all other aspects of the building trade) demand for architect-designed thatched houses remained brisk throughout the rest of the period. Even when overtaken by Modernist preferences in the 1930s, the rural 'rightness' of thatch was so heavily ingrained that when 'Silver End' in Essex was built for Crittals (pioneers of the metal-framed door and window), modernist or plain neo-Georgian houses were joined by a church incongruously sporting a thatched roof (Darley 1978, 253–4).

Occasionally, thatch itself might actually be employed in association with innovative building techniques. Ernest Trobridge at Kingsbury, London created a curious concoction of cottage orné and castellated Gothic. He preferred thatch, on the grounds that it was lighter and required less structural support. As he himself is reported to have said, he had adopted the olde worlde style not 'as an antiquarian enthusiast but as a practical architect'. Unexpectedly, beneath the thatch and timberwork is a prefabricated structural timber framework patented by Trobridge (Lyall 1988, 139–40).

M Paige Wood thought that 'the exigencies of war and the difficulty of obtaining tiles' had somewhat relaxed the stringency of by-laws and Building Acts, to the extent that

> thatch appears for a time to have come into its own again. I have recently come across several cottages in course of building in Sussex, cottages of very different types and in quite different parts of the county, which are being roofed in the primitive fashion ... One example was in a little South Down village where a row of semi-detached cottages of Government pattern was being put up, and the end pair of the row were thatched instead of tiled like the rest. (Wood 1921, 544)

The urbanite influence on maintaining this demand was beautifully captured by A G Street in 1933.

> I have some friends who retired from town business some years ago, and decided to buy a house in the country. They came to me and stated their requirements ... One was the necessity for a large garden, and the other was thatch ... When they used the word 'thatch' a gleam came into their eyes - the same sort of gleam that you can see in a cat's eyes when she is watching a bowl of goldfish. Thatch they yearned for, and thatch they intended to have. (Street 1933, 753)

The Architectural Association Journal featured some new cottages built in 1923 on the estate of Sir Walter Preston at Tetbury, Gloucestershire and designed by Maurice Chesterton. The architect believed that:

> 'to design in thatch one should think in terms of snow.' Snow has other qualities, perhaps rather more abstract, which put one in the right frame of mind for designing in thatch, innocence and simplicity; by innocence I do not mean ignorance, nor by simplicity a lack of understanding. Cleverness is a curse laid upon the artist of to-day, because of his lack of faith, and the curse falls heavily upon those who try to be clever on a thatched roof. (anon 1923b, 61)

The Studio in 1926 also carried an article on 'The Revival of Thatching' in which it was stated that:

> The art of thatching has, of late years, taken on a fresh lease of life. Discouraged, for a long time, by bye-laws drawn up from a townsman's point of view, and condemned by narrow prejudice and vague theories of hygiene, it has been in danger of final extinction. Fortunately more liberal views have prevailed in time to save it, helped, in some measure, by changes in economic influences. Some of our leading architects, whose authority is indisputable, have pronounced definitely in its favour and contributed, in a practical manner to its revival. (anon 1926, 93)

The new, more enthusiastic tone that was now being struck was not confined simply to aesthetic considerations. Experimental work in this period produced some surprising results. In 1929, it was claimed that straw thatch:

is really one of the most excellent of modern building materials. The demerits of the old-fashioned kind were that it required considerable skill to use, and there was always the anxiety of possible fire. These difficulties, however, have now been removed entirely, and modern thatch gives all the old insulation from heat, cold and noise, but the skilled weaving of thatch is needed no longer and the danger of fire is non-existent. (Dodds 1929, 86)

What was this remarkable new material?

This new thatch is made up by compressing straw, reeds, rushes, marsh litter, papyrus and similar vegetable fibres in solid panels under pressure of 100lb per square inch [7.03kg per cm²]. These are tightly bound by parallel steel binding wires running lengthwise on both faces of the panels across the fibres, and the whole is held together by steel hooks passing through the straw. (ibid)

The sheets could be used for interior partitions, or if coated or rendered in some way, on exterior walls or for roofing. Thatchboard was one of the more extreme attempts designed to overcome the 'demerits of the old-fashioned kind' of thatch. But the literature of the period is also full of more mundane, practical advice. The problem of damp plinth walls caused by a lack of eaves gutters on thatched roofs could, for example, be rectified by providing 'a concrete or stone paved causeway ... to carry the water some distance therefrom' (Potter 1914, 43).

The fire question was also tackled during this period. *The British Architect* thought that: 'it seems extraordinary that the obnoxious clauses forbidding its use (except under almost impossible conditions), should not have been cut out of the by-laws long ago' (Morris 1909, 149).

For many people the disabilities of thatch have been perhaps too much emphasized, and its abilities not enough. It is warm and cool. When settled down and solid the danger from fire is not serious, there being no draught possible inwards or outwards to encourage flames. I have known a smithy near Cambridge upon which the sparks had fallen in thousands daily for seventy years without damage; and of a thatched house on fire in which the thatch refused to burn, finally falling upon and extinguishing the burning ruins. (Powell 1923, 859)

It was also pointed out in 1914 that:

the danger from fire ... is more apparent than real, as Lloyds insure brick buildings with thatched roofs for 2s 6d [12p] per cent ... There is a liquid supplied by the Timber Fireproofing Company Ltd, of Townmead Road, Fulham, London, SW, which is said will thoroughly fireproof thatch if it is treated before being used. The Home Office issued a fly leaf some time since advocating 16oz [454g] of tungstate of soda to 12 pints [6.8l] of water, and 2½oz [71g] of phosphate soda mixed with water added thereto. Mr J G Cowell's, of Soham, prescription is 28lbs [12.7kg] sulphate ammonia, 14lbs [6.4kg] lump carbonate ammonia, 7lbs

[3.2kg] borax, 7lbs boracic acid, 14lbs lump alum dissolved in 500 parts by measure of water. (Potter, 1914, 44)

Several companies marketed their own specially devised brands. The British Batavian Trading Company, for example, produced a leaflet advertising the firm's 'Protector' solution 'for protecting all kinds of fibrous materials such as reeds, heath, straw etc' (British Batavian Trading Company *c* 1915). It claimed that 'Nearly half a million square yards [418,000m²] of Thatch treated with our "Protector" are at present in use, and many municipal authorities strongly recommend it'. The 'Proof' was given in 'before' and 'after' photographs, showing a trial roof,

the middle part of which has been covered with ordinary thatch, the parts on either side consisting of thatch which had been prepared eighteen months before the trial. During that period, it had been exposed to all weathers. A trial was made to set the prepared thatch on fire after it had been drenched with paraffin and benzine, the result being that the prepared material was only scorched in a few places. (British Batavian Trading Company *c* 1915)

The notion that thatch attracted birds to nest in it was dismissed by *The National Builder* as something that 'can only seriously apply to inferior or old work. Wire netting is preventive' and in any case, 'some folk prefer the birds' (anon 1933, 238). By the turn of the century, the vermin problem had tended to be hidden away behind several coats of plaster and new build projects were invariably designed to have plastered ceilings below the thatch.

Whether these changes made much difference in preserving thatch was probably of less importance than the fact that fears were being allayed and perceptions altered. Owners now wanted thatch and demand began to outstrip supply. Complaints about the scarcity of thatchers become increasingly frequent after the First World War.

Thatchers are too rare in England, and there is work for many more if they could be found or made. Possibly in some counties scholarships in thatching might be offered. The disuse of the work has caused much hardly-won knowledge to disappear, and proper training by experts would bring back to the work the esteem it deserves but has largely lost. (Powell 1923, 862)

According to *The Builder* corrugated iron was 'usually the result of the property owner being unable to secure the services of a reliable thatcher' (anon 1932, 130).

[in the south west] one or two new houses whose builders wanted thatch had eventually to be roofed with other materials merely because no thatcher could be found to do the required work within the stipulated time. (Ward 1939, 431)

Some people who have built houses on the Devon-Dorset border have been to the expense of bringing both Norfolk thatchers and reed from the Broads 'down West'. This was primarily because they specially wanted roofs of Norfolk

Table 11 *Comparative cost of roofing materials (cost per square in modern pence, labour and materials): 1726 (Neve 1726 [1969]), 1790 (Young 1804b, Lincolnshire Record Office 2), 1901 (Laxton 1901), 1941 (Rea 1941).*

	1726	1790	1901	1941
Straw thatching	20–25	26	62.5	380
Water reed thatching	45	105	157.5	500
Tiling	140–185	70–95	255	400
Slating	150–300	41	245	425

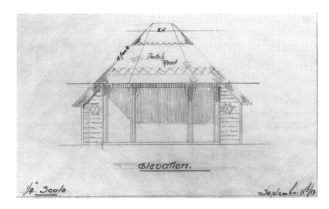

Figure 20   *From drawing to realisation: a garden summer house built and thatched by John Cowell; architect's drawing (11 September 1917) of garden tea room, Irton Manor, Scarborough (Cowell Collection, Cambridgeshire Record Office).*

reed, but there was certainly more than enough work in the locality for indigenous thatchers. (ibid)

The water-reed firms were thus busy expanding.

> Far from suffering a decline, reed thatching is experiencing a period of great popularity. Employers frequently have difficulty in finding sufficient numbers of skilled craftsmen to carry out expeditiously all their contracts. (Deas 1939, 89)

The reason for the spread of water reed at the expense of local straw techniques is not at first sight easily explained. After all, straw was still abundant and cheap, while water reed was costly to buy and to apply. The reed harvest was still an entirely manual operation, while the Broads were hardly well placed to service water reed requirements around the country.

These 'negative' aspects of water reed were, however, turned around and converted into selling points. Straw was cheap, and cheapness tended to be equated with inferiority and 'primitiveness': the fact that straw made economic sense was of little importance, and indeed only

fuelled the notion that if it could be afforded by the masses, then it could not be a status symbol.

Water reed on the other hand was considered to be more durable. It had always been considered the smart and more expensive cousin, as Table 11 illustrates. Not only was it always the most expensive method of thatching a roof throughout the period, but by 1940 the cost of water reed had even overtaken that of other roofing materials, signifying its elevation to luxury commodity status. Architects liked it because it could be ornamented and therefore to a certain extent designed. The bigger firms liked it because reed could be purchased in standardized bundles, was clean to handle and could be transported in bundles around the country. Architects liked dealing with the reed-thatching firms because they

Figure 21   *From drawing to realisation: a garden summer house built and thatched by John Cowell; completed project, Irton Manor, Scarborough (1919) (Cowell Collection, Cambridgeshire Record Office).*

Table 12 Location of jobs undertaken by Cowells of Soham, 1916–1920 (Cambridgeshire Record Office 1).

Berks	2	Herts	6	Somerset	1
Bucks	5	Hants	2	Staffs	1
Cambs	9	Leics	1	Suffolk	1
Cornwall	2	Norfolk	1	Surrey	3
Essex	1	Northants	1	Sussex	7
Kent	4	Oxon	2	Yorks	2

were more commercially-minded and better integrated in the building industry.

An excellent example of this type of capitalist thatcher was J G Cowell of Soham (Figs 20 and 21). Extremely well documented, and deserving a much fuller treatment than can be given here, Cowell's firm is less well-known than the Norfolk business of the Farman family. Yet both were equally active in the first few decades of the twentieth century promoting water reed. The first job recorded in Cowell's notebooks was the repair of the reedwork at the Retreat, Lakenheath in 1898. Cowell was running a weekly advertisement in *The Builder* in 1903, and also placed advertisements in *The British Architect*, *The Builders Journal* and *The Country Gentleman*. His marketing expenditure was just under £12 in that year. In the subsequent year, he had a special *Treatise* on thatching printed, which was in effect an advertisement for the superiority of 'ornamental' water reedwork. Cowell's market is evident in his list of structures considered to be suitable candidates for reed-thatching.

> Reedwork is suitable for any class of roof, viz. Country Houses, Cottages, Gate Lodges, Farm-Buildings, Bungalows, Pavilions, Fruit Stores, Dairies, Summer Houses, etc., and is acknowledged to be the only covering that is warm in Winter and cool in Summer, is noted for its absence of vermin, while its artistic appearance is unequalled. (Cowell nd)

In 1904 Cowell had promotional postcards made showing the firm's work, and subsequently advertised widely in the Country Gentleman's Association *Monthly* and *Annual*, the *Farmer and Stockbreeder*, *The Land Agents Society Journal*, *The Daily Telegraph*, *The Irish Builder*, *Country Life*, *Clerk of Works*, and the *Architect and Contract Reporter*.

Cowell was active as a builder and reed-merchant and also ran a team of thatchers. His ledger for 1916–28 illustrates both the tremendous range of jobs undertaken, and also the geographical extent of the firm's business interests. The bulk of its work was located in the south, and particularly the south-east. In the five year period 1916 to 1920 the firm worked on 51 jobs in 18 different counties (Table 12). Despite using reed from the Norfolk Broads almost exclusively on all these jobs, only once was the material used in its county of origin. Given that Britain was at war for three of these years, the fact that all the supply and transport difficulties were overcome is all the more remarkable. The work was, however, all of a 'polite' nature, and included the thatching of garden shelters at Eastbourne (1916), a fruit-store at Burton-on-Trent (1916), a pavilion at Wargrave (1916). Excluding

repair work, only 14 of the 51 jobs in the five years involved new-build houses.

The Cowells and Farmans never tired of extolling the virtues of reed over those of straw. When M Bateman of Chalfont St Giles in 1931 enquired of Cowell 'do you think all straw would be a satisfactory job.' Cowell had no doubts: 'A roof thatched entirely of reeds, with a ridge of sedge, makes the strongest thatched roof' (Cambridgeshire Record Office 1).

By the 1930s it was becoming clear that this vigorous publicity drive was beginning to pay off. In 1932, *The Builder* remarked that 'Another kind of thatching greatly in demand to-day is that for which reeds are used. This makes a very serviceable roof and lasts indefinitely' (anon 1932, 130). The fact that expert exponents in water reed like the Oldfield family were 'thatchers to HM the King for houses and farm buildings on the Sandringham estate' was also a good selling point (anon 1933, 236).

The reed publicity machine did not, however, stop just at extolling the virtues of reed. Almost imperceptibly, the denigration of straw thatch crept in.

> [reed] is not so easily fired as straw, for reeds are not readily set alight. Thus, when Charles Kingsley wrote in his 'Hereward the Wake' of that hero firing the reeds of Ely against the Normans, he is exercising his imagination against the facts of nature. The fenland reeds refuse to burn, outside the pages of fiction. (Harper 1921, 392)

Harper also remarked that 'the reed-layer of thatch would scarcely see eye to eye with the thatcher in straw' (1921, 392). Another authority in a dogmatic statement made in 1926: 'when speaking of thatch Mr Hepworth reminds us that "one should distinguish between reed and straw"'. Reed roofs, according to Hepworth, could not be easily be set on fire, while 'in the case of straw the risk is greater. Some insurance companies now recognise this and will insure a reed-roofed house at about half the premium required if straw is used' (anon 1926, 93–4).

In 1927, *The National Builder* published the substance of Cowell's *Treatise*, in which the author maintained that 'the life of a straw roof is about 15 years, and is suitable for temporary structures, the cheaper class of rural cottages and farm buildings'. It was also 'impossible to do anything of the nature of pattern work on the surface' of straw (anon 1927a, 35). Six years later, the same magazine not only claimed that 'reed thatching is far superior to other sorts' but also that:

> the difference in appearance and durability between a roof thatched with the poorest classes of corn straw and one thatched with good reeds is so great as practically to make them different things, although nominally classed under a general name. (anon 1933, 236)

Later in the article it was quite categorically stated that 'it is with straw thatch that the danger of fire principally exists' (anon 1933, 238). Water reed had escaped the effects of mechanization and agricultural breeding experiments, both of which were identified as major contributors to a decline in the quality of thatching straw. In the 1930s, E Gunn (1936, 30) thought that the use of thatch in the West Country had declined because of the damage caused by machine-cutting, but usually the blame was laid on the threshing-machine.

Cowell and Farman were the two principal firms operating in the water reed market, and indeed virtually all the well-known architect-designed thatched buildings of the period were tackled by one or other of the firms. It should be stressed that they made a tiny statistical impact on the total stock of thatched buildings, and the essentially idiosyncratic character of those buildings should also be recognized. But the influence that these firms exerted on the course of thatching in the twentieth century was of a quite disproportionate scale.

First, these firms met and catered for the demand for a whole range of buildings of innovative architectural design and serving totally new functions. Secondly, they helped to encourage, in conjunction with the architects they worked for, the notion that water reed was the only material for 'superior' types of work. Thirdly, the firms vied with each other in the extent and complexity of ornamentation applied to their jobs. Their efficient publicity campaigns served to fix the image of immaculate and decorative reed thatch in the popular mind. In their language, thatching was as much an 'art' as a 'craft', and the parameters which they set for the degree of decoration that could be applied to a roof are still very much at the centre of the debate concerning 'style' today. Fourthly, they exploded the popular image of the lone and uncommunicative thatcher working only within walking distance of his home. They harnessed new opportunities such as those offered by the expanding transport network, moving materials and men around the country and even at times outside it (eg to Ireland). They ran their businesses on fully capitalist lines, with a paid workforce who might be hired and fired according to conduct, ability, and availability of work. In turning their backs almost completely on the agricultural world, they elevated the status of the thatcher to that of respectable and respected craftsman.

A more unfortunate consequence of this water reed marketing campaign was that it elevated the notion that reed was the only proper covering for a roof, that it was fireproof, vermin-proof and far more durable than any other material. In denigrating straw roofs, the reed lobby effectively staunched any concerted campaign to promote thatch in general.

6   Conclusion

In 1790 thatch was to be found in all parts of England and on almost every building type. By 1940 the number of thatched buildings had fallen drastically, and thatch was largely restricted to the southern counties. This supports the general perception that thatching has been in terminal decline for at least two centuries. Nevertheless, the analysis of thatch in its different contexts as presented here has suggested that the plotting of this perception as a steep decline is too simplistic and masks some very interesting trends in the period 1790–1940. These can best be highlighted by examining demand in a variety of contexts.

The demand for thatch in most urban areas had been reduced to a mere trickle by 1940. It was not abandoned as early as records of fires would suggest, however, and many towns retained thatch on ancillary buildings well after most dwellings had been re-roofed in more durable materials. Nor was the decline absolute, and in some specialized contexts (eg coastal resorts) thatch enjoyed somewhat of a renaissance. Nevertheless the sample even in 1790 is small compared to the overall number of urban buildings, and the proportion of thatch to other roofing materials is obviously much less significant than in the rural context, due to circumstances peculiar (though not exclusive to) towns which contributed to the incongruity factor. These include the increased fear and risk of fire; the ineffectiveness of fire-fighting equipment, legislative measures, and the physical problems associated with stripping and disposing of old and the storage of new material.

Table 5, showing the number of thatched buildings in the north and the Midlands, demonstrates a precipitous decline over the period, although it is shallower for the Midlands in the first half of the nineteenth century. Industrialization in these regions caused massive urban growth, which in turn swallowed up surrounding settlements. Improvements in transport networks facilitated the movement of durable roofing materials around the region. Finally, the changing agricultural economy and the shift towards pastoralism, most pronounced initially in the north and then in the latter half of the nineteenth century in the Midlands, is of crucial importance in regulating the supply of thatching straw. These trends exaggerated the inter-regional differences which were already in place in 1790. The whole infrastructure of agricultural practice, the emphasis placed on wheat cultivation and rick-thatching in particular, was therefore completely different in the north and south of the country.

In the south, the three sub-regions experienced very different patterns of demand. The south-west sub-region, always regarded as a stronghold of thatch, in fact was experiencing a decline from 1790 onwards and may have lost something in the order of a quarter of a million thatched buildings of all types during the first half of the nineteenth century. Thereafter, the rate of loss was less dramatic than in the rest of England, leaving a false impression of continuous preservation. The survival of thatch in the south west is perhaps surprising given that Devon was more exposed to competition from other roofing materials than most regions.

Plain clay tiles were already predominant in the south-east by 1790, and the demand for thatching was restricted largely to farm and other ancillary buildings. Although the relatively few thatched buildings that were left in the area by this date did decline in the nineteenth century, the popularity of the region as a stockbroker/retirement/leisure area led to a small boom in the latter part of the period.

In the rest of the south, a most interesting phenomenon occurs whereby there is actually a rise in the number of thatched buildings in the first half of the nineteenth century. The explanation lying at the heart of this appears to be an agricultural one, for the emphasis on arable farming became even more marked during the period. This had a twin impact on thatched buildings. On the one hand, agricultural improvements required extensive re-building and enlargements to farm buildings using commonly available materials. On the other hand, the intensification of arable farming demanded an ever larger labour force which had to be housed and the many cheap hovels which sprang up in the region in the villages and on the verges of commons were predominantly roofed in thatch.

Just as the high farming era boosted the area of the country that had hitherto always concentrated on arable farming, so too did the agricultural depression hit arable farms hardest. The impressive rise in the number of thatched buildings was just as speedily undermined, and the south lost more vernacular thatched buildings between 1860 and 1940 than the rest of the country combined. Housing Acts in the twentieth century undoubtedly helped to hasten the elimination of the true humble thatched abode.

Regional analyses should not blind us to the fact that there may have been something like 20 times the number of thatched buildings in 1790 as there were in 1940. The overall loss was therefore mitigated only to a minor extent by the addition of a small number of 'polite' thatched buildings, the majority of which were concentrated in the south of the country. A 'new build' graph for architect-designed thatched buildings would show a rise in the late eighteenth and early nineteenth centuries, as estate landowners took to sprinkling their landscapes with rustic thatched structures. There would be a marked dip in activity in the second half of the nineteenth century as health reformers rejected thatch as a harbourer of vermin and potential disease. This lull was followed by a reawakening of interest at the end of the century as escapees from drab urban centres rediscovered the rural charm of thatch. The Arts and Craft Movement created a demand for a bourgeois version of thatch and a small number of reed thatching firms were not slow to tap into this new market. Their aggressive marketing campaigns did little for the cause of thatch in general, however, for the promotion of water reed was only achieved at the expense of the common and much more widespread methods of straw thatching.

Part II

Thatching materials and their supply

7 Materials and habitats

INTRODUCTION

In the eighteenth and nineteenth centuries the popularity of thatching was determined as much by the supply of suitable materials as by any other factor. Straw was nurtured from seed and for up to a year was exposed to adverse weather, attack by pests and diseases, and eventually to damage during harvest, carting and threshing. Water reed (*Phragmites australis*) was also subject to the vagaries of climate, and its availability was often limited by mild winters, extensive flooding or lack of sufficient labour for its harvest. It too had to be cut and cleaned before it reached the thatcher, and, as with straw, superfluous leaf tissue and weeds were removed in order to enhance its water-shedding capacity and resistance to decay.

The relationship between the supply and demand of materials is thus far from direct or proportional. The supply of straw is obscured by an additional fundamental discontinuity: in arable districts straw was essentially a by-product of grain production, and the qualities of the straw available for thatching varied in response to the needs of cereal producers rather than those of the thatcher. This statement is valid for the entire period, but becomes increasingly relevant after 1900 when scientific plant breeders embarked on hybridization programmes that were to culminate in the development of 'miracle' wheats, dwarf varieties that were indeed miraculous for the large grain producer but disastrous for the thatching industry. Just as significant was the rapid adoption of the combine harvester in the late 1930s which shredded straw into small segments and all but eliminated it as a possible thatching material.

A wide range of materials has been used for thatching in England since the medieval period, either singly or in combination, but nineteenth-century thatchers were rarely free agents in terms of source materials. In most cases, leases or estate custom specified the material that was to be applied to a roof and who would provide it. Access to wild habitats where alternatives to straw could be collected was also governed by a system of common rights enforced by manorial courts. When available, however, materials such as heather (*Calluna vulgaris*), bracken (*Pteridium aquilinum*), broom (*Cytisus scoparius*), gorse (*Ulex europaeus*), water reed (*Phragmites australis*), fen sedge (*Cladium mariscus*) and various rushes, sedges and grasses provided cheap, renewable, and not necessarily low-status alternatives to reed and thatch, which in the nineteenth century were essentially synonymous with straw.

Most thatch in England over the past 300 years has been derived from a fairly narrow range of primary materials, which is understandable given that 1.5 tons of straw, the produce of approximately one acre (0.4ha), is required to thatch a small, one-roomed cottage with a 20' x 15' (6.09m x 4.57m) roof. By the middle of the nineteenth century, alternatives to straw and water reed were simply not abundant enough to be collected efficiently, and in sufficient quantity, to be used as a main coat material in most parts of lowland southern England, and their availability in upland districts had also been seriously curtailed. Similarly, water reed grew in ditches, ponds, lakes and rivers throughout the country, but it was rarely abundant enough to be used for main coat thatching outside of the Norfolk Broads, parts of the Fens and certain coastal districts. A dedicated thatcher or home owner could no doubt collect the amount required from wild sources over several seasons, but this reed was also used for other purposes whereas inexpensive straw was ubiquitous and usually plentiful.

This overview of thatching materials follows the simple habitat definitions used in contemporary accounts. In the somewhat blinkered perspective of the late eighteenth- and nineteenth-century 'improver', the non-arable environment was usually divided into 1) woodland and coppice, 2) grassland and pasture, and various categories of 3) waste which included both dry heathland and wet habitats such as upland moor, bog, salt marsh and fen. These simple divisions allow us to examine the materials derived from each habitat category in relation to the changes that occurred in the landscape during this period. Although the groupings blend into each other and were subject to much regional variation, they are ecologically distinctive and highlight the wide range of materials that was available for thatching in previous centuries.

WOODLAND AND COPPICE

Wood shavings

Woodland and coppice were significant primarily as the source of spars and sways that were used to fix thatch onto roofs. Only one by-product of the underwood industry seems ever to have been used as a main coat material on more than an idiosyncratic basis: wood shavings generated as a by-product of the barrel hoop making industry. The clearest contemporary photograph of a wood chip roof was published by Gertrude Jekyll (1899, opp 169). She wrote that the wood chips employed were 18"–24"

(46cm–61cm) in length and were made up into small faggots that were stacked for 6 months to dry before being used for kindling or for thatching. They were applied in courses 12" (30cm) deep, and produced a thatch 'warm in winter, and cool in summer, and durable, for if well made it will last forty years' (op cit, 169).

> The roof was prepared with strong laths nailed horizontally across the rafters as if for tiling, but farther apart; and the chips, after a number of handfuls had been duly placed and carefully poked and patted into shape, were bound down to the laths with soft tarred cord guided by an immense iron needle ... Only the ridge has to be of straw, because straw can be bent over; the chips are too rigid. When the thatch is all in place the whole is 'drove,' that is, beaten up close with a wooden bat that strikes against the ends of the chips and drives them up close, jamming them tight into the fastening. After six months of drying summer weather he came and drove it all over again. (op cit, 169–170)

Several wood chip roofs have been found to have survived in the Sussex-Hampshire region hidden beneath top coats of straw thatch, and several others have been stripped and rethatched with straw or reed within the past decade (Rod Miller, pers comm). The roofs in question shelter houses rather than simple garden sheds, which suggests that the practice was more widespread than hitherto believed. Although of minor significance in the overall history of English thatching, the use of wood chips is instructive as it reinforces the point that almost any material could have been used to form a reasonably durable thatch when available in sufficient quantity.

GRASSLAND AND PASTURE

Many nineteenth-century writers divided grassland and pasture into simple wet and dry categories. Wet grassland included water meadows on which flooding was controlled to stimulate grass production, hay meadows which flooded naturally in winter and washes which were deliberately flooded when water levels in adjacent rivers were very high in order to prevent more damaging flooding downstream. In all three cases the regular cutting, and subsequent grazing, of livestock discouraged the growth of reedy vegetation on the meadows even though fringing reed swamp may have choked nearby ditches, ponds and rivers.

Wet acidic grassland, which was common on heavy clay soils before the advent of proper underdrainage in the mid nineteenth century, was often dominated by rushes (*Juncus* spp) and sedges (*Carex* spp) which grew in dense patches to 28" (71cm) or more in height and could be gathered in bulk for thatching shelters and outbuildings. Members of the soft rush group (*J. effusus, J. conglomeratus, J. acutiflorus* and *J. articulatus*) were probably the most significant in this respect, along with a range of medium-height sedges. Rushes were recovered from two buildings, having been used to repair a main coat layer on the hip of a cottage at Clipstone, Buckinghamshire (Appendix A:A5), and as a base coat and

ridging material on a stone cottage at Lyndon, Leicestershire (Appendix A: A14).

The rethatching of a medieval building near Chipping Sodbury, Gloucestershire, in 1967 revealed a basal layer described as 'sedge grass', composed of a 3:1 mixture of tufted hair grass (*Descampsia ceaspitosa*) and creeping soft-grass (*Holcus mollis*) (anon 1967). *Descampsia* grows to 6' (1.8m) in damp grassland, meadows and woods throughout England, while creeping soft-grass rarely surpasses 31" (79cm) in woods on moderately acid soils (Clapham et al 1987, 638–40).

Roadside verges were formerly managed as grasslands for animal fodder and were occasionally cut for thatch (Apendix A: A9 Cambridgeshire). The rush 'stob' sample from Clipstone, Buckinghamshire (Appendix A: A5) contained abundant grass, as did an early sample from a medieval building in Milton Keynes, Buckinghamshire (Appendix B: B3). Grass cut from dry pasture in the late summer could be used for repair, as a winter cover for crops and animal shelters (Jones 1927, 77) or as a 'poor man's thatch' that might last for two or three seasons.

DRY WASTELAND

In the nineteenth century non-straw thatch came primarily from what agricultural writers called 'waste', land that did not produce 'useful' arable crops or pasturage. Wastes of various descriptions had, in fact, been managed for centuries for a variety of essential purposes, including thatching, but this did not stop agricultural improvers from waging war on heaths, bogs, moors and wetlands that littered the English landscape. The potentials and limitations of these areas were recognised and respected by local populations, and the use of wastes was regulated by manorial law so as to prevent the abuse of the commons. It was often this communality of landholding that was the focus of the improver's zeal, and the many resources the commons supplied were rarely outlined in the texts that argued for their proscription. Wastes were portrayed simply as barriers to the advancement of modern agriculture on large efficient estates.

The 'improvement' transformed the English landscape and eliminated wasteland products from the repertoire of available thatching materials. Some wet wastes, such as the reed and sedge beds of East Anglia, have survived not only because they produced a relatively high-value commodity, but also because the areas in which they grew so abundantly were not amenable to agricultural improvement. Only fractions of these habitat categories have survived into the present day. Although much of the knowledge of how these distinctive habitats were managed has been lost, it is clear that they generated large amounts of heather, gorse, broom, bracken, rushes, sedges, turf and fixing materials for use in thatching throughout the country.

Coastal foreshore and sand dune

This is a dry wasteland which occurs in river estuaries and along the sea coast and is dominated by stands of coarse grasses, sedges and rushes including marram grass (*Ammophila arenaria*), cord grass (*Spartina* spp), sharp rush (*Juncus acutus*) and the sea couch grass (*Elymus pycnanthus*). All of these species grow to a metre or more in height, and can be gathered in quantity in favourable locations. Published sources document their use for thatching in Norfolk, Cornwall (Wilson 1871), and Dorset (Lowe 1994, 6). Although no details are available, 'sea couch grass' is reported to have been used in Dorset 'between Wimborne and Poole' (John Lowe, pers comm).

Heath

Most dry wastelands can be subsumed within the term heath, which was used in a broader sense in the nineteenth century than today for scrubby waste ground, wet or dry, lowland or upland. Heathland is an unstable community kept in balance by continuous human interference, and most heaths have developed in areas where woodland was cleared and subsequently maintained as rough grazing.

Heathland is characterized by coarse vegetation, usually less than 6' (1.8m) in height, dominated by gorse/furze/whin (*Ulex europaeus*), heather/ling (*Calluna vulgaris*), bell-heather (*Erica cinerea*), bracken (*Pteridium aquilinum*), broom (*Cytisus scoparius*) and various short rushes, sedges and grasses.

Vast areas of Britain were once covered by heathland. In 1688 heathland and moor occupied over 26% of the land surface in England and Wales, but less than 150 years later no heath larger than 100 acres could be found outside of the Brecklands (Rowley 1981, 280–95). This massive decline was absorbed by an expansion of arable production as farmers responded to the realisation that crops could be produced on these light soils if they were heavily manured and planted in rotation with turnips and grasses. Easily-drained soils formerly under heathland became the focus of 'high farming' in the late eighteenth and early nineteenth centuries. By 1838 the Brecklands had been reduced to half its previous size, but still covered almost 900 km² and extended for 16 miles (21.5km) between Newmarket and Thetford (Darby 1976, 133). Thousands of acres of heathland also existed in other counties both in rural districts and near large towns such as London; Surrey held at least 70,000 acres (28,328ha) of waste and heathy commons, primarily in the west of the county; vast areas of dry heathland extended over the Sandlings of east Suffolk and north-eastern Norfolk, the Lincolnshire Wolds, the Lower Greensand and chalk belts of Kent, Surrey, Sussex and Hampshire, the New Forest and eastern Dorset; and pockets of heathland also occurred on light soils in Berkshire, Oxfordshire, the Midlands and well-drained upland areas of the West Country.

Broom (*Cytisus scoparius*)

Broom is a widely distributed leguminous shrub that can be locally abundant on acid, sandy soil on heaths and in woodland. Its green, glabrous stems provided a firm and easily-packed thatching material for internal or external use.

It was used in Sussex in the medieval period (Martin & Martin 1978, 37) and at least one medieval example of broom survives *in situ* at Dunsford, Devon (Letts 1999). Anecdotal information suggests that it continued to be used for this purpose in the Dartmoor region into the last century, and was actually planted specifically for use as thatch (Woods 1988, 58). It is rarely mentioned in nineteenth-century agricultural texts, however, and it may have fallen out of use more rapidly than heather, bracken or gorse.

Bracken (*Pteridium aquilinum*)

Bracken is today considered an aggressive weed of pastures and grassland, but it was once a valued resource and was managed for a variety of purposes including thatching. It grows most prolifically on light, acid soils where it spreads rapidly via rhizomes. Over the last two centuries it has come to dominate large areas formerly occupied by heather and rough, acidic grassland.

> *Pteris aquilina*, the brake ... abounds both in rocky and heathy mountains of our pastoral districts, and in many of the rich and luxuriant grasslands of our plains ... It was formerly in great request for thatch ... but, except in the meanest hovels, it has been completely superseded by heath, straw, tiles and slates. (Wilson 1871, **1**, 525)

Campbell (1831, 184–190) provided detailed instructions on how to thatch with bracken in Scotland, where it was the most common material used.

Figure 22 Thatching with heather (Fearn 1979, Museum of English Rural Life).

Bracken was a popular thatching material in Lancashire in the late eighteenth century (Holt 1795, 16). It was recorded as an undercoat on two roofs early this century, one in Yorkshire and another in Derbyshire, although how much of a local tradition these buildings reflected was questioned (Innocent 1916, 213).

Heather/ling (Calluna *and* Erica *spp*)

The term heather subsumes several shrubby species of the family Ericaceae (Clapham et al 1987, 336). The commonest species (and the most important for thatching), *Calluna vulgaris*, is an evergreen shrub that grows to 40" (102cm) on heaths, moors, bogs and open woods on acid soils throughout the British Isles.

Heather was used in both southern and northern England, but particularly in the north where it was referred to as ling-thack, hedder, hather, heath-thack or black-thack on account of its sombre colour compared to straw or water reed thatch. In the northern counties, as in Ireland, Scotland, Wales and France, it was used both externally and in base coats and often in association with turf (Fig 22) (Peate 1944, 23; Evans 1957, 52; Lucas 1960, 133–43; Le Vegetal 1977; Fenton 1978; Manners 1979; Chapman 1982; Gailey 1984; Emery 1985; Souness 1992). In the south it seems to have been used primarily in base coats, although records and anecdote suggest that it was also used externally in areas where it was particularly abundant such as parts of Sussex and Dartmoor (Taylor 1972, 283). Many older straw-thatched buildings in the New Forest and in West Sussex still shelter base coats of heather applied in the early nineteenth century (Tom Whiteley, Peter Brockett, pers comm), and several experienced thatchers have reported stripping heather base coats from buildings from this region over the past decade. At least one garden shed thatched with local heather is also known to have survived until the late 1980s near Goring Heath, Berkshire (Mick Godfrey, pers comm). Massingham briefly referred to the use of 'ling thatch' by bodgers in the South Chiltern woods.

> The walls were beech-posts with infillings of the very shavings that curled out of their pole-lathes, while the roof was thatched, in the Bourne End [Buckinghamshire] region, with ling, the first I had heard of heather-thatching so far south and so little time ago. (Massingham 1943, 159)

Heather thatch was more common, and is thus better documented, in the north because alternatives were simply not available in sufficient quantity for thatching. Houses at Rothbury, Northumberland, were said in 1760 to be

> mostly thatched ... cover[ed] with sods for warmth, and thatch[ed] with heath, which will last thirty years. (Hodgson 1914, 223; and see p15, this volume)

Heather thatch was common in the Pennines, particularly on their eastern flanks from the Cheviot Hills down through West Durham. 'Ling' was used 'only in the western parts of the county' according to the County Agricultural Report for Durham (Bailey 1810, 58). According to Bishop Pococke in 1760 the people of Stanhope, County Durham,

> thatch their houses with a very thick coat of heath, and make the roofs steep [so] that the melted snow may not soak into the thatch, and lay loads across the top of it to keep out the water. (Hodgson 1914, 209; and see p15, this volume)

Heather thatching survived early this century in the villages around Barnard Castle, County Durham, where heather moorland remained unenclosed until 1859. The roofs of most buildings in this region were very steeply pitched, and several heather thatched barns survived until recently at Bowes, County Durham, Eggleston, Hurst and Hexham, Northumberland. Heather-thatched buildings also survived into the early part of this century at several locations on the North York Moors. Many thatched roofs in this region were replaced by solid materials during the military occupation of the area in the Second World War (Chapman 1982, 9–12). Heather thatching was apparently much more common throughout the Yorkshire Dales 'up to about 70 years ago' according to Hartley and Ingilby (1978, 1022). Houses were being rethatched with heather in the Hawes region in the 1930s by the Kipling family, who were the only surviving professional heather thatchers in the district. Keld Farm, north of Hawes, was thatched with ling 'about a foot thick' (30cm), and numerous buildings in the area retained their heather thatch into the 1930s (Hartley and Ingilby 1986, 55). At the Rufford Hall Estate, Lancashire, in 1856, buildings were thatched with straw, but ling was applied to gables to provide greater durability (Lancashire Record Office 1/7). In parts of Yorkshire heather was also used to cover stacks of peat (Hartley & Ingilby 1968, 166).

Heather thatching declined at different rates and for different reasons in the north and the south, and in the wet, upland moors as compared to districts with abundant lowland heath; in the south and the lowlands it declined as the lighter wastes were cleared for arable; in the north and in the uplands, good quality heather for thatching became increasingly rare over the course of the nineteenth century due to the expansion of grazing and grouse shooting. It thus survived the longest in remote upland districts in Northumberland, Durham and Yorkshire, but disappeared from Hampshire, Sussex, Dorset and the Brecklands in the late eighteenth and early nineteenth centuries with the expansion of 'high farming'.

> When durability is intended, the quality of the heath is of paramount importance ... The best heath for thatching is found growing in close beds, with a slender feeble stem, to the height of 18 inches or 2 feet [46cm, 61cm], so weak and slender as to be unable to support its own weight without leaning, – and this kind is the most durable that can be obtained. (Collier 1831, 191–2)

Other accounts confirm that the best heather grew on 'good ling ground' and that 'long, straight ling was

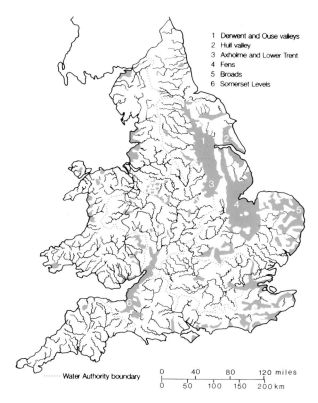

1 Derwent and Ouse valleys
2 Hull valley
3 Axholme and Lower Trent
4 Fens
5 Broads
6 Somerset Levels

········· Water Authority boundary

| 0 | 40 | 80 | 120 miles |
| 0 | 50 | 100 | 150 | 200 km |

Figure 23 Past distribution of wetland (Judith Dobie, after John Letts, after Brown & Bradley 1995).

chosen, as rainwater lodged in the joints of rough, crooked stuff' (Hartley & Ingilby 1978, 1022). The highest quality material came from dense, mature and lightly-grazed stands 15 to 20 years old, although grazed 'drumstick' heather and younger plants were also probably used. Thatching and heavy grazing were incompatible uses, and overgrazing led to a gradual replacement of heather by a narrow range of unpalatable grasses. Grazing and cutting were thus closely regulated, burning was forbidden by manorial law and large areas on the moor were set aside specifically for use in thatching.

Heather was collected preferentially in the late autumn or winter after the flower had set and shed its seed. It was usually pulled rather than cut, this being faster and less likely to damage the crop. Handfuls were bound into bundles with a heather band, 24 bundles making one threave, weighted so that they would keep their shape when drying, and left to dry through the summer for use in the autumn (Collier 1831, 190–95). An average building consumed 200–400 threave, and an experienced worker was expected to pull and bind five threave a day. Early this century, an apprentice thatcher with no previous experience might begin by pulling three threave a day, and could build up to ten per day over time.

> On one red-letter day, [Jonathan Graham, of Swinton, Yorkshire] walked five miles [8km] and pulled five threave, went on into Nidderdale, where he washed two lots of sheep, and returned to pull another five threave, for which he was paid £1 in all, the most he had ever earned in one day. (Hartley & Ingilby 1978, 1022).

Gorse (Ulex europaeus)

Gorse is a spiny, evergreen shrub with yellow pea-like flowers common on light, acid soils throughout England (Clapham et al 1987, 186). The common species (*U. europaeus*) grows to 7' (2.1m) or more, whereas the western gorse (*U. gallii*) is much shorter and locally abundant only in the West Country. In sharp contrast to broom, its stems and leaves are extremely spiny and difficult to handle without thick gloves and protective clothing, but it was nevertheless a popular fuel and roofing material in past centuries (Stevenson 1809, 453–4; Wilson 1871, **1**, 573). The factors that made it such a good fuel (its waxy cuticle and leathery leaves) also made it ideal for use as an undercoat for thatch, for it is extremely resistant to rotting even when in direct contact with water. Its thorns also provided a useful physical barrier to rodents. Crushed young gorse was also used as fodder (and cultivated) in many areas in the eighteenth and nineteenth centuries (Baxter 1834, 256).

According to Innocent (1916, 214) gorse was commonly used on barns and stables in the nineteenth century. One of the half-dozen surviving gorse-thatched buildings in England was recently dismantled in the village of Stanton St John, Oxfordshire (Appendix A: A17). This cart shed, constructed around 1801, contained no rafters. Instead, its shape was provided by faggots of gorse and hawthorn stacked into a pyramidal shape and over-coated with crushed straw. Few structures of this kind are known to have survived, primarily in Gloucestershire, Oxfordshire, Somerset and Devon, at least three of which are still being used as cart-sheds and two as dwellings. All of the extant examples appear to date from the early nineteenth century, but the records suggest they were commonly used in past centuries and in many parts of England.

WET WASTELAND

Wet wastes have been pushed even further than heathland into ecological oblivion by agricultural improvement over the past two centuries. More than a quarter of Britain was once wetland, and as late as 1800 a quarter of the land now in arable production was waterlogged for much of the year (Rackham 1986a). At the beginning of the period under review most English counties harboured significant expanses of fen, bog or marshland, with the bulk being concentrated in the Fenland and Broadland districts of East Anglia and Lincolnshire, the Trent Valley, the Humber Lowlands, eastern Lancashire, the Sandlings of the Essex coast, the estuary of the Thames and the north Kent Marshes, the Romney Marsh, the Somerset Levels and a handful of river estuaries and coastal backwaters along the south coast (Fig 23). Four thousand acres (1,619ha) of wetland, the largest remaining inland bog in southern England, also survived at Otmoor, near Oxford and significant boggy wastes also survived in Shropshire, Worcestershire, Leicestershire, Lincolnshire and Bedfordshire (Darby 1976, 130).

The ownership of these areas was often unclear and access usually difficult, but well-structured use and supply networks nevertheless evolved over centuries of use to satisfy the demand from local communities for a variety of fenland products such as peat, reeds, rushes, withes and *Sphagnum* moss. They were managed and regulated in common as with heathland, and in the same way were enclosed and forced into arable production or grassland with little recognition of local tradition or ecological constraints on their use. Wilson was typical of nine-teenth-century agricultural writers when he wrote of wetlands as:

> the ulcers of the earth, which blur the fair face of nature, where all should be beauty; and from these infectious sores the langour of death extends afar and wide of all that should live and flourish. (Wilson 1871, **1**, 168–9)

Such improvers cannot be relied on to record the impor-tance of fenland products to local communities, and two centuries of drainage have further skewed our perception of the range of materials the fenlands once produced. Wetland species other than water reed rarely receive more than a passing mention in modern descriptions of thatching materials, except for the sedge *Cladium mariscus*, whose fen-dwelling habit and ability to savage those unfamiliar with its character perpetuates the mythical spirit of the medieval fenman.

The wet wastes can be divided into four distinct habitat categories.

Moorland and bog

Moorland occurs in upland regions with short growing seasons and high rainfall, and on soils that have become acidic due to the leaching of nutrients from the topsoil. It is the most common natural vegetation type in much of northern England (Grigg 1989, 35). In contrast with most heathlands, however, moorland is a stable climax community of dwarf plants and not an ecological artefact of human intervention, although clearance and grazing has allowed it to spread southwards and to lower altitudes.

Bog is essentially a wetter version of moor, and the terms are often used interchangeably. Bog develops in areas of high rainfall, usually in upland regions but also as raised bog in lowlands where poor drainage encourages the build up of semi-decayed plant material. Rainfall leaches nutrients from the surface layer producing an acidic peat that is inhospitable to most plants other than *Sphagnum* moss. In the early nineteenth century *Sphag-num* bog covered large areas of northern England, as well as parts of Cheshire, Staffordshire, Lincolnshire, Oxford-shire, East Anglia, Somerset and the south east (Darby 1976, 130–33).

Wet, acidic bog produces little plant materials suitable for thatching, although it can support dense stands of purple moor grass (*Molinia caerulea*) and bog heath (*Erica tetralix*) in areas with high rainfall and reasonable drain-age. Unimproved moorland, however, with its abundant heather, bracken, and moor grass is much more valuable and was widely used for this purpose in the past. Although it was used in many other countries the only English

reference to moor grass encountered so far is Burton's mention of 'coarse grass and rushes from the top of a moss' that were cut for thatching stacks, barns, outhouses and cottages (Burton 1891, 168). Bog vegetation blends into heather moor in drier areas, and in very acidic locations mono-dominant stands of black bog rush (*Schoenus nigricans*) sometimes occur. This species is more com-monly encountered in lowland bogs in fen districts, and was occasionally used for main coat thatching in the nineteenth century as evidenced by the layer of bog rush revealed by a roof excavation in Huntingdon, Cam-bridgeshire (Appendix B: B10).

Most references to rushes in the literature seem to refer to the reedmace or bulrush (*Typha angustifolia* or *T. latifolia*), but a few refer quite specifically to the cutting of rushes from moors and bogs (Innocent 1916, 214). Moor-land and bog also supplied heathery turf which was used as an undercoat and for ridging in parts of northern England.

Coastal salt marsh

Salt marsh occurs in tidal estuaries and coastal lowlands which flood at high tide. This regular flushing removes much of the dead vegetation that would otherwise accumulate as peat. True salt marsh contains few plants that can be used for thatching, the principal exception being sea rush (*Juncus maritimus*), a tough-stemmed, perennial monocot that grows to a metre or more and forms dense stands in suitable conditions (Clapham et al 1987, 543). Sea rush applied as a base coat and in an overlying external coat were recently recovered from the basal layers of a thatched roof in Dorset (B21) (Lowe 1994, 6).

The water reed cut from salt marsh along the coast and in river estuaries grows primarily in reed swamp at the back of the marsh where salt concentrations are very low. Traditionally, these areas were used for seasonal grazing, but many coastal marshes have been embanked against the sea and are now under permanent pasture or arable. Because of the regular flushing of dead plant material from the beds during flood tides, coastal and estuarine reed beds can survive for generations without regular cutting, unlike inland beds which can rapidly fill in and succeed to woody carr if their annual production is not removed by cutting. Large amounts of sea reed were once cut from coastal beds in the Wash, on the Suffolk and Essex coasts, and in the estuaries of the Thames, the Humber, the Severn and numerous smaller rivers in north Kent and along the south coast.

Fen and fringing reed swamp

For our purposes a gamut of distinct habitats can be subsumed under the general term fen. Fen develops in lowland areas with high water tables where dead vegeta-tion accumulates as peat, but where nutrient-rich soils and freshwater prevents the development of acidic con-ditions. Fen is an ecosystem in transition, an intermediate phase between open water and dry land whose botanical inventory is determined primarily by the depth and nutrient quality of the water. Dense stands of water reed or sedge are ephemeral phases in this natural process of succession, and they inevitably give way to woody plants as peat accumulates and raises the soil surface. This build-up occurs at different rates in different parts of a fen depending on local conditions resulting in a mosaic of habitats which attract a diversity of flora and fauna. The opportunistic cutting of natural stands of reed gradually evolved into management, perhaps when it was recognised that regular winter cutting actually improved the quality and abundance of reed in a patch. A managed reed bed is in a state of ecological suspended animation, poised between reed bed and carr. Its botanical structure is skewed by regular winter cutting, and it survives as a distinctive habitat only by virtue of regular human manipulation of water levels and harvesting.

Most of the fen species used for thatching also grow along muddy shores, in the shallows of ditches, ponds and rivers, and on waterlogged, nutrient rich soils throughout the country. Most are tall, rhizomatous monocots that spread vegetatively and can quickly dominate large areas, the adaptation that allows most of them to be managed successively in pure stands. The most important in terms of thatching are the common reed (*Phragmites australis*), fen sedge (*Cladium mariscus*), bulrush (*Schoenoplectus lacustris*), reedmace (*Typha latifolia*) and the lesser bulrush (*T. angustifolia*), reed canary-grass (*Phalaris arundinaceae*), reed sweet-grass (*Glyceria maxima*), several tall rushes of the genus Juncus, the pond sedges (*Carex acutiformis* and *C. riparia*) and the wild flag (*Iris pseudacorus*). Black bog rush (*Schoenus nigricans*) and purple moor grass (*Molinia caerulea*) can also form extensive stands in nutrient-poor locations. The water reed, fen sedge, bulrush, reedmace and reed grasses grow to 6' (1.8 m) or more in height and have long been the preferred wetland species for thatching houses and outbuildings. An intermediate group of rushes, sedges and grasses averaging 3'–6' (91cm–183cm) is less clearly associated with thatching, although some are known to have been used for this purpose and others were widely used for rush lighting, plaiting, strewing and other purposes.

The identity of many of the wetland plants mentioned in the early literature remains a mystery due to linguistic and taxonomic confusion. Reed is an Old English term for a tall, tubular plant stem and was once widely applied to straw, sedges, rushes, reedmace and a host of other species in addition to water reed (Sylvia Haslam, pers comm). A sedge in Norfolk is a bulrush in Somerset, but a rush in Somerset is botanically a sedge that is called bulrush in most counties, reed in some and boulder in Norfolk. To a botanist the distinctions are clear: reed mace (*Typha angustifolia*) is called sedge in Norfolk and bulrush in Somerset, but the term rush in Somerset refers to the bulrush (*Schoenoplectus lacustris*) - a member of the sedge family Cyperaceae. Fitzrandolph and Hay's attempt to clear the confusion poured oil on the fire.

> Botanically, the plaiting rush and one kind of reed belong to the same natural order; the common reed, however, belongs to an entirely different order. To the ordinary observer the reed is easily distinguishable from both rush and sedge, whereas these two last, although belonging to different orders, have a general resemblance. (Fitzrandolph & Hay 1926, 88)

The issue is not simply a concern for botanical accuracy. The evidence suggests that water reed and the fen sedge now widely used for ridging are but two of a wide range of wetland plants that were familiar to thatchers and to the general public well into the post-medieval period. Contemporary records contain a plethora of dialect and common names such as starr, ruskumbard, rish, boulder, and sparte which seem to refer to distinct species, but which all are subsumed under the simpler terms rush, sedge and reed by the late eighteenth century. This linguistic convergence undoubtedly reflects a general loss of familiarity with these species, and their names have disappeared from common usage commensurate with the decline in the prevalence of the wetland habitats in which they grew.

During the period under review the term reed usually referred to water reed *Phragmites australis*, but on occasion to fen sedge *Cladium mariscus* or reedmace *Typha* spp. (Boardman 1933, 563). Reedy vegetation included many of the taller fen species listed above. This older meaning has been retained in the term reed swamp, but is used more specifically in reference to natural stands of water reed in salt marsh or in mixed fringing vegetation in shallow freshwater. River engineers still occasionally use the term reed in a wide sense for any tall reed swamp species. In 1926, Fitzrandolph and Hay stated categorically that both water reed and fen sedge were called reed by 'old Norfolk plaiters and horse collar makers,' and that neither species was used for plaiting due to their hard stems (Fitzrandolph & Hay 1926, 88–9). Water reed and the plaiting rush *Schoenoplectus lacustris* were widely thought to be the same plant, the rush cut in the summer while still soft hardening to form reed, a confusion still shared by thatchers in the region today. The reedmace *Typha* spp. was known under several names including rush, bulrush, poker rush, cattail and sedge, boulder or gladdon in Norfolk. Gladdon is also a common name for the wild *Iris foetidissima*. Reedmace is distinctive in the late summer for the compact poker flower it bears at the apex of its 3'–6' (90cm–180cm) stem, but at other times of the year its leaves are almost indistinguishable from those of many other reed swamp plants.

Sedges and rushes were widely considered to be the same plant, the former simply having grown in poor soils. Botanically, the sedges are members of the Cyperaceae genus *Carex*, a large group of trigonous-stemmed perennials with rhizomatous roots many of which grow to 70cm or more in height. The term rush indicates a member of the rush family Juncaceae, usually of the genus *Juncus*, but as we have seen is also applied to the bulrush *Schoenoplectus lacustris* of the sedge family Cyperaceae. *S. lacustris* has long been used for plaiting, chair making and to some degree for thatching, whereas the common rushes of the Juncaceae were collected for rush lights, mats, cordage and to a limited degree for thatching. The term rush has also been applied to the flowering rush *Butomus umbellatus*, the naturalized aromatic sweet flag *Acorus calamus*, junior members of the sedge family Cyperaceae such as black bog rush *Schoenus nigricans* and the fen sedge *Cladium mariscus* as well as reedmace.

Managed fen

Sedges, rushes and 'shoof'

FEN SEDGE (*CLADIUM MARISCUS*)

Fen sedge is a stout, perennial member of the sedge family Cyperaceae, and its long, sword-like leaves have long been the bane of marsh men and thatchers on account of their razor-sharp margins. It is a flexible and durable thatching material but is today used only for ridging, usually in association with water reed, but sedge was once used for main coats in parts of the Fens where it was abundant (Innocent 1916, 213; Taylor 1972, 281; AppendixA: A9 Cambridgeshire and Appendix B: B9 Cambridgeshire). It was formerly a common plant in fen districts throughout England, and much of the peat used today as fuel and for horticultural purposes is derived from accumulated deposits of partially decayed fen sedge. It has been extirpated from the Somerset Levels and is now common only in managed beds in the Broads and in a few residual fens in Cambridgeshire.

Fen sedge grows to 7' (2.1m) or more in good conditions, and like water reed spreads via a creeping rhizome to form dense mono-dominant stands. Unlike reed, it is restricted to well-established fens and grows in shallow water over peat in alkaline but nutrient poor conditions (Clapham et al 1987, 593; Sylvia Haslam, pers comm). Natural stands of fen sedge develop in the early stages of carr formation, and they contain a rich variety of wetland plants. The sedge used for thatching, however, is composed primarily of *Cladium mariscus*, along with a small amount of wild impurities such as reedmace (*Typha* spp.), bog myrtle (*Myrica gale*), willow (*Salix cinerea*), water reed (*Phragmites australis*), and various small sedges (*Carex* spp.) and grasses (Gramineae).

It is unclear when wild stands of sedge began to be managed in the Broads or the Fens, but many working beds in the Broads sit on abandoned peat diggings and have been managed for centuries. Wild stands contain plants of uneven height, and cutting would have greatly improved the quantity and purity of sedge in the bed. In managed beds plants are uniformly taller, and a dense surface of dead proto-peat prevents other species from invading. As a result, sedge beds are ecologically tenacious and unlike reed beds they can survive neglect or abandonment for a decade and be brought back into commercial use.

Sedge is usually maintained as a complementary crop to reed in adjacent beds, but in contrast to reed water levels in sedge beds fluctuate in keeping with the natural hydrological cycle: they are flooded to 12" (30cm) or more in winter and drained in the early summer to allow cutting in the summer months. Sedge is an evergreen, however, and can be cut at any age and at any time of the year if required. Commercial sedge is cut every three or four years in order to produce material of sufficient length for thatching, and larger producers maintain four beds in rotation. More frequent cutting reduces its length and suitability for ridging and allows competing scrub to become established. Cutting in the late summer is preferred as this prevents water reed and other plants from encroaching, and also allows some regrowth to occur before the winter floods. In the past sedge was cut with a scythe, but it is now cut by machine and left on the marsh to wilt before being tied into standard-sized bunches. Sedge cutting traditionally provided alternative summer employment for reed cutters and increased the overall profitability of Broadland estates.

In the early nineteenth century, sedge beds were considered to be as profitable as newly enclosed arable land (Gooch 1811, 177) and were valued primarily as a source of fuel rather than of thatching material. Sedge was prized for kindling and as a fuel for drying malt (Purseglove 1988, 30), and East Anglia's early prominence as the centre of the English malting industry was fuelled by the sedge beds of the Broads region.

Fen sedge was recovered from two predominantly straw-thatched buildings over the course of this research. At Westley Waterless, Cambridgeshire (Appendix A: A8) fen sedge was used both as a base coat as well as a main coat in later levels, and near Huntingdon, Cambridgeshire (Appendix B: B9), it was spar coated onto a base of crushed straw and was tied into place with a braided rope of river rush (*Schoenoplectus lacustris*). These finds are not surprising for the Fens where sedge was abundant, but in most areas it was simply not available cheaply, painlessly, and in sufficient quantity to be widely used as a main coat or even for ridging. This is surprising given its present popularity and assumed ancient association with water reed thatching. The Cowell papers, however, suggest that there was little commercial demand for fen sedge for ridging in the Fens, the Broads or anywhere else very early this century, and that ridges in these districts were usually formed from threshed straw (Smedley 1976, 50). This may explain why it is rarely differentiated from other wetland plants in agricultural texts that otherwise describe rushes, reeds and thatching in detail (Wilson 1871, **1**, 289–230).

In summary, it appears that fen sedge may be an ancient, but, until earlier this century, unpopular, thatching material that was used for base and main coats as frequently as it was for ridging in areas where it was abundant. Many sedge beds must have fallen out of commercial production in response to the decline in its use as a fuel in the late nineteenth century, and an alternative market developed when architects and builders discovered that it maintained its decorative finish longer than straw and was available at an acceptable price.

BULRUSH/RIVER RUSH (*SCHOENOPLECTUS LACUSTRIS*)

Like most other wetland species used for thatch, the bulrush or river rush is a rhizomatous, perennial monocot that forms extensive stands in ideal conditions. It grows to 12' (3.6m) in up to 7' (2.1m) of still water in ponds and lakes, and 4' (1.2m) of water in slow-moving streams, rivers and canals. Its long, rounded, tapered and leafless stem can measure 1" (2.5cm) in diameter at its base and carries a tuft of small brown flowers laterally near its tip (Haslam et al 1975, 313; Clapham et al 1987, 591).

Bulrush was once very common in south-eastern and central England but has been eradicated from many areas as a result of dredging and the use of herbicides for aquatic weed control. The literature suggests that it was used for thatching in areas where it was abundant, but was valued primarily for plaiting and the manufacture of rush seats (Purseglove 1988, 123). Traditionally it was cut from canals and river beds as a regular part of the maintenance cycle, but it was also managed in beds as on the Ouse at Pavenham in Bedfordshire, along the Cherwell at Islip in Oxfordshire, on the Avon in Wiltshire, and at various locations in Huntingdonshire, Northamptonshire, Norfolk and Somerset (Crampton 1935, 9; Crampton & Machrie 1931, 3). Bulrushes from the Norfolk Broads were considered to be particularly durable.

Clear references to bulrush in the historical literature are rare, and the term was used interchangeably with reedmace (*Typha* spp.) and dwarf rushes of the genus *Juncus* in many areas (Roffey & Cross 1933, 3).

To the authors' knowledge, bulrush has been recovered from only two English roofs: the first example from a village of Ickford in Buckinghamshire (Appendix A: A6), an area where rush was once harvested on a commercial basis, and the second from a small cottage roof in a village near Huntingdon (Appendix B: B9). In neither case had the rush functioned as thatch proper. In Ickford, a bundle had been folded into a roughly bound dollie the size of a bread loaf that was used for packing a hole near the eave of a roof thatched with crushed straw. The thatcher who discovered the sample during rethatching had never before encountered this material on a roof, although he was familiar with the species and its use for chair making. In Huntingdon, a rope made from braided bulrush was used to secure a base coat of fen sedge.

Black bog rush (*Schoenus nigricans*)

Black bog rush is a densely tufted perennial with tough, wiry stems that rarely exceeds 30" (76cm) in height. It is quite widely distributed but rarely abundant in England, and must have been maintained in fairly extensive beds in the Huntingdon region in the last century as it was occasionally used for main coat thatching. An 8" (20cm) thick layer of black bog rush, sparred onto a base coat of stubble and overlain by crushed straw, was recorded on a cottage roof in Great Stukeley, Cambridgeshire (Appendix A: A7). It also occurred as a secondary component within a base coat sample of fen sedge recovered from a roof in Wennington, Cambridgeshire (Appendix B: B10). Black bog rush is more exacting in its habitat requirements than fen sedge, bulrush, reedmace or water reed, and is restricted to damp, peaty, alkaline and nutrient poor areas both inland and at the back of salt marsh (Clapham et al 1987, 593; Sylvia Haslam pers comm).

Reedmace (*Typha* spp)

The records indicate that reed mace or poker rush was also once widely used for thatching, particularly on ancillary buildings and often in association with water reed. Its leaves look very much like a host of other wetland species being long, flat and sword shaped, but it is easily distinguished by the long brown flower head that forms at the tip of its stem in the late summer. English reed mace consists of two species: the greater reedmace *Typha latifolia*, also called the bulrush or cat's tail, and the lesser reedmace *T. angustifolia*. Both are stout, rhizomatous, perennial herbs with erect stems and grow in shallow waters throughout England. The greater reedmace grows to 7' (2.1m) or more in silted areas with abundant decaying plant material, and is the species that was most commonly used in thatching. The lesser reedmace is locally common but much less widely distributed. It rarely exceeds 6' (1.8m) but can grow in deeper water than *T. latifolia*. It is also less tolerant of pollution than the greater reedmace, and its range has been much reduced in recent decades (Clapham et al 1987, 586). Reedmace is usually one of the first plants to colonize newly created shallow water habitat, and like water reed spreads rapidly by rhizomes to form dense, mono-dominant stands. It is a principal component of fringing reed swamp along the edges of ditches, rivers and ponds, and usually occurs in smaller amounts in managed reed and sedge beds.

Reed mace is commonly referred to as rush or bulrush by thatchers and the general public, but it was widely known as sedge, reed or gladdon or boulder in the past. It was commonly used for plaiting and basket weaving prior to the Second World War, particularly in Norfolk (Roffey & Cross 1933, 3), and the down from its poker flower head was occasionally used to stuff pillows. Pure reedmace was still used for thatching in East Anglia earlier this century, and base coats of reedmace are still sometimes encountered on older buildings (John Cousins pers comm).

> One occasionally sees various kinds of farm shelters and boathouses entirely covered with *Typha Angustifolia* ... but it is considered cheap and untidy and not up to the standard of *Arundo Phragmites* [ie water reed]. Where one has a combination of the two types of reed it is known as Mixed, and in many circumstances this is to be preferred to Best Reed by itself, but it is far from popular among architects, probably more on account of its unfortunate title of Mixed than from a true consideration of its merits. Reed-bed owners who obtain a harvest of Mixed stuff off their marshes are rightly indignant with the profession when they find that they can only obtain a price for their crops of £3 per hundred less than those with the Best Reed beds, and it has been said with some truth that, in this case at least, architects are biased when they ought not to be. (Boardman 1933, 563)

Although mixed reed would not be considered an acceptable material today, in the 1930s most reed thatchers considered it to be more durable than pure reed (Deas 1939, 91). It weathered to a coarse and mottled coat, however, and its softness prevented it from being dressed tightly into position as with reed (Boardman 1933, 563; Cowell nd).

Marsh hay (shoof)

There are references to the use of marsh hay or fenstraw for thatching at least some of which probably refer to the shoof or sheaf that is still cut on the Broads and is occasionally used for thatching (Peter Brockett, Charles Cater, M and A Dodson, pers comms). The meaning of the term seems to vary between thatchers and regions. In the Broads it indicates a grassy, reed-dominated mixture cut from those parts of the reed bed which do not produce high quality thatching reed, whereas in the Fens it can include any fringing reed swamp vegetation cut from ditches or dykes. Others have defined it as the waste fraction derived from cleaning grassy reed or the nutritious fodder cut from marsh pasture in the early summer. Although all of these categories are probably distinctive botanically, they can be taken together as a broadly defined and poorly-documented material cut from land that was too wet for regular grazing but yet unsuitable for reed production.

Water reed (Phragmites australis)

Water reed is a tall, stout, perennial monocot that grows throughout England in permanently damp soils and in the shallow waters of ponds, ditches, rivers and lakes (Clapham et al 1987, 648; Haslam 1972). Each year its rhizomes produce tall, slim, jointed stems 3'–9' (0.9m–2.7m) in length that have long been valued for use in thatching, construction, as fuel and for other purposes. Water reed will grow in soil that is dry in summer or covered by up to 6' (1.8m) of still water (or less if it is saline or fast flowing). Its roots can penetrate anaerobic clay in river estuaries to form large mono-dominant stands at the back of coastal salt marsh, and reed also flourishes in all but the poorest and most acidic soils. Only a small proportion of the seed produced each year on a reed plume is viable, and only a fraction of this seed germinates to establish new populations with novel characteristics. As a result, local reed beds are largely composed of vegetatively-produced clones that are identical to the parent plant.

Phragmites reed bed is a freshwater fen habitat that survives as reedswamp due to controlled seasonal flooding and the regular removal of much of the year's annual production in the form of thatching reed. Natural stands of *Phragmites* are an ephemeral stage in the natural process of ecological succession, and many of the reed beds cut for thatching in England exist only because they have been managed for centuries for this and other purposes. Natural fens are wet in winter and spring, and dry out in the summer which allows competing vegetation to become established. In managed reed beds, however, the natural hydrological cycle is reversed using sluice gates and pumps: water levels are kept high in summer, and low in the autumn and winter so that cutting can take place on semi-solid ground. The beds are reflooded in the early spring to protect young shoots (colts) from frost, stimulate fresh growth and discourage competition from weeds.

Distribution

Existing reed beds are a remnant of what was once a much more valued and plentiful resource. A 1982 survey revealed only 109 reed beds in Britain larger than two hectares, with a combined surface area of approximately 2,300 hectares (Bibby & Lunn 1982). One sixth of this was managed for thatching in the Broads district. Many of the 109 beds were also of recent origin.

During this period water reed was cut from both natural stands and managed beds, both inland and along the coasts. The sources of supply can be grouped under four broad categories:

- Managed reed beds along the coasts, cut for local and regional use, located primarily in Norfolk, Suffolk, Essex, north Kent and the Romney Marsh, parts of Lancashire, Cheshire and Lincolnshire and in the Humber Lowlands.
- Managed inland reed beds cut for local and limited regional use, which survived in parts of the Fens, the Somerset Levels and in some river valleys such as the Trent.
- Natural *Phragmites*-dominated reed swamp cut opportunistically, and on a limited commercial scale, from river estuaries in the south east and along the south coasts of Dorset, Hampshire and Sussex.
- Natural fringing and shallow water *Phragmites*-dominated reed swamp that was cut on an opportunistic basis and for local use from ditches, rivers, ponds and pockets of fen throughout the country.

The Fens

No study of thatching materials can avoid discussion of what was the largest wetland area of Britain, the Fens of Cambridgeshire and Lincolnshire. A large-scale project to improve the Fens for agriculture, funded by London investors and large landowners, was begun by the Dutch engineer Vermuyden in the early seventeenth century (Darby 1976, 34). His work was a short-lived success: the new drainage systems that were created were often flawed in design. Many of the wetlands drained in the seventeenth and eighteenth centuries had relapsed into wetland, or survived as wet pasture, by 1800. Large areas of re-flooded fen were again reclaimed during the Napoleonic wars, but catastrophic flooding remained a common occurrence until the introduction of steam-powered pumps in the 1820s. Efficient steam pumping allowed the last large stretches of open water in the Fens to be drained by mid-century (Rackham 1986a, 186). The records indicate that Cambridgeshire reed was becoming scarce by 1790.

> Reed. Nothing pays the occupier equal to this crop. Its cultivation, however, is rapidly decreasing, owing to the improvement of the fens. (Gooch 1811, 178)

Reed was still being cut from the Rosewell Pits at Ely in 1902, and at Burwell, Water Beach, Ramsey, St Ives and Holme Fen in the early 1900s (Cambridgeshire Record Office 1), but the Fens had long since ceased to be a major supplier of reed to the thatching industry. Today only a miniscule fraction of the 1,200 square miles (3100km²) of wetland that once formed the Fens survives in natural parks such as Wicken Fen.

THE NORFOLK BROADS

The uniqueness of the Broads region was vividly portrayed in Wilkie Collins' *Armadale* in 1866.

> The face of the country began to change as the carriage approached the remote and lonely district of the Broads. The wheat-fields and turnip-fields became perceptibly fewer; and the fat green grazing-grounds on either side grew wider and wider in their smooth and sweeping range. Heaps of dry rushes and reeds, laid up for the basket-maker and the thatcher, began to appear at the roadside. The old gabled cottages of the early part of the drive dwindled and disappeared, and huts with mud walls rose in their place ... All the strange and startling anomalies presented by an inland agricultural district, isolated from other districts by its intricate surrounding network of pools and streams – holding its communications and carrying its produce by water instead of by land – began to present themselves in closer and closer succession. (Collins 1866, **1**, 239–40)

The Broads are largely anthropogenic and the place name evidence suggests that none of the broads existed until at least post-Norman times (Rackham 1986a, 85). Research by Lambert et al (1960) revealed that most of the broads began life as peat diggings which evolved into lakes, some a mile (1.6km) or more in breadth, which are now partially filled with mud and peat. Two-thirds of the Broads region has been filled in or drained since 1850 and the remaining broads are shallow and are silting in rapidly. Nevertheless, the area has survived the past 300 years of improvement relatively intact primarily because most of the broads were too deep to be used for agriculture. In the past they provided high quality thatching reed as well as marsh hay for horses and cover for shooting.

> Before motor cars and lorries took the place of horse-drawn vehicles forage was much sought after in Broadland. Reeds and rushes were cut green and sent far and wide as food for horses. This gave employment to an army of workers and produced a steady income for owners and tenants. In addition excellent snipe-shooting over the freshly mown swamps was provided. Now, however, snipe are locked out by great areas of boggy ground rank with tons of sedge reeds and rushes which are allowed to rot. (Vincent 1941, 1119)

Reed cutting and shooting were profitable and complementary, and careful management allowed many bird species to flourish alongside productive reed beds.

The quality and durability of Norfolk reed has long been appreciated.

> The covering [in Norfolk] is of three kinds, Dutch tile generally for the houses, and the common pan-tiles for stables and barns, or sea or marsh reed, which is excellent in quality,

and neatly put on ... No covering is so good as this, and it will preserve a roof twice as long as tile. (Kent 1796, 112)

Reed could be hauled only 20 miles (32km) in 1796 before the cost of haulage equalled that of thatching a standard square of 10' x 10' (3.05m), but this was only one third of the cost of the 'hundred fathom' of reed required to thatch one square (anon 1807, **1**, *Thatch*). Norfolk reed was carried 'perhaps 40 or 50 miles [64km–80km] into the central and northern parts of the county' for thatching (Kent 1796, 181–3), which would include all of Norfolk east of the Brecklands (where straw thatch was more widely used). Transport by canal or river boat up the Broadland rivers into central Norfolk may well have been economic in the nineteenth century, but the cost of additional carriage into Cambridgeshire and beyond was probably prohibitive until rail haulage became a viable option early this century.

THE SOMERSET LEVELS

There is little evidence for the use of reeds, rushes, or sedges for thatching in this region for the period under review. Until the early nineteenth century most of the Somerset Levels were flooded during the winter and early spring, but much had been drained, enclosed and divided by navigable 'rhynes' into cultivable fields by 1850. Fringing reed swamp containing water reed and reedmace survived in neglected corners and rhynes, but as in the Fens and Broads, drainage and regular ditch cleaning has kept stands of potential thatching reed at bay. The fen sedge which was the source of most of the area's peat had been extirpated from the Levels by the Second World War.

ESSEX, KENT, SUSSEX AND THE THAMES ESTUARY

Early this century reed was being cut on a regular basis from marshes at Manningtree, Brightlingsea, Stanford-Le-Hope on the Thames and at other locations along the Essex coast (Rural Industries Bureau 1956; Cowell nd). Reed has long been used for thatching in parts of Sussex, and numerous references to its use in the past are recorded in the Rape of Hastings surveys (Martin & Martin 1978 and 1979).

> In some parts of *Sussex* and *Kent*, they Thatch with Reed instead of Straw. Some Workmen tell me, That this kind of Thatching will endure 40, 50, or 60 Years. They also tell me, That Reed is sold by the Thousand, *viz* A Thousand handfuls, each handful being about 8, 9 or 10 inches [20cm, 23cm, 25cm] in Circumference, bound up in a lattle Band; a Thousand of which will cost 15 or 16s [75p, 80p] and will cover about 3 Square of Roofing. For laying of which they have 4s [20p] per Square. (Neve 1726 [1969], 257)

Large quantities of reed were cut from marshes in north Kent, the estuaries and seaward flood plains of the Thames, the Medway the Swale and the Stour. Reed was also cut from the Romney Marsh and Pevensey Levels in south Kent. In 1831 Loudon wrote that the Romney Marsh comprised 24,000 acres (9712ha) of wetland and was 'one of the most extensive and fertile fresh-water marshes in Britain', with the neighbouring Walland and Dinge marshes adding a further 20,000 acres (8094ha) (Loudon 1831, 748). Even if only a third of this area was cut for reed, it would have produced approximately 60,000 bundles, a third of the annual production of the Norfolk Broads in 1982. According to Phillips (1975, 4), the best natural reed once came from the Woolpack and Beaconsfield fleets (Filmer 1980, 32). Between 1904 and 1910, Cowell was buying water reed from a Mr Norman of Snodland, Kent, and in 1913 sampled reed from a small grower at Hoo near Rochester. Pockets of original marsh or fen in the south east have survived in hunting reserves and in areas with particularly poor drainage (Phillips 1975, 4, 67), but most of the original wetland has now disappeared.

The south coast

One of the most significant reed beds in southern England was at Abbotsbury on the Fleet River north-west of Weymouth in Dorset, and Abbotsbury spear was commonly used in the area early this century. It was generally considered to be a coarse reed with an average lifespan of only fifteen years (Ward 1939, 431). Small amounts of water reed were cut from marshes at Radipole, Wareham, Poole, Weymouth and Lymington within living memory (John Lowe, Rod Miller, pers comm), and south Hampshire also produced reed on a limited scale. Some of these beds became commercial sources of reed only when they began to be managed for use in thatching. Cowell wrote to the owner of a reed bed at Lee-on-the-Solent in 1912 asking to purchase any reed available.

> You have growing (my thatcher says) some reeds which if properly cut and tied into bundles would do for thatching roofs. (The Norfolk Reeds: 600 bunches weigh 2½ tons. Girth about 24 inches [61cm] (measured 18in [46cm] from butt). Norfolk workmen are now cutting, some with a hook, some with a scythe: gather into bunches, use a small rake to scrap[e] out grass. Some tie with Willows, some with string, others tie with the Reeds. Wages paid: 6/- [30p] for 100 bunches to cut, and clean, and tie). If you care to sell yours, a/d to Railway Station F.O.R. They should be cut now helps the young shoots spring up. (Cambridgeshire Record Office 1)

Vidle Van Farm, at Lymington, Hampshire, was selling reed locally at 6s 6d (32p) per score in 1911, as were White & Co (Builders) and a Mr Reason at After Farm, Freshwater, on the Isle of Wight. Cowell stated that the summer of 1911 was the first year within living memory that the beds owned by Mr T J Wiltshire at Totton, near Southampton, had not been cut. These beds must have extended for almost 10 acres (4ha), as they were reckoned to be able to produce 2000 bunches per annum when kept from grazing cattle. The south coast reed industry had probably been in decline for some time by 1911, and its fate was sealed by the First World War, as was the fate of many experienced thatchers and marshmen.

Devon

Water reed was once cut from marshes on the Devon Coast.

> Near Dartmouth an abundance of reeds used in thatching grows in marsh behind the beach, and an old thatcher has been engaged there for 40 years. When he dies he is unlikely to be replaced. (Gratton 1936)

The marsh in question was probably Slapton Sands, south of Dartmouth. According to Rogers (1976, 27) 'thousands of bundles' of reed were once cut from the Sands each year, but were generally used in plastering and wall construction rather than thatching. Reed cutting in the marsh was interrupted when it was mined by the army of the United States of America in the Second World War (anon 1959b).

Inland reed

Inland reed was much more abundant in 1790 than it is today, and even small stands in poorly drained locations along river courses, below springs and in seasonally waterlogged depressions on heavy boulder clay could provide useful amounts of reed. Inland reed is inevitably softer than managed Norfolk reed and would not have performed as well.

> In the vale of Trent, upon the estate of the Earl of Moira [north Leicestershire], and elsewhere, are considerable patches of reed (*Arundo phragmites*); they are equally valuable with good meadow land, being sold to the builders to lay under plaster floors. They are also more durable than straw for thatching, and make screens to keep off the cold wind in gardens: and are, I believe, good food for horses, cut green and carried to the stable. (Pitt 1809b, 161)

Before the development of effective sub-surface drainage in the mid nineteenth century, much of the what is now considered to be the best arable land in the country was too heavy and waterlogged to be used for anything other than wet pasture. Some improvement could be effected by steep ridge and furrow ploughing, and it is possible today to find reed swamp growing in the wet furrows of lightly-grazed grassland. But water reed cannot tolerate intensive grazing, and significant stands would not have survived 'the grazing of the stubble.' In the past the drainage problem was particularly acute in the northern counties, the east Midlands plain, parts of Essex and Suffolk and in Sussex and Surrey, whereas the south west and most of Norfolk were relatively well drained. Darby (1976, 23) estimated that 30% of the soils in England (9.6 million acres, 3.9 million ha) were composed of heavy clay, which if properly drained were the most fertile and suitable for cereal production. A 1968 estimate calculated that 39% of the farmland in England suffered from 'impeded drainage' and an additional 18% was 'poorly drained' (Phillips 1989). Efficient underdrainage using clay tiles revolutionized tillage on the clays in the mid nineteenth century (Grigg 1989, 32) and eliminated most of the small pockets of inland reed swamp that had survived the 'improvements' of the previous century.

Theoretical calculations of the amount of water reed that can be cut from ditches and ponds supports the

Figure 24 Water reed used as a key for plastering, Lancin Farmhouse, Chard, Somerset (John Letts).

contention that *Phragmites* reed could not have been used for house-thatching in any significant amount in arable inland districts in 1790. This does not mean it was not used on smaller farm buildings, shelters and ricks. It was certainly gathered for other purposes, such as a key for plaster (Fig 24), and was probably used as commonly in mixtures with other reed swamp species as in the pure form in which it is used today.

A surprising amount of reed is required to thatch a roof to the modern standard. Thatchers work on the basis of one bundle per ft² (11 per m²) so that 1,600 bundles of reed are required to thatch a small cottage with a roof 40' x 20' (12.1m x 6.1m) to a side. At least 800 bundles would be necessary for even a basic coat thatched to half the modern recommended depth. A well-managed reed bed in Norfolk produces about 400 bundles per acre (990 bundles per ha), so that a small cottage could be expected to consume two acres (0.8ha) of reed. The 1982 survey revealed only 109 reed beds in England larger than four acres, with a total surface area of approximately 4,600 acres (1860ha) in the United Kingdom (Bibby & Lunn 1982). Many of these are of recent origin and only a quarter are managed to produce thatching reed. Even if every one of these 109 beds was managed for reed, they would together generate enough reed to thatch only 1,200 small cottages to the modern recommended depth. Without imports there is enough reed cut in Britain each winter to thatch about 150 cottages to this standard.

If a managed reed bed can produce 400 bundles per acre (990 bundles per ha), an overgrown drainage ditch is unlikely to have produced more than 100 or would not have functioned very well as a ditch. Fringing reed swamp could perhaps be expected to produce no more than 50 bundles of *Phragmites* per acre (123 bundles per ha). In practice, not all of this ditch reed would be of sufficient quality for thatching, although, on the other hand, a pure crop is not necessary to provide an acceptable mixed reed thatch that would last 10 years or so. A 9' (2.7m) wide ditch would therefore yield one bundle every 26.3 yards (24m) at a production figure of 75 bundles per acre (185 bundles per ha). Based on these figures almost 9 miles (14.5km) of ditch would have to be cut to thatch a small cottage to a basic minimum depth.

An average farm with three 15 acre (6.1ha) fields, three acres of pasture, and a two acre (0.8ha) reed-infested pond would harbour a maximum of 2.3 miles (3.7km) of ditches and produce no more than 250 bundles of reed each year. Perhaps only half of this amount would actually be available for cutting due to labour shortages or conflicting demands from neighbours with joint ownership of principal ditches. On the same basis, a much smaller 20 acre (8.1ha) farm would generate no more than 60 bundles of reed each year. In the past, drainage ditches were cleaned every four or five years and reed is unlikely to have been as plentiful in ditches in the early nineteenth century as it sometimes is today. It must also be remembered that the reed fleeking once commonly used as a support base for both reed and straw-thatched roofs can easily consume 30 bundles per roof, and water reed was also much in demand as a key for plastering and for fuel.

The figures suggest that it might have taken five years or more for a self-sufficient farm of 50 acres (20ha) to collect enough water reed to thatch a small farm cottage to a basic minimum depth, and even longer for a smaller farm with access to fewer ponds and ditches. In 1790 thatching with water reed in arable inland districts was possible only if significant local reed beds were available, or perhaps abundant ditches on a large estate with a great deal of labour to cut them. The costs of transporting reeds from afield may well have been the more economic option for a landlord determined to thatch his house with reed, but this was unnecessary when good quality thatching straw was widely available at little cost. The evidence suggests that over the period 1790 to 1940, pure reed similar to what is applied to roofs today was rarely used in arable districts, and that where reed was abundant many houses and outbuildings were thatched with mixed reed, reedmace, dwarf rushes and straw. In general, this accords with the evidence from Ireland and parts of continental Europe where water reed was either ignored, or used on a very limited basis for thatching, even in areas where it was abundant.

THE WATER REED INDUSTRY FROM 1890 TO 1940

Growers

Early this century the ownership of many reed beds in the Norfolk Broads and the Fens was unclear. In some areas there were large landlords who employed gamekeepers and bailiffs to manage estate beds. In others there was a complex web of owners and rentiers. Some owners let their beds to forage merchants or company thatchers such as John Cowell in Cambridgeshire, who would then assume responsibility for harvesting and marketing the reed they produced. In the early 1900s, Cowell was in contact with at least 46 reed growers, most of whom were based in Norfolk, but with one in Essex, two in Kent, three in Hampshire, two on the Isle of Wight, three in Cambridgeshire and three in Huntingdonshire. Reed was also imported on a small scale from Holland. Bearing in mind that one bundle thatched approximately one square foot (or one 'fathom' of six bundles for six ft² in thatcher's measure), then some of the growers were supplying only very small amounts each year. Cowell took over the tenancy of a bed at Ellsfoot, Ormesby, in 1915 for £8 per annum. The previous tenant had paid this sum yearly to the landlord for an annual cut reckoned at 500 fathoms: at 400 bundles per acre this would represent the annual production of approximately eight acres. E Gurney of Sprowston Hall, Norwich, cut 1,200 fathoms from c 20 acres (8.1ha) in 1906, made up of 100 long, 500 short, and 600 mixed bundles of reed and gladdon (reed mace). In 1905 C Dyson at Burwall cut 3,500 fathoms of 'small bundles' from c 55 acres (22ha), and Mr H Smith of Hickling Broad cut 850 fathoms from c 13 acres (5.3ha). In 1911 Cowell cut 2,000 fathoms of single-wale reed from a c 30 acre (12ha) bed at White-Slea Lodge, on the Hickling Broad, while a smaller grower nearby at the Old Rectory offered an additional '10 hundred'. The previous year Cowell had bought 500 fathoms or 'half the total crop' from this source, presumably of double-wale reed managed in two beds. At least some of these figures refer to beds cut annually (single wale) rather than every two years (double wale) as is the usual practice today, in which case the acreage stated does not need to be doubled to obtain the total acreage of the bed (Cambridgeshire Record Office 1).

Both the water reed and the thatchers employed on Rothschild's model village at Ashton Wold, Northamptonshire, in 1902–3 were supplied by Cowell. Over 2,700 fathoms (16,200 bundles) were obtained from seven different Norfolk growers, the largest consignment of 730 fathoms and the smallest of 90 having both come from Ranworth in Norfolk. In 1990 the entire East Anglian production of reed was estimated to be c 38,000 fathoms (227,000 bundles) cut from 750 acres (Bateman et al 1990). At this level of production the village of Ashton Wold alone would have consumed 7% of the annual crop.

Harvest

The fragmented nature of the reed supply network was compounded by the isolated nature of many of the beds, as well as the independent nature of reed cutters and marshmen.

> The shore in these wild regions was not like the shore elsewhere. Firm as it looked, the garden-ground in front of the reed-cutter's cottage was floating ground, that rose and fell and oozed into puddles under the pressure of the foot. The boatmen who guided the visitors warned them to keep the path, and pointed through gaps in the reeds and pollards to grassy places, on which strangers would have walked confidently, where the crust of the earth was not strong enough to bear the weight of a child over the unfathomed depths of slime and water beneath. The solitary cottage, built of planks pitched black, stood on ground that had been

steadied and strengthened by resting it on piles. A little wooden tower rose at one end of the roof, and served as a look-out post in the fowling season. From this elevation the eye ranged far and wide over a wilderness of winding water and lonesome marsh. If the reed-cutter had lost his boat, he would have been as completely isolated from all communication with town or village, as if his place of abode had been a light-vessel instead of a cottage. Neither he nor his family complained of their solitude, or looked in any way the rougher or the worse for it. (Collins 1866, **1**, 251)

It is perhaps surprising that water reed survived at all as a thatching material during the period under review, as its supply was unpredictable even in the geographically circumscribed regions in which it was abundant. The timing of the harvest imposed grossly unpleasant working conditions (Vincent 1941, 1119), although this is not always apparent in artistic portrayals.

> The work of reed cutting must surely be one of the loneliest, coldest and toughest of occupations. Cutting has to be carried out in the winter months ... and goes on into early spring ... The work is often undertaken under near-arctic conditions of snow and ice, in the cutting east wind for which that coast is notorious and which the natives proudly boast is 'uninterrupted by any land between here and the North Pole'. (Elson 1959, 527)

Flooding could often limit the harvest:

> I have today received a note from Marshman in reply to my Enquiries about reeds; they have not yet finished cutting [and] high tides have kept them back this past fortnight. (Cambridgeshire Record Office 1)

Reed beds were managed by reversing the natural hydrological cycle using dykes, sluice gates and pumps. In natural reed swamp water levels are at their highest in the winter and spring and lowest in summer. In managed beds water is drained away in the late autumn so that cutting can occur on a shallow or semi-hard surface in winter. The beds are then flooded in spring to stimulate growth, to protect young shoots from late frost, to discourage competition from weeds through the summer and to clear the beds of accumulating plant debris. The reed was cut with a scythe or a sickle (McDougall 1958, 493; Blackburn 1982, 9). Cutting began after frost knocked the flag leaf off the dead stem in early winter (December), and the harvest continued into March or April when the young 'colts' of the new crop appeared.

> April 6 is the recognised day to stop reed-cutting, and it is surprising how very near that date the scything ceases year by year throughout the Broads. If the reed were to be cut when in full flower, during the months of July or August, the plant would probably be killed. (Boardman 1933, 564)

The best quality reed is cut every year, but most beds are cut on a two year rotation in order to maximize yields while minimizing labour costs (Greenacre 1958; Haslam 1972; West 1987, 24; Bateman et al 1990, 73–5). Reed beds are therefore divided into at least two beds which are cut in alternate years. According to Cowell, an average bed produced *c* 300–400 standard bundles per acre single wale and 400–500 bundles double wale.

> Reed beds can be cut every year, but it is not advisable since yearly cutting seems to thin out the reeds and encourage the growth of other smaller plants, ultimately turning the bed into a sedge marsh. Some thatchers prefer to work with the single wale, or one year's crop, but from the reed-bed owner's point of view, it is undesirable to cut the beds more frequently than every second year, hence the 'double wale' or two years' crop is universally employed. (Deas 1939, 92)

Reed was cut with a scythe or sickle, as low on the stem as possible and below water level if necessary. The cutting, tying, boating, loading, cleaning, trimming, stacking and transporting of reed were all laborious tasks (Jobson 1949, 1187) and labour shortages were common because pay and conditions were always poor. The reeds were cured under cover for several months before being used for thatching, and well-seasoned reed was often difficult to obtain (Cambridgeshire Record Office 1).

In practice, the reed usually contained small amounts of reed mace (*Typha angustifolia*), boulder (*Schoenoplectus lacustris*) and other minor components, and was sometimes called mixed reed as opposed to best reed which was cut from the purest *Phragmites* beds. Mixed reed was commonly employed on shelters and outbuildings and provided a cheap alternative to the pure reed preferred by architects. Mixed reed also generated reduced profits for reed bed owners (Boardman 1933, 563; Cowell nd; Cambridgeshire Record Office 1). Reed cutting was mechanized in the late 1950s and 1960s.

Purchasing reed

Shoves, fathoms, bolts and bundles

Reed was sold in a confusing variety of measures which were often unfamiliar to thatchers or reed dealers from other regions. This is due in part to the marsh men and cutters, who like many of the most skilled rural craftsmen used traditional or idiosyncratic methods of reckoning. Vincent (1941, 1119) noted that one reed cutter marked a 'snotch' for every 'tally' of 50 shoves (sheaves) cut. In 1940, reed throughout the Broads was cut and sold by the 'hundred fathom' which weighed approximately 2½ tons (Cowell nd). A fathom usually contained five or six shoves with girths of 18"–21" (46cm–53cm) measured 14"–18" (36cm–46cm) from the butt end, or sufficient reed to produce a fathom with a six foot girth at its binding. 'One hundred fathom' could be expected to thatch 600 ft^2 (1 bundle/ft^2) to a depth of 12"–15" (30cm–38cm) (Vincent 1941, 1119; Deas 1939, 92), but this varied depending on the length of the reed, local tradition and the depth of material applied. As with the 'baker's dozen', a 'hundred' actually contained 120 fathoms, with

a 'short hundred' containing 100 fathoms (Deas 1939, 92). Reed was sold either in 'bunches' of 100 or in 'scores' in Hampshire in 1911, and in 14lb (6.4kg) bolts with 32" (81cm) girths in Kent. The term bolt has usually been used with reference to osiers used in basketry rather than reed, and the term does not appear to stem from a straw thatching tradition.

Prices and labour costs

Reed thatch continued to be used for thatching in Norfolk into the early part of this century because it compared favourably with pantiles in terms of durability, availability and cost. Nevertheless, the selling price of reed was subject to factors that could fluctuate wildly beyond the control of the thatcher, the landowner or the middleman. Aside from wages paid to marshmen to manage the bed, the primary costs included:

- leasing of the bed
- commissions to growers and agents in the field
- assessing the quality of reed in the field
- cutting
- transport to the bankside and staithes (ie wharfs)
- cleaning, sorting and retying
- transport to a nearby station (train or canal) or to the dealer's yard
- transport to the thatching site or the thatcher's yard

The thatching itself then involved additional costs, but these are difficult to establish as each marshman and his workers negotiated with landowners and reed dealers on an individual (and usually unrecorded) basis. The Cowell papers indicate that the First World War was a watershed for the British reed industry. According to George Applegate in 1910 'it is very uncertain what a man can earn per day as "weather rules". If the weather is favourable they can earn 3/- to 4/- [15p to 20p] a day' (Cambridgeshire Record Office 1).

Applegate paid 4d–6d per bundle of reed (48s–72s [£2.40–£3.60] per hundred) 'depending on how much trouble it was to collect' (Cambridgeshire Record Office 1). Marshall (1790) recorded the cost of cutting as 25s (£1.25) per hundred for reed and 30s (£1.50) for gladdon (reedmace). This suggests that there was little significant movement in the wages of reed cutters over the course of the nineteenth century. The First World War was a watershed for the industry, however, and figures taken from Cowell's records chart a dramatic rise in the labour cost of cutting a hundred of reed over the war period (Table 13).

The cost of cutting reed more than tripled from its previously stable figure of approximately 30s (£1.50) per hundred to over 100s (£5) in 1920.

> Every hundred reed is costing us 102s [£5.10], apart from cost of boats, to cut ... and boat it up. Does the price of 120s [£6] per hundred for best reeds, [and] 82s [£4.10] for mixed appear reasonable to you? [The] price of sedge stands as it is, though there is not much profit on this. I only submit these prices for your approval, owing to the present conditions of

Table 13 Rise in labour costs for cutting a 'hundred' of reed, 1902–21 (Cambridgeshire Record Office 1).

1902	29s (Eels Foot, Ormesby)
1906	30s (or 29s + beer)
1910	30–32s (Hickling Broad)
1911	35s (Hickling Broad)
1912	35–37s or 45s (single wale)
1913	39s (double wale)
1914	40s
1916	50s (Hickling Broad)
1917	60s (Hickling Broad)
1918	60s (Hickling Broad)
1919	80–85s
1920	110s
1921	100s

labour, as I want to act in all fairness to you ... my employees and the men. (Cambridgeshire Record Office 1)

By 1941, reed cutters were still receiving approximately 100s (£5) per hundred, while the reeds sold for 120s–140s (£6–£7) per hundred (Vincent 1941, 1119).

The rise of the middleman

In the first half of this century it was generally much more difficult to secure sufficient supply of water reed than in the present day, and many thatchers sought to purchase or rent reed beds to reduce the unreliability and cost of supplies. The history of John Cowell's thatching and reed distribution business is interesting in this respect. Initially reed was purchased from a plethora of growers, but the logistical problems involved in obtaining sufficient reed from a large number of small growers for large projects encouraged him to purchase entire crops still on the bed. In 1910 Cowell negotiated with the agent of Hickling Broad to purchase the next year's entire cut, and arranged for its cutting and transport by a local forage merchant.

The following year Cowell sought out smaller growers in the area as well as purchasing all of the main crop from Hickling Broad. Eventually, Cowell became a grower as well as a distributor, and in 1915 he took up the abandoned tenancy of the reed beds at Eels Foot Inn which produced 500 fathoms per year. His timing was astute for the price of reed to the thatcher more than tripled its value over the course of the First World War. Even with ownership secured, the notoriously independent marshmen could 'sell away'. Every stage of the supply network involved costs and risks that were often assumed by the reed dealer rather than the grower or the thatcher. This was particularly so when the reed was purchased 'in the field' and its cutting became the middleman's responsibility. Poor management of water levels, or the encroachment of livestock from adjacent pastures, could greatly reduce the quality of the crop, yet the conflicting demands from adjacent landowners also had to be taken into account (Cambridgeshire Record Office 1). Problems could arise when locating a suitable place for stacking thousands of fathoms of reed in an area which was flooded for most of the year. Transportation was often difficult, and carting by road was more efficient and reliable than boating when the marshes were dry enough to support a cart and horses (Cambridgeshire Record Office 1) (Fig 25). Reed was occasionally transported directly to a railway siding or to a dealer's yard, but fires could be triggered by sparks from passing trains (Cambridgeshire Record Office 1). Bundled reed could also be damaged in storage by constant rain (Cambridgeshire Record Office 1) as mature reed is very slow to dry out once wetted. Without this middleman to absorb the risks and concentrate supplies from many different beds, the reed grower could not be certain of selling his entire crop nor the thatcher of obtaining sufficient supplies.

Figure 25 Harvesting water reed in Slapton Lea, Devon, c 1940 (Museum of English Rural Life).

Cowell's papers are the earliest records of an emerging middle tier of dealers and distributors within the reed industry, a belated English version of a system that had long worked well for reed producers and thatchers on the continent. It is the rise of the middleman that made possible the rediscovery and popularization of reed thatching by architects and turned a decentralized and disjointed local industry into a viable commercial one that could supply high quality reed on demand at a national level. The devastation of the First World War probably assisted this development by loosening many of the traditional social and economic bonds that governed the interaction of marshmen, reed cutters, landowners and thatchers. A large section of the local industry never returned from the battlefield, large estates were sold or dismembered, and once productive reed beds grew rapidly into impenetrable carr. This process was accelerated by the depression of the 1930s, and by subsequent government drainage schemes designed to increase food production in the Second World War and in the post-war era. In spite of the many challenges faced by the industry early this century, reed beds remained a profitable way of managing low-lying land for many landowners when labour could be obtained and the reed sold to a middleman.

Importation

Although the importation of water reed is usually considered to be a recent phenomenon, the fragmented and unpredictable supply of reed from Norfolk early this century encouraged at least one thatching firm to look abroad for supplies. In 1911 John Cowell met the director of the Nederlandische Cooperatieve from Sliedricht, Holland, a company that represented a group of mainly small growers who between them managed over 1,200 acres (486ha) of water reed. Compared to the Norfolk industry, the Dutch supply system was efficient and produced reed of standard high-quality. The company exported water reed to Germany, France, Austria and Belgium as well as to a building firm in Cardiff, Wales, where it was used as a key for plastering ceilings. Dutch reed growers were guaranteed 8d (3p) per bundle, and surveyors were employed to enforce standards of size and quality, in contrast to the variability in quality and bundle size encountered in Norfolk.

Cowell ordered 110 'bunches', the equivalent of 22 Norfolk fathoms, of Dutch reed in June, 1911, which was shipped from Rotterdam to King's Lynn and eventually moved by truck to Soham in Cambridgeshire (Cambridgeshire Record Office 1). This reed was applied to a roof at Burgess Hill, West Sussex, in September, which carries the dubious distinction of being the first building in England to be thatched with foreign reed. The economics of the transaction were not particularly favourable: Cowell purchased the reed at 95s (£4.75) per 100 bunches, the growers receiving 66s (£3.30), the Dutch marketing company 29s (£1.45), and the carriage firms 66s (£3.30) for transporting the reed via King's Lynn to Soham. The total cost of reed delivered to the dealer's door was thus 161s (£8.05) when good quality Norfolk reed was available for approximately 35s–45s (£1.75–

£2.25) at source with a further 30s–40s (£1.50–£2) in transportation charges. Norfolk reed at the dealer's door thus cost in the region of 65s–85s (£3.25–£4.25) per fathom, or less than half that of imported reed. The economics of the transaction were not particularly attractive, and imports did not resume until the late 1950s (Rural Industries Bureau 1958–9).

Summary

Several distinct trends can be observed within the history of the supply of wetland thatching materials from 1790–1940:

- an abandonment of the use of reedmace, bulrush and alternative wetland materials for thatching as a result of drainage and enclosure of wet wastes in the early nineteenth century;
- a retraction of production and use of water reed into the Broads district due to competition from alternative roofing materials. Reed beds producing secondary quality reed switched production to marsh hay and bedding for London and other urban markets, and a much reduced number of prime beds continued to be managed for 'pure' thatching reed;
- the abandonment of fen sedge as a profitable fuel crop for kindling and drying malt, and its rediscovery as a ridging material by architects and water reed thatchers in the inter-war years;
- the emergence of middlemen reed dealers early this century, and the expansion of what had hitherto been a 'local' craft into a more mechanized, and market-driven, industry that could supply materials to thatchers on a regional and national scale;
- a near collapse of the reed thatching industry between 1914 and the mid 1920s due to the disruption of the First World War, followed by a rediscovery of reed thatching by architects, builders and wealthy home owners.

CULTIVATED CROPS

Flax *(Linum usitatissimum)*

Flax is the only non-cereal arable crop that has been grown specifically for use as thatch. English farmers were offered strong incentives to grow flax throughout the eighteenth century, but production dwindled in England after export bounties were abolished in 1829. Production increased briefly in response to the American Civil War which cut cotton imports to Britain, but it remained a significant crop only in Northern Ireland in the late nineteenth century (Bell & Watson 1986). Its cultivation was briefly revived on the warm, loamy soils of the Somerset Levels and the Fens during the two world wars, but it remained an uncommon crop.

Both flax and reed were used to repair thatched roofs on the Wantage Estate north-east of Northampton late last century. The flax was probably used for ridging, interestingly, by a thatcher from Whittlesea in Cambridgeshire who must have had access to sedge in abundance (Northamptonshire Record Office 3). Innocent (1916, 214) recorded the memory of its use in Derbyshire where it had been 'formerly favoured'. It is unlikely to have been used for anything other than patching on poorer cottages in England, and only on large estates could it have been produced in sufficient quantity for routine use.

Cereal straw

Straw has probably been used for thatching in England for over 3,000 years, and the roots of both the combed wheat reed and long straw methods now used stretch back into the mists of antiquity. Contrary to popular opinion, long straw did not originate with the threshing machine, although it did increase its popularity and the use of the term. The key to understanding this surprisingly controversial issue is quite simple: there are only so many ways in which cereals can be processed to extract their grain. Hence, there are a limited number of straw products that have been available for thatching through the centuries and the history of straw thatching is to a large degree the history of crop processing.

The earliest *in situ* evidence of straw thatching has only recently come to light with the discovery of late medieval thatch preserved in the base coats of former open hall houses in southern England (Letts 1999). This research has highlighted the fact that English wheat has probably changed more in the past century than it did over the preceding five centuries. Before the early nineteenth century all of the straw used in thatching was derived from tall, genetically diverse land race varieties of wheat, rye and occasionally oats and barley. The straw used for thatching in 1790 would have been closer to that used by the Anglo Saxons than to the combed wheat reed used on holiday cottages in Dorset in the 1930s.

The changes that occurred over this period may be classified into four broad categories.

The industrial revolution and Parliamentary enclosure (1790–1840)

By 1790 the industrial revolution was transforming the English landscape and the social structure of its people in both urban and rural areas. Cities were expanding at an unprecedented rate and creating new markets for agricultural products. Increasing demand for flour products, combined with the disruptions in trade caused by the Napoleonic wars, forced an unprecedented rise in grain prices and consequently an expansion of cereal production as farmers sought to cash in after decades of depressed prices. The boom was short-lived, however, and the instability of grain prices, and hence the supply of thatching straw, returned with the cessation of hostilities.

At the start of this period England was also in the final stages of a revolution in land holding that greatly influenced the materials and methods used in thatching. Much of the common land in the country had been enclosed in the sixteenth and seventeenth centuries, but the process intensified in the late eighteenth century with the enclo-

sure by Parliamentary decree of the last expanses of open field in common ownership. Half of the common arable in England was enclosed before 1790, and the final seven million acres (2.8 million ha) was taken into private ownership between 1790 and 1815 (Mathias 1969). Landed improvers decried common ownership as the prime obstacle limiting agricultural progress and national prosperity, and argued that enclosed land could be farmed scientifically to maximize yields. In reality, parliamentary enclosure was fuelled by the pressure of large landholders eager to raise their cereal output in order to take advantage of high grain prices. Common ownership stressed reliability and security of yield over maximal output, and hence slowed the rate of adoption of innovative crops and production practices. But change was possible and open fields survived as long as they did because they were responsive to pressures for change within manorial economies that valued secondary products such as straw, and the survival of the local community.

Commoners able to substantiate their claims were compensated at enclosure with plots of unimproved land that were often too small to support a family unit. The smaller farms were often incapable of paying for the improvements in fencing, drainage and machinery demanded by law, and were unable to compete with adjacent estates farming better quality land. Eighty percent of the arable land in England was cultivated by tenanted farmers or large landowners by 1780. New cottages were built to house the growing estate workforce, which in turn stimulated a demand for professional thatchers and thatching straw. Although this process of consolidation varied tremendously from region to region, it is undoubtedly responsible for part of the increase in the number of thatched properties in southern England recorded in the insurance papers discussed above.

Enclosure restricted access to the bracken, broom, heather, rush and stubble straw that had covered the poor man's hovel in earlier centuries. Such alternatives were also unacceptable on the progressive landlord's model farm, and the increased popularity of straw for thatching was inevitable as its production became centralized on the estate. Stubble straw gathered from the open fields had long been used by commoners and the rural poor for thatching and for fuel. Enclosure constrained access to the open field stubble, and new cereal varieties and farming practices gradually eliminated the production of tall stubble altogether. Enclosure thus altered both the availability of straw and the way in which it was used for thatching, just as the drainage of wetlands and the enclosure of heaths banished traditional 'wild' alternatives from the repertoire of available materials.

Agricultural improvement

In 1790, bread wheat (*Triticum aestivum*) and rivet wheat (*T. turgidum*) were staple crops on clay soils, whereas rye (*Secale cereale*) yielded better than any other cereal on light and acidic soils. Rye was routinely interplanted with wheat to generate grain for the staple loaf, and its straw was very commonly used for thatching. Barley (*Hordeum vulgare*) and oats (*Avena* spp.) were grown throughout England for bread, beer and fodder, and although they performed best on light soils, they provided an insurance crop for clay farmers because they could be sown in the spring if the autumn crop failed. Oat straw produced the best quality fodder, while mature rye, wheat and barley straw was reserved for bedding. Cereals were grown even in pastoral districts for stock feed and home use, and the straw was used for fuel, bedding and thatching.

In general terms England was divided into eastern corn and western grazing counties, including Yorkshire, Nottinghamshire, Lincolnshire, Northamptonshire, Huntingdonshire, Buckinghamshire, Hertfordshire, Berkshire, south Wiltshire and Dorset in the corn district (Caird 1851). This division was essentially climatic: the grain counties received less than 40" (102cm) of rain a year and enjoyed a longer, warmer and drier growing season than other parts of Britain (Coppock 1964, 32–3). Enclosure led to higher yields only when farmers had access to the new crops, tools, fertilisers and techniques promulgated by agricultural improvers and organisations such as the Bath and West of England Agricultural Society (1777), and the Royal Agricultural Society (1838) (Prothero 1901). 'High farming' methods revolutionized English agriculture by eliminating the fallow and shattering the notion that light soils were incapable of supporting regular cropping.

Much of the farmland taken into cultivation in the late eighteenth and early nineteenth centuries had been under heathland for millennia. The new crop rotations turned the barren heaths of East Anglia into cereal fields, and farmers who could afford the risk shifted their cereal production onto lighter soils (Mathias 1969, 72). Throughout the country wheat fields on heavy clay were abandoned to grassland. This shift to 'high farming' was fuelled by high grain prices and expanding urban markets for bread, beer and meat, but the peace of 1815–35 revealed a tremendous level of over-production and brought a dramatic slide in grain prices despite protective corn laws and expanding markets. The resulting collapse had a disproportionate effect on the wheat farmers who had continued to till the better-drained clays, and for whom the introduction of cheap and effective underdrainage in the 1840s came too late (Mathias 1969, 311; Prothero 1901, 21–2). 'High farmers' could adopt improved varieties with better baking qualities, and the lighter soils supported more flexible crop rotations and specialisation. Clay farmers had no choice but to continue using the traditional, lower-yielding land races that were more reliable, but much less profitable, than the new varieties on poorly-drained heavy soils. The advent of efficient sub-surface drainage in the 1840s and 1850s regenerated farming on clay soils, and underdrainage spread rapidly through Essex, Bedfordshire, south Cambridgeshire, north Hertfordshire, Norfolk and parts of Lancashire, Staffordshire, Derbyshire and Leicestershire. It generated new opportunities for wheat production in grazing counties, and led to a more even distribution of production within eastern and southern England. This led to the creation of new estates and reinvigorated older ones, which in turn stimulated a demand for new thatched cottages to house their workforces.

In general terms, an estimated 58.5% of all dwellings in the south west were thatched in 1800, which would have consumed much of the cereal straw produced in this predominantly grazed region. This figure plummeted from 400,000 to 150,000 by 1862–3 leaving only 16.6% of insured buildings thatched. This would have eased pressure on the demand for thatching straw in the region, but the statistics still indicate that only five acres (2ha) of arable land was potentially available for the production of thatching straw per thatched building. This is a low figure compared to other regions if the coats applied approached the 1.5–2 acres (0.6ha–0.8ha) of straw used on a cottage roof today. However, coats were often much thinner in the past, particularly on outbuildings and poorer dwellings. The insurance statistics indicate that the number of thatched buildings in southern England peaked in the first half of the nineteenth century, with the ratio of arable land per building dropping almost to the level of the West Country by 1862–3 (Table 14). Since a portion of the arable acreage was, of necessity, planted to non-cereal crops, and straw was used for a great variety of non-thatching purposes, the supply of straw may not have satisfied the demand for thatching straw in many areas. In practice, a great number of agronomic, social and architectural changes were occurring at this time so that a simple direct relationship between straw production and thatching cannot easily be drawn for this period.

Northern England is today associated with heather thatching, but the literature indicates that straw was by far the most common thatching material employed during the nineteenth century.

According to Watson and McLintock (1979, 16), most surviving old thatch is of 'wheaten straw ... carefully chosen and thrashed with a flail so as not to damage the reed'. Over 200 purchases of straw for thatching are recorded in the papers of the Rufford estate in Lancashire in the mid nineteenth century. Heather is recorded only once, when it was apparently used on gables in combination with straw. Straw was supplied by 115 different named suppliers, a general practice that is confirmed by the records of other estates and which suggest that straw sufficient to thatch a large building was difficult to find (Lancashire Record Office 3).

Table 14 Arable acreage to thatch building ratios: 1800 and 1862–3 (Guildhall Library, London, 1, 2 and 3; 1866 Agricultural Returns).

	total arable acreage	1800 total thatched buildings	1800 arable to thatch ratio	1862/3 total thatched buildings	1862/3 arable to thatch ratio
south west	731205	411805	1.8	150069	4.9
south east	372726	26568	14.0	9695	38.4
south	3205571	330318	9.7	573544	5.6
Midlands	1983196	128909	15.4	95209	20.8
north	1241902	59646	20.6	13344	93.1

A comparison of the numbers of insured thatched buildings for 1862–3 with the Agricultural Returns for this region in 1866 suggests that over 100 acres (40ha) of arable land was potentially available for the production of cereal straw for each thatched building, compared with only five acres (2ha) in the south and south west, 21 acres (8.5ha) in the Midlands and 3 acres (1.2ha) in the south east. This figure is misleading, however, for in practice much less cereal was grown in the north than in other regions, and much of what was tilled was planted to oats. In all areas changes in the supply and demand of thatching straw operated at the local level and varied tremendously from year to year.

The late nineteenth-century agricultural depression (1840–90)

By 1850 English agriculture was once again in the midst of a golden age. The threshing machine and the mechanical reaper had revolutionized cereal production in the north and in other regions where labour costs were high, but their adoption was delayed until the 1850s and 1860s in the south where labour was abundant. A profusion of new cereal varieties also flooded the market enabling progressive farmers to experiment in order to tailor varieties to specific growing conditions. The demand for straw litter also increased in rural areas as farms maintained larger herds of livestock, and also in urban centres due to an increase in horse transport. Straw was also much in demand for packing, cob walling, straw plaiting and for stuffing mattresses and horse collars, but these were minor demands compared to the amount of straw used in thatching and bedding (Middleton 1798, 252; Young 1804a, 223; Young 1804b, 314; Batchelor 1808, 392; Vancouver 1808, 173; Stevenson 1809, 431; Pitt 1810 [1969], 316; Rudge 1813, 119).

This golden age came to a sudden end in the 1870s, provoked by a string of poor harvests. These were underlain by overcapacity and increased competition from new overseas producers. The impact of plummeting prices was, once again, felt most severely by the clay farmers of Lincolnshire, East Anglia and the East Riding of Yorkshire, who were unable to switch production to alternative crops or dairying (Grigg 1989, 27–61). Essex, once the granary of London, was abandoned to low intensity grazing. Barley and oats rose rapidly in importance to become the principal cereal crops in arable districts (Mathias 1969, 316). Estates collapsed as imports of high-quality baking wheat from North America confined English wheat to use in pastries and biscuits, and the English wheat industry was gradually pushed to the edge of extinction (Coppock 1964, 39; Bingham et al 1991).

The decline was to continue into the 1930s. At the outbreak of the Second World War cereals were grown on only half of the acreage planted to grain in 1875, and production had retracted onto the drier, flatter soils of eastern England. While wheat production plummeted, barley output rose steadily on the light soils of East Anglia, Humberside and the chalk lands of southern England. Fodder oats covered more acreage than any other cereal crop in 1900, but dropped rapidly in subsequent decades

as horses were displaced by the combustion engine in transport. The decline in horse traffic also reduced the demand for rye straw litter, and rye production retracted onto soils too acidic or infertile to support other crops, such as the Brecklands and the Sandlings in Suffolk (Coppock 1964, 68–80).

Between 1790 and 1940, few farmers or thatchers could have ignored the revolutions in transportation, housing, plant breeding and mechanization that occurred over this period, but it is also probably true that a small amount of straw was always available for thatching in rural areas no matter what larger economic changes were occurring. All of these changes affected the demand for thatch as well as the availability and character of materials. In 1790 thatch was the only roofing material available to a large section of the rural population. In 1940 it survived largely because of cultural momentum, and the production of thatching straw had become incompatible with high-input farming systems in which straw was essentially a by-product of the conversion of fuel into grain.

The cultivation of land races

In 1790 cereal crops were composed of genetically diverse land races very different from modern varieties. Land races are a hallmark of traditional agriculture and develop whenever crops are grown over many generations from seed obtained from the previous year's harvest (Frankel 1976, 29). Their underlying genetic variability is a product of semi-natural selection: a plant runs a gauntlet of ecological stresses such as high rainfall, drought, late spring frost, low soil fertility, and pest and disease attack before ripening its seed. Those plants that have advantageous combinations of characters contribute a disproportionate amount of seed to the harvest, and over many generations a unique land race variety develops that is well adapted to local growing conditions and cultural practices. Land races were also interplanted with other cereals, providing a buffer of physiological diversity that ensured that most of the plants in a field survived all but the most disastrous of seasons. Reliability of yield was obviously essential to a subsistence-oriented farmer, and was maintained at the cost of lower yield and baking quality. High-yielding characteristics were of use only when associated with other adaptive characters such as disease resistance, cold tolerance, or stiff straw that allowed the yield advantage to be expressed.

One of the most striking characteristics of older cereal land race varieties was their height; the product of semi-natural selection for tall straw over centuries of cultivation in densely planted, weed-infested fields. In all ecosystems plants compete for light and nutrients with their neighbours, and in cereal fields individuals able to grow quickly and dominate their local environment will capture more sunlight and thus contribute more seed to the harvest. The genetic propensity for tallness that accumulates over many generations differs from the rapid stem elongation (etiolation) that can occur in response to high nitrogen levels and very dense sowing. Etiolation weakens a stem's lower internodes and leads to lodging (stem breakage) in wet and windy weather. Selection for height over many generations was countered by the greater risk of tall plants lodging and failing to contribute seed to the harvest. Unimproved land races had ears that were much lighter than those of nineteenth-century and later selections, however, and lodging probably occurred primarily because of etiolation due to uneven sowing and fertilization. Traditional English land race varieties of wheat and rye grew to over 185cm (6') and averaged between 140–180cm (4' 8"–5' 10") judging by the straw recovered from late medieval smoke-blackened buildings (Letts 1999). Le Couteur (1836, vi) referred to a wheat variety 7' (2.1m) tall on display at the Royal Agricultural Society in the 1830s. Most of the improved varieties available in the early nineteenth century matured at between 140–160cm (4'5"–5'3"), and this had been reduced to 120–140cm by 1900 (Donaldson 1847, 4; Percival 1921). Straw is today considered inferior for combed wheat reed-style thatching if it falls below 3' (80cm), and high-yielding hybrid wheats are now being released that mature at less than 20" (50cm). Tall-stemmed cereals provided ample straw for litter, craft industries and thatching, and although mature wheat and rye straw were not much used as fodder they were highly valued for manure.

In practice, cereal crops often remained genetically diverse even when purified varieties became available, due to accidental mixing of grain from different fields during harvesting, threshing and storage. The custom of obtaining fresh seed from a distant region every three or four years to strengthen the seed also encouraged a mixing of varieties. A change of seed was widely claimed to produce a yield increase equal to half a dunging, but yields generally returned to normal in subsequent years as the novel genetic types were out-competed by plants better adapted to local growing conditions. Many agricultural writers also advocated the deliberate mixing of distinct varieties arguing that this encouraged a more complete use of soil nutrients and produced larger and more reliable yields (Vilmorin-Andrieux et Cie 1880, 167).

Agricultural improvement

Underdrainage

Land races out-perform improved cultivars in heterogeneous and unpredictable growing conditions. One of the major causes of heterogeneity in English cereal fields between 1790 and 1940 was poor drainage, and land races retained their popularity on undrained, heavy clays long after improved varieties had been adopted on lighter soils. Historically heavy soil was ploughed into ridge and furrow to increase the rate of surface runoff and reduce infiltration (Brewer 1972). The coexistence of wet furrows and dry ridges led to great unevenness in plant height, ripening time, yield and grain quality within one field, whereas the lighter soils could be ploughed flat, manured, and sown evenly by machine with more uniform, higher-yielding varieties with improved baking qualities. In the early nineteenth century, arable land was classified simply as heavy or light, and agricultural writers claimed that most heavy soils were in desperate need of

underdrainage. It was considered a key indicator of improvement, and although clay tile drains were introduced in the early nineteenth century, they became accessible through mass production only in the 1840s. In the eighteenth century, fields were underdrained by digging trenches that were filled with stones and wood brash to provide a channel for water to drain away. Cheap clay tiles were more efficient and longer-lasting, and their advent led to a boom in underdrainage works that was capped only by the recession of the 1870s.

Underdrainage was initially adopted in the eastern counties and the Midlands, and particularly Essex, Hertfordshire, Bedfordshire, south Cambridgeshire, Norfolk, and adjoining parts of Leicestershire, Derbyshire and Staffordshire (Grigg 1989, 32). Once underdrained, ridge and furrow fields could be evenly cross-ploughed, fertilized with dung and artificials, planted with a drill and weeded with a row cultivator (Prothero 1901).

The advantages of cultivating a land race were greatly reduced with the increasing uniformity of growing conditions, and the superior yield characteristics of individual plants could be noted more easily once environmental heterogeneity had been controlled. Plants which would formerly have grown to average height in an infertile corner of a ridge and furrow field now grew tall and lodged on well-drained, fertile soil. Plants that could survive severe waterlogging in the furrow during the winter, but which grew less vigorously than most plants in drier conditions, were reproductively disadvantaged on the improved field and gradually eliminated from the population. Uneven ripening produced an inferior flour for commercial baking, and improvements depended upon reducing heterogeneity of growing conditions as well as rigorous plant breeding. Underdrainage allowed wheat to return to the heavy clay soils of the Midlands and the eastern counties, but by this time growers were cultivating shorter improved varieties rather than tall land races.

Soil fertility

Few issues in thatching attract as much controversy as the use of artificial fertilizers, and particularly the impact of nitrogen on straw length and durability. Nitrogen (N) is essential to plant growth, along with phosphorus (P), potassium (K) and a host of secondary nutrients. Whether they arrive in rainfall, manure or in artificial fertilizer, a fair supply of N-P-K is required if a crop is to produce its maximal yield of grain. Abundant nitrogen will lead to lodging, however, as it also stimulates rapid stem growth. But high fertility was rarely a problem for wheat producers in the past, except in naturally fertile soils such as the Fens, and precocious growth was simply grazed by sheep or cut for fodder.

Full-scale dunging of cereal fields had become more commonplace by the late eighteenth century, although this was tempered by the increased risk of lodging this provoked (Loudon 1831, 815; Ward & Lock 1880, 156–7). The larger quantity of manure applied was supplied by an increase in the number of livestock kept through the winter and fed with imported feed. Organic fertilizer was also available from a variety of what now appear to be unusual sources such as bullock's blood, woollen rags, malt dust, town sewage, pigeon dung, rotted fish, oilseed cake and soot (Middleton 1800, 37–43; Wilson 1871, **1**, 135–61; Burn 1878 [1889–1904]; Wright 1891, 66–178). Most of these became more widely available after the development of railways and canals, although they were of local use long before (Clapp et al 1977, 145–7). Organic fertilizers could also be obtained from green manures that were grazed by livestock and ploughed under. Calcareous manures such as chalk, marl, sea shells, sea sand and lime, and naturally fertile soils and silts dug from ditches, river mouths and swampy areas were also widely used well into the late nineteenth century. Cereals were usually grown after a fallow, a leguminous crop or a grass ley, and a certain amount of dung was usually applied at some point in the rotation (but not immediately preceding wheat) to help prevent nutrient deficiencies and improve moisture retention on light soils.

A new era in crop production began in the early nineteenth century when the chemical basis of plant nutrition began to be understood. In 1840 the German professor Liebig concluded that inorganic fertilizers could be used to maximize plant growth and raise yields, although he incorrectly assumed that nitrogen supplements were of no importance (Salmon 1964, 21). Lawes and Gilbert carried out a series of experiments at Rothampstead in 1841 that challenged Liebig's theories and examined the effect of mineral nutrients on wheat yields (Burn 1878 [1889–1904]; Sykes 1981, 60–265). Their results engendered a debate that continued into the late nineteenth century. Lawes and Gilbert classified crops as either restorative or exhaustive depending on the degree to which they consumed nitrogen. Wheat was an exhaustive plant, and required added inputs of nitrogen to maximize yields. New crop rotations, used in conjunction with appropriate artificial fertilizers and manures, allowed the alteration of exhaustive and restorative crops in perpetuity without reducing soil fertility. Their results were gradually accepted and stimulated the development of the artificial fertilizer industry.

Initially, nitrogen for fertilizer production was obtained from ammonium salts and soot. This was joined in the 1870s by sulphate of ammonia produced as a byproduct of natural gas production, which was itself superseded by synthetic nitrogen in the First World War. All nitrogen in artificial fertilizer is now derived from the fixation of nitrogen gas in the atmosphere by the burning of natural gas which produces anhydrous ammonia. The price of artificial fertilizer fell steadily after 1923, and new forms of compounded fertilizer greatly eased the farmer's efforts to maintain a proper soil nutrient balance.

Weed control

Many of the weeds that once plagued British cereal fields are now extinct or extremely uncommon. Before the introduction of effective pesticides weeds were controlled by the age-old practices of crop rotation and fallowing. Copper sulphate was first used in France in the late nineteenth century, and the sulphuric acid used briefly in England early this century was too corrosive for popular use. The contact herbicide DNOC (dinitro-orthocresol) was developed in the early 1930s, but the first truly successful synthetic pesticide, MCPA (methylchlorophenoxyacetic acid), was introduced in 1942.

The elimination of much of the micro-environmental heterogeneity in cereal fields over the course of the nineteenth century altered both the quality and availability of thatching straw in England. Wheat could now be produced on light soil as well as heavy clay, and although eastern England remained the principal wheat growing district, the historical boundary between east and west was blurred as growing conditions fell increasingly under the control of the farmer. Nevertheless, more thatching straw was available in the south than in the north, in the east than the west, on heavier drained clays than on lighter soils, in lowland areas than in uplands, and on improved estates and large farms with access to fertilizer and machinery than on smaller subsistence-oriented farms. But even in agricultural backwaters straw was available for thatching, and it was in these areas of limited straw production, as opposed to core districts, that thatching straw was husbanded, threshed, combed and applied very carefully in order to maximize its life on a roof. Conversely, it is in these core districts that crushed straw was available in abundance and in which straw thatching suffered its first blows from the threshing machine.

Botanical changes in straw

Plant improvement

Farmers have been selecting and improving their cereal crops for thousands of years. In the case of cereals this usually involved choosing the most desirable plants, or a portion of the best seed from the year's harvest, for the following year's crop. Wheat is a self-pollinating plant, and every plant is essentially a pure breeding line. Traditionally, English wheat fields were planted to land races which are collections of pure breeding lines. Mass selection, simply saving a portion of the best seed from the best field from year to year, was widely practiced within land races but with relatively little effect. More rigorous selection in which seeds from a single outstanding ear were multiplied to form an improved variety distinct from the wider parental stock (pedigree or pure line selection) produced more rapid success, however, due initially to the immense genetic diversity present in the existing land races. Unfortunately this diversity was rapidly exhausted, and by the start of this century it had become clear that continued progress in cereal breeding would depend upon hybridization programmes that could combine useful characteristics from different gene lines (Lupton 1987a, 53).

Early plant breeders succeeded in eliminating the tallest gene lines from the older land races, but struggled to reduce the average height of new varieties and improve their purity while maintaining yields. Selection for shorter, stiffer straw generally reduced overall plant vigour and grain yield. Dramatic changes in the 'harvest index', a measure of how much of a plant's photosynthetic energy is directed into grain rather than straw and foliage production, became possible only with the perfection of hybridization techniques early this century, and particularly when dwarf Japanese wheats were successfully crossed with high-yielding English wheats in the 1930s (Lupton 1987).

Little significant increase in grain yield was achieved by selection within land races after 1800, and many of the multitude of varieties available in 1850 were minor variations of a theme. Breeders sought out novel genetic material from abroad, some of which was grown successfully in Britain but most of which was unsuited to conditions in the United Kingdom. Spring wheats, in particular, were obtained from around the world, and improved selections were also made from the old English spring wheat *April* (also known as *Fern/April Bearded*). Many improved varieties of winter wheat were generated from land race stock obtained from France, Holland and other parts of Continental Europe. Once growing conditions within fields had been made uniform through underdrainage, fertilization and mechanization, a wider range of improved varieties could be grown in uniform conditions and their yields tested objectively in relation to soil type and climate.

The shift to mechanization after 1850 provided a powerful new incentive for breeders to develop varieties better adapted to mechanical reaping and threshing. Forty thousand mechanical reapers had displaced the sickle and scythe on a quarter of English wheat fields by 1870, and the threshing machine had largely supplanted the flail in arable districts by 1880. Mechanization encouraged the use of pure crops with uniform straw height and ripening time, and that threshed efficiently and had stiff straw resistant to lodging. The first mechanical reapers were developed in Canada and the USA for cutting short-strawed spring wheats. Most of the reapers and threshing machines used in Britain from the late nineteenth century until the introduction of the combine harvester were physically unable to process crops taller than *c* 140cm (55"), and had to be modified to cope with tall English land races and improved land race selections.

With the shift to mechanical reaping, the development of reliably shorter varieties became as important a goal for plant breeders as improvements in grain yield or baking quality. This change probably improved the quality of the straw for thatching, but even ripening also increased the risk of over-ripening when the harvest was delayed by labour shortages or inclement weather, which remain two of the biggest problems faced by thatch straw growers. Improvements in 'threshability' reduced the amount of grain remaining in straw which could subsequently sprout on the roof and attract birds. The breeding of shorter, stiffer varieties probably improved the quality of reed straw, but may have reduced the quality of crushed straw thatch because of the greater damage that occurred when the new varieties were threshed mechanically.

Wheat taxonomy and varieties
Considerable confusion exists as to the origin and characteristics of the many wheat varieties that are available

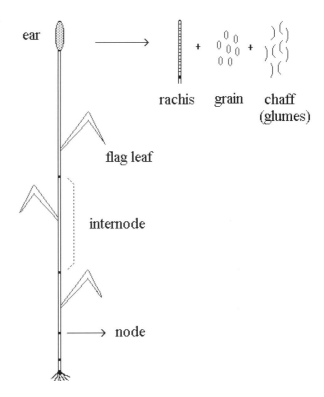

Figure 26 Parts of the wheat plant (John Letts)

for thatching. Long straw and combed wheat reed are often described as separate 'varieties' of wheat, and the relatively modern varieties now used for thatching as 'almost extinct species'. Almost all of the wheat cultivated in Britain over the past 1,500 years has been derived from two species: common bread wheat (*Triticum aestivum*) and English rivet wheat (*T. turgidum*).

<small>BREAD WHEAT (*TRITICUM AESTIVUM*)</small>
The early nineteenth-century literature on wheat is often confusing and riddled with anecdote accepted as fact. To most farmers wheat generally meant autumn-sown bread wheat popularly classified as winter or Lammas wheat (*Triticum hybernum*). Summer wheat (*T. aestivum*) and dense-eared compact wheat (*T. compactum*) were also recognised and grown to some extent, but true spring wheats became popular only in the early nineteenth century. Dense-eared or compact varieties do not seem to have been widely grown in Britain until the late eighteenth century. Some writers correctly classified all of these forms into one species (*T. sativum*) (Fyfe 1863, 297–325), but confusion increased through the century as seed merchants flooded the market with a plethora of new British and foreign selections.

Winter wheat was sown from September to December, overwintered as a young plant and ripened its grain the following summer. It was generally awnless (Fig 26), in contrast to the rivet wheats and spring wheats (Donaldson 1847, 4; Le Couteur 1836), and was generally divided into red and white varieties on the basis of bran colour (Oldershaw & Porter 1929, 14–17). White wheats had thin bran and produced high quality flour, but were lower yielding, less hardy and less disease resistant than red-grained wheats (Lankester 1832).

Hundreds of named varieties were available to English growers in the mid nineteenth century. A contemporary source listed over 200 varieties of red and white wheat in common cultivation at mid-century, although only 30 white and 20 red wheats were considered worthy of recommendation (Fyfe 1863, 297–325). Many of the varieties grown were very similar to other selections taken from the same ancestral land race and were of no advantage to the farmer. Whereas modern farmers cultivate only one or two varieties every year, it was not unusual for a progressive nineteenth-century farmer to grow a dozen named varieties with different soil preferences, ripening times, straw lengths and grain qualities. At least 24 named varieties were grown at Bratton Farm in Wiltshire in the 1840s (Morrison 1993). Some winter varieties provided tall, rigid straw for thatching and poor quality grain that could be used for domestic purposes, whereas improved spring varieties produced lower yields of high quality grain for sale and short straw that could be used as fodder.

Tall-strawed *Red Lammas* wheat, one of many selections from the original land race of this name, was the most common red-grained wheat cultivated in the mid nineteenth century (Morton 1862, 365). A similar selection known as *Blood Red* gradually superseded *Red Lammas* in the West Country, while a shorter form called *Golden Drop* became popular in the northern counties. *Browick*, a hardy, high-yielding wheat with stiff straw was popular throughout the century, and was similar to Burwell which was popular in the Midlands and the north. These two varieties were members of a large group of old, dense-eared wheats that included *Teverson*, *Red Standup* and *Squareheads Master* (Percival 1921, 303). *Squareheads Master* was first recorded in 1830 and several improved forms were marketed in the late nineteenth century. The most successful version was developed by a breeder in the West Midlands in the 1880s and was recommended for cultivation by the National Institute of Agricultural Botany until 1960. It was a hardy, red-grained wheat with 110cm straw, and yielded well in a range of soil and climatic conditions (Percival 1943, 109). Its stout, stiff straw was considered ideal for thatching, and it is the oldest (and the only non-hybrid) wheat currently grown in England for this purpose.

Spring wheat (*Triticum aestivum*)

For countless centuries English wheat has been autumn-sown, usually in September or October, so that the plants were well established before the onset of winter. In fact, autumn sowing was essential because old English varieties need a long period of exposure to cold weather after germination in order to flower and set seed successfully. When labour shortages or inclement whether delayed sowing beyond December or January farmers not only obtained reduced yields but also risked complete crop failure. True spring wheats, on the other hand, require very little cold to satisfy their vernalization requirements. Some can be sown as late as early May and still produce a good crop, although most are susceptible to winter frost and cannot be sown safely before March or April. Spring varieties also ripen a little earlier than most winter varieties, and produce a lower yield of harder grain well suited to commercial baking. Such wheats were obviously very useful as they could be planted instead of barley or oats when autumn sowing had been delayed by poor weather, or could be raked into patches of winter wheat killed by winter frost or waterlogging. True spring wheats were widely grown in Continental Europe, but the records suggest that they were uncommon in Britain before the late eighteenth century (Banks 1807; Loudon 1831, 812; Burke 1834–40, **2**, 152; Young 1813a, 149).

One of the first popular spring wheats grown in England was *April*, an improved variety derived from an old land race known as *Fern* wheat (Morton 1862, 539; Percival 1943, 33; Peachey 1951, 28). *April* seems to have been the parent of *April Bearded*, a popular nineteenth-century selection that was still being cultivated and used for thatching in 1940.

Some older winter varieties could be sown up until late February or early March and still produce an acceptable crop. Such intermediate varieties were often called spring wheat in the literature, but later planting was unreliable in the absence of controlled studies. Having recognised the value of reliable spring wheats, growers and plant breeders began experiments with improved land race selections and foreign varieties. Most yielded poorly in British growing conditions, and English growers were unable to take advantage of high-quality baking wheats such as *Red Fife* that fuelled a rapid expansion of wheat production in the North American prairies in the second half of the nineteenth century. It thus appears that spring wheats were not widely used for thatching until the early part of this century when varieties became available that were better adapted to English growing conditions (Arthur Hannabuss, pers comm).

Rivet wheat (*Triticum turgidum*)

Much of the straw used for thatching in the nineteenth century was derived from land race varieties of a species of wheat known as rivet wheat (*Triticum turgidum*), a wheat now unfamiliar to farmers and thatchers. The archaeobotanical records suggest that rivet wheat spread throughout most of southern England after its introduction in the Norman period, and the evidence from medieval records and ancient thatch suggests it was valued as much for its straw as its grain. Medieval land races of rivet wheat were extremely variable in characters such as ear density and straw length, and presumably also in growing characteristics such as ripening time and tillering ability (Letts 1999).

In the nineteenth century 'turgid' wheats were usually classified into two groups: *Egyptian wheat* (*T. compositum*) with its unusual branched spikelet, and the standard form (*T. turgidum*) which included many old English varieties (Fyfe 1863, 297–325; Percival 1943, 89). *Egyptian wheat*, one of the tallest wheats in cultivation, was also known as *Mummy* wheat in the mistaken belief that it was an ancient variety that had been returned to cultivation after having been found in an Egyptian tomb (Lupton 1954).

Percival (1921, 241-58) classified the English rivet wheats fell into four varietal groups. The *Iodurum* group included many of the most popular and productive rivet wheats available such as the white, grey and blue cone wheats, *White Pollard*, *Turkey* and *Duckbill* wheat. Most were tender, tall (150cm+), solid-strawed, late to ripen and carried dense, cone-shaped, and velvet-chaffed ears with indurate glumes that were difficult to thresh unless harvested when fully ripe. *Pole Rivet* was hollow-strawed, as was *Rampton Rivet*, a selection from *Blue Cone* released by the National Institute of Agricultural Botany in 1939. *Dinurum* varieties were better adapted to northern climates and poor soils, and included the popular *Red Rivet* and *Red Pollard* or *Clock wheat*. Most were velvety-chaffed, hollow-stemmed and grew to 130cm or more in height. *Speciosum* varieties, *Red Smooth Rivet* being the most popular, had glabrous chaff, solid stems, and were usually shorter and smaller-eared than *Iodurum* or *Dinurum* varieties. The single member of the *Gentile* group, commonly known as *White Rivet*, was similar to *Red Smooth Rivet* but with shorter awns and a shorter, narrower grain. It was popular in East Anglia and the Midlands in the early nineteenth century.

Many foreign rivet varieties were introduced over the course of the nineteenth century, particularly glabrous-chaffed varieties from France with both hollow and pithy straw. By 1900 English rivet wheats were the tallest wheats in cultivation, with varietal heights ranging from 130cm to 160cm or more. In many ways they were the miracle wheats of traditional English farming; they thrived on heavy clay soils, never lodged on account of their stiff, thick-walled straw, and yielded more than any other variety when grown on heavy land; most were immune to the rusts, mildews and other diseases; their scabrid awns discouraged attack by birds; many produced acceptable yields even on poor soil; they produced very tall straw well suited for use as litter, fuel or thatch; and all produced fine-grained, good tasting flour that could be used in pastries and home baking. The rivet wheats also had their drawbacks, however, which led to their gradual decline over the course of the nineteenth century; mature straw was thick-walled and often solid with pith rendering it unpalatable to livestock; many were sensitive to frost and performed adequately only when thickly sown on rich soils in southern England; rivets also had to be planted early in the autumn, for they flowered and ripened very late which maximized yields but carried the harvest into the late autumn.

Rivet wheat was also more difficult to thresh than most varieties of bread wheat, which worked against its popularity when mechanized threshing became the norm in the second half of the nineteenth century. Tradition-ally, cereals were cut while the nodes were still green and the bound sheaves were stooked in the field for several weeks to ripen. This arrested further lignification of stem tissues and prevented the straw from becoming brittle and inflexible. Delays in harvesting increased the loss of grain due to shattering at harvest, and reduced the quality of the straw for litter and fodder, while premature cutting reduced grain quality. Traditional varieties of rivet wheat rarely shattered, and its glumes clasped the grain tightly unless the crop had been harvested when almost fully ripe. Before the introduction of the threshing machine this problem could be overcome by selective and vigor-ous hand flailing, but this became one of its most annoy-ing characteristics after threshing machines began to dominate the landscape. This was an even greater prob-lem in genetically diverse land race varieties or impure selections of rivet wheat which ripened very unevenly.

References attesting to a preference for the straw of rivet wheat for thatching are common in nineteenth-century sources.

> [The rivet wheats] also have the advantage of being decidedly productive in both straw and grain; and their straw, though too hard and firm and semi-solid to be relished by cattle, is admirably adapted, by these very qualities and by its length, for the purposes of thatching. (Wilson 1871, **1**, 719)

Perhaps the most important factor contributing to the decline in the popularity of rivet wheats in the nineteenth century is the fact that they produced an off-white flour rich in bran and low in gluten, and were thus inferior to imported hard wheats for commercial baking. Only *Rampton Rivet* was grown to any extent after the Second World War and rivet wheat has gradually become a relict crop (Percival 1942, 52).

Hybridization

The first hybrid wheats were exhibited in England in the mid nineteenth century. Shireff released numerous suc-cessful hybrids in the 1860s and 1870s, and cross-breed-ing was routine by the 1880s, but full-scale hybridization programmes had to wait several more decades until plant breeders had exhausted the potential for crop improve-ment using simple pure line selection (Beaven 1909; Palmer 1970; Bingham 1979, 1–17). Support for hy-bridization programmes was assured by the rediscovery of Mendel's work on inheritance at the turn of the century, in the midst of a crisis in the British wheat growing industry. English varieties had long been recognised as amongst the best in the world in terms of yield, texture and flavour, but produced soft, low gluten flour that was considered inferior to imported hard-grained wheats by commercial bakers. British stone mills were unable to grind the imported wheats without contaminating the flour with finely ground bran and damaging their stones. The milling industry responded to the drop in the demand for British-ground flour by introducing roller mills in the 1880s, which separated the bran from the grain in a separate grinding process and produced a superior product (Humphries 1911). Wheat growers could not respond so quickly to the flood of imported grain, and by 1900 home-grown wheat was almost unmarketable in England even in time of shortage (Halliwell 1905).

The survival of the British wheat industry demanded the development of improved varieties, and a Home Grown Wheat Committee was established by the Asso-ciation of British and Irish Millers in 1901 to work with

Figure 27 Decrease in height of wheat varieties due to plant breeding (l-r: T. turgidum var. Mummy, T. aestivum var. Red Fife, T. turgidum var. Rampton Rivet, T. aestivum vars. Squareheads Master, Maris Huntsman and Brock) (John Letts).

the university-based plant breeding stations and the Board of Agriculture to this end. State-funded plant breeding stations were soon set up within university departments at Cambridge, Aberystwyth, Edinburgh and

Belfast, and Roland Biffen was appointed to the Department of Agriculture at Cambridge in 1896 to apply the new knowledge to English wheat breeding (Biffen & Engeldow 1926; Palmer 1970; Bingham et al 1991) (Fig 27). Thousands of wheat varieties from around the world were assessed to locate lines that could be crossed with English wheat to reduce the incidence of lodging while maintaining yields and improving baking quality. At Reading University, John Percival evaluated over 1,500 accessions for valuable characteristics, but the straw requirements of the thatcher were never a major concern (Oldershaw 1944, 64).

A few of the early crosses made by Biffen and his team are still grown in England for thatching and many were used as stock for later breeding work (Fig 28). Early this century Dutch breeders crossed *Squarehead* with *Talavera* to produce *Victor* (1908), a high yielding, white-grained wheat with stout, 110cm straw that was well regarded by thatchers and recommended for general cultivation until 1957. Biffen crossed *Squareheads Master* with the hard Polish spring wheat *Ghirka* in 1910 to produce *Little Joss*, a variety with good disease resistance that is still grown on a small scale for thatching. *Browick* was crossed with the Canadian spring wheat *Red Fife* to produce the relatively short-strawed variety *Yeoman* (1916), the first high-yielding wheat with good baking qualities available to English growers (Lupton 1987a).

In 1800 all of the wheat grown in Britain was derived from genetically diverse land races, land race selections and mixtures of improved selections. By 1900 land races were cultivated in only a few isolated areas with difficult growing conditions, and land race selections and mixtures were rapidly giving way to a much narrower range of modern hybrids (Beaven 1909). In 1929 over 80 named varieties were still in common cultivation (Patterson 1925, 99; Percival 1943) and a list of the most popular varieties grown during the first half of this century includes:

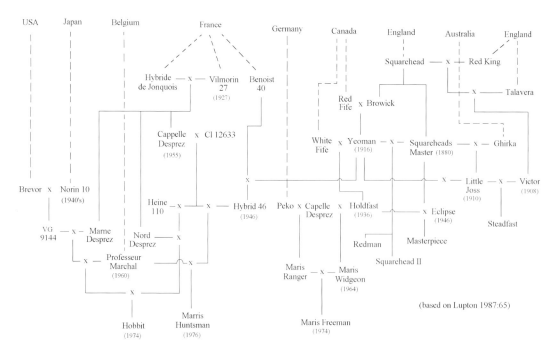

Figure 28   Lineages of modern varieties of baking and thatching wheats (T. aestivum) *(John Letts, after Lupton 1987, 65).*

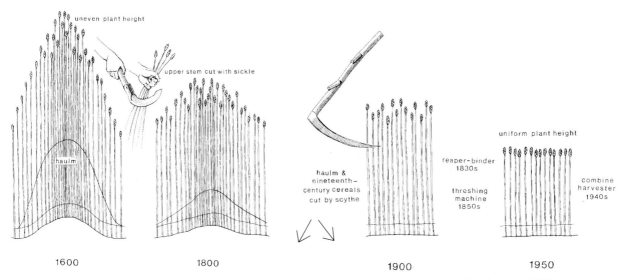

uneven plant height

upper stem cut with sickle

haulm

haulm & nineteenth–century cereals cut by scythe

uniform plant height

reaper-binder 1830s

threshing machine 1850s

combine harvester 1940s

1600   1800   1900   1950

Figure 29 Changes in harvesting methods, straw height and height uniformity; medieval to 1940 (Judith Dobie, after Letts 1999).

- *Browick* (1844)
- *April Bearded* (nineteenth century)
- *Squareheads Master/Red Standard* (nineteenth century)
- *Red Marvel* (1904)
- *Starling* (1907)
- *Partridge* (1907)
- *Victor* (1908)
- *Little Joss* (1910)
- *Wilhelmina* (1910)
- *Yeoman* (1916)
- *Vilmorin's Hybrid 27* (1927)
- *Rampton Rivet* (1934)
- *Bersee* (1935)
- *Holdfast* (1936)
- *Juliana* (1936)

The development of *Bersee* and *Holdfast* marked a transition for the thatching industry. These wheats were well adapted for mechanized harvesting (Fig 29), and like many of the newer hybrids they performed poorly in low input (ie low nitrogen) systems. *Bersee* was used as breeding stock for many of the wheats that dominated cereal production after the Second World War.

The early hybrids produced acceptable combed wheat reed and perhaps slightly lower quality long straw than the older land race selections due to their stiffer straw, but with the introduction of semi-dwarf wheats the bulk of the straw grown in England was for the first time in its history too short to be used in thatching.

Other cereals

R YE (*SECALE CEREALE*)

Rye was a staple grain throughout England until the post–medieval period, and almost every agricultural writer of the last three centuries comments on its use for thatching. It was usually the first cereal to be grown on moorish soils and recently enclosed acidic heathlands, and although its mature straw was useless as fodder, it was always much in demand for thatch, litter, fuel and plaiting. By the mid nineteenth century, however, rye was grown primarily as a green fodder crop that was planted in the late summer or early autumn for feeding sheep and horses (Loudon 1831, 821–2; Lankester 1832; Hillyard 1837, 28; Rham 1845, 443–5, Percival 1942, 518–20). Unlike wheat, rye tillers primarily in the autumn and prior to the mid nineteenth century winter rye was almost always sown early in the autumn.

As late as the mid nineteenth century rye was interplanted with wheat in some parts of England to produced maslin (Low 1843, 343–5; Rham 1845, 443–5). A rye/wheat mixture yielded more reliably than either species planted as a pure crop, particularly in fields with variable growing conditions, and the taller rye was thought to provide shelter and support for the wheat (Burke 1834–40, **2**, 167; Ward & Lock 1880, 212–4). English winter rye grew to 6' (1.8 m) or more in height in average conditions, but this has been reduced by plant breeding while grain yield and size have been increased (Gill & Vear 1969, 80–2).

All nineteenth-century writers refer to its use in thatching (Young 1813b, 39; Low 1843, 343; Loudon 1831, 821; Lankester 1832; Rham 1845, 443; Ward & Lock 1880, 212–4; Bowick 1883, 57). It was used as unbruised reed and as crushed straw, but since rye threshed less cleanly than wheat extra care had to be taken not to cause inordinate damage to the straw required for thatching (Dickson & Stevenson 1815, 317). Rye straw was used for main coat thatching as well as ridging, and was generally thought to perform as well, if not better, than wheat straw. In Dorset, until the late 1950s, rye was cut green before the grain had formed and left to dry before being used in thatching (Rod Miller, pers comm). This obviated the need for threshing and eliminated any problems of sprouting or of bird damage. Immature rye straw is frequently encountered in base coats of thatch that have survived from the medieval period (Letts 1999). The records also indicate that rye stubble was used for thatching (Woodward 1984, 63).

Rye seems to have maintained its popularity as a food grain and as a thatching material for longer in the West Country, perhaps because of the well-entrenched tradi-

Figure 30 Experimental reaping leaving tall stubble; Goring Heath, Berkshire (John Letts).

tion of reed straw thatching, and the regional emphasis on livestock production rather than arable. According to Vancouver rye was once much more common in Devon.

> [it] seems confirmed in a striking degree, from the vast quantity of rye straw which is found to form the lower layer in all the ancient thatched buildings. (Vancouver 1808, 170)

Rye straw was processed in same way as wheat reed in the West Country (Marshall 1790, 181); the grain was extracted with the least possible injury to the straw, either by thrashing the ears lightly with a flail, or by beating them across a cask or a frame, before the reed was suspended from a roof beam and combed with a long-toothed rake. Hand combed rye reed straw was believed to be the equal of water reed as a thatching material, and was also prized as litter.

Barley (*Hordeum vulgare*)

According to several nineteenth-century writers, barley straw was 'too soft, too difficult of assortment into lengths [ie straw of uneven lengths], too pervious by rain, and too liable to rot' to be used for thatching (Loudon 1831, 823; Morton 1862, 54–65; Wilson 1871, **1**, 141). Although barley threshing waste was often used in medieval base coats, it is unlikely to have been used to any great extent

for external thatching as long as wheat and rye straw were preferred and available. In southern England, barley was mown when dead ripe, usually in July, and could be reaped and bound into sheaves or scythed and raked into shocks to dry, before being threshed with a flail or by machine. It was always the most difficult crop to thresh and had to be passed through the threshing machine twice after having been hummelled to remove as many awns as possible.

Oat (*Avena sativa* and *A. strigosa*)

Oat straw has not figured significantly in the repertory of thatching materials used in England over recent centuries, and is dismissed by thatchers as too soft for high quality house thatching. It is one of the most common thatching materials used in Ireland.

Henry Best (Woodward 1984, 226) believed 'haver' straw was 'as tough and lastinge' as wheat or rye straw, but was also more prone to attack by vermin. The literature almost never refers to oat straw for thatching even though it was the most widely planted cereal in terms of acreage over most of the seventeenth to nineteenth centuries (Oldershaw & Porter 1929). Pure samples of combed oat reed thatch are occasionally encountered on ancient buildings in Devon (Letts 1999), and oat was occasionally used for thatching earlier this century (Arthur Hannabuss pers comm). A spar coat of oat reed applied to a relatively steep roof near Cullompton in the 1940s was replaced after a respectable 26 years.

Oats could be grown on a wide variety of soils, and formed the staple loaf in northern England, Scotland and Wales in the nineteenth century (Rham 1845, 353–355) for it yielded well on poor, wet soils in areas with cool, short growing seasons. In southern England the crop was usually scythed rather than reaped unless it was very heavy or lodged, and the straw was raked into mows, carted, and threshed in a pile in the barn. Like most grain, oat was cut before being fully ripe which made threshing more difficult, but semi-threshed oat straw was also a useful way of regulating the amount of oat grain fed to animals (Ward & Lock 1880, 181).

THE MECHANIZATION OF CEREAL HARVESTING AND THRESHING

The impact of mechanization on British agriculture in the late eighteenth and nineteenth centuries is a popular research topic amongst agricultural and economic historians. The technical changes that occurred are well understood, as are the impacts of the mechanical reaper and the threshing machine on grain prices, wages and rural employment, but little has been written about its effect on straw and thatching. The topic cannot be examined without reference to the botanical changes which were already in process, and which mechanization encouraged by creating a demand for varieties better suited to mechanical reaping and threshing.

In 1790, genetically impure crops of wheat were grown primarily on heavy, poorly-drained soils, grew unevenly within one field, ripened unevenly late in the season and produced grain with inferior baking qualities.

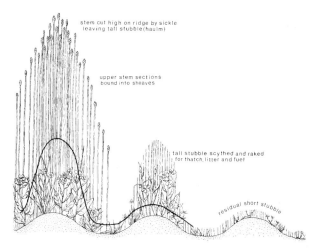

Figure 31 *Tall stubble produced by reaping high on stem on ridge and furrow fields (a & b) (Judith Dobie after Letts 1999).*

But they also produced ample straw and reliable yields of grain, and out-competed the improved products of scientific plant breeding in poor and unpredictable growing conditions. By the mid nineteenth century, a plethora of imported varieties and impure selections from English land races were available which allowed farmers to grow wheat profitably in a much wider range of growing conditions, and by the end of the century plant breeding had added relatively pure varieties to the list so that crops could vary enormously between fields as well as farms.

Reaping

Changes in the characteristics of the varieties grown parallel the changes that occurred in reaping technology and practice (Collins 1969, 1970). Until the late eighteenth century, the serrated reaping hook and the heavier smooth sickle were the principal tools used to reap wheat and rye, and in some areas barley and oats. The scythe was used primarily to cut hay, barley and oats, although it was also used for wheat and rye when labour was scarce, crops were lodged or when rain threatened to spoil a ripe harvest in the field. Tall, weak-strawed or lodged crops are more difficult to cut efficiently with a scythe, and hand reaping ensured a thorough harvest at a time when harvest labour was cheap and plentiful. The literature is replete with descriptions of hand reaping, which essentially involved taking a handful of straw in one hand and drawing the hook back to cut the stems in one smooth motion. The smooth reaping hook, and later the heavier fagging hook, used a hacking action and left a messier sheaf and stubble. Handfuls of cut straw were laid onto a straw band and tied into a sheaf when a sufficient quantity had been reaped. The manner in which this reaping was organised in the field varied from region to region, but it inevitably involved large gangs of men, women and children. Reaping was a laborious task, as was the subsequent stooking, carting, ricking and threshing.

Cutting high on the stem increased the efficiency of the harvest by reducing the size and weight of the sheaf, and also reduced the amount of straw that had to be stored in the barn or rick prior to threshing (Fig 30). In arable

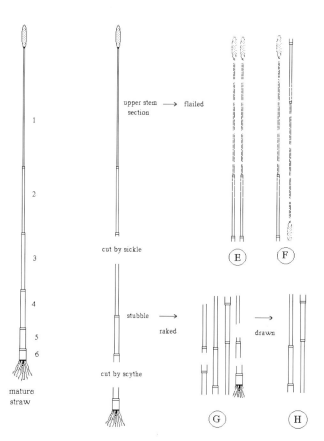

Figure 32 *Diagram of stubble straw (John Letts).*

districts with open field systems, the pressure to cut as high as possible was encouraged by the commoner's traditional right of helm-bote, to collect tall stubble for thatching, fuel and bedding. This was of no great consequence to landowners until the mid nineteenth century when stubble became an increasingly valued commodity for manure. Most grain-bearing ears in a medieval-type land race crop *c* 150cm in height would have been produced on stems *c* 120–180cm tall. Also, at least 40cm of straw is required to bind a cut stem into a sheaf so that it will not fall apart during handling. As a result, grain yield and reaping efficiency coincided when an average crop was reaped between *c* 50–80cm above ground level producing a 100–130cm sheaf, although these values obviously varied from area to area depending on variety and local custom. An average sheaf could not have fallen much below *c* 100cm in length if it was to include the bulk of the grain-bearing ears. The remaining coarse stubble could be scythed later in the season once the harvest had been secured, and would have been composed primarily of lower stem segments *c* 40–70cm in length. In general, only half of annual straw production was actually cut and stored leaving about 40% as tall stubble and about 10% in the field as residual short stubble.

The evidence also suggests that cereals usually grew taller on the ridge than in the furrow of an unimproved ridge and furrow field on heavy soil. According to Henry Best in 1642:

> the strongest and ablest of your shearers yow shoulde allwayes putte to the ridge, because there the corne is rankest and strongest. (Woodward 1984, 44)

As a result, a crop had to be cut at ground level in the furrow in order to match the 100–130cm sheaf obtained from cutting high on the stem on the ridge (Figs 31 and 32). The harvest would then be composed of sheaves of approximately equal length, except perhaps for sheaves reaped low on the ridge specifically for thatching. This two-fold harvest and the uneven stubble it left in the field persisted in some parts of England until the late nineteenth century, and was frequently portrayed in stylized form in medieval sources. It was not practiced in the West Country and other areas where ridge and furrow was uncommon and where the entire crop was reaped at ground level for use as thatch.

Stubble thatch

Traditionally, the stubble of the open fields was grazed by sheep and cattle after the harvest. The coarse lower stems of mature cereals have little nutritional value, however, and it was primarily the weeds, grasses, dead leaves and dropped grain and ears that provided food for livestock. Scythed wheat, rye and barley stubble were offered as fodder only when oat straw and hay were unavailable (Marshall 1790, 181), and the popularity of stubble as an ingredient of mixed fodder increased only when the cattle population rose rapidly in the mid nineteenth century (Low 1843, 312, 341; Burke 1837, 136; Rham 1845, 548, 247; Woodward 1984, 150).

Stubble was mown and raked into 'haulm baulks' in straw yards to provide winter shelter for animals (Rham 1845, 247; Burke 1834–40, 193). It was a common fuel in the medieval period (Tusser 1586, Fitzherbert 1534) and stubble was still being burnt as fuel in the early nineteenth century, although most agricultural writers decried the practice (Young 1813a, 318; Wilson 1871, **1**, 628).

Stubble was short and long wearing, which made it ideal for sparring or bedding into the layer of wet mud that was routinely employed on the top of mud or stone walls in some areas to secure the base coat of thatch at this point (see Appendix A: A15 and A14). Stubble was frequently employed to thatch mud walls, and the evidence from sampling ancient roofs indicates that stubble was also frequently used as a base coat. In several samples, short stubble still with its roots and adhering mud was tied in courses, roots-up, against a fleeking of water reed and covered with a layer of fen sedge and later spar coats of straw.

The use of stubble in English thatching has so far gone unrecognized in part because of confusion between the words haulm, halm, helm and stubble. Halm, of Anglo-Saxon derivation, is used in Old English as a general term for straw with helm as a possible southern variant (Johnston 1827; Baker 1854). To halm is to cover with straw thatch. Helm, however, is in its own right an Old English word for a covering or shelter. Haulm has also been defined as the straw made up straight into bundles for use in thatching with haulming the process involved, and in this sense it is perhaps linked to the modern long straw terms yealm and yealming. Threshed straw was thus 'heaped up together in order to be helmed' (Lisle 1757, 236), and

Worlidge in 1694, referring to West Country practice, could state that the best straw for thatching

> is call'd *Helm*, that is long, and stiff Wheat-Straw, (with the Ears cut off,) bound up in Bundles unbruis'd; which well laid, lies thin, lasts long, and is much neater than the common way [ie threshed and drawn straw as used in other parts of England]. (Neve 1726, 256)

Numerous passages support the use of the term haulm for both the material produced (reed straw or stubble) and the drawing process itself. Haulming is also used to describe the process of mowing stubble in the field, as in Innocent's interpretation of haulming wheat stubble in Essex in 1811 (1916, 113). The term stubble was also used in reference to both tall haulm and the short stubble that remained in the field after mowing.

> The stubble is horse raked. The rakings are tied up and when carted away ... are not allowed to be mixed with the rest of the crop. (Bacon 1844, 265)

Thus, the passage quoted above might, at first, appear to describe the raking of tall haulm, but a previous line indicates that the crop in question had already been scythed leaving only residual short stubble.

> The common thatch covering used in the neighbourhood of Gloucester, and Upper Vale, is made of the straw, threshed in the usual way, or of stubble, which is the ground stalk of the wheat left by the reaper, about a foot long, and afterwards mowed. (Rudge 1813, 46–7)

Rudge distinguished between the short stubble cut from 'the Hills' (to clear the land for ploughing), and the taller stubble from 'the Vale' which was

> mowed like grass, left in swathes, and afterwards raked into heaps: then it is 'drawn,' or picked, and, being tied up into small sheaves, is in a ready state for thatching. (op cit 118–9)

When the stubble was too short it was mixed with longer flailed straw for use in thatching, although this was thought inferior to the 'whipped' helm straw most commonly used in the region (op cit, 46–7).

Thatching with stubble would have been most common in areas where large cereal acreages and a limited demand for animal litter encouraged reaping high on the stem. The right of helm bote ensured that poorer members of the community had access to the stubble of the open fields for thatching in open field districts where there were few alternatives, but the practice was driven into the history books in the mid nineteenth century by enclosure, a rising demand for straw for animal bedding and manuring, and the breeding of shorter cereal varieties better adapted to mechanical reaping and threshing. Outside of the West Country, stubble was simply replaced by threshed and drawn straw on roofs, stacks and ricks - which did not last so long according to at least one observer (Marshall 1790, **1**, 64).

The use of stubble for thatching was becoming increasingly uncommon in the Gloucester region by the late eighteenth century due to the rising demand for manure. The Reports of the Board of Agriculture indicate that the cutting of stubble for fuel, thatch or litter was still fairly widespread in 1800, although the practice was strongly discouraged by agriculturalists. In Kent:

> On most of the middle and small-sized farm-houses and offices, thatch is the common covering; which is put on, particularly in the eastern part, much worse than in any other part of the kingdom ... The stubble of wheat is raked up for this purpose; which being often done in the winter, when, by rainy seasons, it is become half rotten, of course, cannot last a long time on a building. (Boys 1805, 32)

In Berkshire:

> after the wheat is cut with a sickle and carried home and secured, a certain number of labourers are employed in mowing with a scythe the stubbles, which are made into haulm, and used for thatching and for litter, as occasion may require. (Mavor 1809, 197)

The use of stubble for thatching was also reported in Leicestershire (Pitt 1809b, 379–80), Northamptonshire (Pitt 1809a, 309), Rutland (Parkinson 1808, 67) and Huntingdonshire (Marshall 1818, 486).

> In the application of stubble as a thatch for ricks, it is mostly put on by sticking one of its ends into the roof of the stack in a regular and exact manner, so that it may stand very close and thick; when the other, with such loose straws as may occur, is to be cut over or pared off with the thatching knife, or a very sharp tool for the purpose, so as to form a neat and impenetrable thatch, having the appearance of a newly thatched house-roof; the whole being well secured in its place by short pegs made for the purpose ... [The] same rules in some respects to be followed [for houses], only the materials are to be laid on to a considerable thickness, and be more firmly secured. They are applied in regular ... courses, from the eaves of the building to the ridges ... secured by short sharpened sticks thrust in where necessary; and bended sticks sharpened at each end are sometimes made use of near the ridges, being thrust in at each end ... [then] raked over from top to the bottom, so as to render it completely smooth and even, and take away all the short straws. (Loudon 1831, 517–18).

Stubble thatching became increasingly uncommon in the last decades of the century, and it survived only as a memory by the 1920s when the following description was recorded in Buckinghamshire:

> We used to ketch holt uv a handful a standin carn, drah the sickul acrass th' alm, and ar-ur a few handfuls were pleeaced togither we tied em up into a sheeaf, so when the shocks were maiad up they stood no higher than the

Figure 33 Distribution of stubble thatching c 1790 (Judith Dobie).

standin alm about em. When the shocks were carried they used to let th' alm stand till it got a few frastes an it, and then men used to goo and beeat it down wi poles, fur then as soon as it was touched it broke awf as brittul as glass. But the best way to saiav laiabur was to drive a flock of ship through the feeuld backurds and forruds. They ood soon fet moast an it down and what was left could very soon be boshed down bi poles. This was called 'baggin th' alm.' The straw was then reeaked up into cocks carrd, and it was the best strah for thecking. (Harman 1929, 91)

The increasing tendency to overwinter animals had diverted most stubble away from roofs and into stock-yards by the mid nineteenth century. Numerous passages attest to the use of stubble for this purpose, and the archaic practice of reaping high on the stem was strongly discouraged by agriculturalists (Wilson 1871). Stubble was particularly valued in areas where straw was not abundant (Davis 1811, 66). The Country Agricultural Reports abound with references to the use of stubble for litter (eg Buckinghamshire: Priest 1810, 183–4; Leicestershire: Pitt 1809b, 102).

In summary, stubble was cut over a large areas of south-central England well into the nineteenth century, primarily for use as litter and on a more restricted basis for thatching in parts of Berkshire, Oxfordshire, Kent, Gloucestershire, Rutland, Northamptonshire, Huntingdonshire and Leicestershire (Fig 33). Stubble was also probably once used for thatching in other regions in which stubble is recorded to have been used only for litter. The practice survived the longest in the Midlands in arable districts with heavy soils and persistent ridge and furrow topography suited to the cultivation of older land races and land race selections, rather than in the main cereal growing districts of East Anglia and south-central England. Low cutting was preferred in the north, and in upland and pastoral districts where straw was at a premium. Stubble thatching seems to have been practiced by cottagers and labourers as much as by professional thatchers. References to the cutting and use of stubble become less common after 1850, but it was still used on occasion to thatch stacks in some areas early this century (Stephens 1908, **2**, 199).

Stubble thatching disappeared for a variety of reasons: mowing with the scythe or reaping machine, and the cultivation of shorter cereal varieties, eliminated the option of a stubble harvest altogether; cereal production and the stock of thatched rural buildings became increasingly concentrated on large estates that were usually the first to adopt advanced agricultural practices such as the husbanding of straw for manure and mechanized reaping and threshing; urban expansion created a lucrative market for undamaged, full-length straw for animal litter; labour costs, and easier access to storage space for straw, argued against high reaping and a second harvest of stubble; and most importantly drawn, threshed straw produced a very acceptable alternative to stubble for thatching. A brief rise in the number of recorded thatchers in stubble areas in the late nineteenth century can perhaps be linked to a professionalization of the craft as stubble, and the lower quality structures onto which it was usually applied, was abandoned and more respectable full-length crushed straw became the principal material used on the thatched houses and outbuildings that remained.

Mowing

In 1790 all wheat and rye in England was cut with either a sickle or a reaping hook (Loudon 1831, 372–8; Collins 1970). The scythe was widely used for mowing hay, barley and oats throughout England, but the corn scythe, with its bow and cradle attachment that allowed the cut grain to be thrown neatly into a swathe, was used for cutting wheat only in the East Riding of Yorkshire, east Kent, south-west Essex, east Dorset, south Hertfordshire and parts of Norfolk and Shropshire, areas without strong stubble traditions. According to Collins (1969, 247), a 'hand tool revolution' occurred between 1790–1814 in which the reaping hook and sickle were replaced initially by the much heavier fagging hook and eventually by the corn scythe, a move triggered by a rise in cereal production in response to high grain prices caused by the Napoleonic wars. The initial revolution was followed by a period of stasis and agricultural depression from 1815–33, and then another revolutionary shift to mowing as grain prices recovered from 1834–51. The fagging hook and corn scythe cut more efficiently, more evenly, and lower on the stem than the sickle in experienced hands, and also left a shorter (c 12"/30cm) stubble (Baxter 1834, 645; Rham 1845, 548).

The scythe and fagging hook were adopted initially in areas with a pre-existing low reaping tradition, such as parts of northern England and Scotland and in upland areas with limited cereal production. Labour factors were obviously very important, and industrialization in the north in the early nineteenth century drastically reduced the rural workforce and forced up rural wages, which

provided a strong incentive to adopt labour-saving technologies. In the south, however, the agricultural workforce continued to expand until the 1840s, providing an abundant, low-paid labour force for hand reaping. In many arable districts, roving gangs of low-paid harvest workers were often employed to reap the cereal crop (Wilson 1862, 309). The demand for thatching straw and for high quality litter in this region also encouraged a shift to mowing and fagging low on the stem (Rham 1845, 431), and throughout the country, especially on lighter soils farmed using the new rotations, every stem of straw was increasingly valued for its potential use as manure (Loudon 1831, 519). Although the cereal acreage increased (doubling in Berkshire between 1831 and 1866) most of this increase was in the production of barley and oats on light chalk land soils rather than wheat, and any stubble or waste straw in these areas was soon ploughed back into the soil as manure.

The shift to shorter wheat varieties simply eliminated the option of high reaping, and improved the efficiency of mowing. But the scythe was more efficient than the sickle only in experienced hands, and was impractical in many situations such as on strongly ridged and furrowed fields. Numerous advantages and disadvantages were enumerated by agriculturalists: scythed straw was usually less tightly bound in the sheaf than sickled straw, and thereby dried faster in the stook (Burke 1834–40, **3**, 107; Rham 1845, 431; Wilson 1862, 309); mowing reduced grain loses due to shattering, as it involved less handling of the crop (Loudon 1831, 516; Ward & Lock 1880, 171); the scythe was difficult to use when cutting heavy crops; sickled wheat was generally clean in the sheaf; and the greater evenness of the scythed sheaf also allowed it to be machine-threshed more easily (Loudon 1831, 516). Practical issues such as these conditioned the adoption of new reaping methods, but the sickle continued to be used for harvesting lodged crops, and for opening the field for the mechanical reaper, well into the first half of this century (Arthur Hannabuss, pers comm).

The mechanical reaper

The first patent for a corn reaping machine was issued in London in 1799, but the first successful machine was developed in the late 1820s by a Reverend Bell of Forfar in Scotland (Fig 34). Only a dozen of Bell's 'shearing machines' were ever used in Britain, and their adoption

Figure 34 Patrick Bell's 'shearing machine' (1826) (Partridge 1973).

led to riots in various parts of England (Partridge 1973, 130). Two similar machines built by the Americans Hussey and Cyrus McCormick were demonstrated at the Great Exhibition in London in 1851. These machines were expensive and not terribly efficient, but 1,500 had been sold in Britain within two years (Rham 1845, 433; Partridge 1973, 128), and by 1853 Hussey-type machines, modified for British field conditions, were being manufactured under license by 11 British firms. A flurry of new machines hit the market over the next two decades, with the most notable innovation being the 1858 addition of a continuous canvas belt that neatly conveyed the cut straw from the cutter bar to the side of the machine. Approximately 40,000 reaping machines, cutting one quarter of the cereal acreage, were at work in Britain by 1871, primarily in Scotland, northern England, and specialist corn-growing districts in East Anglia (Partridge 1973, 162) (Fig 35). As with the scythe, the reaper-binder was adopted less readily in southern England where wages were low and labour abundant, and hand reaping persisted the longest in the south Midlands, the Fens and the Border counties in the north (Collins 1970, 236).

The cutting height of the reaper-binder could be raised from 10cm to 40cm above ground level if necessary when reaping on uneven or stony ground (Loudon 1831, 427), but usually left a stubble that was too short to be used for thatching. The ability to adjust the cutting height was essential because the standard cutting bar and conveyor worked most effectively on straw 38"–48" (100cm–120cm) in length and could not usually cope with straw longer than 55" (140cm). Many older British cereal varieties were simply too tall to be cut efficiently with the reaper binder, and its introduction created a demand for improved varieties with shorter and stronger straw better suited to mechanical reaping.

Initially, the reaper simply cut the crop and hand labour was required to bind the straw into sheaves. An automatic binder mechanism was perfected in 1878, but was rare in English fields before 1890. By 1900 80% of the cereal acreage was cut by reaper-binder (Collins 1969; Creasey & Ward 1984, 11). The reaper-binder eliminated the labour required for reaping and hand tying, as well as the flexible immature straw that was used for sheaf bonds. It also allowed the farmer to delay the harvest until the crop was almost fully mature, which increased the quality and uniformity of the grain but in some cases may also have increased the brittleness of the straw. In fact, the adoption of the reaper binder was inevitable, in part because the new cereal varieties introduced in the late nineteenth century ripened much more evenly over a much shorter time period, and it would have been almost impossible to harvest a large acreage devoted to one improved variety by hand without significant grain losses due to shattering. A large pool of labour was still required to stook, cart, and stack the crop, but the ability to cut a rapidly ripening crop quickly gave a grower much greater control over harvesting time and probably improved the uniformity and quality of straw for thatching.

Figure 35 The reaper-binder, Somerton, Somerset (John Letts).

Hand threshing and combing

The simplest way of producing straw suitable for thatching is simply to cut a crop before it has set its seed. A crop without grain does not need to be threshed, although combing would remove weeds and leafy tissue that might retain excess moisture and reduce its longevity. Immature cereal obviously cannot sprout on the roof nor attract birds or rodents, two of the principal reasons for repair. As we have seen, unripe straw remains strong and flexible once cut whereas mature straw is hard and brittle at maturity. How common this practice was in the past is hard to say, as the loss of grain from such a harvest would have been a disaster for any small or medium-sized farmer. It was perhaps a means of salvaging some worth from a crop that simply failed to mature due to late sowing, poor growing conditions or disease attack. Historically, rye has almost always been considered inferior to wheat as a bread grain, and the loss of a rye crop grown on fallow or on a field of poor soil was perhaps acceptable once a decade, particularly as much of the nutrient extracted from soil by a cereal plant is used to produce grain. At later periods, the price of rye grain in the market may simply not have justified the cost of the labour involved in growing the crop to maturity specifically for its grain. If deliberate, the advantages of using immature straw in thatching have been very well accepted, and it is probable that it would have been used more commonly on larger estates that were able to devote acreage to straw production for this purpose.

Immature rye is common in late medieval and post-medieval reed straw thatch from Devon, and until quite recently tenants of the Palmer Estate at Hampstead Norries, Berkshire (Appendix A: A3), were required to grow winter rye for thatching buildings on the estates. The rye was cut immature, combed at its butt end and applied as with combed wheat reed (Appendix A: A4). Earlier layers of thatch on several of the estate buildings surveyed were of rye and wheat long straw. Immature uncombed rye was also used in combed wheat reed-style thatching in Dorset in recent decades (Rod Miller, pers comm).

Flailing

Before the development of mechanical threshing, cereal crops were threshed either by lashing handfuls of ripe cereal against a solid object such as a wall, wooden racks or a barrel, or by striking the ears repeatedly with a stick or flail. In Yorkshire gangs of men trod the ripe grain from oat sheaves placed in a circle (Marshall 1790, 20).

The reason for the violence is obvious: grain must be forced out of its protective husks before it can be eaten. Old English cereal varieties were genetically impure and ripened very unevenly within one field, so that a crop would inevitably contain both overripe and underripe ears when harvested. This clearly reduced grain yields, and the residual grain in the ears was a problem for thatchers in that it attracted vermin and could sprout on the roof once wetted.

The best straw for thatching is obtained from crops cut while still a little unripe. It is also the case that the grain-bearing ears of older English varieties might range over 60cm within a sheaf 100cm–140cm in length, and ripened very unevenly. Where straw was less abundant various ways were developed for removing the grain while leaving the straw uncrushed for thatching. In the principal cereal-growing districts it was accepted that a sheaf had to be battered over much of its length in order to extract most of the grain from the ears, and by far the most common tool for this purpose was the flail. There are surprisingly few descriptions of flailing in the literature, perhaps because it was simply too common to describe. It was a skilled and onerous task, and one of the best paid jobs for farm labourers who relied on it as a sole source of winter employment. Poor quality flailing would greatly reduce grain yields as well as damage the straw for use as thatch or litter. In most cases, the straw bond securing the sheaf was loosened prior to flailing. An experienced worker concentrated his blows onto the grain-bearing portion of the sheaf, thus reducing the effort required to dislodge the grain and preserving the bulkier butt end of the sheaf for thatching and litter. In general, the repeated blows gradually moved straw out of the sheaf leaving the threshed straw in a jumbled heap with ears and butts mixed, although this tendency varied depending on the skill of the thresher and the crop being flailed. Mowed and raked crops, and the rakings of the stubble, were also more difficult to thresh than a crop of bound sheaves as they arrived already jumbled. This removed the option of concentrating the flail's blows onto the grain-bearing portion of the crop, and produced a straw that was inevitably more crushed than straw flailed in the sheaf.

On small farms the cereal crop might be stored indoors and threshed when grain was required for domestic use. Cutting high on the stem reduced the amount of straw that had to be stored indoors, and the shift to fagging and mowing, combined with the introduction of shorter wheat varieties and a rapid expansion of cereal production in the early nineteenth century, encouraged the practice of storing the unthreshed crop in large thatched ricks while awaiting threshing. The Victorian rickyard with its thatched stacks of wheat would have been unfamiliar to the medieval farmer. Flailing was usually done inside the barn on a specially prepared wooden or stone-packed clay surface, and, depending on storage space, the threshed straw was stored indoors or reformed into a thatched straw stack in the rickyard.

Flailing methods varied from region to region, but the following description of threshing in Buckinghamshire in the early twentieth century is typical:

> A good thrailer ull thresh all the kurnuls out quite as clean as a threshin machine; but a cu-urse, it teeaks him longur. ... when ye be a-thrailin bi yurself ye a perhaps three ur fu-ur down layin bi the side uv aich other an the flu-ur. Ye then hot [hit] the swinjul [top portion of the flail] streeat acrass the bunches a eeurs, but the sheeavs must be hot flat wi the swinjul to git the best results. When two men wurk togither two rows uv perhaps half a dozen sheeavs ur moour are pleeaced an the midstid, the eeurs feeacin aich other, and the butts on the outside. Then the thrailurs feeace aich othur and they hot one up, one down, and tis wonderful how they do it - they do it jest like a machine. To get to the middul a the row they ull teeak a step forrud and then backurds and theeur they kaip an all day long. Ivvery now and then one an em will put the thrail under some an it and tass it ovur fur the tuther to hit. (Harman 1929, 83–4)

Middleton's comments about threshing, written in Hertfordshire at the end of the eighteenth century, indicate that straw was crushed and jumbled by the flail as much as it was with the new threshing machines:

> In places more distant from London, they ... strike perpendicularly, but incessantly without changing hands, or reducing the force of the blows, till the principal part of the corn be thrashed out on one side; they then turn the sheaf, and repeat the operation on the other side - they next change hands and strike in an oblique direction, which draws the straw from the sheaf an inch or two at every such blow; till the whole is completed. This gives them an opportunity of seeing and hitting every ear, till it be cleared of the grain. I have observed them often, and I think there is no other method of thrashing clean by the flail. This practice, it is true, tosses the straw into every direction, as much as is usually done by the mills now coming into use, and it is, therefore, nearly as much bruised. (Middleton 1798, 174)

This passage infers that the usual method of flailing in arable districts 'beyond London' gradually removed the straw from the bound sheaf and 'tossed it into very direction'. Contemporary passages indicate that straw was treated much more carefully outside the principal cereal producing districts.

The demand for undamaged, full-length straw for horse litter probably influenced threshing practices close to London (Middleton 1798, 174–5; Young 1804a, 92). Unbruised litter-straw was not necessarily suitable for thatching, because the residual grain would have attracted birds and vermin and sprouted on the roof once wetted.

> Many of the farm-houses, and most of the out-buildings in this county [Middlesex], are thatched; but it appears, in

some places, that sufficient attention is not paid to the straw being very cleanly threshed, which in thatching is a very material circumstance, as otherwise the corn will sprout after the straw is laid on the roof, and soon let in the rain. (Foot 1794, 79)

Straw that was to be apex-flailed for use in thatching was chosen carefully for the purpose. Only the tallest straw would provide the necessary length because the more thorough threshing that was required, combined with the uneven spread of ears within the sheaf, damaged much of the upper portion of the stem. According to Marshall, 'thrashing lightly with the flail' and lashing handfuls of straw against a solid object, were the most common methods of threshing used in Devon and throughout the West Country, and such processing was 'highly profitable ... while straw continue[d] to be used as thatch' (1790, 181–3). After an initial light beating with a flail to dislodge the ripest grain, the reed was

> formed into small sheaves, returned to the floor, and the ears thrashed again with the flail ... [or] thrashed by hand over the cask, to free it effectually from any remaining grain, which the former beating might have missed. (Marshall 1790, 181–3)

Apex-flailing could obviously be used in combination with other methods, such as in parts of Dorset where earless versions of modern combed wheat reed were prized for thatching.

> In some places, the sheaves are partially thrashed, without striking the straw further than the principal part of the ears extend, and the short straws and unthrashed ears are afterwards separated with a wooden comb. (Stevenson 1812, 220)

The shorter straw that remained in the Dorset 'pitching press' after the tallest had been drawn for thatching were rebound into sheaves and apex-flailed (Stevenson 1812, 146, 153). In Wiltshire early this century, sheaves of wheat were placed in two rows with overlapping ears, and heavy timbers or railway sleepers were placed near the top of the sheaves to keep them in position and to prevent the flail from damaging the lower portion of the stem (Alan Fuchs, pers comm). A similar method was apparently used in parts of Devon early this century (Hubert Snowdon, pers comm).

The rhythmic beating of the flail against the threshing floor disappeared from the rural winter soundscape over the second half of the nineteenth century, but in a technical sense the two types of thatching straw that it produced, unbruised, full-length, apex-flailed reed straw and crushed straw, have survived into the modern day as combed reed and long straw. Both have an ancient pedigree and were traditionally generated as by-products of hand threshing.

Lashing

The practice of lashing a sheaf against a stone, barrel, bench, racks or a door set on its side in order to dislodge

Figure 36 Experimental threshing: lashing wheat against a 'brishing horse', Blackhawton, Devon (John Letts).

the grain has undoubtedly been used in Britain for as long as cereals have been grown. Lashing was an economic method of threshing cereals on subsistence farms and in pastoral districts where machine threshing was simply not available and where straw was scarce and valued for thatching and other purposes. It was used routinely, throughout the British Isles, to separate seed grain for the following year's crop, as it did not damage the grain and produced a cleaner product (Fig 36).

In the early nineteenth century, lashing was employed to some degree throughout the British Isles, and references occur to its use in northern England as, for example, in Lancashire.

> Where lashing out the grain over a stone, or other contrivance for the purpose, is still employed, the expense is commonly something higher, as the work is more heavy and labourious. By this method the best part of the grain is only stricken out; the remainder being afterwards thrashed out by the flail. (Dickson & Stevenson 1815, 309)

Lashing was widely employed in the West Country, and the practice survived into the early part of this century due to the demand for unbruised thatching straw.

> The method of thrashing wheat, in this district and throughout the West of England, is too singular to be passed without notice. While straw continues to be used

Figure 37 Threshing 'webble': Somerset, mid nineteenth century, in Somerset County Museum (John Letts).

as thatch, the practice is highly profitable. ... The object of this method ... which is applicable to rye, as well as to wheat, is to extract the grain from the ear, with the least possible injury to the straw. To this end, the ears are either thrashed lightly with the flail, or are beaten across a cask, by hand; until the grain be got pretty well out of them. (Marshall 1790, 181–3)

The practice of whipping out grain is resorted to in some districts with wheat, when the straw is much wanted for thatch. The operator takes a handful, and strikes the ears repeatedly against a stone, the edge of a board, or the face of a strong wattled hurdle, till the corn is separated. (Loudon 1831, 519)

Various items could be used as a threshing object, the most common being a barrel, a tree trunk, a door set on its side, a wheel barrow, a barn floor and various racks, frames and trestles that were usually called 'webbles' in the West Country. In Devon, handfuls of lashed straw were suspended from a roof beam or door jamb (using a rope looped around the ears) and combed clean of weeds, short straw and flag leaf. In Somerset, threshing trestles often had a row of metal spikes through which the straw was drawn to comb it into shape (Fig 37).

In one instance, I saw a frame, for beating the ears over, instead of a cask; the construction somewhat resembling that of a very wide, short, crooked ladder, supported nearly horizontally, with its convex side upward; the cross bars being set edgeway, and a few inches from each other; and with an angular piece of wood running lengthway through the middle of the frame, and rising above the cross bars, – to separate, and spread with greater ease, the ears of the corn; and thereby to render the strokes the more effective. (Marshall 1790, 181–3; and see Laycock 1920, 183)

The usual manner of thrashing corn, in the lower parts of Cornwall, deserves notice, as it seems peculiar to this part of the county, and has its advantages. A frame, which they call *barn boards*, is formed of four or five sycamore or ash planks, on three ledges, or transverse beams; this frame is about seven feet by four, and about ten inches in height. Care is taken that each plank is set about the third of an inch

from its neighbour, that the grain may fall through. By this mode of thrashing, little or no corn is bruised, which, with the flail on the common floors, is so much the case, as to occasion a considerable waste, both of seed and bread-corn. (Worgan 1811, 44–45; see also Laycock 1920, 183)

Lashing was still used to produce reed straw in parts of Dorset and Devon in the 1930s. Cowell clearly considered it to be superior to threshed straw for thatching in 1925, when he visited Charmouth, Dorset, where his East Anglian thatchers were thatching a roof in straw.

Three samples of Straw had been delivered on job: The best was prepared with all the corn-ears cut off with hand knife, combed and tied into bunches about 14lbs [6.4kg] Second grade had been 'whipped out' - that is the corn is knocked out on a piece of wood. Chaff and ear is left on. Straw then tied as above. Third grade has been thro' a Machine as all [sic] done - but after leaving drum it goes into a machine for tieing into bunches with string. Straw is bruised. Ear and some chaff left on straw - not a good sample. (Cambridgeshire Record Office 1)

The practice of lashing continued in Somerset and Gloucestershire until the turn of the century (Hennell 1934, 174), but was soon replaced by combed wheat reed after the introduction of the mechanical comber (Laycock 1920, 183).

Pitching

The simplest method of separating the grain from a wheat plant without bruising the straw is by clipping off the ear, a technique called pitching, which was commonly practiced in the wheat growing districts of Somerset, Gloucestershire, east Devon and west Dorset (Stevenson 1812, 150, 467). In Somerset:

Wheat is seldom threshed with the straw, but the ears are cut off, and the straw bound in sheaves tied very tight; the circumference of the sheaf at the bond should be six feet [1.83m]; ... A good acre [0.4ha] of wheat will produce three dozen sheaves, ...★ and each sheaf should weigh fifty-six pounds [25.4kg].

★ Ear-pitching is the provincial term for this management, and the sheaves thus prepared are called reed-sheaves. They are in general use for the purpose of thatching, for which, indeed, they are solely intended. The practice is not confined to Mendip, but is in common use through a great part of the district. The workmen are very dextrous in making, and the thatchers no less expert in using it; and at the same time that it makes a covering more durable than any other of straw, it is of such superior neatness, that the thatched buildings of this neighbourhood excite the admiration of many strangers coming from other parts where this practice is not known. (Billingsley 1798, 97–8)

After one of his trips from Somerton to Shepton Mallet, Marshall noted that 'Somersetshire reed' was 'different from that of Devonshire ... as having the ears cut off ... consisting of clean straight unbruised stems only' (1790, 203). In 1805 Dickson defined 'Somersetshire reed' as 'nothing more than the strongest wheat straw which can be met with' (quoted in OED, 1989, 321).

Pitching was widely believed to produce the best thatching straw possible. For thatching stacks it was suggested that one should use

> well-drawn rye or wheat straw, of the toughest kind, with ears cut off, in equal lengths, which since the introduction of thrashing mills, is a more difficult matter than formerly. (Burke 1834–40, **2**, 195)

> Unthrashed wheat straw, without the ears and provincially called reed, is the favourite thatch in the counties of Devon, Dorset, and Somerset, and possesses eminent advantage above thrashed straw, which ought to recommend it into use in all parts of the kingdom. It lasts nearly as long again as common straw, and does not offer the temptation, arising from the grains of imperfectly thrashed corn, which induces mice and birds to infest the building, and to make holes in the thatch. The mode of preparing it is simply to take a sheaf of wheat, and to place it in a press, made of two pieces of timber 10' [3.05m] long, and put on a stool, and to have women to lay hold of the ears and draw them out and cut them off, and then to bind up the sheaf for thatch. A covering with this straw is not only neat but elegant, while one with threshed straw is aged and slovenly; and it has, in many instances, been preferred to all other coverings for cottages ornées in consequence of its picturesque effect. (Wilson 1871, **1**, 625)

In Dorset:

> in drawing of reed, a frame is made use of, which is frequently four or five yards [3.66m, 4.57m] long, and supported on four legs at a convenient height, having an upright piece at each end passing loosely through a mortise in the upper piece of timber, which, by its pressure on the sheaves, holds them in their place. The work is performed by women and children, who place a number of sheaves in the frame, with the ears all one way, and pull out all the longest, and form them into a kind of gleans, with the ears all close to their hand till it is full, when the ears are cut off with a reap-hook, or any other sharp instrument. The ears, together with the short straw, which is not worth drawing, are laid by themselves, and either thrashed by the flail, or put twice through the thrashing machine ... The practice of drawing reed is very prevalent in the west and northern parts of the county, but not so much in the east and south-east parts, beyond Blandford and Bere Regis. At the last-mentioned town I was informed, that reed was seldom drawn, because the landlords would not repay the expense to the tenants. (Stevenson 1812, 220)

Cowell (nd) believed that pitched reed straw was the best thatching straw available in Dorset early this century, but the technique was no longer used by the Second World War due to the introduction of the mechanical comber.

Removing the ears of a crop to produce reed straw is quickly dismissed by older Devon thatchers who insist that ears were necessary to hold the rope that was looped around the sheaf to allow it to be suspended from a barn beam for combing (Arthur Hannabuss pers comm). In the Dorset method, however, the straw was pulled from the press before the ears were cut off, while in Somerset the ears were cut off before the reed was combed over the spiked webble. Drawing and pitching continued to be used in Dorset into the 1930s, perhaps because this method selected only the tallest straw for thatching from a sheaf increasingly reduced in height from its Victorian counterpart. The production of thatching straw gradually became a more specialized activity, however, as cereal producers adopted improved varieties with shorter straw much less suited to thatching. Nor could the Dorset process be mechanized as effectively as the Devon combing procedure, and in both areas hand processing was discontinued before the Second World War due to the combined effect of a reduced demand for thatching straw and the introduction of the combine harvester and the mechanical comber.

Hand combing

Combing is a secondary activity used to clear both reed straw and crushed straw of extraneous material: short and broken straw segments, weeds and leaf tissue can channel rainwater towards the interior of the thatch, and retain moisture that will prevent the roof from drying out quickly after being wetted. The excess moisture stimulates fungal decay which largely determines the lifespan of a thatched roof.

The threshing and combing procedures have become confused in recent years because the mechanical comber attachment on the threshing machine performs both operations at the same time, one series of combing pegs stripping leaves and rubbish from mid-stem towards the butts, and the other series stripping the ear and most of the flag leaf. These were separate processes in the past, and ear-threshed straw was not necessarily combed as thoroughly as in the modern combined procedure. In fact there was no reason to comb threshed reed straw towards the ear unless the reed was very short, for the upper half of a course lays beneath or above the fixings and was never exposed. Only the leaf tissue, tiller and broken straw in the lower half of the sheaf needed to be removed in order to maximize its water shedding properties, and this is easily accomplished using a small hand rake. Combing of the upper half from mid-stem towards the ear removed superfluous short straws, but could not have been intensive as the upper portion of the straw was already crushed and the ears interfered with the raking process.

Hand reaping left cereal sheaves relatively free of weeds, for a skilled reaper simply avoided cutting them in the field. The scythe and reaper-binder are more indiscriminate, however, and included any weed tall enough to reach the scythe or cutting bar. Stooking was essential not only to let the grain ripen, but just as importantly to allow the weeds to dry out so they would not spoil the crop in the stack. More thorough combing was required

Figure 38 'Industrial' reed straw production, early nineteenth century (Judith Dobie, after anon 1791).

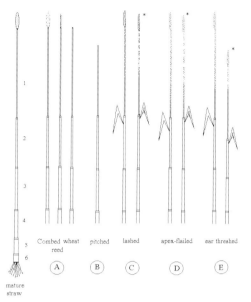

'Reed-straw' (1790-1940)

* indicates breakage possible at any point of damaged section

NB: - cutting height varies from internodes 4-5 (scythe & reaper binder) to 3-4 (sickle)
- C, D & E may also be combed towards their ears to remove upper flag leaves

Figure 39 Variations in forms of reed straw produced c 1790–1940 (John Letts).

to produce West Country-type reed straw or halm after the adoption of the scythe and the reaper, whereas threshed straw required drawing irrespective of the amount of weed contaminating the sheaf.

The Dorset drawing and pitching method of producing reed straw may well be an indigenous development, but the hand comb and webble were widely used for cleaning thatching straw in many parts of the British Isles and mainland Europe. The Dorset method relied on the tension of the beam press to hold the straw in place while selected strands were vigorously drawn out, stripping the flag leaves from the stem. In the more general West Country version, a handful of reed straw was placed in a small clamp, or more commonly a rope was tied around the ears of a sheaflet and suspended from a beam, and a hand comb was used to draw weeds, short straw, leaf and detritus from the reed straw. Conversely, in many areas the sheaflet was held in the hands and drawn through the stationary spiked webble which produced the same stripping effect. Descriptions of such webbles are not uncommon in the literature (Rudge 1813, 119; Hennell 1934, 156).

An interesting attempt to industrialize the production of reed straw was drawn for patent purposes in the early nineteenth century (Fig 38). Wooden clamps were used in Somerset to hold the sheaflet while it was combed with a hand rake:

> Before the machine was used sheaves had to be made by hand ... a man considered himself lucky if he had fifteen made in a day at two pence [1p] a sheaf payment. Taking a couple of handfuls of straw with the corn still in, he knocked it on the side of a wheel-barrow till the grain was all thrashed out. It was then put into a wooden clamp to hold it firm while the ribbins were raked out. (Albino 1946a, 90–3)

> The next operation is to suspend the straw, in large double handfuls, in a short rope, fixed high above the head, with an iron hook at the loose end of it; which is put twice round the little sheaflet, just below the ears, and fastened with the hook's laying hold of the tight part of the rope. The left hand being now firmly placed upon the hook, and pulling downward, so as to twitch the straw hard, and prevent the ears from slipping through it, the butts are freed from short straws and weeds, by means of a small long-toothed rake or comb. This done, the rope is

unhooked and the 'reed' laid evenly in a heap. (Marshall 1790, 181–3)

Combing methods have changed very little, and a very similar description can be found in 1934 (Hennell 1934, 159).

An experienced worker was expected to comb between eight and twelve 28lb [12.7kg] nitches of reed straw per day, each of which contained 20 smaller bundles (Arthur Hannabuss, Ian White, and Alfred Howard, pers comms). The work provided extra income during the winter months, but was tedious and strenuous. Hand combing survived for longer in Devon than in other parts of the West Country, in part because of the steady demand for high-quality reed straw in a region that was, historically, better suited to raising animals than wheat. Its persistence also probably encouraged the retention of taller varieties of wheat and rye which produced a better quality reed than many of the shorter improved cultivars. According to a report written in 1934:

> the 'reed-comb' [is] falling out of use altogether in South Devon ... [but] a Kingkerswell farmer, Mr Rakeman, near the Arch, still combs his reed with an old hand-comb, and I am told by Mr Parkhouse, thatcher, of Barton, Torquay, that this method still prevails to some extent in North Devon. (Fielden 1934, 363–4)

Pre-mechanized reed straw production – conclusion
The historical evidence indicates that largely undamaged straw was used in much of England in the past, although most assiduously in the West Country. Even within the West Country there were local variations in the way in

which this reed straw was produced. The grain-bearing portion of a sheaf might be pitched, lashed, or flailed and the butt end combed with a hand rake, or a webble. However it was produced, the thatch that resulted was largely uncrushed over at least the lower half or its length and was butts-together in the sheaf (Fig 39).

The reasons for this commitment to reed straw in the West Country are both ancient and practical, and involve architectural, climatic and economic factors. This is a region of heavy rainfall compared to central and eastern England. The abundant moisture, combined with more sunshine and significantly warmer year-round temperatures than other parts of England, provides ideal conditions for fungal growth and straw decay. West Country thatched roofs are generally flatter-pitched than their counterparts in central and eastern England, and therefore shed water less rapidly. This encourages a greater ingress of water, which combined with the greater precipitation, higher ambient temperatures and more sunshine creates ideal conditions for the breakdown of thatch. Rapid decay is not a problem if straw is cheap and abundant, but the West Country is primarily a pastoral district where straw was husbanded for use as litter as well as thatch. Most farms grew rye and wheat for domestic purposes in the past, and processed the straw in order to extend its useful life as thatch for as long as possible. The statistical evidence suggests that less than five acres [2ha] of arable land was available for each thatched building in the south west in 1862–3, less than any other region, despite a dramatic decline in the number of thatched buildings in the region over the first half of the nineteenth century. The scarcity of wheat straw in the region was often noted.

> It has been disputed, whether reed [ie reed straw] thatch would last longer than that from thrashed straw; but there seems to be no doubt on the subject in this county; where, on account of the great number of thatched buildings, and the comparative small quantity of arable land, it is important to make the most economical use of the wheat straw. The practice of reaping very low, and that of mowing the wheat crop, are both useful in this point of view. (Stevenson 1812, 221; see also 86–7)

Combing removes surplus vegetation that might increase the sponge effect and provide additional moisture for fungal decay. Unbruised straw will also dry out more quickly than crushed straw because of the greater air circulation that can occur around the stem and within its central bore (lumen), if the reed straw is not fixed too tightly into position. Smooth stemmed reed straw will stay in place without excessive fixing on a flat-pitched Devon roof, but tighter fixings, which will reduce air circulation, are necessary on more steeply-pitched roofs in other parts of England to prevent slippage.

The West Country has the longest growing season in England. Old English wheats were very long-seasoned, with some of the rivet wheats taking a year or more to mature - but with bountiful results. These older varieties were ideal for producing reed straw, particularly when grown on a small scale and reaped by hand.

Figure 40 Distribution of reed straw thatching c 1790 (Judith Dobie, after James Moir and John Letts).

The historical evidence seems sufficient to justify a generalized distribution map of West Country reed straw use in 1790 (Fig 40). Its eastern boundary ran from the Severn estuary down through Dorset to the west of Blandford Forum. Within this region, ear-flailing, lashing, pitching and combing were the norm, with hand combing being more popular in Devon, fixed combs in Somerset and pitching in east Devon, west Dorset, Somerset and south Wiltshire.

The historical and *in situ* evidence for the use of reed straw beyond the West Country is discussed below. The evidence suggests that the leggats and combing devices of the West Country were eschewed by southern English halm thatchers who recognised the importance of using uncrushed straw, but prepared and applied it in much the same way as straw crushed and mixed by the flail. This halming tradition initially received a boost by the introduction of the mechanical thresher, but gradually faded from view in face of the massive quantities of relatively inexpensive, but equally useful, crushed straw generated by the shift to mechanization and the expansion of arable farming.

Drawing crushed straw (long straw)

Straw bruised by the thresher and drawn into order has been the dominant thatching material used throughout most of England outside of the West Country for at least two centuries (Fig 41).

Drawing from a bed is simply a method of stripping leaves from the stem once it has been crushed (Figs 42 and 43). It is also the most efficient way of realigning the stems within a jumbled heap while at the same time removing short straws and weeds that would otherwise affect its performance as thatch. Today the term drawing is used specifically in reference to the preparation of long straw, but pitched reed was drawn in Dorset in the early nineteenth century as was ear-threshed halm in various southern counties. In this respect, drawing is simply another version of combing performed in reverse, the heap acting as the rake and the material itself being pulled instead of the rake.

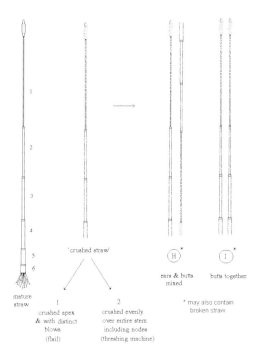

Figure 41 Variations in forms of crushed straw produced c 1790–1940 (John Letts).

Figure 42 Drawing long straw, Reading, Berkshire (John Letts).

Drawing is labour-intensive and exhausting, but the performance of a thatched roof depends as much on the good preparation of material as on the skill of the thatcher, and it is for this reason that drawing and yealming are performed with almost religious attention to detail by modern long straw thatchers. The principal drawing method that has been used in southern England can be divided into four main steps:

1   shaking the straw into a loose bed
2   wetting the bed to soften and lubricate the stems and leaves so that they are more easily stripped
3   drawing the straw from the bed into a row in front of the bed, and
4   collecting the row into a tight and neat yealm ready for fixing.

The yealm acts like a tile, and a well-prepared yealm will remain intact when stacked into a yoke and laid in position on the roof. One of the earliest records of this procedure was provided by Henry Best writing in seventeenth-century Yorkshire (Woodward 1984, 135).

Loudon's short description from the early nineteenth century is significant primarily because it emphasises the fact that drawing produces two products, a long straw and a short straw.

> With articles of the straw kind the usual method is this: the substances, after being well moistened with water, are drawn out in handfuls perfectly straight and even, into regular lengths, and the short straw separated from them, leaving them placed in convenient bundles to be carried to the thatcher by the person who has the serving of him. (Loudon 1831, 517)

Rham provides a similar description in reference to both ricks and house thatching.

The straw is prepared by moistening it, that it may more easily bend without breaking. It is then forked up in a loose heap, the straws lying in every direction, and somewhat matted. Portions are now drawn out from this heap in handfuls, which lays the straws again in a more parallel order: these are placed in a forked stick, which will hold several of these bundles or handfuls, and are thus carried to the thatcher. (1845, 513)

The description of drawing and yealming in *The Thatcher's Craft* is one of the most reliable descriptions and clearly reflects nineteenth-century practice. There are two stages to the work, preparing the heap and actually drawing the yealms.

Figure 43 Yealming long straw, Reading, Berkshire (John Letts).

The straw must first of all be wetted in order to make it flexible and less stubborn, and to enable it to be compressed when applied to the roof. This is done with a two-tined hay fork. A quantity of straw is taken from the load as delivered and thrown forward into a layer, using a shaking action to separate the bunches. One or two buckets of water are thrown across each layer of straw. The bucket should describe an arc, and the water will then be evenly distributed over the whole layer. This process should be repeated, layer upon layer, always building on to the back of the heap. An occasional light beating with the fork tightens the heap and makes it more shapely. When a sufficient quantity has been treated, it is known as the bed and should then be allowed to steep for a few hours before use. By this time the straw has become well soaked.

The yealms are prepared by drawing double handfuls of straw from the bed:

> Standing to the *front of the bed* ... Working from the extreme right-hand side ... good double handfuls of straw are drawn out, one after another, and laid side by side on the ground. Walking slowly backwards, the thatcher continues this process throughout the complete width of the bed. The part of the straw which is grasped in the hands is known as the large end. The small end is that end nearest the bed. Care must be taken in laying the large ends in as straight a line as possible. Bunches of the straw are then worked tightly together towards the feet to the required width of one yealm. By running the fingers through the straw the short waste will be removed ... superfluous straws are pulled out from both ends. (Morgan & Cooper 1960, 8–9)

Crushed straw has probably been drawn for use as thatch for millennia, but our earliest *in situ* evidence dates only to the post-medieval period and particularly the eighteenth and nineteenth centuries. The smoke-blackened thatch recovered from medieval buildings is composed primarily of threshing waste and reed straw used as base coats for external layers that have not survived (Letts 1999).

References to the term long straw have not been discovered prior to the early nineteenth century, but this does not mean that a crushed straw product that would easily be recognized by a modern thatcher as long straw was not used in the past. An early use of the term occurs in the records of the Duke of Grafton's estate in Northamptonshire. On 15 September, 1807, 'a load of long straw' was sold from the estate, presumably for use as thatch, as most other entries in the documents refer to the sale of 'halme', stubble, wheat straw and straw for this purpose (Northamptonshire Record Office 4). Whether this long straw was produced by a mechanical thresher or a flail is not clear.

In East Anglia in the mid nineteenth century, threshers crushed the straw but a winnower was used to separate the short straw from the long straw used for thatching (Wilson 1871, **1**, 633). Wilson had to use the term 'long in the straw' wheat when referring to straw that had grown tall in the field because the term long straw had already acquired a specific meaning in reference to

thatch. The term was well entrenched by the early decades of this century. According to Patterson (1925, 131), in passing through a thresher straw was sorted into 'long straw, consisting for the most part of stems, and the cavings which include broken stems and leaves.' The term long straw thus seems to have entered the thatcher's lexicon in the early nineteenth century and was popularized as the thresher spread through the English countryside.

The threshing machine

The first mechanical 'thrashing' machines were constructed in the mid seventeenth century by attaching short lengths of wood to a revolving crank that attempted, usually unsuccessfully, to duplicate the flailing process (Ransome 1843, 137–71). A much more practical machine, which used a rotating drum with wooden pegs rather than revolving flails, was patented by Andrew Meikle of East Lothian, Scotland, in 1786 and was widely acclaimed. In Meikle's machine, a drum with pegs rotated at high speed within a second concave drum, and grain-bearing ears passing between them were held back by the concave drum long enough for the rotating pegs to knock out the grain. The wooden pegs were soon replaced by beater bars, but this basic 'drum and concave' principle was used in all of the threshing machines built over the next century and a half. Meikle's thrasher was well received on large cereal farms in Scotland, northern England and East Anglia, areas where farm labour was expensive, and had become fairly common in parts of southern England by 1815. The early machines were driven by horse, water or hand power, and from the mid 1840s by fixed steam engines. The cost of setting up a mechanical threshing operation was well beyond the means of most small and medium-sized farmers, and the gentleman's debate over the utility of the thrasher in the agricultural literature of the period is conducted with relatively little concern over the social conditions that slowed its acceptance. The cost of a new threshing mill was a regular complaint in the literature (Rudge 1813, 85). The high purchase price was compounded by equally high running and repair costs (Batchelor 1808, 210–11).

The flood of threshed straw was unprecedented and required a change in storage practices. Hitherto, it had become available in measured quantities as flailing proceeded through the winter months, and was used for animal bedding, thatching, fuel and other purposes as required. Machine threshed straw was very dry and preserved well in the barn, but unfortunately most barns were not large enough to hold all of the harvest (Low 1843, 323; Wilson 1871, **1**, 633). For many growers, the only solution was to stack the surplus threshed straw outdoors in a thatched rick, a practice that became increasingly common during the Napoleonic wars as producers attempted to take advantage of soaring grain prices.

The inefficiency of the early threshing machines was a common source of complaint. Long-stemmed cereals were difficult to thresh because of the large volume of straw that had to be processed per unit of grain extracted.

There is a thrashing machine at Southoe [Huntingdonshire], power[ed by] four horses, which thrashes when the wheat is good, and the straw short, thirty loads a day, of five bushels; but when the straw is long it thrashes but half that quantity. (Parkinson 1811, 293)

This might well have encouraged reaping higher on the stem with a consequent increase in stubble. Nor did the early thrashers remove all of the grain from the ears (Burke 1834–40, 197; Wilson 1871, **1**, 635), which reduced profits and also caused problems for the thatcher when the grain sprouted. A farmer remarked that the ricks of a farm on the borders of Hertfordshire were 'almost as green as a meadow, from the corn left in the straw by a thrashing-mill' (Batchelor 1808, 210–11).

The early thrashers could be adjusted to some degree to maximize grain extraction while minimizing damage to straw, but thorough threshing usually resulted in very damaged straw. This presented no great change of tradition for thatchers in arable districts in south-central and eastern England who had always used crushed straw for thatching, but was unacceptable to thatchers in reed straw districts or to growers who valued their straw for sale as litter.

> The markets of London have been long supplied with straw drawn straight in handsome trusses. This makes it supposed, that straw thrashed by the mills will be less saleable, on account of being more bruised, and less sightly in the truss. (Middleton 1798, 175)

One solution was simply to cut the ears off of straw intended for thatching, and to thresh the ears, and the portion of the crop not wanted for reed straw, by machine:

> Mr Goodenough, of Frampton [Dorset] has a thrashing-machine ... Five women and two men are employed in attending the thrashing ... but it is difficult to obtain correct accounts of the quantity of wheat that may be thrashed by machines in this county, as Mr Goodenough and many others, very generally thrash only the ears, which are always put twice through the machine. (Stevenson 1812, 145–6)

This passage is highly significant for it suggests that reed straw, in this case Dorset pitched reed, continued to be produced even though all of the ears were being threshed by machine. The damage inflicted on the straw, as well as the efficacy of grain extraction, varied tremendously depending on the construction of the machine and how it was operated. Peg drums replaced beater bars in the early nineteenth century because these were gentler on the straw (Bell & Watson 1986, 213). Long-stemmed straw could pass through the drum very slowly, while short straw passed through largely unthreshed. The process also varied depending on how the machine was fed, a point that is always stressed by older thatchers and farm workers with threshing experience.

When straw was not needed for thatching the sheaves were untied and fed into the drum ear first. The straw was bent, broken and crushed inside the drum, and tossed out

the other end onto walkers that shook it clean of grain and short straw and dumped it into a trusser or a jumbled heap. By feeding the sheaf sideways or at a slight angle, however, the straw passed through the drum threshed but in much better shape, and left the walkers with a larger proportion of stems in the butts-together order in which they were fed (Alan Fuchs, Arthur Hannabuss, pers comms). The process was obviously constrained by the length of the drum. A standard 54" (138cm) drum was in use by the Second World War, but drums as small as 18" (46cm) were marketed in the nineteenth century (Bell & Watson 1986, 213). In 1808, the drum of Mr Den's threshing machine in Tempsford, Bedfordshire, measured 48" (123cm) in width (Batchelor 1808, 199). Drums smaller than this would have been unable to thresh a standard sheaf of tall English wheat without damaging the straw. As a result, the introduction of the threshing machine provided a strong incentive to grow shorter varieties of wheat in areas where unbruised straw was valued for thatch and for animal bedding.

In the early years the grain had to be shaken from the threshed straw by hand. The addition of walkers, which separated the grain and short straw (also called colder or cavings) from the long straw, greatly improved its appeal to farmers as well as thatchers, as it reduced the amount of drawing and cleaning that was required to turn the threshed straw into thatch. Improvements in portability brought the threshing machine within reach of most farms in England by the 1850s, and machine-threshed straw quickly became the dominant material on thatched roofs in arable districts.

> The thrashed straw of wheat, with the ears on it, is the thatch most generally in use throughout the plains and valleys of Britain; and when well laid, forms at once a very neat, a quite secure and a sufficiently... durable covering for most structures to which it is applied. (Wilson 1871, **1**, 625)

Long straw-style thatching using machine-threshed straw and a variety of fixing techniques was unquestionably the dominant type of thatching used throughout most of central, southern and eastern England over most of the nineteenth century. How much lashed or ear-flailed reed straw was used in long straw areas in past centuries would be difficult to establish, but it is unlikely to have been used to any great extent once the threshing machine had become a practical, affordable and portable option. No memory of a reed straw tradition had survived by the end of the century, and hand threshing survived only in remote and geographically isolated areas such as Devon where the small width of country lanes physically precluded the advance of the thrasher. Most thatchers operating outside of the West Country at the turn of this century would never have had occasion to use any thatching material other than threshed straw, and it is significant that complaints about the damage caused to straw by machine threshing are rarely encountered in the literature in the second half of the nineteenth century.

In general, no alternative was available due to the almost total commitment to machine threshing, and complaints only reappear in the early part of this century

Figure 44 Patent illustration of 'Mr Harding's pedal for not breaking the straw' (Young 1807, 157).

promulgated by thatchers and middlemen with a vested interested in encouraging the use of water reed. The quality of the threshed straw available for thatching certainly varied in crushed straw districts for a variety of reasons including the collapsing markets for high quality animal litter and thatching straw, but straw was assuming its modern role as a low-value by-product of the grain production industry. This decrease in status was reinforced by the introduction of increasingly short, and brittle-stemmed, hybrid varieties, and in the late 1930s by the combine harvester. Long straw became scarce, expensive and unreliable in quality, a situation that did not improve until a new generation of specialist producers, dedicated to growing straw specifically for thatching, emerged in the 1960s.

The mechanized production of reed straw

No matter how a crop is threshed, and whether combing is done by hand or by machine, reed straw becomes reed straw when the stem is left unbruised and the butts lie together in the bundle. In this sense, the development of mechanical combing marked only a quantitative change in the amount of thatching straw that could be produced per man hour of labour, rather than a significant change in appearance, quality or performance. Growers were initially quite wary of mechanical threshers because of the damage they inflicted on straw, but rising labour costs and an increasingly lucrative and competitive market for grain made their eventual adoption inevitable. The first machines were used as a substitute for ear-flailing.

> In some places [in Dorset], the sheaves are partially thrashed, without striking the straw further than the principal part of the ears extend, and the short straws and unthrashed ears are afterwards separated with a wooden comb. In the vicinity of Sherborne, the thrashing machines are made to answer the same purpose, by holding the wheat in the hand in small parcels, and withdrawing it when the ears are thrashed. (Stevenson 1812, 220–1)

Adjustments were made on some machines to improve the ease with which the straw could be withdrawn from the drum (Fig 44).

> Mr Daw, near Evershot [Dorset], has a thrashing-mill which belongs to the farm. It has six wooden wheels, which appear to increase the velocity about 80 times. The drum is an open one, 3½ feet [1.07m] in diameter, and the lower fluted cylinder may be depressed by treaders, when it is desired to draw back the straw for reed-thatching. (op cit, 162)

Ear-threshed reed straw was obviously available wherever a threshing machine was available to produce it, just as lashed or ear-flailed straw had previously been available wherever cereals were grown. Ironically, the thresher increased the efficiency of producing (uncombed) reed straw in crushed straw districts, while at the same time increasing the amount of threshed straw available for crushed straw style thatching. According to Mavor, writing from the long straw county of Berkshire:

> R Tull, of Chamber House, Thatcham, has a hand machine, [made] by Balls, turned by four women, and which employs ten persons in all, although only one man is necessary. The only saving Mr Tull finds in its use is in making reed for thatching, which is much more durable

and neat than when the straw is broken. The straw is drawn back as soon as the ears are threshed, instead of being allowed to pass through the machine'. (Mavor 1809, 138)

Purpose-built mechanical reed straw combers were manufactured in the West Country at least as early as the mid nineteenth century, powered initially by a hand crank and eventually by horse, water and eventually steam and tractor power. They have attracted very little attention from devotees of old agricultural machinery and their early history is poorly understood. Many were made to local specifications, but several versions were marketed by agricultural machinery firms in the late nineteenth century. They were, in essence, mechanized versions of a webble that combined the combing and threshing processes into one operation. Handfuls of straw were inserted into the comber where the flag leaf and grain was stripped off by a rotating drum with spikes (Ian White, Richard Wright and Arthur Hannabuss, pers comm). The handful was then turned around and re-inserted to clear the butts of weeds and short straw. A final combing in the barn, and on the roof when being applied, ensured that the straw was free of contaminants that might lessen its longevity.

In Devon the barn comber (Fig 45) was preferred by growers who valued their straw for thatching as it stripped both the grain and extraneous leaf and short stems from the sheaf in the same process. The eventual application of the straw comber to the thresher in the late nineteenth century must have been prompted, at least in part, by the less satisfactory performance of the ear threshed reed straw the thresher produced, but it may also be linked to the reduction in average stem height. Only the basal portion of a stem need be stripped of its upper leaves to improve its performance as reed straw. The upper portion of the stem, with its leaves bent down towards the butt end of the course, is hidden from the

elements below or above the fixings. The removal of these leaves becomes increasingly desirable as straw length decreases, however, both to reduce the retention of moisture and to maximize the length of stripped straw available for weathering, particularly in the West Country. Barn combers were dangerous to use, but increased the amount of reed straw that could be produced in one day by at least ten-fold. An experienced comber could produce up to a hundred 28lb [12.7kg] nitches of high-quality reed straw per day, but the improved efficiency was not enough to stimulate its adoption in other parts of England (Arthur Hannabuss, Richard Wright and Ian White, pers comm). Undamaged reed straw, carefully ear-threshed in a threshing machine for sale as high quality litter, could always be combed by hand to produce a good quality combed wheat reed when required.

A combing mechanism that could be attached to the top of any standard threshing machine was developed at the turn of this century for the hatting industry. It used the same basic principle as the barn comber, the rotating spiked drum, to thresh the straw as it was combed, and used the power of the thresher to turn the spiked drums and to pass straw over them using a belted conveyor delivery system (Figs 46, 47 and 48). By this means a straw grower could thresh the bulk of his crop in the usual way and turn the remainder into high-quality reed straw. In practice, the combing attachment was expensive and difficult to attach, and was adopted primarily by farmers with a special interest in producing combed wheat reed. The comber attachment greatly increased the efficiency of the combing process, and unlike the barn comber produced tied bundles of reed straw and cleaned grain in one operation. The comber was a familiar sight in the West Country before the First World War (Rogers 1976, 26), and by the late 1930s almost all of the thatching straw used in Devon was produced using a comber-thresher (Fielden 1934, 363).

As with the thresher, the quality of the combed reed straw varied depending on the machine, the manner in which it was fed and the straw that was combed. Cereal varieties that produced straw between 90–110cm in length were preferred, as the standard 60" (153cm) combing box was incapable of combing straw much taller than 47" (120cm). Thus, as with the threshing drum a century earlier, the comber attachment probably encouraged specialist producers in the West Country to abandon the tallest, traditional varieties that remained in cultivation in favour of improved cultivars that produced a shorter and more even straw.

The comber made its first appearance outside of the West Country in the inter-war years, and a description of its first demonstration in south-eastern England appeared in *The Architect* in 1922.

A demonstration of the Isaac Reed Comber, the product of Messrs W Isaac & Sons, of Braunton, was given under good weather conditions at Rochford, Essex, on March 31 ... This is the first machine of its kind that has been seen in the East of England; Mr E J Halsey, of Rochford, is charged by the manufacturers with its introduction into Great Britain, except in the Western Counties, where it is already known.

Figure 45 Mechanical barn comber, Holsworthy Museum, Devon (Museum of English Rural Life).

Figure 46 *Late nineteenth-century threshing machine (Museum of English Rural Life).*

Figure 47 *The portable threshing machine with reed straw comber attachment, Goring Heath, Berkshire (John Letts).*

Among those present at the demonstration was Mr Thompson Close, of the machinery branch of the Ministry of Agriculture (who are taking a keen interest in the matter), and who also represented the Ministry of Health, who see in the production of improved straw reed a cheap roof-covering for dwelling-houses in rural districts. (anon 1922a)

No further trace of this experiment has been found, but it marks the beginning of a period of interest in the use of West Country thatching methods and materials in other parts of England.

The straw trusser

Prior to the invention of the sheaf binding mechanism in the late nineteenth century, cereal cut by the reaper was tied into sheaves by hand using straw bonds. The reaper-binder mechanized this procedure and greatly reduced the labour required at harvest time. The binding mecha-

Figure 48 *Reed straw comber attachment, Goring Heath, Berkshire (John Letts).*

Figure 49 *Portable threshing machine with straw trusser attachment, late nineteenth century (Museum of English Rural Life).*

nism was soon adapted for use on the threshing machine, and the trusser was available as a standard addition to the thresher by the 1880s (Fig 49). Hitherto, the crushed straw that emerged from the back of the threshing machine fell into a jumbled heap that was stacked loose or bundled in a straw barn, or with the increase in cereal production from the late eighteenth century in a thatched rick (Loudon 1831, 818). Feeding sheaves ears-first into the thresher produced a heap of straw that was jumbled in terms of ears and butts. When fed horizontally, however, most of the straw emerged more or less in the same orientation as it was put in, and was tied into bundles by the trusser after being shaken clean of grain, short straw and detritus. Tying facilitated subsequent handling, stacking and transportation, and was essential if the straw was to be sold off the farm for use in thatching or as litter. Straw drawn directly from a rick of trussed bundles would thus have produced a more regular yealm of butts-together straw, but the usual practice was to shake the compressed bundles into a loose bed that was then drawn into yealms mixed in terms of ears and butts.

Straw was usually stacked loose in a stack before the invention of the trusser (or when a trusser was not available), for retying threshed straw into bundles involved additional labour costs and was unnecessary unless the straw was to be sold off the farm. Straw could be drawn directly from the stack or a bed in the stackyard when required for thatching. The trusser facilitated the sale and transport of undrawn bundles off the farm, and allowed owners to save on thatching costs by drawing the straw themselves rather than having to purchase straw drawn from the stack by the grower.

The specialist straw producer

Straw was clearly a valued resource on subsistence-oriented farms in England prior to the rise of industrial agriculture in the last century. It was essential for thatching and for animal bedding, but was also used as a fuel and for a variety of minor purposes. It became increasingly valued as a source of manure. But three factors conspired to drive straw steadily towards the category of waste product: the discovery of artificial fertilizers, the development of mechanized harvesting and threshing and the breeding of shorter and higher yielding varieties better suited to the new industrial agriculture. By 1900 the straw once processed in small amounts on a weekly basis and carefully husbanded for use as manure was now available en masse, threshed in bulk over a period of a few days and stored in large ricks, or simply burned in arable districts where it had little value for thatch or for bedding. Unfortunately, this growing surplus did not necessarily increase the thatcher's opportunity to select better quality straw for thatching due to the tendency to delay harvesting and the crushing impact of mechanized threshing.

In the mid nineteenth century, plant breeders began to produce improved cereal varieties that were better adapted to mechanized cereal production, higher yielding, shorter and stiffer-stemmed varieties that ripened more evenly, threshed more efficiently and produced grain with improved baking qualities. A farmer might grow a dozen or more named varieties including a low-yielding foreign spring wheat that produced high-quality flour for commercial baking, a traditional English winter wheat that minimized the risk of total crop failure and generated tall straw for thatching, and a red wheat of moderate yield and moderate straw length that produce good-tasting flour for domestic baking and sturdy straw for animal bedding.

Subsequent increases in wheat yields and the eventual emergence of specialist straw producers after the Second World War, are linked to the development of improved forms of *Squarehead* wheat, an old English land race variety with tall, stout straw and dense ears that produced respectable yields of soft-grained wheat suited to traditional bread and biscuit production.

A selection retaining the ancestral name was developed from a single plant discovered in a field of *White Victoria* wheat in Yorkshire in 1868. *Squarehead* wheat became very popular towards the end of the century, and is the English grandparent of most of the wheats that are used by thatchers and cereal growers today (Percival 1921, 296). A variety called *Squareheads Master* (syn *Red Standard*) was first recorded in 1830, and an improved version released by a breeder in the West Midlands in the 1880s was the most popular winter wheat in England until the late 1930s. *Squareheads Master* was hardy, yielded well in a range of soils and climates and produced stout, stiff straw *c* 110cm in length (Percival 1943, 109).

Success for cereal producers spelt failure for thatchers. Short-stemmed straw will obviously wear out before longer-stemmed straw applied to an equivalent depth, and the shortening of the average length of straw from *c* 120cm to 80cm between 1790 and 1940 reduced the longevity of a new coat by at least 25–50% over the 1790 values. This change probably affected thatchers in the principal cereal-growing districts more than in secondary reed straw areas, as the crushed straw thatchers were largely recipients of straw produced as a by-product of grain production. West Country growers retained their taller, older varieties as their straw was more highly prized for thatching in an area without abundant cereal production. Varietal heights plummeted in the 1920s and 1930s with the release of *Yeoman* (1916) and other semi-dwarf products of intensive plant breeding, and although a yealm could accommodate some reduction in straw length, its performance was still ultimately governed by the length of its individual components. In addition, the new varieties ripened more evenly and were generally left to ripen more fully before being harvested, and so were generally more damaged by the threshing machine. A roof thatched with *Yeoman* in 1925 might have had half the life expectancy of a coat of *Squareheads Master* applied in the same manner by the same thatcher 20 years before, and the situation worsened with the adoption of even shorter varieties.

The shortening of straw length from *c* 120 cm to 80 cm between 1790 and 1940 thus has obvious and striking implications: it would have reduced the longevity of a roof by about 20 years, ignoring the fact that the shorter material was also applied to a shallower pitch. For this reason West Country reed straw growers and thatchers retained their tall older varieties longer. The shortening of varietal heights could have been compensated to some degree by extending the yealm, but the length of the yealm and the performance of the layer is still ultimately governed by the length of its individual components.

8 Fixings

SPARS AND SWAYS

Most of the spars and sways used to fix spar coats of thatch to existing base coats are today made from coppiced hazel (*Corylus avellana*). The evidence from medieval and early post-medieval roofs, however, suggests that roundwood of a variety of species was once much more frequently used than split wood (Fig 50). Well-preserved twig spars of bramble (*Rubus* spp.), snowberry (*Symphoricarpos albus*), willow (*Salix* spp.) and several other woody species that would never be used by modern English thatchers were used routinely in Ireland earlier this century. The preliminary data from England suggest that a transition from roundwood to split hazel (and presumably short rotation willow coppice and pollard) occurred at some time in the seventeenth or eighteenth century. This evidence is biased, however, by the fact that the better built houses have survived to be sampled, and their owners may well have had greater access to high quality underwood than many rural workers whose smaller homes and hovels have disappeared.

Coppice woodland was maintained for a variety of purposes throughout most of England from the medieval period until the late nineteenth century (Rackham 1980; Crowther & Evans 1986). It was most plentiful in areas of intensive sheep farming such as Hampshire, south Wiltshire, West Sussex and Dorset where there was a large demand for hurdles. In most cases coppice was maintained as a mixed growth of many species including hazel, ash, field maple, sweet chestnut, hornbeam, lime, birch, sycamore, aspen and oak depending on soil conditions. Growing conditions within a coppice encourage the rapid growth of long, straight rods ideal for splitting

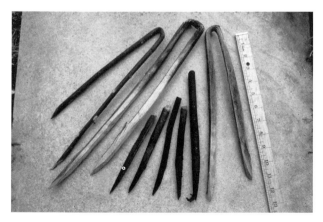

Figure 50 Fixings: medieval roundwood and post-medieval split hazel spars (John Letts).

into spars and liggers, but suitable wood can also be obtained from hedgerows and mature trees if available. For thatching, sways must be as strong as spars are flexible, as the latter had to be bent into a U-shape without snapping. Less discrimination was required when using peg and rope fixing as the pegs were simply pushed into the thatch without bending.

Traditional hazel coppice was cut on a 4–10 year rotation depending on the purpose for which the underwood was required. Ideally cutting occurred from October to March when sap levels were low, and summer wood was 'sappy', weaker and more prone to insect and fungal attack. The coppice stools were cut back to ground level and the *c* 2" (5 cm) diameter 'spar gads' (rods) were cut into 2–3' (60–90 cm) lengths for splitting into spars, c 1" (2.5 cm) thick and 8' (2.4 m) long sways for fixing courses and shorter liggers for external and decorative use. An average modern roof consumes about 8,000–10,000 spars as well as a large number of sways and liggers. One acre of good hazel coppice produces 10,000–12,000 10'–15' (3.05m–4.57m) long rods which can be cut into about 75,000 spars. A good spar-maker can cut 1,000 spars a day using just a billhook. Exposed liggers made from good quality hazel can last ten years or more, but poor quality wood degrades after only a few years.

Dialect dictionaries provide upwards of 25 different terms for spar as used in the late nineteenth century, many being variations of spar, spray, the Middle English term broach and buckle, gooseneck or scallop (Wright 1905). Straight pegs (pricks/prods) were also known under a variety of names in different areas. This rich vocabulary reflects the ancient origin of the practice, and stands in striking contrast to the present day where the vast majority of spars are known to thatchers as either spars or broaches.

Spars are cleft with a bill hook or spar hook, and it takes some time to master the craft so as to produce straight spars of even diameter efficiently (Fig 51). Spars made from coppice wood were often made during the winter months or on rainy or windy days unsuitable for thatching. They were usually made by the thatcher or the thatcher's mate, but also by professional spar-makers who were paid by the bundle. A spar is bent double (into the shape of a hairpin) before it is used to clamp a sway or straw to the underlying thatch. Dry wood will usually snap before it bends, so a split wood spar is usually thinned in the centre, soaked for at least a day, and twisted as it is bent in two which allows the wood fibres to separate rather than snap. The fibres of many woody species will

Figure 51 Woodcutter 'riving' spars for thatching. James Minns, or 'Rough Jimmy' (photographed 1901) was born in Ditchling, Norfolk, in 1826 (Museum of English Rural Life).

not separate as easily as those of hazel or willow. Thick diameter roundwood is very difficult to twist even if cut only a day or two before use. One drawback to using green willow for spars is that they can sprout on a roof if the wood is cut from a dormant tree and sparred onto a roof that is permanently damp. Spars are usually bent so that one tine is a little longer than the other, and are inserted so that the longer tine is towards the ridge. Their ends are also sharpened to a two or three-faced point depending on their diameters.

ROPE AND CORDAGE

A wide variety of plant materials was used to bind thatch to roofs in England, but the evidence suggests that most of the base coats applied over the past two centuries are tied down with tarred or untarred hempen twine. The botanical identification of rope fibres is a difficult task, however, and examples from most of the buildings examined during this study have been retained for future analysis. Historically, the most important material used for making tarred rope was hemp (*Cannabis sativa*), but coir, manila fibre and sisal were also commonly used in more recent times. Many English towns had their own rope-making industries. For maritime use ropes were soaked in tar distilled from coal which acted as a preservative, but tarred rope found ready use in other industries and activities where rope came into contact with mois-

ture. Several improvements in the methods of manufacture of tar rope were made in the late eighteenth and early nineteenth centuries.

In 1803 W Chapman from Newcastle upon Tyne perfected a system of adding suet, whale, linseed or rape oil to 'common tar' to prevent the tarred and spun rope from becoming brittle. Tarred rope found favour with thatchers not because it shed moisture, but because the foul taste of the tar kept the rope from being eaten by rodents, and it was widely used once it became available cheaply and in quantity. Most of the historical evidence for the use of tarred rope in thatched roofs dates from the late eighteenth and early nineteenth centuries. Patents for the production of tarred cord on an industrial scale were issued at the end of the eighteenth century (Dundonald 1794, 145–8; Chapman 1798, 1–44), and it was being used for thatching in Norfolk in the 1830s (Loudon 1831, 518). It was embraced by thatchers not because it was any stronger or cheaper than the non-tarred product, but because it was less subject to attack by rodents and thus provided a more secure fixing. Unfortunately, it cannot be given a specific date of introduction, and non-tarred hempen rope continued to be used throughout the nineteenth century. Some of the early descriptions of thatching in the literature probably refer to the non-tarred product, as in Gooch's reference to 'spits and rope' in Cambridgeshire (1811, 288). The reed applied in 1944 to the oldest section of the building recorded in Lingwood

(Appendix B: B30 Norfolk) was clamped into position by sways tied to the rafters with two-ply hempen rope (David Farman, pers comm). Short segments of tarred cord survived from the base coat stripped from the younger section of the roof in 1976.

Surprisingly strong and flexible 'rope' can be made from a variety of plant materials including coppiced hazel rods and saplings – a skill that is now unfamiliar to most thatchers. As in bending a spar, however, the key to the process lies in twisting the rod in such a way that the wood fibres separate rather than snap – as with spars. Younger saplings, willow withes, clematis stems and dethorned bramble stems are much easier to use and are extremely strong, and selecting suitable bindings was undoubtedly an important aspect of the thatcher's craft in past centuries.

A few of the buildings sampled over the course of this project had base coats fixed with straw rope and straw bonds were commonly used by English thatchers in the past in combination with spars when wooden sways were unavailable.

TURF AND CLAY

Turf cut from bog or rough pasture was used more widely as a base coat and a ridging material in the northern counties (Harrison 1989, 1991). A possible turf ridge was stripped from a house in Kings Sutton, Northamptonshire, in 1994, but references to the use of turf in southern England are rare (Wood-Jones 1963, 247–8).

Clay was obviously abundant and available free of charge, and it is likely to have been used more commonly on poorer buildings in areas where underwood for spars and sways was less plentiful. Clay mixed with chopped straw or other organic material was used in some districts to cap ridges on reed roofs. Clay ridges were recorded on two buildings sampled as part of this project, one in Great Doddington, Northamptonshire (Appendix A: A15) and the second in Lyndon, Leicestershire (Appendix A: A14), both of which had reed fleekings supporting multi-layered roofs of straw thatch. In England it appears to have been used on ridges in the same way it was used to seal eaves and gable courses onto the wall plates, by overcoating a layer of mud with thatch which was then anchored into place by being sparred and bedded into the wet clay below it. Anecdotal evidence suggests that clay may have been used for ridging in Oxfordshire as well as the Northampton-shire-Leicestershire region, but how common it was in any area is difficult to establish.

Part III

Thatching techniques

9 Performance and technical change

Many of the thatching methods and materials used in the nineteenth century are no longer used in England, and any attempt to present a technical history of the craft is doomed to generalization and simplification because of the biases inherent in the *in situ* record. A manor house or cottage orné is unlikely to have been thatched in exactly the same manner as the cattle shed or outhouse in the adjacent garden, but it is inevitably the manor house that has survived. It is often forgotten that a huge swathe of poorer housing, much of it thatched using a variety of methods and materials, was swept away by housing reforms early this century. We have been left with a distorted and incomplete subsample from which we must attempt to reconstruct the larger picture.

LOCALITY

Regional thatching styles cannot simply be grafted onto the principal walling traditions because thatching methods do not slavishly follow geological realities. The link between geology and thatch occurs via surface geology, which along with climate broadly determines natural vegetation cover and the way in which a region can be farmed. Hence, heather was cut for thatching in districts with light sandy soils that later produced rye straw when the cultivation of wastes became profitable. Both materials were applied successfully to the same roofs.

Regional traditions can be quite variable or extremely uniform depending on how much or how little detail one includes in the definition. These traditions are commonly linked to constructional details for which there is little *a priori* justification. For example, the apparent link between water reed thatching and timber framing in East Anglia exists only because this region is particularly rich in both timber-framed buildings and water reed thatch. The steepness which has been a feature of roofs in this region since the early medieval period does maximize the longevity of water reed thatch, but these roofs can also be thatched successfully with crushed straw, river rush or fen sedge.

The form of dormer windows, contrary to what is sometimes inferred (Gunn 1936, 30) is not influenced by any one type of roofing material or technique. In cases where a long sweep of roof was not available to accommodate a wrapped dormer, the best option was usually to roof in an entirely different material such as tile.

Judging by the buildings examined to date, the timber structure of a roof seems to have had little influence on the way in which it was thatched after the first base coat had been applied. In England, similar sorts of thatch occur on king, queen and crown-post roofs as on jointed, full or upper-cruck roofs, but this evidence is biased as the roofs that have been examined have survived largely because they were well constructed and could support heavy accumulations of spar coats. Rafter and battening structures influence the way in which the first base coat is applied to a thatched roof. They also affect the longevity of a roof through their effect on physical processes such as air flow and slippage, but as long as this base coat remains secure the substructure plays a minimal role in the roof's subsequent thatching history. Nor do structurally significant factors such as bay spacing or ridge construction seem to have influenced external thatching techniques. The ridge rolls that provide the solid base into which the external ridge cap is sparred can be tied either to the ridge beam, or in buildings in eastern England which do not have a ridge piece, to the uppermost battens without changing the method in which the ridge is subsequently fixed or finished.

It is perhaps in the junction between the rafters and the wall plate that roof structure most directly influences the way in which thatch is applied. In many older reed thatched buildings in East Anglia the rafters descend to the inside of the wall and rest on a wall plate that runs along its inner face. This leaves a significant gap between outer edge of the wall and the feet of the rafters. A long and stiff material such as reed will flex as it crosses over the outer edge of the wall, producing a kick that tightens the eaves to the top of the wall and reduces the risk of slippage (Deas 1939, 101).

A similar gap, and kick, occurs at the top of the wall in older cob-walled buildings in the West Country. Buildings in other regions thatched with long straw generally have flush or oversailing rafters that carry the eaves courses as far over the outer wall face as possible. Where the rafters rest on the inner top of the wall, the gap can be filled by additional straw or alternating layers of mud and thatch that provide a draft-proof seal and a firm base into which the first eaves course of crushed straw can be sparred. When these buildings are converted from long straw to combed wheat reed or water reed, the only change they usually require is the addition of a tilting fillet to provide the missing kick.

PERFORMANCE CRITERIA

Thatching is not the 'changeless craft' beloved of writers on England's heritage. Traditionally it has always been in a state of flux as with most other building crafts that have survived into the modern era. Traditionally, thatchers were trained through apprenticeship with the inevitable idiosyncracies this generated, rather than through standardized courses and vocational qualifications. The materials used varied from year to year and from season to season, and new methods, fixings and materials were incorporated into existing 'traditions' when they were shown to keep out the rain more efficiently, reliably and inexpensively. Change may have been slow, but change did occur. The transition from a patched and gulleyed past to the clipped and regimented present has occurred gradually and imperceptibly, leaving fossilized remnants of unique practices and materials beneath the surface at every rethatching.

Performance, rather than style, material or regional tradition provides one of best ways of assessing technical change in thatching through the centuries. The most important technical factors governing the craft are universally accepted, and although ranked in different ways by different thatchers, a list inevitably includes consideration of pitch, material quality, orientation and maintenance regime. Few of these have ever been under the thatcher's control, certainly not the orientation of the roof, or even the quality of the material used as this was usually provided by the home owner, a local farmer or the landlord. Not even the pitch to which a new coat is applied is under the full control of the thatcher for this will be conditioned by the pitch of the rafters, the pitch of the existing base coat, the length of the new material being applied, the depth to which it is being applied and the manner in which the new coat is to be fixed. The only thing that has remained relatively stable is how a roof will perform within a given set of technical and climatic conditions.

Pitch

Pitch is one of the most important factors influencing the performance and longevity of a thatched roof. Whatever the material employed, thatch works by moving water laterally from ridge to eaves as quickly as possible while limiting the degree to which it soaks into the surface coat. Although the speed of this downflow is obviously constrained by the nature of the material used, it is always the case that the steeper the pitch of the thatch the lesser the rate of infiltration and the longer the roof will last.

There are three different pitches that must be considered when thatching: the pitch of the rafters, the pitch of the existing base coat and the pitch of the material being applied. In the present day tiled roofs are usually pitched at 45° and slate roofs at 30°. Thatched buildings are usually steeper, averaging 50° in the Midlands and 60° in East Anglia, but only 40° or even less on combed wheat reed roofs in the West Country. The pitches of the buildings recorded for this project fit the expected pattern and range from 38° on a seventeenth-century timber-framed cottage near Bedford (Appendix A: A2 Bedfordshire) to 60° on a stone cottage of similar age in Lyndon, Leicestershire (Appendix A: A14 Leicestershire). The three East Anglian buildings were quite steeply pitched at 56° while the three examples from Devon were shallowly-pitched at 42°. The average pitch of the remaining buildings from Buckinghamshire, Bed-

fordshire, Northamptonshire, Oxfordshire and Wiltshire was fairly high at 49°, although this was skewed by the steeper pitches of the Leicestershire and Oxfordshire examples. On most of these roofs more ancient thatch survived towards the ridge than at the eaves due to disproportionate stripping prior to rethatching. This remains a common practice, and the evidence suggests that it has raised the surface pitch of some roofs by 10° or more above the pitch of the underlying rafters (eg Appendix A: A1 Bedfordshire).

The pitch of a roof is always much steeper than the pitch of the thatch which is fixed to it. The material pitch is a product of three variables: the taper and length of the material, and the depth to which it is applied. All thatching materials are tapered. Water reed has a very gradual taper compared to that of a yealm of long straw or a bundle of modern combed wheat reed. As a result of this taper, reed straw would quickly begin to lie flat if bundles were simply stacked on a roof in overlapping courses, and a thatcher must smooth each bundle into place by pushing the top portion of each wedge of material applied up the roof until its exterior face assumes the required line of pitch. The relationship between the length of material used and the depth to which it is applied is a little more difficult to visualise. An experienced thatcher will understand intuitively that the pitch at which a bundle of thatch is fixed decreases as the thickness to which it is laid increases, or, conversely, that short straw will lie at a flatter pitch than longer-stemmed straw when applied to an equivalent depth. This relationship is given by the formula $m° = r° - \sin^{-1} D/L$, where $m°$ is the pitch of the material on the roof, $r°$ is the pitch of the underlying rafters, D is the depth to which the material is applied (in practice, measured from the fixings), and L is the length of the straw applied.

A working out of this formula for various pitches, depths and lengths of materials is revealing and relates directly to thatch performance (Fig 52). Rough figures indicate that the pitch angle of the material drops by 8° (20cm) for every additional 4" (10cm) of material applied when the material is 31" (80cm) in length. A thin 10cm spar-coat of 100cm straw applied to a 45° roof will lie at an acceptable 40°, but this value drops to 34° at a 20cm depth and only 28° in a 30cm coat. Any further increase in the depth of the material applied would cause the straw to lie almost flat on the roof. Similarly, shortening straw length by 10 cm while maintaining the same depth of material reduces the material pitch by about 2°. The figures indicate that in terms of material pitch, increasing the depth of material on a roof has three times the effect of decreasing material length, or in other words, maintaining a steep material pitch is primarily a question of controlling the depth of thatch applied.

The implications of these figures are significant historically and in the present day. A coat of 90cm combed wheat reed laid to a 30cm depth actually lies at a pitch of only 26°, and the standard 80cm straw of Maris Huntsman or Maris Widgeon can be laid to only 20cm before the material pitch falls below 32°. In contrast, the *c* 40cm decrease in average straw length that occurred between

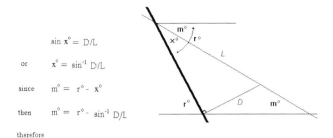

$$\sin x° = D/L$$

or $\quad x° = \sin^{-1} D/L$

since $\quad m° = r° - x°$

then $\quad m° = r° - \sin^{-1} D/L$

therefore

$x°$ will increase if L decreases and D remains constant

$x°$ will decrease if D decreases and L remains constant

rafter pitch (P_A)	depth of thatch (cm)	straw length (cm)			
		80	100	120	140
50	10 (4")	42.8	44.3	45.2	45.9
	20 (8")	35.5	38.5	40.4	41.8
	30 (12")	28	32.5	35.5	37.6
	40 (16")	20	26.4	30.5	37.6
45	10	37.8	39.3	40.2	40.9
	20	30.5	33.5	35.4	36.8
	30	23	27.5	30.5	32.6
	40	15	21.4	25.5	28.4
40	10	32.8	34.3	35.2	35.9
	20	25.5	28.5	30.4	31.8
	30	18	22.5	25.5	27.6
	40	10	16.4	20.5	23.4
35	10	27.8	29.3	30.2	30.9
	20	20.5	23.5	25.4	26.8
	30	13	17.5	20.5	22.6
	40	5	11.4	15.5	18.4

Figure 52 Relationship between roof pitch, depth of material and straw length (John Letts).

1790 and 1940 decreased the pitch of the straw on a 45° roof thatched to a standard 20cm depth by *c* 10°. The taller straw available in 1790 could obviously have been applied to a greater depth without the material pitch falling below the optimum, with a corresponding improvement in performance. The implications of these figures are perhaps most striking for the West Country and provide at least a partial explanation for the development of the combed wheat reed tradition, or more accurately, the West Country obsession with maximizing the water-shedding capacity of straw by careful threshing and combing. On a Devon roof with an average 40° pitch, a 30cm coat of reed straw 80cm long lies at an unacceptable 18°, whereas it would lie at 34° when applied to the same depth on a steep 55° roof in the Midlands. A 10cm coat of this material would lie at a more tolerable 32°, and the material pitch increases to 36° for a 10cm coat using the 120cm straw available in 1790.

The figures indicate that shortening straw length from 120cm to 80cm has four times the impact in reducing material pitch at a 16" (40cm) depth than at a 4" (10cm) depth. Hence, the shortening of straw length in the last century would have had less of an impact in areas with a tradition of thin spar coating, and a negligible effect on rick and stubble thatching. The reduction might have encouraged the use of thinner coats in order to maintain the material pitch, although the decrease was so gradual that the change in pitch may not have been noted. The average decrease in straw length from 1790 to 1940 can

be assumed to have decreased the pitch angle by at least 6°, which would need to be countered by a 4" (10cm) reduction in depth to maintain the status quo. The evidence, however, suggests that thatch is now put on more thickly than in the last century. Spar coats thicker than 6" (15cm) were probably uncommon in the West Country because the resulting material would simply have lain too flat, particularly when the reed straw was shorter than average due to a poor growing season. This same factor probably helped fuel the export of Devon combed wheat reed to other parts of England over the course of this century: tall reed straw was reserved for use on shallow, local roofs whereas shorter reed was sold up country for use on steeper roofs where the flatter pitch this shorter material required was less recognised and less of a problem.

Steeply pitched thatch on a steeply pitched roof will shed water very efficiently, but stronger fixings are also required on such roofs to prevent the material from slipping out of place, particularly in the case of smooth-stemmed materials such as combed wheat reed and water reed. This is a particular danger with water reed whose stems are long and woody and consequently very heavy. The final dressing tightens the reed in its fixings 'like a tapered pin in a socket' and all but eliminates the risk of slippage. The extreme pitch of both the rafters and the reed on East Anglian houses ensures maximum longevity only as long as the fixings remain secure. It is for this reason that water reed roofs generally carry only one coat of reed, and that reed is never fixed to an underlying coat with spars, on a steeply pitched roof, as these are unable to hold the reed under sufficient tension to prevent it from slipping. Spar coating with water reed is successful in the West Country because the new reed is applied at very shallow pitch and is not dressed into position with the leggat as vigorously as in the Norfolk manner, and most importantly because the base coats of combed wheat reed offer a secure grip for the new spars (Appendix A: A11).

A similar situation exists with combed wheat reed. Although much shorter and lighter than water reed, it too can slip from its fixings when spar-coated onto a steeply pitched roof with a base coat that provides too little bite for the spars. Spars can also be loosened if the finished coat is dressed too vigorously with the leggat. In contrast to both reed straw and water reed, long straw thatch rarely suffers from slippage even on very steeply pitched roofs because it is flexible and bites the spars more securely.

The problem of slippage on reed straw and water reed roofs can be solved by the use of iron crooks and sways, but overly solid packing and fixing can also reduce a roof's ability to 'breathe' and release moisture from beneath the surface layer in dry weather. It is for a similar reason that water reed performs no better than good quality combed wheat reed on roofs in the West Country. The shallower pitch encourages the reed to absorb more water, and the woodier nature of the reed ensures that the stems do not dry out between wettings. This provides an ideal environment for fungal activity in which decay can proceed uninterrupted by climatic fluctuations. The water reed stem's greater natural resistance to decay relative to reed straw is thus countered by

Figure 53　Thatching straw (var. Maris Huntsman*) ready for harvesting, note the green nodes and 'rainbow' of colours in upper internodes (John Letts).* See also colour plate 1.

Figure 54　Stooking thatching straw cut with a reaper-binder, Somerton, Somerset (John Letts). See also colour plate 2.

the greater degree of fungal activity it supports, thereby eliminating any advantage it has in the eastern counties.

Material quality and longevity

Generally speaking, traditional West Country thatchers prefer combed wheat reed that is tall, straight, evenly tapered and free of leaf and weeds. The ideal straw stands 100cm–120cm in the field and produces a cut length of 90cm–110cm. Reed is considered unusable if it falls below 70cm, which is not far below the modern *c* 80cm–90cm average. Medieval reed straw in Devon ranged from 100–160cm (Letts 1999) judging by samples recovered from fleekings and underlays. Undegraded reed straw survives to be measured only if it is protected from weathering. Only one such example was recovered from the five reed straw roofs excavated during this project, a late nineteenth-century 100cm long straw that was used to fill a depression prior to the spar coating of a full top course on a building near Cullompton, Devon (Appendix A: A12). Most of the samples recovered were weathered to between 40cm–60cm (Appendix A: A3 Berks, A10/A11/A12 Devon, A13 Dorset), in practice, just before the fixings are exposed. This provides the basis for a direct calculation of a degradation quotient that may help to explain some of the reduction in longevity experienced by thatchers early this century. Accepting an average longevity figure of 25 years between recoats, a straw length of 100cm and the necessity of leaving at least *c* 50cm above and beneath the fixings, an average layer degrades at *c* 2cm per year, or 10cm every 5 years. As previously described shortening of straw length from *c* 120cm to 80cm between 1790 and 1940 would have reduced the longevity of a roof by about 20 years, ignoring the fact that the shorter material was also applied to a shallower pitch.

Thatchers tend to prefer pale-coloured straw with a dull shine and a waxy surface, and glossy reed is widely believed to reflect an over-generous use of nitrogen fertilizer. In reality, this sheen probably reflects genetic and climatic factors more than nutrient levels. Waxy straw will shed water more readily and absorb less water when being yealmed or wetted prior to application. Most

experienced thatchers will also choose a coarse wheat reed over a fine one even though the latter produces a better finish. Straw strength is thought to reflect durability and is usually measured by twisting a few strands into a coarse rope that is pulled until it breaks. Brittle reed will produce a frayed rope that breaks easily, whereas durable reed produces a strong and flexible rope. Hardness is also thought to reflect durability, and is assessed by the ease with which a stem can be crushed at its butt end. Good quality wheat reed is believed to have a distinct smell with little of the mustiness that indicates improper storage or the sweet smell of straw that has not been properly matured. High quality long straw shares many of the characteristics of good combed wheat reed with a greater emphasis on length and flexibility. Long straw must also be clean, evenly crushed and free of grain to stop it sprouting on the roof.

The best combed wheat reed and long straw are derived from slow-growing winter wheat, produced on fairly heavy and well-drained soils with low to moderate fertility. The straw must be harvested before it is fully ripe to stop the lignification of the stem, and left to ripen naturally for at least a few weeks in a stook or barn before being threshed or combed. The timing of the harvest is crucial. The genetic purity of modern varieties causes them to ripen very evenly within and between fields, which can cause problems when labour is not available in sufficient quantity or at short notice. The straw must be cut while the nodes are still green and a rainbow of colours separates the yellowing lower stem from the rapidly ripening ear (Figs 53 and 54). The grain must be cheesy whereas grain producers combine their crops when the grain is dead ripe.

The underlying edaphic and biological factors that govern the performance of thatched roofs have generally been constant. All organic material decays if sufficient moisture is present for microbial growth, which in thatch involves both ascomycete and basidiomycete-mediated decay (ie fungal white rot) of the cellulose in both the thatch and its fixings (Kirby & Rayner 1986; 1988). The processes involved are very similar to those operating in a natural ecosystem such as forest, or perhaps more accurately, a grassland such as a tall-grass prairie with a

Figure 55 Water reed (John Letts). See also colour plate 3.

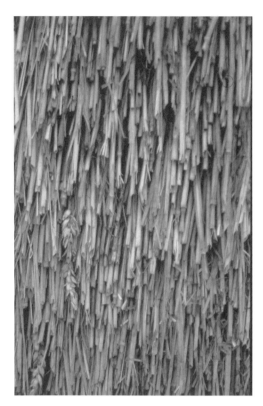

Figure 57 Long straw (John Letts). See also colour plate 5.

Figure 56 Combed wheat reed (John Letts). See also colour plate 4.

Figure 58 Fen sedge (John Letts). See also colour plate 6.

fluctuating moisture regime and a straw-rich litter layer. Fungal communities in such habitats can develop in many directions, and fungi adopt different life strategies depending on the resources that are present. The rate of fungal growth is obviously influenced by temperature, pH and the availability of nutrients, but its main determinant is obviously moisture. A thatched roof works because the material on its outer face has been processed and applied in such a way that moisture levels, and hence the rate of decay, beneath the surface are reduced sufficiently for the material to be considered a viable roofing material. The decay has been controlled, but not arrested.

Thatch can be made from any material that can be stacked in such a manner that its constituent segments overlap to form a tiled surface that sheds water efficiently (Figs 55–58). Any technical or material change that improves the speed at which water falling onto the ridge is carried to the eave and thrown clear of the roof will reduce the availability of moisture for fungal growth and extend the longevity of the roof. The *in situ* evidence demonstrates that thatch can survive for over five centuries in almost perfect condition as long as it remains dry, but it will then degrade as quickly as any compost heap when sufficient moisture becomes available for microbial growth. Multi-layered roofs invariably contain thick layers and pockets of decay that are botanically unrecognisable even under the microscope.

A thatched ridge fails not so much because the thatch itself has decayed, but because the exposed wooden spars and liggers that hold it in place have degraded and no longer provide a secure fixing. Identical spars and roundwood sways are sheltered within the main course and remain viable for centuries. The quality of the fixings, or more specifically, the degree to which they absorb water and resist fungal decay, is thus as important in determining the longevity of a ridge as the ridging material itself. As a result, it is the quality of the external fixings that determined the longevity of the external peg and rope thatch so prevalent in England in the last century, and speculation as to the quality of the straw employed is largely immaterial. Such roofs are unlikely to have lasted any longer than an average ridge, perhaps six to eight years, depending on whether the spars were cut from good quality hazel coppice or from assorted woody species from the hedgerow.

Fungal activity depends upon the presence of moisture, but its intensity is conditioned by additional factors including nutrients such as nitrogen. Nitrate fertilizers have been linked to poor performance in both combed wheat reed and water reed thatch. This issue becomes a matter of concern only towards the end of the period under review as in the past nitrogen inputs were rarely so inexpensive that they could be applied in as generous or wasteful a manner as they are today.

The longevity figures presented in *The Thatcher's Craft* of 'Water reed, 50 to 60 years; Combed wheat reed, 25 to 40 years; Long straw, 10 to 20 years' (Morgan & Cooper 1960, [vi]), have been used in debate, in publications and for marketing purposes even though they were heavily caveated and are widely known to be misleading, particularly with regard to long straw. The 10 to 20 year figure is probably more appropriate for water reed used in the West Country, or even for poor quality combed wheat reed in East Anglia. The evidence suggests that it is the middle figure of 25 to 40 years that more accurately describes the average longevity of long straw. In truth, all longevity figures can be grossly misleading, because the underlying factors that condition performance vary tremendously from building to building and from region to region.

The 40 to 60 years suggested by the RIB in 1953 is probably average for a roof of good quality Norfolk reed in East Anglia, but the figures decrease considerably with corresponding reductions in roof pitch. Forty years for combed wheat reed seems realistic in the West Country, but the higher figure reflects its longevity only on steeper

roofs. The reed on the northern half-hip of Homestill Cottage near Coleford, Devon (Appendix B: B19) has shed water efficiently ever since it was applied in 1936. Combed wheat reed would undoubtedly perform well on steeply-pitched roofs in the Midlands and East Anglia when fixed in a way that prevents it from slipping, but without having been packed so tightly that it cannot breathe. Long straw may well have survived for only ten years on many roofs in the Midlands and southern England in the 1940s when straw quality hit rock bottom. According to an article on Dorset thatch written in 1939:

> A little further to the east [of Abbotsbury], and also to the north (in the New Forest and up in Berkshire, for example), there was thatch in which many of the straws had the heads or ears pointing downwards. It was called 'tatt-entail' (top-and-tail?), and was said to last from six to twelve years. It looked vastly inferior to Devon thatch. (Ward 1939, 431)

Roofs in East Anglia thatched with long straw in the early 1940s continue to protect the base coats of crushed straw beneath them (Stanford, pers comm). A 20 to 30 year figure is probably more accurate for long straw, and although the lower value may better reflect the situation in the Midlands and shallower-pitched roofs in the southern counties, nowhere does it drop today to the lower figure offered by *The Thatcher's Craft*.

Longevity estimates in the literature for water reed range from a century for a reed roof in Norfolk (Albino 1946, 68) to only 15 years for a south Dorset cottage thatched with Abbotsbury spear (Ward 1939, 431). According to Marshall in 1807 a reed roof would last 50 years without any attention and another 30 to 40 with only minor repair and redressing (anon 1807, **2**, Thatch). Cowell believed that a roof of Norfolk reed would last 60 to 70 years 'if cleaned down and knocked up about once in 7 years' (Cambridgeshire Record Office 1). Boardman (1933, 567) was a little more generous in claiming 80 years, but few modern reed thatchers in East Anglia will offer a figure of more than 40 or 50 years (David Farman, pers comm). The figures hover around 25 to 30 years for reed straw and from 10 to 50 years for long straw (anon 1807, **2**, Thatch; Rudge 1813, 46; Albino 1946, 68), but the lower figures for long straw are, once again, a reflection of the situation in the 1940s and 1950s rather than the last century or more recent decades.

Orientation

Many people would instinctively suggest that a thatched roof will degrade more quickly on its north face than on the south because the northern aspect is inevitably wetter, colder and more covered with moss and lichen. In fact, the southern face of a thatched roof will usually degrade more quickly because rapid changes in temperature can occur at the surface of a thatched roof when it is first struck by the warming rays of the sun (Peter Brockett, pers comm). This temperature explosion not only stimulates fungal activity, but also apparently pumps moisture towards the core of the outside layer of thatch in a manner not yet fully understood. This moisture stimulates microbial activity beneath the surface and increases the rate of decay. Micro-climatic conditions are much more stable on the north face of a roof, however, and although the roof may often be much wetter on this side, it is also usually cooler so that fungal activity proceeds steadily but at a slower rate.

This aspect-induced differential in decay has had a significant impact on the record of thatch that survives *in situ*. In the past, roofs were generally rethatched when required and not simply when they had begun to look a little weatherbeaten. This might usually involve patching only the most decayed portion of a north face, but an entire rethatch of the south face. As a result, the north face of a roof whose main axis runs east/west can often provide a much better preserved and stratified sequence than its southern face whose earlier layers are almost always patched and pocketed by decay. The chronological build-up on one face may thus only partially reflect the materials and methods used on the other. Eleven of the 20 buildings recorded in detail for this report presented this potentially significant difference in aspect. Sequential series of samples were obtained from the northern faces of eight – two of which also provided samples from the southern face, but only because these two buildings were derelict (Appendix A: A17, A19).

Maintenance

Maintenance and repair have always been an essential part of the thatcher's craft and provided more of his bread and butter in the past than in recent decades. In the nineteenth century, however, the distinction between maintenance and rethatching was blurred by the propensity to patch or rethatch sections rather than recoat entire roofs as in the present day. The approach was largely functional. A thatcher would have maintained the roofs in his patch on an annual basis, replacing wooden fixings, repairing ridges, removing moss and lichen and patching gulleys and bird holes as required to keep out the rain. Larger surfaces were rethatched when straw (and labour) were abundant or when the burden of regular and extensive patching began to outweigh the cost and effort of complete recoating. Appearance was much less of a concern than it is today, particularly on ancillary buildings, but it had become a more important factor in the equation by 1940. A golden patch of new straw contrasts sharply with a worn main coat. It is now a common perception that the presence of patching implies that the home owner does not have the resources to maintain the roof in an immaculate state, or by inference, the status and lifestyle now associated with owning a thatched house. Modern roofs usually receive a complete recoating even though only a small portion of the roof might actually require attention. The chronological build-ups that have survived therefore reflect a chronic state of patching and repair within a longer cycle of more extensive rethatching. Unfortunately, it can be difficult to differentiate between a patch and a full spar coat when a sample is observed only briefly during a rescue excavation.

In the past, as today, most repair work would have been directed towards the weak points of a roof, the ridge, gables, valleys, dormer windows, eaves, bird holes, depressions and gulleys that gradually develop in response to wind damage, uneven runoff and decay. Repairs were often made with materials different from those used in the main coat. The *in situ* evidence indicates that straw roofs were patched with pasture rush (Appendix A: A5, A14), grass (Appendix A: A5, A14; Appendix B: B3), river rush (Appendix A: A6), flax (Appendix B: B1) or straw (Appendix A: A3, A9, A11, A17; Appendix B: B26, B39) and degraded sections of straw thatch have been replaced with water reed (Appendix A: A18). In Long Hanborough, Oxfordshire (Appendix B: B39) a patch of crushed straw was fixed to a coat of similar material by a course of mud in combination with spars. Whatever the material used,

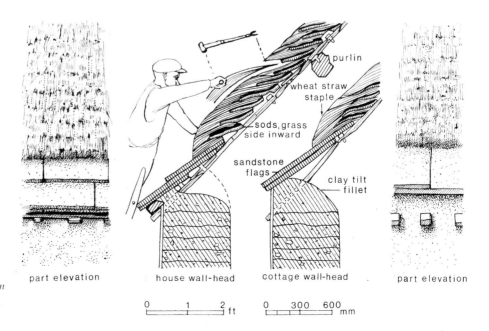

Figure 59 *Thrust or stapple thatch in Cumberland (Judith Dobie, after Harrison 1989, 145).*

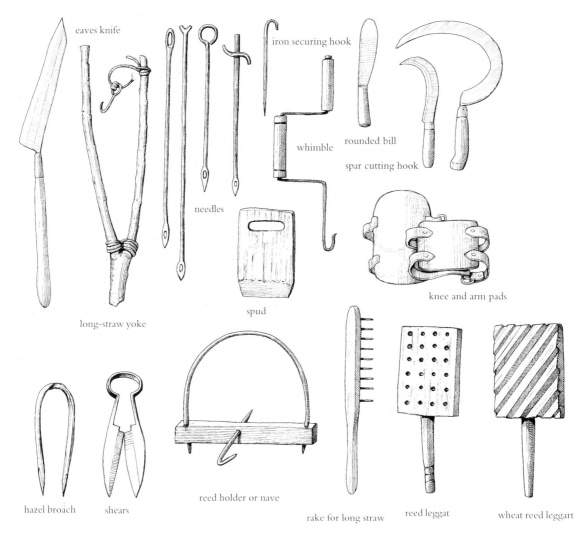

eaves knife

iron securing hook

whimble

rounded bill

spar cutting hook

needles

knee and arm pads

long-straw yoke

spud

hazel broach   shears

reed holder or nave

rake for long straw   reed leggat   wheat reed leggart

Figure 60 Thatching tools used by long straw, combed wheat reed and water reed thatchers (Judith Dobie, after Seymour 1984).

it was applied in overlapping courses as in the main coat, and its spars and sways could either be hidden at each course (except the uppermost) or applied externally.

Bird holes in straw roofs were blocked by simply stuffing a fist-sized stob of thatch into position. Holes in combed wheat reed and water reed roofs were blocked by pulling out a rim of reed surrounding the hole and dressing the new plug and rim back into position with a leggat (Jobson 1949, 1187). A similar ancient, but poorly

Figure 61 Patched and moss-covered thatch in Kent, late nineteenth century (Quinton 1993, copyright J Salmon Ltd, Sevenoaks, England).

documented, thatching technique that appears to have been common in parts of England in the past involved forcing handfuls of new reed, stubble or other stiff material into a worn main coat where it was then held in position without additional fixings (Fig 59). The new material was forced into a gap created by a short, flat-bladed tool known as a spud. A long-bladed version, used within living memory to locate rafters when crooking new reed into place, survived in the tool kits of some reed thatchers until early this century (Fig 60). The spud is often confused with a similar technique of stinging or stuffing flexible thatching materials into position using a forked spartle (spurtle, crammer, gillet, swallow-tail or battledore), a technique still used in parts of northern England.

Older records suggest that build-ups of moss and lichen were common on thatched roofs in the last century (Fig 61). In fact, many nineteenth-century roofs could probably have been described as successional ecotones because of the wide variety of species that seem to have colonized them. Pitt mentioned the presence of stonecrop on thatched roofs in Northamptonshire in the early nineteenth century.

To Charwelton ... the farmhouses crowded in villages a whole parish together. Many houses thatched, and the

Plate 1. Thatching straw (var. Maris Huntsman*) ready for harvesting (NB green nodes and 'rainbow' of colours in upper internodes (John Letts).* See also Figure 53, p 96.

Plate 2. Stooking thatching straw cut with a reaper-binder, Somerton, Somerset (John Letts). See also Figure 54, p 96

Plate 3. Water reed (John Letts). See also Figure 55, p 97.

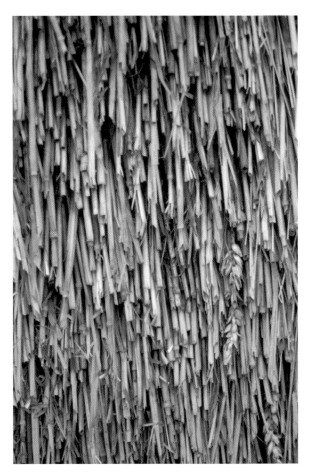

Plate 5. Long straw (John Letts). See also Figure 57, p 97.

Plate 4. Combed wheat reed (John Letts). See also Figure 56 , p 97.

Plate 6. Fen sedge (John Letts). See also Figure 58 p 97.

Plate 7. Moss and lichen colonizing a long straw roof in Bedfordshire (Appendix A: A2 Beds) (John Letts). See also Figure 62, p 101.

Plate 8. External liggering applied to a sedge ridge on a water reed roof (Appendix B: B30 Lingwood, Norfolk) (John Letts). See also Figure 70, p 106.

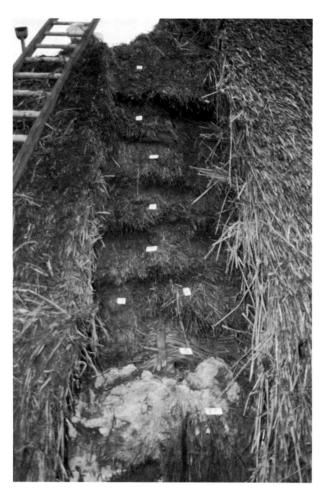

Plate 9. Stepped trench excavation of late medieval to modern thatch (Appendix A: A15, Great Doddington, Northamptonshire) (John Letts).See also Figure 94, p 130.

Plate 10. Thatch excavation: exposed ridge section with layers of clay (Appendix A: A15, Great Doddington, Northamptonshire) (John Letts). See also Figure 95, p 130.

Plate 11. Thatch excavation: decayed ridge with 'hedgehog' display of spars (Appendix A: A18, Bacton, Suffolk) (John Letts). See also Figure 96, p 131.

roofs abounding with house-leek, and different species of stone-crop. (Pitt 1809a, 297)

Straw thatch could be raked and water reed roofs re-dressed to remove excessive buildups of moss and lichen and reestablish a shaggy water-shedding coat (Fig 62). Many thatchers believe that this cleaning reduces the longevity of a roof, for removing moss and lichen exposes more thatch to the elements and perhaps increasing the moisture pumping effect previously described. Moss and lichen certainly interfere with the downflow of water and provide a more stable environment for fungal growth, but they also reduce the impact of UV light, heat and the physical damage of rain droplets. This situation is compli-cated by the use of wire netting, which has been used since early this century to prevent bird and rodent damage, particularly on long straw roofs in the Midlands and East Anglia. Unfortunately, netting can trap frag-ments of straw, leaves and other debris whose breakdown provides nutrients for accelerated fungal growth. Some thatchers believe that the danger of damage by birds is greatly exaggerated, and was never a problem in the past. Others have been known to mix lime or sandy grit with straw to discourage nesting and foraging activities (Peter Brockett, pers comm).

HEATHLAND AND 'SOLID' THATCH

In situ evidence of heathland thatching traditions now survives in the south primarily as base coats of heather or broom in multi-layered straw-thatched buildings in the New Forest and Dartmoor, and very rarely in semi-derelict barns and cottages in the north. None of these buildings was examined as part of this project, and the following discussion is based primarily on historical evidence.

Broom *(Cytisus scoparius)*

Broom formed an ideal base for a spar coat of straw, as it was a firm, tightly packed material that provided good bite for spars driven into it. As a top coat it would have functioned like straw or reed, whether it was tied to the roof in courses with sways, spar-coated to an existing base or clamped in place between the members of a wattled base.

Heather *(Calluna vulgaris)*

Heather's coarse and woody structure forced it to be used in a broadly similar way wherever its abundance allowed its use in thatching, whether as a base coat or as an external coat. The best heath for external use was long, straight-stemmed and stood 2' (60cm) in the field or slightly longer after 'pulling' (Collier 1831, 190–5; Hartley & Ingilby 1978, 1022). Grazed heather could be used as a base coat over brushwood or battens, but not as a top coat as it would not shed water efficiently due to its more dissected stems. It occurs only in the base coats of eighteenth- and nineteenth-century straw-thatched build-ings in the New Forest (T. Whiteley, pers comm), perhaps because of intensive grazing in this area. A

Figure 62 Moss and lichen colonizing a long straw roof in Bedfordshire (Appendix A: A2 Beds) (John Letts). See also colour plate 7.

heather thatch settles gradually over time, and its per-formance actually increases as it acquires the sombre, dark colour that gave it the name of black thatch in the north east (Chapman 1982, 9; Emery 1986, 91).

External heather thatch was often supported on a base of brushwood overlain by a layer of turf, as at Fell Close Farm, Durham (Emery 1986, 91–6). The heather was laid in courses as in straw thatching, stem side up, which were fixed with turf, clay, rope, spars, pegs or nails. There seems to have been a propensity to fix heather from the outside rather than tie it to the roof structure, due either to a lack of resources to pay for a second thatcher inside the roof, or more likely to the difficulty of stitching through a thick layer of branched and woody heather underlain by a layer of sod and a base coat of brushwood. Whatever the fixing method employed, the finished roof showed no external liggering on the main coat although the ridge was capped with heather and liggered as in any straw roof.

One of the best descriptions of heather thatching was compiled by J Graham at the end of the nineteenth century at Low Ashhead on the moors between Masham and Nidderdale in the North Yorkshire Dales (Hartley & Ingilby 1978, 1022). The thatching of this roof was paid at the same rate as the pulling of the heather it consumed. Both were measured in threave each containing 24 loggens (or bundles) composed of five handfuls of stems bound by a heather band. Five threave were pulled, and 20 applied, to a roof in one day, and from 200 to 400 threave were required to thatch one roof. The usual practice was to lay a layer of flagstones on top of the wall (usually of clay) to protect it from water. The rafters were laid to a very steep pitch with battens fixed at 15" (38cm) intervals. Loggens were laid roots upwards in courses, and heavy stones were applied to each course for a few hours to force the heather to bed down prior to fixing with hazel spars and sways. The gap at the ridge was bridged by heather wrapped 3' (92cm) wide over the apex in small bundles alternating in their orientation in terms of roots and flowering end. Turves about 6' (1.8m) long x 1' (30cm) wide x 3" (7cm) thick and cut preferentially from a 'rooty bog surface growing bilberry' (Hartley & Ingilby 1978, 1022) were laid tile fashion over the ridge with a 6" (15cm) overlap and pegged down with 18"–24" (46cm–61cm) hazel pegs. As with all thatch, the pegs were driven in horizontally and slightly upwards to prevent the ingress of water. The barges were also pegged down with spars and sways, and the thatch was sheared with a sharp blade or scythe to produce a smooth finished coat.

At Hurst, County Durham, at about the same time, heather was laid onto a roof battened with thin branches that were nailed vertically at about 12" (30cm) intervals between two horizontal purlins. The heather was applied in 'gangs' (courses) tied to the battens and purlins using 'spelks' (sways) and straw rope. A heather ridge was pegged flush without an overcoat of turf (Hartley & Ingilby 1968, 166; 1978, 1024). The most approved method of fixing, recommended in part because of its immunity to attack by mice and rats, involved sealing every two or three courses to the underlying turf with clay, followed by a ridge capping of clay mixed with straw and again covered by turf. At Rothbury, Northumberland, in 1760 houses were said to be

> mostly thatched ... cover[ed] with sods for warmth, and thatch[ed] with heath, which will last thirty years. (Hodgson 1914, 223; and see pp15 and 46, this volume)

Heather could also be used in combination with straw, as in mid nineteenth-century Lancashire, where heather was sparred over straw on a gable to improve the longevity of the roof at this point (Lancashire Record Office 1/7).

A worn-out roof of heather could be renewed either by spar coating, or by stinging a new coat of heather into the existing coat using a forked implement of wood or iron. This was an essential part of the thatcher's tool kit in heather districts, and roofs were patched and repaired on a regular basis as with straw roofs. Individual branches were simply pushed into the existing thatch and the new material was held in place by friction, interlocking branches and the pressure of the thatch above it (Hartley & Ingilby 1978, 1024). As with straw roofs, regular re-stinging and maintenance made it difficult to estimate the average longevity of a coat of heather, but figures of about 30 years or a little less seem to have been accepted by contemporary writers.

The performance of a heather roof was more dependent on proper ventilation and air circulation than straw or reed thatch because heather soaks up more water in its woodier leaves and stems and thus takes much longer to dry out after being wetted. In fact, heather thatch functions in a very different way from straw or reed thatch. As with all thatched roofs, the battle on a heather roof is to move water laterally towards the eaves as quickly as possible in order to reduce its rate of infiltration due to simple gravitational forces. Heather provides a much less successful barrier to water ingress, but at every millimetre it descends rainfall is met by thousands of stems and leaves held at a pitch that help channel water towards the eaves. A 3' (92cm) thick layer at the ridge simply provides an additional time factor for this lateral flow to occur before water infiltrates to an unacceptable degree. Several feet of heather on the eaves would provide no additional protection as the water would already have seeped a considerable distance into the roof by the time it reached the eaves. To improve the speed of lateral flow, and as a result of the need to lay more material on the ridge, heather roofs were always very steeply pitched (55°–60°). According to Hartley & Ingilby (1986, 55), many of the barns on the Yorkshire Dales had their gables raised at the eaves to slacken the pitch when their heather thatch was replaced by slates.

Bracken *(Pteridium aquilinum)*

Bracken was once widely used for thatching both in northern and southern England. Campbell (1831, 184–90) provides one of our only descriptions of bracken thatching, and the English method of application is unlikely to have differed greatly from the Scottish method he describes. Whichever way it was used, the fronds were pulled rather than cut while the stems were still yellowish, and before the first frosts, so that they retained some flexibility. The first step in rethatching was to consolidate the existing coat, stripping off vegetation and filling holes and gulleys to ensure a solid base for the new spar coat:

> Before beginning to lay on the thatch, it is necessary to pull out all the tufts of grass and weeds that may have grown on the roof, and then sweep it with the branch of a birch tree. (Campbell 1831, 186)

'Long turfs taken from rough ground' were applied to the wall tops, and a 5"–6" (13cm–15cm) thick brow course of cut bracken was secured 'by introducing their points under the turfs ... to answer the same purpose as the first course of slating ... called the "easing"'. The main coat was then applied in courses, in Campbell's description using a *c* 20' (6m) beam stretched between two ladders which acted both as a support for the thatcher and as a guide to ensure an even depth of application. Half a dozen stalks were stripped of branches towards their root end and adjusted so that their upper tips were in line. Each handful was then bent 'almost to breaking ... to make them lie the closer' and applied root-end up with the tips of the fronds resting on the beam. Once the beam was covered, the thatcher would raise one end of it up the ladder 6"–8" (15cm–20cm), descend this ladder and pick up more bracken, climb up the second ladder and raise the beam at this end, and then apply the next beam-course in like fashion. The ridge was eventually capped with turf (Campbell 1831, 186–7).

> The next object of consideration is to secure the thatch from being blown off by the wind – a matter of greater importance than would appear to be attached to it, from the number of accidents of this kind that occur. The degree of precaution to be adopted ... must depend in a great measure on the situation of the building ... if exposed to strong gusts ... the best thing for securing thatch is ropes made of heath, or pliant birch-twigs ... one set of ropes running from side to side over the roof, and fastened by wooden pins put into the turf covering the side-walls, and the other set running horizontally along the roof, and fastened into the turf on the gables. Where these ropes are not to be had conveniently, light spars made of common fir may be substituted in their place. Where ... less security is required, the same substances may be used, only in much smaller quantity. Care should always be taken, where pins are driven into the thatch, that they be made to slant *upwards*. (Campbell 1831, 188)

Campbell was well aware of the fact that a roof performed better if steeply pitched, but shallower roofs were also less susceptible to wind change. The pitch was increased with the application of every spar coat 'so that, by the time a house gets a third covering, the slope which was originally 6" below the square, comes to the square itself' (ibid). We are also told that an 'active' man could pull a cart-load of bracken each day, which would cover just over six square yards of roof. An average house 40' x 13' (12.2m x 4.0m) carried a roof of 115.5 square yards (96m²), consumed 18 cart-loads of bracken and took an experienced man 17 days to thatch.

> If done properly, and by an experienced hand ... [bracken] will last on the south or sunny side of a house for eighteen or twenty years (in some instances it has been known to endure for thirty years); while, on the north side, its duration cannot be calculated on much beyond eight or ten years ... If the house, however, were built north and south, as barns generally are, the duration of the thatch on *both sides* might be reckoned on for ... eighteen or twenty years. (op cit, 188–9)

Wilson (1871, **1**, 525) claimed a 15 to 20 year lifespan for a bracken thatch. The figures suggest that bracken performed differently from straw in terms of its decay, as straw will generally survive longest on a north face. Bracken perhaps provided a barrier to the pumping effect that forces moist air up the stems of tubular materials such as water reed and straw when they are struck by the first warming rays of the sun. This moisture carries fungal activity in its wake, and straw and reed thatch therefore decay more slowly on a north face where the sun never shines. Bracken is a very different material from straw in a structural sense, and it inevitably degrades in a different

way, or, more properly, is degraded by a different group of fungal decomposers whose activities may have been more constrained on the relatively warmer and drier southern side of a roof. Indeed, Holt, writing of Lancashire, considered bracken to be the best material available for thatching 'being naturally dry, and not apt to ferment like straw' (Holt 1795, 16).

Innocent (1916, 214) observed bracken being used as an undercoat in buildings near Sheffield, Yorkshire, as a base for a layer of sods, and also as a base for a straw thatch. These roofs are thought to have been copied from examples their owners had observed in adjacent Derbyshire.

Gorse (*Ulex europaeus*)

Although it could not be used as a top coat, gorse is nevertheless the most important component of what was one of the most historically significant thatched roofs recorded over the course of this project, the solid thatch of gorse that until 1995 formed the roof of an early nineteenth-century cart shed at Stanton St John, Oxfordshire (Appendix A: A17). The gorse used in this roof was cut in the late summer from mature bushes or small trees and tied into 25lb (11.3kg) faggots with hazel and gorse bonds. These faggots contained a considerable amount of the bracken that must have grown alongside the gorse, along with mature stems of field bean (*Vicia sativa* ssp *minor*) whose presence remains a mystery. These faggots were stacked onto beams spanning the wall plates to form a flattened pyramid of solid gorse, capped by several ridge-rolls of hawthorn and several overcoats of straw thatch.

Solid thatch

Roofs have been identified throughout much of England where the stacked material is of brushwood, threshed stems of broad beans, straw bales or several other materials so that the phenomenon of solid thatch is not restricted to the use of gorse. They were once quite common and the very few that have survived perhaps provide one of our closest links to the rough-hewn houses of our ancestors in prehistory. Most solid thatched roofs seem to have been quite shallowly pitched. The external thatch on the cart shed in Stanton St John, Oxfordshire, sloped at about 37° on its eastern face and 42° on the west, in contrast to the steep *c* 50° faces of its internal core.

The Stanton St John example is one of the few solid thatch roofs to have come up for analysis or repair in the past decade, but other examples, mostly derelict or recently destroyed, have been noted in recent years in Gloucestershire, Oxfordshire, Leicestershire, Suffolk, Devon, Somerset, Sussex, Hertfordshire, Northamptonshire and Lincolnshire. That any original examples have survived into the modern era is a testament to their structural success, as well as their adaptability, for in at least one example (at Harwell, Oxfordshire) what began life as a cart shed has functioned successfully for generations as a very well-insulated cottage. All those that have survived are threatened with destruction through neglect or by repair that invariably replaces the solid thatch with

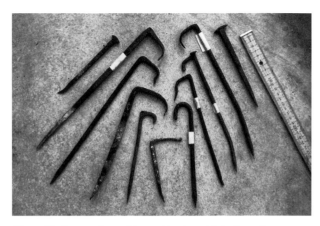

Figure 63 Iron crooks used in combination with horizontal sways (John Letts).

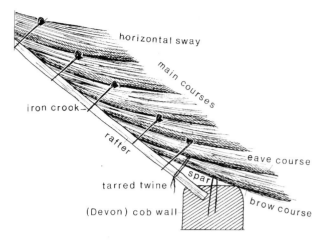

Figure 64 Fixing thatch with iron crooks and sways to a cob wall (Judith Dobie, after John Letts).

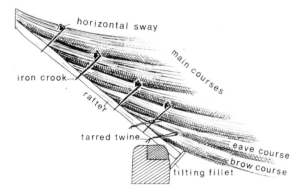

Figure 65 Fixing thatch with iron crooks and sways, with inserted 'tilting fillet' (Judith Dobie, after John Letts).

a standard roof of rafters and battens. Solid thatched roofs encapsulate a true vernacular tradition in which local resources were used to provide shelter for man or beast with minimal expenditure or embellishment. On permanent structures solid thatch provided a dry, warm and most importantly breathable roof that eliminated the problem of condensation that occurs in less well ventilated barns with stone or tiled roofs. Temporary helms were often used to store the harvest or the unthreshed sheaves bearing the seed grain for the next year's planting, and would not have been used to shelter animals at the same time. They would also have been topped by a rick thatch designed to last no more than a couple of seasons (Meirion-Jones 1976, 50; Airs 1981; Meeson & Welch 1993).

The most common core materials in solid thatch roofs seem to have been gorse, brushwood, hedge clippings, heather, bean stalks and bundles of straw, but almost any bulky material would probably have sufficed. In the Second World War farmers were encouraged to use hay bales for temporary shelters and to thatch them with straw (Peters 1977).

THATCHING WITH WATER REED

Water reed (*Phragmites australis*)

Water reed thatch is generally associated with East Anglia, but a more focused study of thatching in the region would demonstrate that there was considerable diversity in the methods and materials used, including the common use of 'crushed straw' for main coat thatching as well as ridging, even in the heart of the Broadlands (Peter Brockett, pers comm; Kent 1796, 163). Traditionally, Norfolk reed arrives in bundles that vary in coarseness and range from 3' to 9' (0.9m–2.7m) in length; short, strongly tapered bundles are saved for ridge courses and for turning hips, valleys and corners, whereas longer reed is used to fill valleys and for main coat work.

The method used to apply water reed in the early 1960s, which, as with straw, reflects nineteenth-century practice, is described in *The Thatcher's Craft*. It is applied in courses running up the roof from eaves to ridge. Particular care is taken to ensure that the first eaves and gable courses are securely fixed as they provide the

footing for all subsequent courses. It is still standard practice to tie in this first course with strong cord. The rafter feet of older buildings in East Anglia were inserted just inside the outer edge of the wall plate so that bundles laid and fixed in line with the rafters would be kicked up by the outer edge of the wall. A similar situation was provided by a raised gable wall or barge board, although thatched roofs in many areas have traditionally been hipped. A bundle of semi-woody reeds offers considerable resistance to being bowed at its centre, and it is the tension produced by this camber that is carried up the roof at every course and forces each new bundle to bed firmly onto the reed below it. Such a kick is unnecessary when reed is fixed as a single coat onto a shallow pitched roof without dressing, or as a spar coat over straw, but a tilting fillet is routinely added to the eaves of formerly straw-thatched roofs when these are stripped and converted to reed, in order to create the necessary camber.

The first gable course is either tied into place in the same way as the eaves course, or is fixed with 'sways and crooks'. Sways were traditionally hazel or willow rods about 2cm–3cm in diameter. Each bundle of reed applied along the gable is wedged under the sway, which is then clamped at intervals to the gable plate by long iron nails with hooked tops called crooks (Fig 63). Traditionally, these crooks were hand smithed and used in situations where normal tying was not possible or insecure for material and manufacturing costs could be prohibitive.

Figure 67 Overhanging barge of water reed with an adjacent 'rolled' barge of straw, Great Brington, Northamptonshire (John Letts).

Figure 66 Dressing water reed with a leggat, Crediton, Devon (John Letts).

A brow course is laid over the first eaves course and held in position temporarily with a few strands of reed pegged to the underlying eaves course with steel pins or twisted wooden spars, called broaches in Norfolk. When a few bundles are in their final position, they are fixed permanently to the roof with sways and crooks that are nailed into the rafters. This basic procedure is carried up the roof in courses, each bundle being applied in line with the material below it and running as close to vertical as possible to ensure that rain runs off the roof as rapidly as possible (Figs 64 and 65). A thatcher must also ensure that every bundle of reed applied is bedded imperceptibly into the bundle adjoining it in order to prevent the formation of gaps that could channel water and lead to premature decay.

A backfill of loose reed is tucked in between the top of every new course and the underlying battens. This lifts the apex of the fixed course and hence tightens the bundles at their butt ends. More importantly, it provides a solid base over which individual stems can slide when they are dressed into position with a leggat, a flat, nail-studded mallet unique to the craft (Fig 66). Loose reed can be moulded into an acceptable shape with just the hands, but the sharp woody butts limit the pressure that can be applied without dressing. Dressing forces the reeds up into their fixings, and since the reed is tapered it becomes tighter in its fixings the further back it is driven. Attaining the correct tension evenly over the face of the

roof so that wear will occur evenly is a skill acquired through years of practice. The leggat is also used to dress the eaves and gables into position, unlike long straw and combed wheat reed thatch in which these are moulded into place but eventually cut to the desired shape. Gables are usually dressed square with the gable wall, whereas an eaves overhang is created of sufficient depth to allow runoff to drip free of the wall tops while minimizing the surface which is then exposed to damaging winds, 10" (25cm) usually being sufficient (Fig 67). Reed is usually applied to provide a depth of between 10"–14" (25cm – 35cm) to the top of the fixing, but each roof will have an optimum depth that reflects the range of technical factors that will govern its performance.

Although the bulk of the reed on a roof is applied in the relatively straightforward procedure described above, greater caution is exercised when courses are swept around chimneys and dormers to ensure that the reed always lies as steeply pitched and near to the vertical as possible. Additional packing is used to lift the valley and create a wider surface to disperse the downflow that concentrates at such points, and lead or mortar flashing is used to provide an additional seal at the joints between reed and brick or stone. Anything that interferes with the downflow of water poses a potential challenge to the longevity of a thatched roof. The ridge, in particular, must be applied with great care achieving a balance between the aesthetic demands of the home owner and performance.

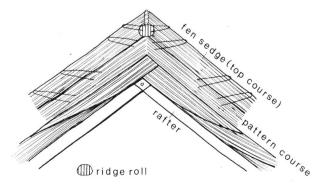

Figure 68 Schematic cross-section of a sedge ridge (Judith Dobie, after John Letts).

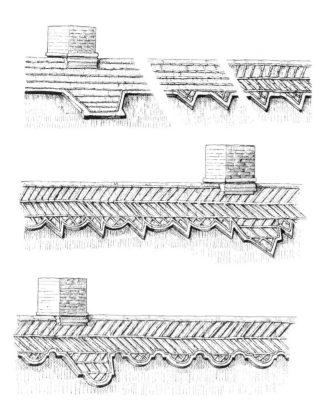

Figure 69 Designs for external liggering used on ridge of a water reed roof (Judith Dobie, after Boardman 1933).

Ridging

Reed is an inflexible material that, unlike straw, cannot be bent over the crest of a roof to form a ridge. In England reed ridges are almost always made from fen sedge (*Cladium mariscus*), although crushed straw seems to have been the most common material employed until early this century. Their methods of application are broadly similar, and they are occasionally used in combination when a heavily patterned ridge is required (Fig 68). Special treatment of the ridge begins with the final courses of reed applied to the main coat. The first course to oversail the apex of the ridge is cut flush with the angle of the exposed rafters on the other side of the roof. The top course of reed on the other side is then fixed with its apex nestled snugly against the cut face of this first coat, with any oversailing reed being trimmed to form a tight crest. A skirt course of sedge, previously yealmed to draw the leaves into alignment and eliminate short segments and detritus, is sparred onto this reed to a handful's depth. A ridge roll of water reed about 6" (15cm) in diameter running the entire length of the ridge is sparred into the sedge and underlying reed to provide a relatively narrow crest over which to wrap the final top coat of sedge. The bundles making up this top coat of sedge are forced tightly together to prevent any water from penetrating to the underlying layers, again avoiding gaps or flat areas that could interfere with the flow of water off the roof.

The top coat of a ridge is fixed with a series of liggers, wooden sways split into two, and broaches, the first running along the crest of the ridge from gable to gable (Figs 69 and 70). Two or three additional liggers are usually fixed on either side of the crest joined by cross-rods producing a herring-bone or 'diamented' pattern, with great care being taken to insert the broaches horizontally and at an angle to avoid creating gaps or directing water towards the interior of the ridge. In some areas, additional sedge is built into a raised pinnacle on the apex

Figure 70 External liggering applied to a sedge ridge on a water reed roof (Appendix B: B30 Lingwood, Norfolk) (John Letts). See also colour plate 8.

Figure 71 Stitching long straw, c 1940 (Museum of English Rural Life).

of a gable because the underlying sedge at this point lies almost horizontally and is thus subject to more rapid decay. Additional patterning is provided by trimming the skirt course down to the surface of the main coat of reed a few inches below the bottom ligger producing a raised block effect, traditionally along a straight edge but more commonly today with a scalloped or jagged edge. The roof is finished with a last trimming of the sedge cap and a redressing of the main coat where required. Some thatchers wire their sedge ridges to avoid bird damage, but the sharply serrated edges of sedge leaves provide a natural barrier to the depredations of birds and rodents, and wiring is an advantage only on older ridges where the sedge has softened through decay and the spars and liggers have degraded. At this point, a new ridge must be applied, and the main coat repaired and redressed, the latter outliving the former by a factor of at least three to one.

Tying

A secondary way of fixing, tying sways using a thatcher's needle, tarred cord and an apprentice (Figs 71 and 72) is described by Deas.

In many old buildings, especially in the Broads district, sways were tied down with brambles, but nowadays there are two alternatives – three-thread jute (spun yarn or 'spunnion') or iron hooks. It is for the former that the thatcher has his binding needle, the procedure being as follows; The spun-yarn is first tied to a sway, then threaded through the eye of the needle and after a rafter has been located by prodding, the thread is pushed through thatch and flaking to the thatcher's boy. He passes the spun-yarn around the rafter and re-threads the needle which is then drawn up again by the thatcher who again ties the spun-yarn to the sway so that two knots occur the width of a rafter apart. This occurs at every rafter, great care being taken to see that the sway is held tightly. Under no circumstances are sways bound to the battens. If the rafters have been boarded, or for any other reason tying is impracticable, sways must be held down with iron hooks spiked into the boards or rafters. (1939, 105)

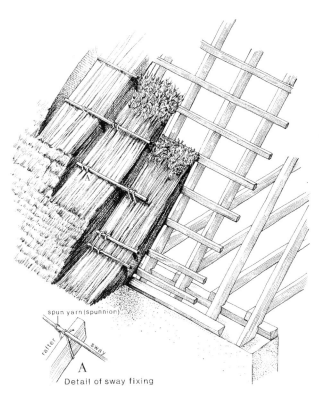

spun yarn (spunnion)

rafter

sway

A

Detail of sway fixing

Figure 72 Method of stitching water reed in Norfolk (Judith Dobie, after Boardman 1933).

Tying to battens facilitated the operation, and could be essential when rafters were widely spaced, but the tension required to fix reed securely with a camber could break thin battens or pull them off the rafters. The best thatchers used sways that were flexible enough to be used on hips and corners, but strong enough not to bow between rafter fixings. Batsford and Fry's comment probably reflects poor practice.

The thatcher takes tar rope in his foot-long [30cm] steel needle and passes it through to his assistant in the building, underneath the rafters. The rope is twined round the horizontal laths laid across the rafters, which are much more widely spaced than for a tiled roof; occasionally the twine is tied at the intersection of laths and rafters. (Batsford & Fry 1938, 74)

It should be noted that reed was tied to the roof in individual bundles only at the eaves (Cowell nd), whereas all of the remaining reed was fixed with sways tied as described. Old roofs could be retied or simply cleaned and redressed if the fixings were secure. One or perhaps two thin spar coats could be tied through a standard base coat, but this consumed a large amount of cord and the upper coats were held less securely and were more likely to slip. Broaches would simply not hold a new coat of tensed reed securely onto an existing base coat of water reed.

Lost traditions in reed thatching

It is always dangerous to view modern practice as reflective of the past. Early eighteenth-century estate records of the Whitaker family in Wiltshire indicate that local reed was reserved for thatching outbuildings rather than houses

(Pamela Slocombe, pers comm). Just as modern combed wheat reed and long straw traditions are distilled and codified versions of what was once a more diversified craft, so is modern water reed thatching the end product of generations of difficult adaptation to rapidly changing market conditions. And although it is today viewed as the supreme example of the thatcher's craft, it too suffered from the general decline in the popularity of thatching in the last century. This was due to the replacement of thatch by alternative materials, as well as to the loss of the bulk of the reed beds in Norfolk and of wetland in general throughout England. Unlike crushed straw thatching, however, reed thatching was able to reform itself to fit the idyll demanded of it by a new generation of architects and home owners.

In the past, up to a quarter of a bundle could often be composed of stems of bulrush or flag, which was preferred by many thatchers for use on dormers and gables (Jenkins 1965, 139; Peter Brockett, pers comm). Entire roofs thatched with 'more bulrush than reed' are still occasionally encountered in the Broads region (David Farman, pers comm). A much wider range of reed of variable quality was used in the past. This is even more true outside of the Broads where reed quality seems to have varied tremendously, ranging from the poor quality reed cut from ditches in Oxfordshire or the Fens, to the reed of intermediate quality cut from the shores of the river Arun in Amberley, Dorset, the tidal pools of Slapton Lea, Devon, or the spear beds of Abbotsbury, Dorset. Over the past century, those beds that were the least viable, either because they produced low quality or insufficient reed, or were difficult to manage in terms of water levels, were abandoned leaving the more reliable Norfolk beds as the principal domestic suppliers. River reed must be cut by hand much higher on the stem producing a shorter bundle with softer butts.

It is estimated that East Anglia lost almost 3,500 square kilometres of fenland, including much of the Broadlands, over the last three centuries. The characteristics that make a certain reed plant desirable for thatching are not necessarily the same as would make it a successful plant within a wild stand of reed, and selection and management have undoubtedly increased the relative preponderance of high-quality reed at the expense of more successful wild plants that produce reed stems of secondary quality for thatching. In the Norfolk Broads reed has essentially become partially domesticated. Quality reed is produced not simply by good management but also by selection of quality stock as with any crop.

The availability of reed has also changed drastically over the past century.

> At no time in the past 40 years have Norfolk reeds been more abundant than they are to-day, and the supply is ever increasing. For centuries they have been used for roofing ancient barns, churches and houses in Broadland, but it is only during the last 30 years that they have been employed extensively all over England. (Vincent 1941, 1119)

Written evidence

There are numerous references to the use of water reed in medieval and post-medieval sources, but no technical descriptions of thatching appear to have survived. Thatching was simply too common to be considered worthy of recording. Fleeting references nonetheless confirm that reed was used outside of East Anglia. In 1773, '400 [bundles of] reeds' were applied to the pigeon coop of the Manor House in Gedney, Lincolnshire, using 'rush rope' and a ridge fixed with 'broaches'. Other references in the Yarborough estate papers confirm that reed was commonly used in the district for thatching as well as a key for plastering walls. Interestingly, there are also numerous passages clearly referring to thatching with crushed straw that was watered, drawn and 'broached' to roofs, including that of a boat house at Newsham, Lincolnshire, that was presumably ideally situated to receive a shipment of reed had it been desired or available (Lincolnshire Record Office 2). Reed was clearly used to some degree, but not necessarily in the Norfolk manner, in eighteenth- and nineteenth-century Lincolnshire (Young 1813b, 39), Leicestershire and Northamptonshire.

> In the Vale of Trent [Leicestershire], upon the estate of the Earl of Moira, and elsewhere, are considerable patches of reeds (*rundo phragmites*); they are equally valuable with good meadow land, being sold to the builders to lay under plaster floors. They are also more durable than straw, for thatching, and make screens to keep off the cold wind in gardens; and are, I believe, good food for horses, cut green and carried to the stable. The pannicles are used in Sweden, to dye woollen green. (Pitt 1809b, 161)

Both reed and straw thatching cost 4s 2d (21p) a square in Norfolk in the late eighteenth century (Kent 1796, 163), but reed was less expensive than straw thatching in the heart of the Cambridgeshire Fens a few years later.

> Reed thatching is done in a masterly way in this county ... At Whittlesea, reed thatching is done at 3s 6d [17p] per square, the thatcher finding spits and rope; straw-thatching at 4s 2d [21p] per square. (Gooch 1811, 286).

Archaeological evidence

No reliable archaeological evidence for water reed thatching has come to light in England, either as macroscopic plant remains or in any other form. The earliest conclusive evidence rests with the smoke-blackened fleekings of reed that have recently been located in a handful of late medieval cottages in southern England (Letts 1999). This does not mean reed was not used for thatching in antiquity, as there is a similar paucity of evidence for the use of straw or any other material for thatching in England. Ancient thatching practices have simply not survived, or at least have not been recognised in excavations.

Fleeking

The presence of water reed fleeking in a roof does not imply that reed was used for main coat thatching in that area. Marshall provided one of the earliest descriptions of reed fleeking as it was apparently used in Norfolk in the late eighteenth century.

Figure 73 Post-medieval water reed fleeking (Appendix A: A15, Great Doddington, Northamptonshire) (John Letts).

No laths being made use of, in laying it a little of the longest and stoutest of the reed is scattered irregularly across the naked spars, as a foundation to lay the main coat upon: this partial gauze-like covering is called the fleeking. On this fleeking the main covering is laid. (Loudon 1831, 518 quoting Marshall's *Rural Economy of Norfolk*)

The *in situ* evidence suggests that there were several ways in which fleekings were constructed in previous centuries, 'scattering the reed irregularly across the naked spars' perhaps being one of the least common (Fig 73). Four examples of smoke-blackened fleeking of medieval ori-

gin have been recorded (Appendix A: A15; Appendix B: B11, B13, B20). Medieval methods of fleeking were clearly carried into the post-medieval period. Eight buildings without battens and with non-sooted fleekings were recorded in eastern England and the Midlands (Figs 74 and 75). In six of these cases the reed was woven *in situ* into a coarse mat as in the medieval examples (Appendix A: A7 Cambridgeshire; Appendix B: B12 Cambridgeshire, B30 Norfolk, B34 Northamptonshire and B36 Northamptonshire). In the Norfolk example, the fleeking was tied to the rafters with tarred cord only in the oldest section of the roof. In two buildings handfuls of reed were stitched horizontally into mats with grass twine, and these mats were then clamped onto the roof with laths nailed to the rafters (Appendix A: A1 Bedfordshire, A14 Leicestershire). In the Leicestershire example, a stitched mat was used below purlin height, replacing the original fleeking of coarse reed clamped in horizontal bundles to the rafters, part of which survived above the purlin. In all of these roofs the fleeking supported the entire weight of the overlying straw thatch in the gap between adjoining rafters. Fleekings composed of reed laid horizontally in bundles or mats had been clamped into position prior to thatching, but woven fleekings were generally held in place by the weight of the overlying thatch and extended up the roof as thatching progressed. In the Tavern Barn in Bacton (Appendix A: A18 Suffolk), a coarse fleeking of reed was laid horizontally between adjacent rafters, but with occasional reinforcement with roundwood rods. The examples from Weston-on-the-Green, Cherwell (Appendix B: B37 Oxfordshire) and Horbling (Appendix B: B28 Lincolnshire) were not examined *in situ* but both appear to have been fleeked with water reed.

No matter how it was applied, a fleeking provided:

- support in the absence of battens
- a firm base against which the tops of the reed could slide when dressed
- a smooth underside to the thatch when viewed from ground level
- a potential key for plastering independent of the main coat

The necessity of having a firm base against which the reed can slide when it is dressed up into its fixings has already

Figure 74 Early nineteenth-century water reed fleeking (Appendix B: B30, Lingwood, Norfolk) (John Letts).

Figure 75 Late eighteenth-century water reed fleeking (barn, Ranworth, Norfolk) (John Letts).

been discussed, and on reed roofs an additional backfill was usually required to ensure the tops of the stems were not blocked by the horizontal bands of the fleeking when their butts were dressed. Marshall's statement about reed being 'scattered irregularly across the naked spars' makes much more sense if one assumes that he omitted to mention the backfill that was inserted beneath the main coat and the 'gauze-like' fleeking he describes. A fleeking's main purpose was to provide a strong support structure for the overlying thatch without using battens (and in some straw roofs, to hold up the base coat of fragmented threshing waste that formed the base coat for external spar coats of full-length straw). The implication is that reed was often more plentiful, or at least cheaper, than battens, and performed the task just as well.

A good portion of the weight of a mass of ancient thatch is actually carried on the rafters rather than the fleeking, and on a moderately pitched roof gravity holds the fleeking tight to the rafters. On such a roof, a little bowing in the fleeking between the rafters was probably an advantage as it would have helped to equalize the tension created by uneven tying and dressing of reed of uneven length. On a more steeply pitched roof, however, the forces act over a shorter lateral distance and the reed stands at a steeper angle thus increasing the risk of slippage, particularly if there is any slack in the fleeking or fixings. Although it may now be impossible to prove, logic suggests that fleekings might have been more common on reed roofs with moderately steep pitches (45°–55°) while steeper roofs were more often battened. The five reed-fleeked roofs whose pitch was accurately recorded averaged 52° and all of those recorded in Appendix B are also believed to fall within this moderate group.

External thatch

As with fleekings, logic based on technical understanding suggests that there are only a few ways in which reed can be applied to a roof:

1 clamping reed between the elements of a wattled sub-structure without any additional fixings;
2 clamping reed to rafters and battens using iron crooks and sways;
3 clamping reed onto a fleeking or battens using sways that are tied to rafters with cord or organic bindings, a method used for both main coats and spar coats;
4 stinging a worn coat by lifting the butt ends of a course and inserting new reed into the gap;
5 tying individual bundles of reed to a battened roof.

Only methods 1 and 5 have not been recorded as main coat thatching methods in England. Method 1 would probably have worked as well with reed as it currently does with broom in parts of France if it was used in the distant past. Method 2 is an extension of a fixing technique that was used only in special situations where tying was not possible, as the iron crooks employed were hand-forged and too expensive for popular use until after the

Second World War. Method 3 forms the basis of the English reed thatching tradition, and late nineteenth-century methods differed from medieval practice only in the use of tarred cord for fixing sways instead of withes, bramble stems or straw rope.

Whatever way the water reed was fixed its exposed butts are moulded into shape with a leggat to provide a regular surface that would repel rainfall evenly and efficiently. It is inevitable that the final finish on a reed roof is more regimented than a multi-layered roof of long straw or dressed combed wheat reed, for water reed is much less flexible than straw and its single coat more closely reflects the underlying structure of the roof. This contrasts sharply with the soft and flowing appearance of a long straw roof, and has been accentuated in more recent times by the increased importance attached to the tilting fillet.

Spar coating with reed

It is generally accepted that the longevity of a reed roof will be extended quite considerably by regular cleaning, redressing and repair approximately every seven to ten years, in practice when the ridge is rethatched (Cowell nd). Once the butt-ends of the reed have worn back to such a degree that the fixings are but a couple of inches beneath the overlying reed the roof must be rethatched, either by stripping and replacing or spar coating. The nineteenth-century literature is silent on the subject of spar-coating with reed, and it was an uncommon, but acceptable, practice in the early part of this-century. This point was emphasized in a letter written to Cowell by thatcher Fred Dickerson concerning the rethatching of Queen Charlotte's Cottage at Kew Gardens. Cowell replied:

> This job can be done two ways. Put on half coat of reeds, or at the rate of about 9 fathoms per square. Leave on old under eaves. All new reeds would be shown on the face of roofs. A good reed eaves is on now. Verges would show all new Reeds. No other part of roofs to be strip'd, just pull out to required thickness. (Cambridgeshire Record Office 1)

At the bottom of this page, Cowell added:

> Not necessary at any time to strip old roofs if reeds. W R D would tell you it is. (Cambridgeshire Record Office 1)

In his treatise on reed thatching written in the 1920s Cowell wrote:

> Old Roofs. A thin coating 6" [15cm] to 8" [20cm] in thickness can be placed over an old reed roof. An old building with new eaves and ridge worked in this way, provided the timber work is sound, is equal to covering with a new whole coat. (Cowell nd)

In 1931, Cowell was asked by a Mr Bateman from Chalfont St Giles, Buckinghamshire, whether it was possible to provide a 12" (30cm) coat of thatch using 9"

(23cm) of straw as a base with 3" (8cm) of reed on top. Cowell replied:

> I cannot remember covering a straw roof with reeds, but if you decide to do your roof in that way, all the face of the roof should show reeds. (Cambridgeshire Record Office 1)

Boardman wrote:

> If a roof does get beyond local repair it is a comparatively simple matter to half-coat the entire surface, using the existing thatch undisturbed as the foundation for the new work. The new work of half-coating works about 9ins [23cm] thick and binding hooks would be used to secure the sways if the rafters have been boarded or a ceiling must not be disturbed. Some of the best-looking thatch on old cottages has been half-coated, and it looks both neat and new to the expert, yet old and beautiful to the layman from the day it is done. (Boardman 1933, 567)

On rare occasions, straw and water reed are known to have been applied within the same coat, as occurred at Barrington Court, Ilminster, Somerset, early this century. Whether provoked by a shortage of water reed, or a particular liking for the straw grower named Billie, the two top courses of what had been a water reed thatch were completed with three tons of rye straw and 360 bunches of 'Billie's wheat straw'. The wheat straw, almost certainly West Country style combed wheat reed, was probably used to complete the main coat, whereas the rye, perhaps threshed, was used for the ridge. The thatch was completed jointly by the East Anglian reed thatcher William Dickerson and a local straw thatcher named Richard Pittard and his son (Cambridgeshire Record Office 1). The roof was probably indistinguishable from any other roof in the area, at least in the initial years before differential rates of decay became visible. Whether the main coat of water reed performed differently from the upper courses of combed wheat reed cannot be confirmed, but the practice does not seem to have been copied to any great extent.

The traditional Norfolk ridge

Norfolk reed ridges have traditionally been made of wheat or rye straw, fen sedge, river rush or gladdon, schoof, or even flax, but never of reed, which cannot be bent to wrap over a ridge. All these materials were applied in a similar manner, and the degree of ornamentation they were given probably reflected the custom of the thatcher and the region as much as the material employed. River rush is extremely easy to cut to a pattern and is surprisingly resistant to decay. Sedge would have been used more commonly in the Fens than in other areas, and since it is much more difficult to cut to a pattern than straw or rush, sedge ridges in this region may not have been scalloped or as heavily ornamented as straw ridges here or in other parts of East Anglia. The writings suggest that the bottom edges of most ridges were cut straight in line with the butts of the uppermost course of reed, not only

because this reduced the work involved but also because a scalloped ridge can concentrate the downflow of rainfall into channels that evolve into gulleys which decay at an accelerated rate. This is generally supported by photographic records from the last century and paintings and drawings from Norfolk which depict thatched roofs (Dickes 1906; Moore 1982; Ben Thomas, pers comm). Sedge's greater resistance to decay is unlikely to have overruled its relatively poor workability, since it is usually the fixings, rather than the ridging material itself, that determines the longevity of a ridge.

Many thatchers clearly preferred applying simple straw ridges for a variety of technical reasons (Jobson 1949, 1187). The heavier the ornamentation on a ridge the larger the number of broaches required, and hence the greater the risk of water infiltrating where the broaches enter the ridge material. Diamenting also consumes a large number of broaches and is a slow, and thus expensive, task that would have been considered a frivolous extra by many home owners unfamiliar with the architectural fashions of the day. If an ancient Norfolk reed ridging tradition can be teased from the literature, it would probably take the form of a block-cut ridge of crushed and drawn wheat or rye straw cut in a straight line below a series of horizontal liggers spanning the roof from gable to gable, much as in the manner described by Marshall for the late eighteenth century.

> A *cap* (provincially, a *roof*) of straw is set on in a masterly, but in an expensive, manner. In this operation, the workman begins ... by bringing the roof to an angle, with straw laid lengthwise upon the ridge, in the manner in which a rick is topped up; and to render it firm, to keep it in its place, and to prevent the wind from blowing it off or ruffling it, he pegs it down slightly with 'double broaches;' namely, cleft twigs, two feet [61cm] long and as thick as the finger, sharpened at both ends, bent double, and perhaps barbed by partial chops on the sides, to make them hold in the better after being thrust down. This done, the workman lays a coat of straight straws, six or eight inches [15cm or 20cm] thick across the ridge, beginning on either side at the uppermost butts of the reed, and finishing with straight handfuls evenly across the top of the ridge. Having laid a length of about four feet [1.22m] in this manner, he proceeds to fasten it firmly down, so as to render it proof against wind and rain. This is done by laying a '*brochen ligger*' (a quarter-cleft rod as thick as the finger, and four feet [1.22m] in length) along the middle of the ridge, pegging it down at every four inches [10cm] with a double broach, which is thrust down with the hands, and afterwards driven with the *legget*, or with a mallet used for this purpose. The middle ligger being firmly laid, the thatcher smooths down the straw with a rake and his hands, about eight or nine inches [20cm-23cm] on one side, and at six inches [15cm] from the first lays another ligger, and pegs it down with a similar number of double broaches, thus proceeding to smooth the straw and to fasten on liggers at every six inches, until he reaches the bottom of the cap. One side finished, the other is treated in the same manner; and the first length being completed, another and another

length is laid, and finished as the first, until the other end of the ridge be reached. He then cuts off the tails of the straw square and neatly with a pair of shears, level with the uppermost butts of the reed, above which the cap (or more properly the *rooflet*) shows an eaves of about six inches thick. (Loudon 1831, 518–9)

Sedge became a much more common ridging material on reed roofs in East Anglia in the 1920s and 1930s.

> Wheat straw has been used in a few instances in the place of sedge for the ridging, but it is despised in Norfolk because it fails in every respect to compete with the latter. It is too light in colour to harmonize with the reed, nearly three times as expensive, and very much more inflammable. (Boardman 1933, 566)

And Deas reported simply that 'sedge is used for all the best thatch ridging' (1939, 94). Dried sedge is prepared in much the same way as long straw:

> Sedge is carted to the site loose in the manner of ordinary hay and before use is formed into a heap which is thoroughly soaked with water for several hours. This helps the thatcher to lay the sedge tight. When ready for use, the sedge is drawn in handfuls or 'halms', as they are called, from the bottom of the heap so that all the fibres are more or less parallel and stretched. After this preparation, the sedge is made up into bundles and carried up to the ridge where it is laid, fibres cross-wise, in a three-inch layer extending 3' [91cm] or so from the apex down each side. Each side is now fixed towards its lower edge with a ligger and brotches. (Deas 1939, 108)

The reed roof examined in Lingwood, Norfolk (Appendix B: B30) carried three previous ridge coats: the oldest of crushed straw (bread wheat) and middle layers (a mixture of fen sedge and grass) were retained, along with part of the last coat of fen sedge applied in about 1976.

REED-THATCHING TOOLS

Marshall's description of thatching in Norfolk in the late eighteenth century suggests a reed thatcher carried a larger tool kit than his straw-thatching colleagues due to his use of both materials. The core of this kit consisted largely of the same tools described in *The Thatcher's Craft* in 1960: a leggat, a 'binding' (stitching) needle, 'setting needles' or pins used as temporary fixings, a mallet for beating in broaches, shears and a sharp knife for trimming straw on the ridge, perhaps a stinger for repair work, ladders, a small side rake for combing ridge straw into line and cleaning off moss and lichen and, apparently, a 'holly bough' used in the final cleaning. As in the present day, eighteenth-century reed thatchers also probably wore leather knee-pads and possibly a leather hand protector if broaches were pushed rather than beaten into place with a mallet. Broaches, liggers and sways were cut and trimmed with a billhook, although a thatcher might well have bought in his 'sticks' ready-made.

The nail-studded leggat was, without question, the supreme tool of the reed thatcher (Jobson 1949, 1187). According to Marshall it was

> made of a board eight or nine inches [20cm–23cm] square, with a handle two feet [61cm] long, fixed upon the back of it, obliquely, in the manner of the tool used by gardeners in beating turf. The face of the *legget* is set with large-headed nails to render it rough, and make it lay hold of the butts of the reeds. (Loudon 1831, 518)

Each leggat was hand made to satisfy a thatcher's individual requirements, although they were all broadly similar.

> in principal all leggets are similar. The head consists of a piece of elm about 7" [18cm] square and 1½" [4cm] thick, studded with common horseshoe nails at about 1½in centres. The nail heads are flattened and protrude about 3/4" [2cm] from the face of the legget. To this head is bolted a handle, which is usually about 2' long [61cm], 1½" in diameter and set at an angle of approximately 35 deg to the head. This form of (reed) legget is a fairly heavy tool and the weight is sometimes increased by hoop iron binding around the edges of the head. (Deas 1939, 94)

Some thatchers used a much smaller and lighter leggat when dressing patterns into the reed, and Deas also described a 'very handy' but uncommon version consisting of an oak block 8" (20cm) square 'with an undersurface stepped diagonally, into which oak or iron spikes are driven' (op cit, 94–6).

Needles also varied in length and form.

> The thatcher possesses several needles, which are usually of iron. Wooden needles were used in the past, but they have been entirely superseded by iron. The needles are made from ½" [1cm] diameter rod in various lengths to suit the different thicknesses of thatch, the heads being finished in the form of a knob to fit the hand, but in the case of large needles, a handle is formed. Some of the thatcher's needles are plainly pointed, whilst the others are flattened and eyeletted. They are known respectively as setting and binding needles. (op cit, 96–8)

Measuring water reed

As with many craftsmen, the illiteracy that was undoubtedly common amongst thatchers in the past was no barrier to the development of great skill in their craft. In thatching, distance, surface area and volume were based on traditional, and usually very practical, measures that had been in use for centuries. Reed is still cut and sold in 'fathoms' measuring 6' (1.8m) in circumference 12" (30cm) from its butt end. This fathom is approximately the distance between the tips of the fingers of two outstretched arms, and its use in the Norfolk Broads could well have been encouraged by the strong maritime traditions of this coastal region. A fathom traditionally contains five or six bundles or bolts each having a diameter of approximately 26" (66cm). Reed was sold by the hundred, which was equal to '6 score' or 120 fathoms, or from 600 to 720 bundles. Thatching was, and still is, reckoned by the 'square', a surface measure of 10' x 10' (3.05m) or 100 ft² (9.3 m²). According to Young (1804b, 318), a 'hundred' of reed was expected to cover five 'square', or at a rate of 1.3 bundles per ft² (14.0 bundles per m²). The traditional value, using standard measures, is 70 bundles per square or 0.7 bundles per ft² (7.5 bundles per m²), but the records suggest that this figure varied a little within the Broadlands and considerably in other parts of the country, as in parts of Kent and Sussex where, according to Neve (1726, 257), just over three 6" (15cm) diameter bundles of reed were applied per ft². Modern figures range from 60 to 160 bundles per square or 0.6 – 1.6 bundles per ft² (6.5 – 17.2 bundles per m²) depending on the size of the bundle and the depth of reed applied (Chris White pers comm).

An interesting reference in Northamptonshire indicates that a 'waggon load' held eight square of reed in 1825 (Northamptonshire Record Office 5). Assuming a standard application figure of 0.7 bundles per ft², this wagon carried 560 bundles or 93 fathoms of reed (at 6 bundles per fathom), the cut of about 1.5 acres (0.6ha) of well-managed reed bed generating 350 bundles per acre (864 bundles per ha). A fathom of reed produces a bundle about 20" (51cm) in diameter. Assuming an average (tapered) length of about 6' (1.8m) per bundle, an overlap of one third in stacking and a stacking height of 4 fathoms (ie to about 6' 8", 2.03m) the reed in question must have been carried on a wagon that measured about 18' (5.5m) long and 8' (2.4m) wide, stacked to take advantage of the reed's taper. This might have provided sufficient reed to thatch a very small cottage in 1803, but an average modern roof would have required 2.5 cartloads of reed to be thatched to an equivalent depth. Since an average thatcher can lay about 50ft² (4.65m²) of reed a day (35 standard bundles), this single cartload would have supplied a thatcher's requirements for 16 days continuous work. In reality, it could perhaps be assumed that reed was applied slightly thinner at this time, thus reducing all of the above figures by 10–20%.

Conclusions

The craft of water reed thatching has survived the centuries because of its ability to adapt to changing economic realities and satisfy consumer preferences. Variations in the methods and materials once used have gradually been lost as the 'prettified' version that best satisfied the demands of consumers and architects early this century emerged from the reed thatching tradition of the Broadlands of Norfolk. This 'new and improved' Norfolk technique was promulgated most successfully by a few family-based thatching concerns that rejected tying and straw ridges in favour of battens, crooked sways and heavily diamented and patterned sedge ridges. This new pattern spread rapidly to other parts of England, adapting only very slowly to local environmental and architectural differences, but everywhere gaining favour relative to long straw and to a lesser degree combed wheat reed.

The English water reed tradition is of great antiquity, particularly in the Norfolk Broads and what was once fenland in Cambridgeshire, and with a few notable (but localized) exceptions there is little evidence that reed was used in any great quantity for main coat thatching beyond these areas. Reed is a valuable thatching material that can perform better than any other material currently available on an appropriate roof, but this superior performance will be achieved only if the underlying factors that maximize longevity are in place.

FLAX (*Linum usitatissimum*)

Flax was recovered from two buildings examined over the course of this project, one forming a main coat on a cottage in Wennington, Cambridgeshire (Appendix B: B10) and in the second example as a 'stob' used to repair a bird hole in a multi-layered straw roof in Hamwick, Bedfordshire (Appendix B: B1). In the Cambridgeshire example the flax lay fixed by spars and wooden sways below a surface coat of reed straw and above base coats of crushed straw, butts-up reed straw and fen sedge. At Hamwick, a thick stob of flax had been pushed far into a bird hole that had penetrated the roof space from what had once been an exterior layer. In both cases the flax had been threshed to remove its seed pods, which left only the upper portions of the stems intact. The material was drawn and yealmed as with long straw and was fixed with spars and sways in the usual way.

A bill from a thatcher from Whittlesea indicates that flax was used in conjunction with reed on at least one building at the Wantage estate northeast of Northamptonshire in 1890, presumably for ridging (Northamptonshire Record Office 3). A flush ridge of retted flax probably provides as much security as a block cut ridge of fen sedge, but it seems unlikely that the Wantage flax was retted and the practice does not seem to have caught on.

THATCHING WITH STRAW

Reed straw

The historical and *in situ* evidence indicates that several different processing methods have been used over the centuries to turn mature wheat straw into reed straw thatch that was largely undamaged and butts-together in the sheaf. The evidence also suggests that there were regional variations in the way this straw was used for thatching, with the modern combed wheat reed technique now popular throughout Britain being a codified version of the principal method used in Devon early this century. Ears might be lashed, flailed, threshed by machine or cut off completely as in the Dorset/Somerset practice of pitching, but the resulting reed straw was essentially the same product and was applied in a similar manner. West Country roofs have been coated with reed straw for centuries, but defining the regional distribution of a reed straw tradition beyond the West Country is a little more problematic.

Figure 76 Straw bond providing a permanent additional fixing to horizontal sways on roof of combed wheat reed, by B Armstrong, Wiltshire (John Letts).

The key difference between reed straw and modern long straw thatch is that the latter is crushed and the former is not. It cannot be defined in relation to the fact that combed wheat reed is generally dressed into place and long straw is not, as reed straw can simply be moulded into position with the hand and fixed without any further dressing. The use of a leggat may well be one of the key technical factors distinguishing the West Country and non-West Country reed straw traditions, but the differences between the two materials are more fundamental. The confusion was probably just as great in the past, and nineteenth-century observers also had to contend with hybrid materials that are no longer used. Tall stubble, for example, could easily have been confused with short combed reed straw.

It is not always easy to distinguish a roof of combed wheat reed from one of water reed or neatly trimmed long straw. It may be a cliche to say that a roof thatched with long straw looks poured on whereas a roof of combed wheat reed bristles like a hedgehog, but these reflect the fact that the materials do exert a fundamental influence on technique. Combed wheat reed is a relatively rigid, tubular material that imposes its form while being applied. It is coaxed into position on a roof with its rigid butts uncrushed at the surface and hence amenable to dressing. Long straw is much softer to work with, sits solidly where it is applied and presents a

mixture of crushed ears and butts to the surface. A combed wheat reed roof is usually given a kick at the eaves by the use of a tilting fillet as with water reed, which holds the reed straw under tension at the eaves and facilitates cutting. This would have little technical value in a roof of long straw and would reduce the pitch of the straw and encourage decay at this point. The lack of kick does, however, make a long straw eaves more floppy and less resistant to wind damage, and so they are secured with external liggers along the eaves and barges.

Charting the changes that occurred in reed straw thatching between 1790 and 1940 is a difficult task for a variety of reasons: ridges are often stripped at rethatching or are too degraded to sample; chronology is often difficult to determine; rescue excavations are limited in terms of both the area of a roof examined and the time and resources available for the task. Four of the 20 buildings recorded in detail were thatched historically in true West Country fashion (Appendix A: A10, A11, A12 Devon, A13 Dorset) while those beyond Devon acquired their reed straw after 1940.

Main coat thatching
As described in *The Thatcher's Craft* (Morgan & Cooper 1960, 48–121) work begins with the preparation of the material on the ground. Combed wheat reed arrives in 28lb (13kg) bundles, tied with binder twine, which are ready for application after they are wetted and left to soak overnight or for no more than a day or two. Work generally begins at the lower right hand gable, whether the new reed is being spar coated or crooked to open rafters. Using tarred twine or plastic binder twine, large handfuls of reed are tied individually into wads that are then tied firmly to the lowermost batten along the eave, and to a vertical sway nailed securely to the battens along the edge of the barge. As with water reed, a kick is provided by a tilting fillet along the eaves and a raised barge board on the gable to tighten this first brow course and facilitate its later trimming. The wads are tied so that they press up against each other, thus preventing the formation of any gaps or gulleys. This brow course is then dressed with a straw leggat which tightens the straw in its fixings.

The first eaves course, and all successive courses, are applied in much the same way as with water reed. A nitch is carried up onto the roof and stored in a cradle fixed to the brow course. A manageable large handful of reed is fixed into position with a temporary sway of straw pinned into place with iron needles about 16" (40cm) from the butt end of the reed. This straw bond can take the form of a continuously extending band of 8–10 straws (Fig 76), or can be created by bending a few strands of straw from an already fixed wad up and over the newly applied one. The course is pushed into its near-final shape with a leggat leaving an undressed lip that is dressed back with the next coat to form an imperceptible joint between the two courses. When several feet of reed have been laid, they are clamped to the rafters and battens about half way up the wad using iron crooks and a horizontal sway of hazel or iron. The temporary sway is then removed and the course

Figure 77 Shearing a newly thatched roof of combed wheat reed (Museum of English Rural Life).

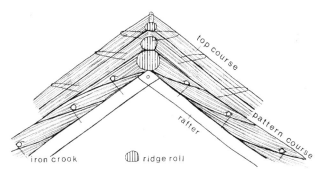

Figure 78 Schematic diagrams of straw ridges: wrapover ridge (threshed straw) (Judith Dobie, after John Letts).

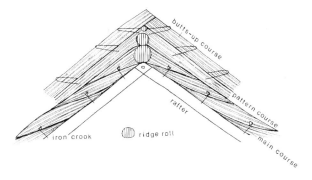

Figure 79 Schematic diagrams of straw ridges: butts-up ridge (combed wheat reed) (Judith Dobie, after John Letts).

is dressed back securely into its final position with the straw leggat.

A thin backfill is also applied against the battens beneath each course to prevent the tops of stems from penetrating into the roofspace when they are dressed into position, and also to provide a smooth base to the thatch when viewed from within the roofspace. The thatcher works his way up the roof laying backfill, fixing loose wads of reed into position with a temporary sway, crooking the new reed to the rafters, removing the temporary sway and dressing the new section firmly into its final position with the leggat. Care is taken at every step to ensure even tension within the fixings and a smooth surface without bumps or depressions. The wads are also bedded closely together, using iron needles for leverage, to prevent the formation of gaps or gulleys that could allow channel water or allow it to infiltrate. The finished coat is given a final raking and a thin shearing to ensure a smooth surface free of short or bent straw that could channel water into the core of the roof (Fig 77).

This crooking technique was already well-entrenched when *The Thatcher's Craft* was published in 1960. The book does not demonstrate the tying method, technically a similar procedure to that already described for water reed, that had been used before crooks became available at low cost. Unlike water reed, however, combed wheat reed was fixed to new rafters in two stages: only the bottom waist coat was actually tied to the roof structure, and the upper coat was sparred to the base coat in the usual way. This waist coat could be tied directly to the battens as well as the rafters as it was clamped to the roof with much less tension and did not run the risk of pulling the battens away from the rafters as with water reed. The waist coat was tied to the roof in individual bundles so that any problem with one fixing did not loosen the fixings of a large section.

As with any thatching material, special techniques are used in dealing with obstructions to water flow such as chimneys, dormer windows, valleys or joints between thatch and a raised barge. The fundamental strategy is to ensure the reed always lies straight as possible, disperses the water evenly away from any junctions, and quickly returns to the vertical after sweeping around any obstruction. Joints are covered with flashing and packing is added to raise valleys and ensure a broad and even downflow. As with water reed and long straw roofs, thatched dormers are particular danger spots as they invariably reduce the pitch of the reed that covers it. A small leggat is used to dress reed into place in tight corners, but unlike water reed, barges and eaves are cut into their final shape with an eaves hook and not dressed with the leggat.

Ridging

Roofs of combed wheat reed are usually finished with either a wrap over ridge or a butts up ridge (Figs 78 and 79). The former is well-described in *The Thatcher's Craft* and differs from the latter only in the way in which the last top coat of reed is applied. Ridges can also be raised (block cut) or flush and finished with complex diamenting or simple horizontal liggering, but all of these methods use roughly the same techniques and differ only in the treatment of the top coat.

The ridge is begun by tying a dolly (ridge roll) of straw securely along the apex of the roof. The main coat courses are crooked into place until they reach the ridge roll, and any oversailing portions are either cut off or folded back over the course and fixed with a straw bond. A second ridge roll is sparred securely onto the first, and handfuls of reed are folded over about 12" (30cm) from their apex and fixed knuckle up against this roll with a straw bond and spars. The third and final ridge roll is sparred into place to provide the final narrow crest of the ridge and a firm and level base for the final ridge course. For a

Figure 80 Spar coating with combed wheat reed, Wroughton, Wiltshire (John Letts).

Figure 81 Spar coating with combed wheat reed in the West Country, c 1930s (Museum of English Rural Life).

wrapover ridge a handful of reed is divided into two and one half is reversed to form a bundle of even thickness. These bundles are wedged tightly into position astride the ridge ensuring there are no gaps between them and are fixed with a central ligger. A second ligger is fixed on either side 8"–10" (20cm–25cm) below the crest ligger followed by further liggers at intervals down the ridge. Ridges can be diamented by adding cross rods between adjacent liggers or they can be left simple, as the extra cross rods do not provide additional security of fixing and may, if not carefully placed, actually provide more opportunities for failure. Finally, the raised block effect is produced by trimming off the surplus ridge material down to the main coat in line with the lowermost ligger using a sharp knife, and the ridge is given a last thin shearing to remove any superfluous straw and provide a neat finish.

The flush ridge, apparently once common on combed wheat reed roofs, differs from the block cut version in that trimming begins just below the uppermost side ligger and continues down the ridge until it runs flush with the main coat, with horizontal liggers being applied as required. Rope ridges have also been used in the West Country and been introduced to other regions, differing only in that each handful applied in the uppermost course is twisted to form a loop at its centre before it is wrapped over the crest of the ridge.

The butts-up ridge is much more common and is largely confined to Devon. Again, it follows the basic pattern, but the butts of the upper coat are dove-tailed into each other, the bundle applied to one face of the ridge oversailing the butt end of the other, to provide an impermeable joint. Such ridges perform well in the West Country, but the paucity of butts-up ridges in other regions to which combed wheat reed thatching has been introduced reflects a view held by thatchers from these areas that butts up ridges do not provide the same degree of security against rain or longevity as the standard wrapover ridge.

Spar coating
The description of main coat thatching described above refers primarily to the application of combed wheat reed to open rafters. This was a rare event in the past as roofs were usually stripped down to a firm base coat and spar coated (Figs 80 and 81). The modern recommended depth is 10"–12" (25cm–30cm), but in the past a much greater thickness was obviously left as evidenced by the thick accumulations of ancient thatch that have survived as superimposed spar coats. It is also common practice to strip out barges and eaves fully in order to ensure secure fixings and maintain a shallow overhang. A spar coat of combed wheat reed is fixed with horizontal sways of wood, cord or straw as with long straw, but extra caution must be taken to avoid over-dressing as this can loosen the reed straw in its fixings and cause slippage.

Tools
Most of the items used in long straw work would have been found in a reed thatcher's tool kit, but it also

included a straw-adapted form of the leggat used for dressing water reed, traditionally called a dreft, beater or bat (Seymour 1984, 46). In earlier decades, the base (waist) coat was stitched into place with tarred twine using a long stitching needle made of iron or wood. Combed wheat reed is fixed into position temporarily using iron fixing needles or pins that are removed when the permanent fixings were applied. Spars and sways are cut with a spar hook, and spars are twisted into the required shape, pushed into place with the palm of the hand and driven into their final position with a wooden mallet. Reed straw is carried onto the roof in nitches and placed in a wooden frame called a beetle that holds the new reed within easy reach. Most thatchers work from a ladder, but in the West Country a short wooden frame with curved spikes that hook into the thatch is sometimes used and provides an independent means of support. Every course of reed straw is raked thoroughly before the next course is applied in order to remove any broken or folded straw that could disrupt the flow of water. These rakes are usually hand made by driving nails through a wooden handle 18" (46cm) to 5' (1.52m) in length, and they are used with a combined beating-combing motion to pack the straw into position as well as ensure that every strand lies vertically. The final components of the tool kit include an assortment of bladed instruments, the large-bladed shearing hook used by many thatchers to trim the surface and provide a smooth finish, a long eaves knife used to trim barges and eaves to the appropriate angle, a smaller knife for cutting the ridge to pattern and hand shears for trimming extraneous straws.

Historical evidence

The methods used to apply combed wheat reed have changed considerably since 1940, particularly outside of the West Country. Some changes that might seem unrelated to thatching, such as the better provision of water in houses, has helped release the craft from climatic influence and moderated the degree to which it is wetted before use.

> In the past the thatcher liked to work in the autumn so as to lay his reeds when damp. Reeds must be watered before laying as they will pack tighter and be easier to dress afterwards. Today, better water supplies enable him to work in fine weather without relying on help from the climate. (Seymour 1956)

Most thatchers agree that some dampening is required to facilitate the laying of combed wheat reed, but many more believe that longevity is greatly decreased when it is put on wet. Wetting was taken to its extreme in some areas in the past. In Lancashire, a traditional method of preparing what seems to have been reed straw was called wet thatching and involved rotting the straw for several months prior to use. Bottles of butts-together reed were dessed (soaked) with water for a week, drawn to remove leaf and short straw, and dessed for another two to three months until the straw was 'black and slippery', which is when it was considered fit for thatching. This straw was fixed externally using spars and sways, and was capped

with a ridge of puddled red clay mixed with chopped straw (Watson & McClintock 1979, 16). This emphasises how low the quality of reed straw could be, and although it may have arrived at the dessing pond in unbruised condition, it could not have been dressed into position on a roof because its stiffness would have been destroyed by the soaking. A soft reed straw cannot be dressed, as it will flex before it is forced up into its fixings.

An early nineteenth-century reference from the Woburn Estate in Bedfordshire suggests that a local reed straw was used for thatching in addition to common threshed straw. With sufficient resources reed straw could also be imported from the West Country. 'Reed straw ... as attainable and done at Woburn' was more expensive than the local crushed material, but was certainly less expensive than reed straw thatching 'as practised where common', ie in the West Country, 'made out from the particulars procured by his Grace'. Both were fixed with 'tarr yarn' and sways, but the West Country version required 'an additional man for new work', presumably to assist with tying in the waist coat (Bedfordshire Record Office 4). The passage makes it clear that West Country reed straw was not being used in Bedfordshire at the time, and the local version was a less common and more expensive product than local crushed straw.

The introduction of the reaper-binder caused a shortening of the average length of reed straw and indirectly influenced the way it was applied.

> An old thatcher tells me that the best *reed* is obtained from wheat reaped in the old-fashioned way by hand, with the sickle or *reap-hook*; as reaping-machines and self-binders tend to a certain extent to bruise the straw, and at the same time longer straw is obtained by hand-reaping, as the machines do not cut it off so close to the ground. (Laycock 1920, 182)

This shortening would have been an even greater problem for thatchers using pitched reed, as this technique removes the 4"–6" (10cm–15cm) ear along with at least a further 10cm of the upper internode, rendering it shorter than the equivalent apex-flailed or lashed product by at least 10" (25cm) or more. This would have reduced the performance of a coat of pitched reed applied to a standard depth as it would have reduced the material pitch by about 15°. Whether a difference in performance was noted is not clear from the records, and any reduction in the average depth of application is hidden within regional, local and individual variations. Reed straw has usually been marketed in nitches ranging from 56lbs (25kg) (Somerset) to 8lbs (3.6kg) (Dorset) standard weight, with Devon reed traditionally sold in either 14lb (6.4kg) or 28lb (13kg) bundles.

According to *The Thatcher's Craft* a new roof requires three nitches of reed per m², half of this for the top coat and half for the waist coat (if following the Devon practice). This translates into 28 nitches per thatcher's square of 100 ft² (9.29m²). Stevenson (1812, 88) noted just this amount for Dorset in the early nineteenth century, whereas the figure for Somerset in the late eighteenth century was a little lower at 24 nitches per square (Billingsley 1798, 98).

Reed crushed at its apex either by a flail or the drum of a thresher was less likely to penetrate a roofspace when dressed with a leggat and thus required less of a backfill. Such reed was generally considered to be inferior to pitched reed. Cowell, visiting Charmouth, Dorset, in 1925 to inspect a rethatching job, noted three grades of straw available for the work: 'the best' had been pitched of its ears and combed; 'second grade' straw had been 'whipped out' but had some ears and chaff still attached; and the 'third grade' straw, 'not a good sample' according to Cowell, arrived in trussed bundles after having been threshed by machine. He also noted that the whipped version was the predominant thatching material used 'on the hills where machines can't travel' (Cambridgeshire Record Office 1).

The records indicate that apex-flailed straw was produced in large quantities for animal bedding in the hinterland of London, and some of it must have been used at least on occasion for thatching.

> The markets of London have long been supplied with straw drawn straight in handsome trusses ... that straw thrashed by the mills will be less saleable, on account of being more bruised, and less sightly in the truss ... will very probably be the case for a short time, till either gentlemen or the grooms discover the value of a softer bed for horses; or till most or all the straw be thrashed by mills, which I hope it will be in short time. (Middleton 1798, 174)

That reed straw was used outside of the West Country in the past is certain, but where exactly, and to what degree, may never be clarified because of the limitations of the *in situ* evidence and the confusion that exists in the literature over the words halm and stubble. Worlidge (1694, 238) was clearly referring to West Country reed straw when he wrote of 'helm' in the late seventeenth century.

> The best straw [for thatching] is helm, that is long, and stiff wheat straw, with the ears cut off, bound up in bundles unbruised ... which forms better thatch than the common way.

The term haulm was used in the West Country early this century in reference to the nitches into which reed straw was bundled.

> The mode of thatching most practiced in the West Country is by good wheat straw drawn into haulms and fastened with spars ... take a bundle of haulmed straw and start by laying the first haulm down on the eaves, butt downwards. (anon 1916, 275)

In Gloucestershire 'helm' fixed with 'spicks and rope yarn' was said to last 30 years (Rudge 1813, 383). This helm was sold in 'boltings', the same measure used for selling water reed in Kent. Four boltings, presumably of helm, were applied to a roof in the region a few years before Rudge's record in association with 'stub' (stubble),

so that stubble and helm are clearly different materials (Gloucestershire Record Office 1).

Neve accepted Worlidge's view of the superiority of West Country 'helm' over the 'common' crushed straw thatch of Kent and Sussex, and also referred to the localized use of water 'reed' that would last '40, 50 or 60 years', but there is no suggestion that 'helm' was used in the region (Neve 1726, 256). A house on the Whaddon Estate in Wiltshire was thatched with 'a dozen of helm' in 1666 (Slocombe pers comm), and the 'helming' of straw for thatching was noted by diarists in the region as early as the eighteenth century (Morrison 1898). In these passages, the term 'reed', once again, seems to refer to water reed as 'reed beds' are specifically mentioned. In Dorset, however, reed, unbruised wheat straw, was drawn and pitched for use as thatch (Stevenson 1812, 220). Vancouver's reference to the cost of 'drawn or yelmed straw' should be read with caution; it may simply refer to the fact that 'drawn' halm (west Hampshire) was no more expensive than 'yelmed' crushed straw (east Hampshire) (Vancouver 1813, 69). The Dorset influence is indicated by the fact that this straw was sold in 14lb bundles, half the weight of a standard Dorset nitch of reed straw.

Early nineteenth-century records from the Duke of Grafton's estate in Northamptonshire also refer to several distinct categories of thatching straw including a 'halm straw' that must be a Midlands version of reed straw. The accounts have regular entries for the sale of stubble straw (7.12.1807), wheat straw (23.1.1808) and halm straw (5.1.1808), but wheat straw and haulm also occur in the same entry (28.7.1807, 10.1808, 4.1808, 20.10.1809) as do stubble and long straw (14.9.1807) and stubble straw and white straw (ie the straw of spring cereal) (10.1.1809) (Northamptonshire Record Office 6). Stubble and haulm were, in this area, very separate products, the latter being the more expensive material for thatching. Wheat straw may well be a synonym for long straw, and the latter might also have included threshed white straw.

There is some surviving folk memory of this non-Devon reed straw tradition beyond the West Country. A building examined in Buckinghamshire (Appendix B: B6) was being rethatched with combed wheat reed applied long straw style, ie without dressing and with the appropriate eaves and barge liggers, by a local thatcher in keeping with local practice. In Dorset in the 1960s, reed straw was laid long straw fashion, in some cases butts down on the eaves to thicken it at this point and butts up elsewhere on the same roof to build up the pitch (Rod Miller, pers comm). The reed was stitched to the roof in individual bundles, without a waist coat, using tarred rope (or withes, blackberry stems or straw rope in earlier years), or sparred and swayed over existing coats. This reed straw coexisted with butts-together long straw produced when a crop was threshed, stacked and drawn so as to maintain the original orientation of the stems. The long straw roofs were sparred on the eaves and barges, finished with a flush ridge and clipped when completed to remove any ears showing on the surface.

The paucity of references to reed straw in East Anglia probably reflect the climatic, architectural and perform-

Figure 82 Flush ridge, c 1920s, Marsh Baldon, Oxfordshire (Centre for Oxfordshire Studies).

Figure 84 Simple raised (block) ridge, c 1900, Stanton St. John, Oxfordshire (Centre for Oxfordshire Studies).

Figure 83 Flush ridge, c 1930, Ardington, Oxfordshire (Centre for Oxfordshire Studies).

Figure 85 Simple raised (block) ridge, c 1916, Uffington, Oxfordshire (Centre for Oxfordshire Studies).

ance issues that mitigated against the development of an independent reed straw tradition, the presence of good quality water reed thatching in the Broads, and the fact that long straw worked very adequately in this area of steep roofs and abundant surplus crushed straw. East Anglia's rapid adoption of the threshing machine would have provided this abundance from the early nineteenth century and may have eliminated much of the evidence for an earlier reed straw tradition.

The thresher's role in increasing the availability of crushed straw is not as straightforward as many believe. In fact, the historical evidence suggests that it actually increased the availability of reed straw in some areas depending on how the new technology was used. In Dorset, wheat straw intended for thatching was 'pitched' of its ears and combed in the normal way, and only the ears were put through the thresher (Stevenson 1812, 145–6). In other regions, the operator simply inserted only the grain-bearing portion of a sheaf into the drum and withdrew the now ear-threshed reed straw for use in thatching (Young 1807 **1**, 157). There is ample historical data to demonstrate that this was a common practice in the early nineteenth century, and that the thresher was recognised as a means of increasing the efficiency with which reed straw could be produced (Mavor 1809, 134).

A greater challenge to the notion that long straw thatching originated with the threshing machine could not be found, as Mavor makes clear that the new technology might well have increased the use of reed straw at the expense of the common crushed straw of the region. The new material was produced as a by-product rather than a goal in itself, and its superiority over crushed straw was a welcomed bonus. The new reed straw was probably applied in the same way as the common crushed straw as there is no mention of dressing, and it could either have been combed in the bundle with a hand rake or drawn in the same manner as crushed straw.

The linguistic evidence also provides support for a once wider use of helm in southern England. The link is perhaps so obvious it has escaped notice: the long straw term yealm (drawn bundles of straw ready for thatching) and halm (unbruised reed straw or tall stubble prepared for thatching) are often indistinguishable in common parlance. The term yealm is actually pronounced hellum in Gloucestershire and several other districts, and is used throughout the long straw thatching districts of southern England. This could be explained by a transference of a widespread term for non-Devon reed straw (halm) to the process of preparing it by drawing (haulming), and its logical extension to include the 'haulming' of crushed straw with the rise in popularity of mechanical threshing.

Figure 86 Base coat of late medieval smoke-blackened thatch adjacent to post-medieval rebuilding, Honiton, Devon (John Letts).

Only the latter association has survived due to the disappearance of the reed straw tradition. We would be unable to distinguish this south-central halm straw tradition in the literature as it was prepared and applied in roughly the same way as with crushed straw, lightly flailed and butts-together long straw or even tall stubble. In contrast, the term yealm seems not to have been widely used in northern England even though reed straw was haulmed (drawn) for use as thatch, perhaps because thatching had already suffered a terminal decline in the north before (or irrespective of) the introduction of mechanical threshing.

The patterned ridge
The historical writings and the *in situ* evidence are all but silent on this issue, but there is fortunately abundant photographic evidence beginning in the middle of the nineteenth century to establish at least one general principle: ridges were generally finished flush and were provided with much less diamenting or raised patterning than is the case today (Figs 82–85).

Changing preferences in external ridging details, which can usually be accommodated with only a limited impact on what underlies the external ridge coat, are probably rooted in architectural movements of the early nineteenth century. Architects influenced by the cult of the picturesque rediscovered thatch in the late eighteenth and early nineteenth centuries and incorporated its 'rustic' qualities into cottage designs. The movement culminated in the cottage orné with its complex roof forms and external detailing, including an emphasis on heavily patterned ridges and the use of reed straw and water reed (Brown 1852). Some of these plans were totally impractical from a thatching perspective and were never implemented, but their general popularity injected an air of ostentation to what had traditionally been a functional approach to ridging. The movement undoubtedly influenced ridge ornamentation throughout England, particularly on roofs whose owners could afford to follow fashion, and perhaps limited on the houses of poorer folk only by the availability of the additional spars, liggers and labour it required.

Crushed straw

The term long straw is now too well-defined and narrowly interpreted for use in a broader historical enquiry of this kind. Crushed straw is a more historically valid term and loosens rigidified perspectives.

The earliest *in situ* evidence for crushed straw thatching in England was recovered during the rescue sampling undertaken over the course of this project. The chronologies of many of the roofs examined are difficult to unravel with any great certainty, but some of the earliest samples are probably post-medieval in origin even if most date to the eighteenth or nineteenth centuries (Fig 86). Multi-layered roofs are almost always thatched with straw, and beyond the West Country they are thatched primarily with crushed straw. The *in situ*, historical and linguistic evidence also supports the former existence of an ancient unbruised halm reed straw tradition throughout much of southern England. As with stubble thatch, however, it had slipped into obscurity by the mid nineteenth century to be replaced either by butts together or butts mixed crushed straw similar to modern long straw. The evidence clearly supports the notion that thatching in southern England from 1790 to 1940 was essentially straw thatching, and over most of the latter part of this period usually employed crushed straw.

According to *The Thatcher's Craft* the process of thatching with long straw begins on the ground with the preparation of the material. The threshed straw is forked into a jumbled heap, wetted and left to steep for several hours. Double handfuls of straw are 'drawn' from this bed and formed into neat yealms about 5" thick and 18" in breadth (13cm x 46cm). Yealms are stacked into a yoke which is carried onto the roof and fixed within convenient reach of the thatcher.

The thatch is usually applied from right to left in section, but can also be applied in narrow strakes from eaves to ridge. As with combed wheat reed, a brow course of bottles is fixed securely along the eaves to form a base for the first eaves course. These bottles are either tied to the lowermost battens and rafters, or clamped to

Figure 87 Cutting dormer eaves, c 1940s (Museum of English Rural Life).

the rafters with iron crooks and hazel sways. The eaves and barge bottles are pinned tightly against each other with spars driven sideways from one bottle into its neighbour, thus preventing the formation of any gaps that could encourage the formation of a gulley between them. A tight brow also facilitates the later cutting of the eaves (Fig 87).

Main coat courses are subsequently applied in much the same manner as with combed wheat reed and water reed, using temporary needles to ensure yealms are tightly bedded into each other and that no folded straw or gaps are left between them. Yealms are laid more horizontally on the barge and sweep towards the vertical as the course moves away from the barge. The eaves course is sparred into the brow course in front of the lower sway using individual spars or a continuous straw bond (scud) fixed with spars. Succeeding courses are laid in pairs, the upper course overlying the lower sufficiently to provide a standard depth from the surface to the batten face. *The Thatcher's Craft* recommends a total depth of 15" (38cm) with about 9" (23 cm) of material left beneath the fixing, or about two thirds of the surface depth, but the optimum depth varies with the length of the yealms being applied and the pitch of the roof. Thin coats will not last so long because less material needs to weather before the fixings are exposed. The second and third courses, and every

succeeding pair of courses, are crooked into place together and the sequence is continued up the roof towards the ridge. When a several square yard section of thatch has been laid, it is beaten and raked thoroughly with a long-handled rake in order to remove any short or unfixed straw, leaf and ears, and to ensure that all of the straws are lying vertically. Additional packing is used in valleys and around dormer windows to produce broad sweeping bends in the surface rather than sharp angular turns which would channel water and lead to rapid gulleying and decay. In the last century, valleys were often tiled or slated to eliminate the problem of accelerated weathering at this point (Wood-Jones 1963, 137).

Combed wheat reed and long straw ridges are interchangeable, but the simple flush ridge that so often occurs on long straw roofs in older photographs is a little simpler and less expensive to apply as it consumes less straw and fewer spars and liggers. On an open raftered roof, a ridge roll is first fixed to the ridge board with strong cord. Side courses are laid and their tops are twisted and sparred down onto the ridge roll to form a base for the top coat. Yealms are divided into two, half of which is reversed to ensure an even thickness of about 6" (15cm) when the yealm is folded over the ridge. A ligger is sparred into place along the crest, followed by additional liggers at intervals down the ridge, three liggers with cross-rod diamenting being shown in *The Thatcher's Craft*. The ridge is swept around a hip end as with combed wheat reed, but extra bottles and yealms must be inserted at the apex of the barge to make up for the downwards slope of the material and to enhance the ridge line. These are fixed by external liggers sparred along the gable, as along the eave, to secure them from the wind. Unfortunately, the pinnacle created at the top of the apex forces the material to lie at an inverse pitch which allows water to penetrate the roof at this point, emphasizing the fundamental advantage of a hipped end. The manner in which this gable apex is finished varies from region to region.

> In Essex and Suffolk a very solid and closely-packed pyramid of straw is imposed upon the missing point so as to convert it to a peaked form; in West Somerset the absence of point is accepted, and the diagonally laid straw is finally worked up into a forward jutting curve secured by strong (and highly decorative) fixings which give a sort of coxcomb effect ... Wiltshire, and Wessex generally, avoids the problem altogether by hipping off the gable in a rounded form. The effect of these three varying solutions of the same problem is far-reaching – the traditional form of cottage building in ... Essex resembling a child's Noah's Ark; Wessex, a tea-cosy; and Somerset in the form familiar to us all. (Gunn 1936, 30–31)

When the ridge and all external liggers have been fitted, the eaves and barges are cut at an angle sufficient to provide a drip from the upper edge of the thatch and to leave about a 4" (10cm) gap between the barge board and the lower edge. The barges and eaves are cut to perfectly straight lines. Extraneous straw is removed with shears, and some thatchers trim off any ears lying on the surface in order to produce a finish not dissimilar to combed wheat reed, although the ears will eventually reassert themselves from underlying layers as the thatch degrades.

The historical evidence
Detailed and reliable descriptions of thatching houses with crushed straw are surprisingly uncommon in the historical literature compared to the extended passages referring to thatching with reed straw and water reed. It is perhaps because the latter descriptions were almost always provided by agricultural writers from south-central England with the express purpose of encouraging the use of these superior materials at the expense of the crushed straw thatch of the common people. Descriptions are more commonly offered with reference to the thatching of ricks, with throwaway passages at the end indicating that a similar method was used for thatching houses, although to a higher standard using a greater depth of material and more secure fixings. Although fixing materials varied, there does not seem to have been much variation in way in which crushed straw was applied. The literature also offers little description of some of the finishings that are linked to long straw thatching in the present day which are simply not discussed.

The first coat of thatch was tied in place with a variety of strong and flexible fixings, the most common being straw, withes, blackberry stems, twisted hazel rod rope and later tarred and untarred cord. Stitching becomes impractical after one or two top coats have been applied, however, and a multi-layered roof will develop only when subsequent coats are fixed with spars and sways

Early nineteenth-century descriptions of thatching with crushed straw usually refer to ricks rather than buildings.

> Where long straw is made use of, the operator or workman usually begins at the eaves or bottom of the roof, depositing it in handfuls in regular breadths till he reaches the top, the different handfuls being so placed endwise as to overlap each other, the upper ends being constantly pushed a little into the bottom parts of the sheaves. In this manner he gradually proceeds, breadth after breadth, till the whole of the roof is covered, which is usually done to the thickness of about four or five inches [10cm–13cm]. In order to retain the thatch in its place, short sharp-pointed sticks are sometimes thrust in, in a slanting direction upwards, and sometimes small sticks sharpened at the ends are bent and thrust in along the top parts and sides; but as the water is apt to follow the course of the sticks, it is a better practice to make use of ropes of twisted straw for this purpose. (Loudon 1831, 517)

The suggestion is that the 'sharp sticks', thatching pegs, used to hold the thatch in place were fixed externally and individually without liggers. The same basic procedure was followed for thatching houses.

> In thatching the roofs of houses or other buildings with any of the sorts of straw, the same rules are in some respects to be followed, only the materials are to be laid on to a considerable thickness, and be more firmly secured. They are applied in regular narrow slips, or what in some districts are terms *gangs* or *courses*, from the eaves of the building to the ridges, the ladder being moved forward as the work proceeds. The thatch is secured by short sharpened sticks thrust in where necessary; and bended sticks sharpened at each end are sometimes made use of near the ridges, being thrust in at each end. In finishing the work, the thatcher employs an iron-toothed rake, with which the whole is raked over from the top to the bottom, so as to render it completely smooth and even, and take away all the short straws. (op cit, 518)

At first glance, this passage seems to describe a method of external pegging similar to that used for fixing ricks, but the fact that the roof was 'raked over from top to bottom' when it was completed indicates that the fixings were in this case 'internal' as expected when maximum longevity was required. The distinction is very important in terms of technical history, but such confusion is rife in the literature and its interpretation. It should be noted that the external pegging method described can be used with various materials and slight differences in the way in which these are laid before they receive their final fixing.

Straw could simply be laid over the surface, or stuffed to some degree into the existing base coat or rick surface.

> [The thatcher] seizes a handful, and bending one end into a kind of noose, he inserts this into the hay or straw near the bottom of the roof, at one end if it be a square roof, or at any convenient part if it be a round one. He presses down the straw which he has thus inserted to about half its length, in order to form the eaves, which extend a little beyond the lower part of the roof. When he has thus laid several handfuls side by side so as to cover about a yard in width, that is, as far a he can conveniently reach without moving his ladder, he begins another row a little above the place where he began, so that the lower end of the straw now inserted may cover the upper part of the first row, as tiles do each other. Thus he proceeds upwards till he comes to the upper ridge of the roof, or to the point of the cone in a round stack ... a rope of straw has been prepared, and many small rods about two feet long, and cut sharp at the point: these are inserted just below the ridge, in a line with it, and about a foot apart; one end of the straw rope is inserted into the stack, and twisted firmly round the projecting end of the first rod; it is then wound once round the next rod, and so on the whole length of the ridge: this is done on both sides. The straws which form the ridge are now cut with shears horizontally, to give it a neat finish, and at each end a kind of ornament is usually made by winding a straw rope around a handful of the projecting straw, forming a kind of knot or bow according to the taste of the thatcher. Rods and straw ropes twisted round them are inserted near the edge of the slanting side and all along the eaves, which prevent the wind from blowing off the thatch. (Rham 1845, 513)

On buildings where greater longevity was required:

> the straw is prepared in the same manner [as for ricks] ... but the ends of the handfuls, as they are put on a lathed roof, are kept down by means of long rods, which are tied to the laths of the roof by means of strong tar twine. A much thicker coat of straw is put on; and rye straw, which has a solid stem, is preferred as more lasting, and less liable to be filled with water than hollow straw. Instead of straw ropes, split willow is used and the rods which are inserted are much nearer each other and more carefully secured. As this kind of thatching is a peculiar trade, it requires a regular apprenticeship to be master of it. The thatching of temporary ricks may be done from mere description, and a very little practice will enable any one to protect his stacks sufficiently by a thatched covering. (ibid)

Although the early records are silent on the issue, it is undoubtedly the case that experienced thatchers in the last century manipulated the orientation of stems within the yealm, and the yealm itself, in order to solve problems of pitch, balanced by the desirability of keeping the butt end of a stem exposed to the elements as it is the toughest wearing portion of the stem. It is possible to draw stems into a predominantly butts-together yealm if the straw has been threshed and stacked so as to maintain this uniform orientation. Such a product weathers slowly in its early life but more quickly as the softer upper portions of the stems are exposed, whereas a butts and ears mixed yealm weathers evenly over its lifespan. However, the softest portion of the stem of the first material is sealed by the fixings and would not be open to weathering in any case. The face of the mixed yealm should pack more tightly than the butts-together roof as it contains both thin upper internodes and coarse butt ends, but it also contains crushed ears and leaf tissue that can interrupt the flow of water and provide foci of fungal activity and decay. A strong butts and ears mixed tradition has survived in East Anglia where the trusser was a late addition to the thresher, but even within one county or locality the practice varies as Bagshawe (1951, 1166) discovered during his fieldwork in the early 1950s.

Stubble thatching

Stubble thatching is one of the most striking lost traditions in English thatching, and no folk memory of it survives amongst thatchers. The historical records clearly demonstrate its popularity, both for thatching ricks and houses, but they are not so clear as to the ways in which it was used. This situation has been improved somewhat by the *in situ* evidence. The records indicate that stubble was cut over much of southern England and references to its use as thatch survive from the historic counties of Berkshire, Oxfordshire, Kent, Gloucestershire, Rutland, Northamptonshire, Huntingdonshire and Leicestershire (Fig 33). It probably survived the longest in arable districts of the Midlands with heavy soils that were less quick to shift to mechanized cereal production. Stubble was used in three principal ways:

1   isolated repair using a stobbing method
2   spar coating and patching (of both houses and ricks)
3   packing and underlay

When used externally it had to be drawn, as with crushed straw, but for internal use it could be applied as it arrived from the field, dirty, fragmented and full of short straw and weeds. Stubble was well soaked before being drawn as it was very coarse. Stubble was also partially decayed before it arrived on a roof, as it had usually stood in the field for several weeks or months before being scythed and raked. According to one observer from Kent:

> on most of the middle and small-sized farm-houses and offices, thatch is the common covering; which is put on, particularly in the eastern part, much worse than in any other part of the kingdom ... The stubble of wheat is raked up for this purpose; which being often done in the winter, when, by rainy seasons, it is become half rotten, of course, cannot last a long time on a building. (Boys 1805, 32)

REPAIR

Stubble makes up the lower internodes of a cereal crop. These segments are naturally more lignified even if cut green, but they are particularly tough and brittle if left to ripen fully as occurs when crops are cut high on the stem. Stiff stubble can be inserted quite easily in handfuls into

Figure 88 Pegged thatch, The Forge, Fringford, Oxfordshire (Centre for Oxfordshire Studies).

bird holes or patched into place with exterior fixings, but is simply too brittle and unyielding to be bent into a knotted 'wisp' so as to be stuffed into a hole or spar coated. It could be used in this way only if it was mixed with longer, more flexible straw (Woodward 1984, 64).

The similarity of the terms stob, plugs of straw used in repairs, and stubb (stubble) is obvious and too close for them not to have been more strongly associated in the past, but the term stob has probably widened over the years to include repair using any material used in this way.

SPAR COATING AND PATCHING

Stubble was applied to houses using external fixings of peg and rope (or spars and sways) identical to those used on ricks. The technique simply involved fixing the thatch from the outside rather than internally with each course covering the fixings of the course below it. Outside thatching never performed as well as inside thatching. The former was associated with rick thatching and the latter with the professional craft, but the longevity of pegged roofs was low not because of poor thatching but because of the inevitable fungal breakdown of fixings and the quality of the stubble employed.

Stubble could rarely have exceeded 24" (60cm) even in the medieval period when cereal varieties grew to 5'–6' (1.5m–1.8m) in height, and in the early nineteenth century probably averaged 16"–20" (41cm–51cm) judging by the historical, botanical and *in situ* evidence. Using the degradation quotient of about 1" (2.5cm) a year previously discussed, and allowing half of this average length for fixing, an average coat of 40cm stubble could be expected to last for no more than seven to eight years at the maximum. The pegged roofs that figure so prominently in photographic records of the last century probably survived for no more than five to seven years with regular repair and maintenance (Figs 88 and 89). Since they were probably thatched by the same people who

Figure 89 Pegged thatch being replaced with crushed straw, 1944, Great Bentley, Essex (Museum of English Rural Life).

thatched local ricks using the same fixings, it can perhaps be assumed that many, if not most, were also thatched with stubble straw in areas where this was available. Hence, the records from Gloucestershire that mention stubb used as a main coat thatch may well be referring to a peg and rope technique:

> 1796. Mr Charles Wherret Do to Thos Clark, to thatching At William Preas, to Laung up 10 Drave of Stub at 1sh 2d [6p] per drave
> 1798. Mr Charles Whearret Dr to John Clark, to thatching at William Reas, to Laing up 20 Drave of Stub at 1s 2d [6p] par Drave, to Laing up half a Drave of Boulting. (Gloucestershire Record Office 1)

For at least three reasons, the term boulting (a Gloucestershire word for unbruised reed straw) was probably used as a fleeking: high quality reed straw is unlikely to have been applied in the form of a butts-up ridge on a poor roof of stubble; a fleeking of some sort would certainly have been required; and stubble roofs were usually finished with either a flush or wrap-over ridge of threshed straw.

Loudon's description of stubble thatching in the early nineteenth century suggests that stubble was often wedged into the existing base coat rather than simply laid upon its surface, presumably to hold it in place prior to fixing.

> In the application of stubble as a thatch for ricks, it is mostly put on by sticking one of its ends into the roof of the stack in a regular and exact manner, so that it may stand very close and thick; when the other, with such loose straws as may occur, is to be cut over or parred off with the thatching knife, or a very sharp tool for the purpose, so as to form a neat and impenetrable thatch, having the appearance of a newly thatched house-roof; the whole being well secured in its place by short pegs made for the purpose ... the same rules are in some respects to be followed [for houses], only the materials are to be laid on to a considerable thickness, and be more firmly secured. They are applied in regular ... *courses*, from the eaves of the building to the ridges ... secured by short sharpened sticks thrust in where necessary; and bended sticks sharpened at each end are sometimes made use of near the ridges, being thrust in at each end ... [then] raked over from the top to the bottom, so as to render it completely smooth and even, and take away all the short straws. (Loudon 1831, 517–8)

The historical records must be read with caution.

> The common thatch covering used in the neighbourhood of Gloucester, and Upper Vale, is made of the straw, threshed in the usual way, or of stubble, which is the ground stalk of the wheat left by the reaper, about a foot long, and afterwards mowed. (Rudge 1813, 46–7)

> In the Vale, it is mowed like grass, left in swathes, and afterwards raked into heaps: then it is 'drawn,' or picked,

and, being tied up into small sheaves, is in a ready state for thatching. (op cit, 119)

However, Rudge also mentions a 'short stubble' cut from 'the Hills' around Gloucestershire simply to clear land for ploughing, providing a contrast with the taller stubble cut from 'the Vale'. In dire emergencies longer straw could be mixed with short stubble to form a thatch that might last a season or two, but the taller product was preferred (op cit, 118–9).

PACKING AND BACKFILLING

Stubble need not have been drawn to be used for packing or base coats which were not to be exposed to the elements. The only condition its use for this purpose imposed was the need for an underlying support base that prevented short stem segments of straw from falling into the roof space. As in medieval buildings, this was usually provided by a fleeking of straw or reed, wattle, brushwood or closely set laths. The stubble was held in position by virtue of the fixings that tied the overlying external coat to the rafters and battens.

Rick thatching

For those who remember rural life as it was before the Second World War a distinction is frequently made in discussions of thatching between the house thatcher and the rick thatcher. The former is usually accorded much more respect as a skilled craftsman, whereas the rick thatcher is seen as a simple farm labourer with delusions of grandeur. A house thatcher could always thatch a rick, but a rick thatcher was usually less capable, and usually less willing, to thatch a house. In the late nineteenth century, however, it is probably true to say that to most of the populace, house thatching was simply an improved version of rick thatching, differing only in the quantity of material applied, the number of fixings employed, the cost of the work and the fact that ricks were never sparcoated. The differentiation between rick thatcher and house thatcher might well have existed more strongly at a social rather than technical level, and a good rick thatcher could usually produce an acceptable thatch on a house for much less cost than the full-time professional. English sources from the last century are filled with descriptions of thatching ricks of corn and hay using a variety of methods.

It was relatively easy to keep rain from spoiling a rick for one winter, but another matter entirely to produce a thatched roof that would last for 15 years or more. A well-thatched rick might well have lasted for several seasons, but this longevity was rarely tested as ricking was a temporary measure provided to keep cereal dry in the sheaf only until it could be threshed. Rick thatchers could thatch quickly, using whatever material was to hand, to keep rain off of essential stocks of fodder or seed for next year's planting. House thatchers worked at their own pace as the opportunity arose and as the demands of the seasonal round of harvest activities allowed. A poor cottager unable to thatch his own roof would usually have preferred to pay a rick thatcher to apply a thin coat

Figure 90 Thatched ricks in Oxfordshire, c 1900s (Centre for Oxfordshire Studies).

of rush or poor quality straw that might last for five years, rather than employ a house thatcher at triple the cost to apply top quality reed straw that could last four times as long with regular maintenance. It is very likely that a large portion of the poor quality housing in rural areas that was cleared away by the reforms early this century and late last century were thatched by occupiers or handy rick thatchers.

The storage of grain in ricks is a relatively new development in English agriculture, linked to the massive increases in cereal production that occurred in the late eighteenth and early nineteenth centuries. Fodder was regularly stored in ricks in southern England as it was in upland and northern districts, but before this period of expansion the bulk of the grain harvest was stored in barns where it lay subject to the depredations of vermin, insects and fungi while awaiting threshing. Storing the harvest indoors was much cheaper than ricking if space was available, but space was usually in short supply and many large farms and estates cut their cereals high on the stem in order to reduce the amount of straw that was carried into storage with the grain. The stubble that remained in the field was harvested later for use as thatch, litter or fuel.

> It is the practice in the greatest part of the district [Lancashire], to secure the wheat crops in the barns ... because ... there is a objection to [ricking] with respect to the straw which is required for thatch, which in many places is very valuable. Mr Perrie ... considers the practice of housing in barns as advantageous in saving straw and thatching, as well as time, and in being more secure from rain and vermin. (Dickson & Stevenson 1815, 307)

In pastoral districts, hay ricks continued to be thatched using ancient roping techniques, and roping was used in Cornwall and parts of northern England into the 1960s. The small amounts of cereal grown for domestic use in pastoral districts were stored indoors, and the straw produced was carefully husbanded for purposes other than thatching when wild materials could be procured. Hay ricks were less plentiful in arable districts and the corn crop was largely stored indoors prior to the late eighteenth century. With rising cereal output, however,

ricking became a necessity, particularly when the threshed straw that was once considered a waste product became a much more valuable commodity (Figs 90 and 91).

Some researchers have suggested that the origin of regional differences in house thatching lie in ancient methods of rick-thatching, and it is generally assumed that the best thatchers and techniques moved from primitive rick to more sophisticated roof. In fact, it is likely that house thatchers influenced the methods used in rick thatching more than in the reverse case, at least in districts where cereal production rose in the late eighteenth and nineteenth centuries. The external peg and sway method employed on ricks, essentially a more rapidly applied version of the internal spar and sway technique, was probably borrowed from the repertoire of methods commonly used by the less professional house thatchers of the period. Stephens (1908, 199), for example, believed that rick thatching with external fixings was simply 'an imitation of thatching cottages' that provided less shelter from the wind than their roped predecessors. This would go far to explain why external pegging on poorer rural housing is so prevalent in photographic collections from the turn of the century, and it suggests that many of these houses were probably thatched with stubble as long as it was available.

Rick thatchers received less money for their services than house thatchers, but payment was calculated in the same way using the thatcher's square.

> As a rule, most of the work was done on a piece-work basis at so much a 'square', there being 100 ft^2 [9.29m^2] to the square. When the thatching of the stacks was completed, the farmer would come along with a tape measure and help my father to measure up the work, on which basis payment would be made. (Parrott 1974, 19)

As with roof thatching, the finer variations in technique and material preparation are too numerous to present in detail. Ricks could be round or boat-shaped with hipped ends, or square or rectangular with gable ends. It was essential that the rick was left to settle for a week or more before commencing thatching, and that the top layer of hay or corn was worked into a smooth surface. This was done by knocking in sheaves that stood out and pulling out sheaves in the hollows. Loose straw was spread over the surface to fill up the holes and bumps that could buckle the thatch and interfere with the downflow of rain water. In a well built rick every sheaf lay at an acute angle with its butts towards the outside, and even without its thatched roof it would shed water well enough to survive a moderate downpour. It was also essential that the thatch was combed thoroughly before any external fixings were applied, in order to ensure that any weeds or short straw were removed and all bent straw combed into line with the rest of the thatch. The 4"–5" (10cm–13 cm) coat of thatch applied to a ricks provided a secure barrier to rain and snow, but was thin enough to allow the rick to breathe and release the moisture that could lead to mildew and decay when the harvest was stored in a barn with poor air circulation.

Figure 91 Thatched ricks, Berkshire, 1940s (Museum of English Rural Life).

It is very good husbandry to top hay or corn reeks with well wetted helms, that they may be well sparred down. (Lisle 1757, 202)

In essence, thatching a rick was similar to spar-coating onto an existing roof, due to the undercoat that provided a solid base for fixing pegs and spars. Most of the descriptions of thatching ricks in the literature refer to the use of threshed wheat straw that was drawn in exactly the same manner as is used today with long straw. Records also attest to the use of rye, oat and barley straw, stubble, wheat reed straw and pasture rushes, or any other materials that could provide an absolutely secure thatch for at least a season. The shorter expected longevity of a rick thatch meant that oat and barley straw, which were usually considered to be too soft for use on roofs, could be used successfully. Interestingly, water reed is almost never mentioned in connection with rick thatching.

APPLICATION
The records suggest that ricks were thatched using one of four methods:

1   Internal fixing: This type of thatching was perhaps the closest technically, and in external appearance, to

higher quality house thatching, in that the pegs, spars and rope or straw fixings of each course were hidden beneath the course laid above it. This method could be used with any thatching material including sheaves with grain still in the ear.

2   External fixing: This was essentially an easier-applied version of the first technique in which the pegs, spars and rope or straw fixings were applied externally onto the surface of the thatch at varying intervals.

3   External roping: A system by which the thatch was held down using ropes strung in various ways and either fixed under the eaves, tied to a main rope at eaves level, or weighted down with stones to ensure that the roof stood firm against the wind.

4   Sheaf fixing: In this last method, handfuls of straw were inserted up to half their length into the butts of sheaves which formed the top layer of the rick, which would hold them into position without the use of any additional fixings, except in very windy conditions.

Methods 2 and 3 required handfuls of thatch to be pushed up a short distance into the butts of the top coat of sheaves so that they could be held in position until the external fixings could be applied. External pegging was a simple method to learn: a long peg was pushed three quarters of

Devon contains c.300 examples of SBT

Counties with <10 examples of smoke blackened late medieval thatch (SBT)

Figure 92 Distribution map of buildings sampled and described in Appendices A and B; A1 = building described in Appendix A, 1 = buildings described in Appendix B (Judith Dobie, after John Letts).

its length into the thatch, and a rope made from tarred twine, straw, hay or rush was twisted around the top of the peg. The peg was then pushed in further to tighten the rope against the thatch. Rick pegs were roughly the same length (2'–3'/60cm–90cm) as untwisted spars, with one end sharpened to a point and the other cut flat to allow it to be pushed into the rick with a hand or mallet. Notches were also sometimes cut into the sides of the peg to help stop it from working its way out of the rick. Numerous passages refer to the pegging of both ricks and house thatch, for example:

> Pegs can be made out of any straight wood that can be got cheaply, and should be of the thickness of one's fingers; thicker sticks ought to be split. For a hay rick it is not necessary to have pegs longer than from, say, fifteen to thirty inches [38cm to 76cm], but for straw or corn ricks pegs from two to three feet [61cm to 91cm] in length are better. The thick end of the stick should be sharpened to a point, and the top end cut off at a right angle to avoid injury to the thatcher's hand. (Bradshaw 1912, 301)

Twisted hazel spars were much less commonly used in thatching ricks: they were more difficult to make and use properly, they left two holes in the thatch rather than one and their tines were not inserted into the stack as deeply as with a peg. Pegs for use on ricks could also be cut from almost any straight-grained wood as they were not expected to last for more than a couple of seasons.

Spars could be used alone or in combination with straw bands or rope, but wooden sways were used almost exclusively on buildings. In Dorset:

> Such of the wheat crop as is not put into barns, is generally laid on square frames, which are supported on staddles ... They are generally covered with *reed thatch* or unthrashed wheat straw, which lasts two years for this purpose. It is

fastened on the corn stacks by spars made of split hazel wood, which are twisted in the middle, and used in this state to bestride and hold together the small handfuls of *reed*, which cross the roofs in a horizontal direction, and perform the same office as the hay-bands and spits of the midland counties. (Stevenson 1812, 219–20)

A straw finial or dozzle in the shape of a bird, an animal, or a sheaf of wheat tied so as to allow the ears to fan out, provided a creative outlet, and an advertisement, for the rick thatcher, along with a convenient perching spot for birds who might otherwise damage the main coat of thatch. On a square rick the finial provided additional coverage for the gable apex which was always the most difficult part of the rick to thatch. However finished, newly-applied thatch was always well raked before putting on any external fixings, in order to remove short and crooked straw that might interfere with the flow of water towards the eaves.

Straw ropes were often used in combination with other fixing methods to provide additional security for a rick in exposed conditions. An important element of this was the fixing of a strong guide rope parallel with, and just above, the eaves line to which the vertical ropes were tied. Similarly, a guide rope was often placed along the crest of the ridge, or around the conical point of a round rick, to provide an upper fixing for the vertical ropes and to prevent them from cutting into the thatch at the ridge. The combine harvester soon dampened the demand for rick thatching, and the development of the one-man needle in the 1930s extended the life of the craft only temporarily.

THE ARCHAEOLOGY OF ANCIENT THATCH

The plant materials preserved in ancient roofs, whether medieval or nineteenth-century, provide an unparalleled resource for reconstructing the history of agriculture and land use, and for characterizing both the crops and the weeds that otherwise survive only in very degraded form on archaeological sites. The search for 20 buildings with multi-layered roofs suitable for excavation began in 1994 and continued into the spring of 1997 (Fig 92). No roofs were excavated in northern England because few thatched buildings have survived in the north, let alone with multi-layered roofs suitable for sampling. On average, only one out of every three vetted buildings visited actually produced a series of samples suitable for analysis.

Recording thatch *in situ*

As with any archaeological excavation, layers are removed one by one to reveal as much about the fixing of each underlying course as possible (Fig 93). Large-scale open-plan excavation is rarely possible, and sampling must proceed within a narrow slit trench less than a metre wide – which makes it difficult to record and photograph basal layers that can be as much as 5' (1.5m) below the surface. Narrow excavations are best accomplished using

Figure 93 Stripping a c 2 m accumulation of post-medieval reed straw, Devon (John Letts).

a stepped trench technique, each main coat layer being removed to reveal about 12"–16" (30cm–41cm) of the layer beneath it (Fig 94). Sampling begins towards the ridge and proceeds down towards the eave, where the fixings of the eaves courses and the structure of the roof at this point are examined in closer detail.

In general, multi-layered roofs are built up through the simple superposition of one spar coat over another, but obtaining sequential samples is more problematic than it appears in theory due to patching, disproportionate stripping and re-ridging. A main coat layer sampled in one discreet location may in fact be a small patch that differs significantly from the layer onto which it was sparred or the patch a few metres away. Similarly, thatchers usually stripped weathered coats only so far as necessary to obtain a solid base for rethatching. Dips and gulleys were filled with packing considered unsuitable for external use; eaves and gables were stripped back to their base coats to obtain secure fixings for the eave course; and ridges were raised and consolidated by the addition of ridge rolls and 'skirts'. The gradual effect was to raise the pitch of the roof by up to 10° or more over several centuries. A series of samples taken from just above the eaves on such a roof would not reflect the full chronology present just below the ridge.

Care must also be taken during sampling not to misinterpret two courses within one layer as two separate layers, particularly on degraded roofs or under difficult sampling conditions. Courses are obviously bedded onto each other with a clean interface and separate very easily when being stripped. Layers are generally separated by a distinct layer of decay containing dead moss and lichen, and are best differentiated by reference to the thatching materials they contain. The pitch of the material in individual courses is also usually shallower than the pitch of the surface of the underlying layer.

Samples were carefully removed from a section face with their fixings left intact whenever possible. They were placed in sample bags with the external portion of each bundle in the bottom of the bag in order to ensure that the sample retained the same orientation in the laboratory as it had on the roof. Damp samples can decay very rapidly in a warm laboratory unless the sample bags are opened and dried out quickly.

Dating

Few multi-layered roofs harbour more than ten layers of thatch. If each layer lasted about 15 years, theoretically the thatch on few of the buildings sampled predate the early nineteenth century. Base coats were replaced infrequently and many of the base coats examined are probably the original base coats applied when the buildings were first constructed. This is clearly the case where base coats are tied into position with saplings, twisted rod-rope or dethorned stems of blackberry. Overlying base coats might be stitched with tarred twine, which was being used for thatching by the early to mid eighteenth century. Early layers were often fixed with spars of roundwood rather than split hazel as in more recent times. Thatching materials do not in themselves offer a firm date for their application. It would be very difficult

Figure 94 Stepped trench excavation of late medieval to modern thatch (Appendix A: A15, Great Doddington, Northamptonshire) (John Letts). See also colour plate 9.

Figure 95 Thatch excavation: exposed ridge section with layers of clay (Appendix A: A15, Great Doddington, Northamptonshire) (John Letts). See also colour plate 10.

to date specific layers based on the morphology of the cereals present, although advances in molecular genetics have opened the possibility of extracting DNA from ancient specimens for comparison with *in vivo* accessions of older varieties with known introduction dates. Few named varieties predate the development of scientific plant breeding in the mid nineteenth century, however, and the morphological diversity of the cereals in many samples from basal layers suggests an earlier origin.

Ridges present particular problems both for sampling and dating. An average layer of straw thatch in England will require re-ridging two or three times during its lifetime, and ridges are generally left to decay more thoroughly before being replaced than a main coat layer. Ridges often survive as indistinct layers of organic detritus, their chronology confused by the degraded remnants of spars, horizontal fixings, ridge rolls and occasionally by clay (Figs 95 and 96). The external appearance of ridges in the past is one of the most disputed topics, but this evidence rarely survives in sufficient detail in ancient roofs.

Analysis and interpretation

The first steps are to identify the botanical constituents of a sample, assess their presence in rough percentage terms and describe the manner in which they are organised and oriented in the sample. Cereals are identified through ear

and rachis characters as straw is largely unidentifiable on its own. The presence of weeds is often very important as they reflect the degree to which a sample has been cleaned by drawing or combing before it was applied. The presence of flag leaf, short fragmented stems of straw or other materials and herbaceous detritus is also important in this respect.

A representative number of straw specimens are measured to provide an average length for the overall sample. Since older wheat varieties usually produced stems with five or six nodes, the average internode length can be used to estimate the probable original height of the crop in the field and the height of the stubble left behind at harvest. Specimens can usually be identified as having been derived from the apex or base of a stem, an observation that has considerable significance in terms of crop harvesting and processing methods employed. For example, scythed stubble should theoretically be composed of relatively short segments of uncrushed basal specimens cut at both ends, the upper end by sickle, the lower end by scythe, and perhaps containing specimens with roots dislodged when the cut stubble was raked. Similarly, it is impossible to tell whether a degraded course of reed straw has been derived from straw cut at ground level or high on the stem.

Specimens are also assessed for the intensity and extent to which they have been crushed during threshing. It is highly probable that an early nineteenth-century speci-

Figure 96 Thatch excavation: decayed ridge with 'hedgehog' display of spars (Appendix A: A18, Bacton, Suffolk) (John Letts). See also colour plate 11.

men showing evidence of distinct blow marks on its internodes, but with nodes largely uncrushed, was threshed with a flail. More even crushing of both nodes and internodes, particularly from later layers, reflects the damage caused by a mechanical thresher. Crushing at the apex of early samples of reed straw indicates either lashing or flailing, whereas later samples may have been threshed by inserting only the ears of the sheaf into the mouth of the thresher. The product, appearance, destiny and performance of both these materials were similar, although they were produced by different methods. As with measurements of length, the evidence for crushing can be distorted when, for example, apex-flailed reed straw is degraded leaving only crushed upper stem sections which are identical to the weathered residue of crushed straw applied butts-together.

Information regarding the cereals is largely restricted to descriptions of ear characters, such as the general size and density of the ear, the presence or absence of awns and more rigorous botanical characters when required (Hervey-Murray 1980; Hillman 1983; Zohary & Hopf 1988; Jarman & Pickett 1994). One very important fact that must be recorded is the presence of rivet wheat (*Triticum turgidum*), a soft-grained English version of the free-threshing tetraploid wheat (*Triticum durum*) that is grown for pasta in Mediterranean countries. The archaeobotanical evidence suggests that land race mixtures of rivet wheat introduced to Britain in the Norman period spread rapidly to become very common on clay lands in medieval times, but were gradually eclipsed over the course of the nineteenth century by improved varieties of common bread wheat (*Triticum aestivum*), better suited to commercial baking. Rivet straw is thicker and stronger than that of any bread wheat, and its presence in thatched roofs, whether medieval or post-medieval, might well reflect its cultivation specifically for this purpose.

Straw thatching in England: the *in situ* evidence

The *in situ* evidence indicates that the multi-layered thatched roofs of buildings in England are almost always composed of accumulated spar coats of cereal straw. Although water reed (*Phragmites australis*) was commonly used in parts of East Anglia and other regions in the past, early evidence of reed thatch generally survives only in the form of fleekings. As expected, the availability of non-arable materials has always been dictated by local vegetation and habitat, hence sea rush (*Juncus maritimus*) has been recovered from a building in coastal Dorset (Appendix B: B23), fen sedge (*Cladium mariscus*) and black bog rush (*Schoenus nigricans*) from cottages in former fenland districts in Cambridgeshire (Appendix A: A9; Appendix B: B9, B10), and bulrush (*Schoenoplectus lacustris*) from a cottage in Buckinghamshire adjacent to a part of the river Thames once noted for its production of bulrush for basketry and chair making (Appendix A: A6).

Multi-layered straw roofs are generally composed of eight to nine layers of reed straw in the West Country and six to seven spar coats of mostly crushed straw in south-central and eastern England. Although the layering on these roofs is discontinuous, they do provide sequential snapshots of the local environment, agricultural activities and the craft of thatching over several centuries and are as fundamental a part of the vernacular history of a building as any oak beam or mullioned window.

The data suggest that roofs of crushed straw were stripped back more often, and more completely, to a sound base before a new spar coat was applied than those of reed straw. This practice varied, however, as 11 main coat layers were recorded on roofs in Wiltshire (Appendix A: A20) and Bedfordshire (Appendix A: A2) and only three or four in Berkshire (Appendix A: A3), Buckinghamshire (Appendix A: A5) and Cambridgeshire (Ap-

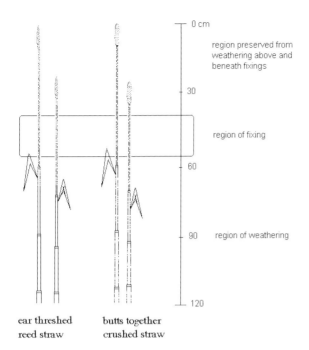

Figure 97 Impact of weathering on appearance of crushed straw and reed straw: convergence of reed straw and butts-together crushed straw due to decay (John Letts).

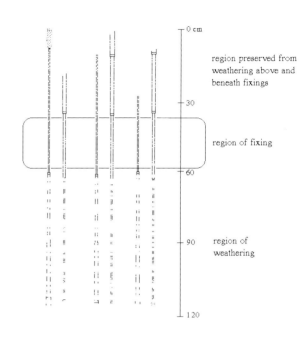

Figure 98 Generalized impact of weathering on appearance of crushed straw/long straw (John Letts).

pendix A: A8). In both regions, the evidence from excavations indicates that base coats were rarely disturbed during rethatching.

The outer layer of a multi-layered roof is usually a good indicator of what lies below it. Hence, a top coat of long straw almost inevitably shelters earlier layers of long straw, just as an external spar coat of combed wheat reed in the West Country generally overlies earlier layers of reed straw. External coats of combed wheat reed beyond the West Country have also been spar-coated onto long straw bases over the past 30 years, as demonstrated by the derelict barn at Hampstead Norries, Bedfordshire (Appendix A: A3), in which an external coat of rye reed straw covered two earlier layers of crushed straw, and the cart shed at Stanton St John (Appendix A: A17 Oxfordshire) in which a top coat of combed wheat reed overlay several spar coats of crushed straw covering a gorse core. The distinction between modern long straw and combed wheat reed is usually very clear even in highly weathered samples, just as ancient Dorset pitched reed is easily distinguished from a layer of jumbled and drawn crushed straw. Other variations in the way reed straw and crushed straw were once prepared and applied are not always so easy to distinguish once they have degraded back to their fixings, for reasons that will become clear once the surviving evidence for the two principal materials has been discussed.

Reed straw, halm and crushed straw

Numerous examples of modern combed wheat reed thatching were observed over the course of this project, but only four ancient reed straw roofs were actually recorded in detail; three from Devon (Appendix A: A10, A11, A12) and one from south Dorset (Appendix A: A13). Four examples provide a very limited basis for comparative analysis, but these buildings nevertheless fit

the expected pattern and are revealing in several ways. The lower layers of the cottage roof in Dorset (Appendix A: A13) were composed of very clean and undamaged pitched reed straw, while the bulk of the Devon material had either been lashed or flailed with the crushing being restricted to the apex of the straw. Surprisingly, a once exposed pre-modern layer from one Devon building (Appendix A: A11) was also composed of crushed straw, applied butts-together and fixed with pegs and homespun tarred twine. Crushed straw is not used for thatching in Devon today, but the find emphasises the fact that a cross-over in technique and material has always been possible even in the heartland of the combed wheat reed tradition.

On these four buildings, the bulk of the reed straw had been laid butts-down, except when it was used for repair or as a base (waist) coat when its orientation could be reversed. A base coat can be identified by the absence of weathering as at Stockland (Appendix A: A10) and Cullompton (Appendix A: A12), and can be smoke-blackened and thus probably medieval in date as at Stockland and Ilfracombe (Appendix A: A10). In both cases, the first surviving weathered coats were post-medieval. This limited evidence suggests that, in Devon, medieval base coats of reed straw or threshing waste were used in the same way as waist coats in more recent times, to provide a solid, unexposed base for external spar coats. The waist coat for a cottage orné in Axmouth, Devon, was composed of full length, unbroken, and apparently well combed crushed straw (Appendix B: B16). In contrast, no separate base coat was applied to the cottage in Osmington (Appendix A: A13 Dorset), and the base coat, applied butts-up and thus undressed, had functioned as an external coat for at least five to ten years judging by the c 8" (20cm) of wear that had occurred. On a newly stripped roof a fleeking is essential to allow the reeds to slide upwards when dressed rather than penetrate the roofspace. No fleeking was required on the wattled roof at Stockland (Appendix A: A10), but both the Cullompton (Appendix A: A12) and Ilfracombe (Appendix A: A11) examples were fleeked even though they were also provided with waist coats, which suggests that these fleekings were actually applied for aesthetic rather than technical purposes.

The historical literature provides considerable support for the former existence of a reed straw or halm tradition in southern England beyond the West Country. Two early examples of butts-together halm were recovered from buildings in Buckinghamshire (Appendix B: B2) and Cambridgeshire (Appendix B: B10). Both had degraded to about 45cm–50cm but were clearly derived from uncrushed straw. Ear-threshed halm need not have been applied butts-together in West Country style, however, and the evidence suggests it was treated in much the same way as crushed straw and drawn from a wetted heap into yealms that were mixed in terms of ears and butts. Such a material would then weather into a sample containing equal proportions of short basal segments and well-crushed upper internodes (Figs 97 and 98). At least six of the 20 buildings recorded in Appendix A contain such mixtures (Appendix A: A2 Bedfordshire, A4 Buckinghamshire, A14 Leicestershire, A17 Oxfordshire, A19 Wiltshire and A20 Wiltshire), and most of this material occurs in early layers. The unbruised lower stem segments are easily confused with true stubble, but they are usually cut at only one end and weathered at the other. It is difficult to explain the origin of such mixtures by reference to any other process, and they provide fairly conclusive evidence for the early use of halm thatch in these areas.

Fifteen of the 65 buildings examined provided samples of what at first glance might easily be called butts-together long straw. Top coats from Appendix A: A1 and A7 (Bedfordshire) and earlier layers from Appendix A: A2 (Bedfordshire), Appendix B: B32 (Northamptonshire) and Appendix A: A18 (Suffolk) certainly fall into this category as they are crushed over their entire *c* 70cm–80 cm length. Butts-together crushed straw also occurs in Devon both as a weathered main coat (Appendix A: A11) and a waist coat (Appendix B: B16). Sample Appendix B: B9 (Cambridgeshire), now degraded to only 35cm, was removed from a layer of mostly butts-together long straw applied in about 1955, a late version of a material now being replicated by header stripping (Appendix B: B26 Hertfordshire) and apex-combing (Appendix B: B39 Oxfordshire) in East Anglia. Early samples from Bedfordshire (Appendix: A1 and A2, Appendix B: B1), Buckinghamshire (Appendix B: B7), Cambridgeshire (Appendix A: A8, Appendix B: B10), Leicestershire (Appendix B: B27), Oxfordshire (Appendix A: A17), Suffolk (Appendix A: A18) and Wiltshire (Appendix A: A20) cannot be lumped into this category quite so easily for a very simple reason: ear-threshed reed straw and butts-together crushed straw are all but identical once they have weathered back to the point of fixing. A mid nineteenth-century reed straw about 39" (99cm) in length could easily have had 20" (51cm) of its apex crushed by the flail or threshing

drum, or about 4" (10cm) beyond its fixings. None of the older butts-together samples examined exceed 50cm in length and all have probably lost at least half of their original length to decay. Since reed straw and crushed straw are fixed to the roof at approximately the same distance within the bundle, weathered examples of the two materials would be indistinguishable unless they had been over-coated well before they decayed to the point of the fixing. As a result, we cannot rule out the possibility that at least ten of the buildings examined might contain additional degraded examples of halm straw.

Most of the samples of crushed straw recovered are similar to modern long straw in being mixed in terms of ears and butts. They also vary greatly in the degree to which they have been crushed, but it would be very difficult to attribute this crushing to either the flail, the (lashing) webble or the threshing machine based on a non-statistical analysis of a degraded sample of 30cm specimens. As is clear from both historical and contemporary evidence, threshers varied in the degree to which they damaged the straw, just as a flail could be used carefully to minimize both the damage inflicted on the straw and the effort expended in thrashing. In general, the thresher crushed straw evenly over the entire length of the stem including the nodes. In contrast, many examples of crushed straw show distinct blow marks on the internodes caused by a flail, while the nodes, and in fact most of the stem, are undamaged. Irrespective of how the straw was threshed, the mixed orientation of stems in terms of ears and butts indicates the material was heaped into a bed, drawn into yealms and applied in much the same way as modern long straw, for undrawn material would not have been used as an external coat on a cottage roof. Whether applied to ear-threshed halm or crushed straw, the drawing procedure clearly dates back to at least the post-medieval period and certainly pre-dates the introduction of the threshing machine.

Stubble

The historical records indicate that stubble was used in many parts of the Midlands and south-central England for external thatching in the late eighteenth and early nineteenth centuries, but since stubble would normally have degraded to leave only a very short length of straw intact, it is not surprising that no examples of external stubble thatch were identified.

Samples of short, about 6"–14" (15cm–36cm) stubble mixed with longer, upper stem material have been recovered from buildings in Bedfordshire (Appendix B: B1) and Buckinghamshire (Appendix B: B7). Both mixtures were used as base coats for external layers of crushed straw. Three unweathered base coat samples of pure stubble were also recovered from buildings in Cambridgeshire (Appendix A: A7) and Northamptonshire (Appendix A: A15), and from eaves packing in Leicestershire (Appendix A: A14), all in situations in which the stubble had not needed to be drawn. Specimens ranged from 8"–24" (20–60cm) in Cambridgeshire (Appendix A: A7), 6"–12" (15–30cm) in Northamptonshire (Appendix A: A15) and 12"–20" (30–50cm) in Leicestershire

Figure 99 Fixings: twisted and dethorned stems of blackberry Rubus sp., *Long Crendon, Buckinghamshire (John Letts).*

Figure 102 Fixings: twisted stem of wild rose Rosa sp. *fixing ridge roll of brushwood (Appendix A: A10, Stockland, Somerset) (John Letts).*

Figure 100 Fixings: c early nineteenth century tarred twine (Appendix A: A1, Cople, Bedfordshire) (John Letts).

Figure 103 Fixings: 'continuous' twisted straw bond (Appendix A: A2, Toddington, Bedfordshire) (John Letts).

Fixing methods

Fixing materials are one of the most variable aspects in the technical history of thatching, and the diversity of materials used in the past stands in striking contrast to the uniform iron crooks and split hazel spars and sways now used. Early base coats seem to have been fixed with just about any material that could be formed into a flexible bond. Withes and blackberry stems were particularly abundant, inexpensive and renewable prior to the widespread clearance of wet wastes in the late eighteenth and early nineteenth centuries (Figs 99 to 112). This decline probably coincides with the adoption of tarred twine and a drop in the diversity of fixings used in both base coats and upper layers.

Figure 101 Fixings: roundwood sways and spars (Appendix B: B30, Lingwood, Norfolk) (John Letts).

(Appendix A: A14), but also included abundant broken stems, leaves and weeds. If drawn, these samples would have produced stubble yealms of about 12"–24" (30–60cm) in length. Using a degradation quotient of 1" (2.5cm) a year and allowing half of the average length for fixings, they would have survived no more than 6 to 12 years had they been used externally. In Leicestershire (Appendix A: A14) and Northamptonshire (Appendix A: A15), the stubble was bedded onto the tops of the (stone) walls with mud to provide a firm base for overlying layers of crushed straw.

Appendix A includes buildings with base coats fixed with both tarred and untarred cord (Appendix A: A2 Bedfordshire, A3 Berks, A5/6 Buckinghamshire, A7/8 Cambridgeshire, A13 Dorset, A18 Suffolk, A19/20 Wiltshire), saplings of blackberry (*Rubus* sp), *Clematis* sp, willow (*Salix* sp) and twisted hazel (*Corylus avellana*) (Appendix A: A4/5 Buckinghamshire, A7/9 Cambridgeshire, A11/12 Devon, A15 Northamptonshire, A16 Oxfordshire), twisted grass rope (Appendix A: A1 Bedfordshire, A9 Cambridgeshire, A14 Leicestershire), straw bonds (Appendix A: A5 Buckinghamshire, A4 Buckinghamshire), braided sedge (*Carex* sp) rope (Appendix A: A7 Cambridgeshire) and twisted bark (Appendix A: A12 Devon). The waist (base) coats at Ilfracombe (Appendix

Figure 104 Fixings: straight peg and braided rope (Appendix A: A14, Lyndon, Leicestershire) (John Letts).

Figure 106 Fixings: 'discontinuous' straw bond (Appendix A: A10, Stockland, Devon) (John Letts).

Figure 105 Fixings: roundwood sways and braided hempen rope (Appendix B: B30, Lingwood, Norfolk) (John Letts).

Figure 107 Fixings: yealms of crushed straw fixed with individual twisted spars (Appendix A: A9, Westley Waterless, Cambridgeshire) (John Letts).

Figure 108 Fixings: course of crushed straw fixed with roundwood sways, split hazel spars and mud (Appendix A: A6, Ickford, Buckinghamshire) (John Letts).

A: A11) and Cullompton (Appendix A: A12) were tied with withes, twisted bark and dethorned stems of black-berry (and later consolidated with tarred twine); the base layer at Stockland (Appendix A: A10) was clamped into position with spars driven into the wattle; and the waist coat at Osmington (Appendix A: A13 Dorset) was tied to the rafters and battens with tarred twine, probably in the mid eighteenth century, at approximately the time tarred twine became available cheaply and in sufficient quantity for use in thatching. A base coat of crushed straw at Cople, Bedfordshire (Appendix A: A1) was tied to the rafters and battens with a two-ply rope of twisted grass similar to the grass rope used at Lyndon, Leicestershire (Appendix A: A14). Although based on a limited data set, there does not seem to be any significant difference between the materials employed in fixing waist coats of reed straw in the West Country and base coats of crushed straw or halm in south-central England.

In practice, base coats were sometimes held in place by the fixings of an overlying coat applied at the same time. Hence, the base coat of muddy stubble on a fenland cottage at Great Stukeley, Cambridgeshire (Appendix A: A7) was held in place by an overlying layer of black bog rush (*Schoenus nigricans*) that was stitched to the rafters and battens (through the underlying water reed fleeking) with untarred cord, withes, and two-ply rope made from braided strands of small diameter sedge (*Carex* sp). Stitching became a difficult and expensive task once two or three base coats had

accumulated, and all succeeding top coats had then to be sparred or pegged into place. Aside from the spars and pegs themselves, the only variation possible was in the horizontal fixings employed. Wooden sways and discontinuous straw bonds could be used only with spars, whereas tarred cord or rope made from twisted grass, bulrush (*Schoenoplectus lacustris*) or straw could be used with either spars or pegs (eg Appendix A: A14 Leicestershire, A9 Cambridgeshire).

Layers could also be fixed with mud on the eaves (Appendix A: A15 Northamptonshire, A14 Leicester-

Figure 109 Fixings: twisted two-ply rush (S. lacustris) rope fixing base coat of black bog rush (S. nigricans) (Appendix B: B10, Wennington, Cambridgeshire) (John Letts).

Figure 111 Fixings: tarred twine and twisted hazel rod in bed of plaster applied from within (Appendix A: A14, Lyndon, Leicestershire) (John Letts).

Figure 110 Fixings: horizontal roundwood sways nailed to rafters (clamping fleeking in position) (Appendix A: A14, Lyndon, Leicestershire) (John Letts).

Figure 112 Fixings: layers of mud and rush (Juncus sp.) and straw surviving on a ridge (Appendix A: A14, Lyndon, Leicestershire) (John Letts).

shire), within the main coat (Appendix A: A6 Oxford-shire; Appendix B: B34 Northamptonshire) and on the ridge (Appendix A: A15 Northamptonshire, A14 Leices-tershire). The use of mud for fixing courses is well-documented in northern England (Harrison 1989; 1991) and was noted in buildings in Buckinghamshire (Appen-dix A: A6) and Northamptonshire (Appendix B: B34). Straw was also bedded onto mud applied to the tops of

eaves and gables in Northamptonshire (Appendix A: A15) and Leicestershire (Appendix A: A14). The mud ridges on these two buildings are amongst the few examples of this practice recorded even superficially in England. Layers of clay were visibly inter-bedded with layers of very decayed straw (and in one case pasture rush *Juncus* sp.), and although only a brief examination of a section face was possible, the evidence suggested that the clay was used as an anchor for a top coat of straw that was sparred into it and not as a surface coping. Ridging with clay was recorded in Leicestershire and several other northern counties in the late medieval period and in later centuries. According to Pitt (1809b, 26), mud walls in Leicestershire were thatched using 'road scrapings' ideally suited to the purpose, while in Lancashire, ridge caps were made from 'puddled red clay mixed with chopped straw' (Watson & McClintock 1979, 16). However it was used, mud was free and abundant and provided a secure means of fixing courses, ridges, eaves and gables even when other methods of fixings were available.

The *in situ* evidence suggests that straw bonds or 'scuds' may have been used more frequently than wooden sways (in combination with spars) on Devon roofs in the past. In contrast, every layer of pitched reed on the lone Dorset roof excavated was sparred and swayed. Spars also seem to have been used on their own, although in some cases the horizontal fixings (especially of straw) associated with the spars had probably degraded and were not recovered during excavation. Spars and sways seem always to have been the dominant fixing method east of Devon, and peg and twine or rope of various sorts appear only sporadically on both reed straw and crushed straw roofs (Appendix A: A12 Devon, A14 Leicestershire, A8 Cambridgeshire). Straw had several advantages over wooden sways: it provided a less expensive, but equally secure, fixing; it was flexible and easy to work with; it ran out only when the main thatching material itself ran out; it was not damaged by woodworm; and it remained strong as long as it was dry and the spars fixing it were intact. These straw bonds look very much like the temporary sways used by combed wheat reed thatchers in the present day, and some of them may well be temporary sways that were left in position after the permanent fixing had been applied simply to provide additional security of fixing. Most, however, were clearly a principal fixing, and the additional use of spars this required probably limited double fixing. The use of straw bonds allowed limited coppice or hedgewood to be saved for making the spars or pegs that are essential for spar coating onto a thick base coat irrespective of the type of horizontal fixing employed.

Wooden sways used on these ancient roofs vary from saplings (Appendix A: A10 Devon) to strong hazel rods (Appendix A: A5 Buckinghamshire, A13 Dorset). As in the present day, there was no benefit in using roundwood sways greater than 2cm in diameter as vigorous dressing will more likely pull a spar out of its base as snap or bend the strong sway it fixes. The use of saplings/withes on a reed straw roof (eg Appendix A: A10 Devon) suggests that stronger sways were either not available, or that the layer applied was not dressed as vigorously or applied as thickly as modern combed wheat reed. Such roofs were perhaps moulded into position with a leggat and sheared to their final shape. The crooks now used as a matter of course for both combed wheat reed and long straw thatching are a relatively recent addition to the craft and provide the ultimate security of fixing when used with an iron sway. They have undoubtedly encouraged more

vigorous dressing to produce a very tight outer surface compared with earlier centuries, and have allowed more secure fixings at the eaves and gables. Traditionally, straw thatch was bedded onto the wall tops of older cob and stone buildings with mud (Appendix A: A7 Bedfordshire, A11/13 Devon, A14 Leicestershire), and the top few inches of a cob wall could easily be reformed to allow the brow course to be sparred into the wet mud, as in the cob-walled barn examined in Coleford, Devon (Appendix B: B22) (Fielden 1934, 364). Crooks can cause damage if driven directly into a dry wall top, and many older buildings have been altered over the past century to accommodate wall plates to provide a base for crooks (Appendix A: A11 and A12 Devon, A13 Dorset).

Cereal species and varieties

There is little doubt that thatching straw in England has generally been derived from common bread wheat (*Triticum aestivum*), although rivet wheat (*Triticum turgidum*), rye (*Secale cereale*), oats (*Avena sativa*) and barley (*Hordeum vulgare*) were used more commonly in the past, and more frequently in some regions than others. This does not mean that bread wheat was acknowledged as a superior thatching material between 1790–1940. Bread wheat occurs on its own in most of the samples recovered during the present study, and only on occasion in combination with rivet wheat or rye. This suggests that English cereal fields were largely composed of mono-specific crops by 1790, although mixtures of bread and rivet wheat continued to be grown in some areas well into the late nineteenth century (eg Appendix A: A18).

Little is known about varietal changes within rivet wheat, and the current project has recovered numerous samples which could elucidate the post-medieval history of this shadowy species. As with bread wheat, the later material seems to be less morphologically diverse than the medieval examples, particularly in terms of ear size, although many of the examples in crushed straw samples might best be described as tillers. Rivet wheat occurs either in pure samples or a significant secondary component in approximately 17% of the buildings examined, including four of the 16 crushed straw roofs detailed in Appendix A (A4 Buckinghamshire, A5 Buckinghamshire, A18 Suffolk and A19 Wiltshire) and seven of the 45 buildings listed in Appendix B (B11 Cambridgeshire, B12 Cambridgeshire, B24 Dorset, B25 Gloucestershire, B26 Hertfordshire, B34 Northamptonshire and B39 Oxfordshire). Rivet wheat was also a significant component within a smoke-blackened base coat sample obtained from a former open-hall building in Stockland, Devon (Appendix A: A10). In contrast, approximately 40% of the 50 samples of smoke-blackened medieval thatch recovered to date contain rivet wheat, usually as a mixture with bread wheat and other cereals but occasionally as a pure crop (Letts 1999). More accurately, rivet is almost absent from smoke-blackened base coats in Devon but occurs in over 73% of the non-Devon examples recorded to date. The evidence from 1790–1940 strongly suggests either that rivet wheat was particularly favoured for fleekings and base coats in the late medieval and early post-medieval periods, or that its use in thatching declined in later centuries commensurate with a general decline in its cultivation over the nineteenth century and early this century.

Rye occurs primarily as a contaminant in crushed straw samples from 10 buildings (Appendix A: A9 Cambridgeshire, B13 Cambridgeshire, A15 Northamptonshire; Appendix B: B9 Cambridgeshire, B11 Cambridgeshire, B20 Devon, B29 London, B34 Northamptonshire, B43 Surrey and B45 Wiltshire). It also occurs in medieval base coats in Devon (A10/11), and as a post-medieval spar coat and later wrap-over ridge at Berrynarbor, Devon (A11). Rye reed straw applied within the last 25 years also formed the external coat for underlying layers of crushed straw on a derelict barn at Hampstead Norries (A3 Berkshire). In general, it occurs in 25% of the buildings listed in Appendix A, and is unlikely to have occurred in any greater amount in the buildings listed in Appendix B. In contrast, bread wheat occurs on its own in most of the samples recovered during the present study, and only on occasion in combination with rivet wheat or rye. This suggests that English cereal fields were largely composed of mono-specific crops by 1790, although mixtures of bread and rivet wheat continued to be grown in some areas well into the late nineteenth century (Appendix A: A18). The results of the present study support the view of a significant decline in the use of pure rye straw for thatching in England during the late eighteenth and early nineteenth centuries, although it appears to have survived as a constituent, or perhaps more accurately, a contaminant, of wheat crops used for crushed straw thatching into the early part of this century. A notable exception is the use of rye reed straw for external main coat thatching in parts of Berkshire, and the once common use of rye for main coat thatching and ridging in Devon and several other districts.

Two-row hulled barley usually occurs exclusively as a minor component of threshing waste in base coat samples of both late medieval (Appendix A: A15 Northamptonshire; Appendix B: B11 Cambridgeshire) and early post-medieval date (Appendix B: B34).

Pure samples of oat straw are rarely encountered but the weathered base coat at Ickford, Buckinghamshire (A6) was composed of roughly equal amounts of bread wheat and cultivated oat.

In 1790 much of the wheat crop was reaped by hand, leaving most of the weeds that grew with the crop in the field to be scythed with the stubble or grazed by livestock. The scythe and the reaper undoubtedly increased the presence of weeds, but improved cultivation and seed cleaning practices may have countered this effect to some degree. However contaminated the crop, both combing and drawing are designed to remove weed stems and flowers along with short and broken straw, and it is not surprising that main coat samples of any date rarely contain weeds. In fact, even the undrawn stubble samples are not particularly rich in weed specimens. The contrast with medieval base coat samples of threshing waste is striking, but understandable given the fact that this material was never destined to be used as an external coat. The most common species encountered, grasses (Gramineae), field poppy (*Papaver rhoeas*), dock (*Rumex* spp), corn marigold (*Chrysanthemum segetum*) and thistle (*Cirsium* spp), are still common in arable fields, whereas many of the species recovered in medieval threshing waste have disappeared from English fields because of improved agronomic practices, seed cleaning and the use of herbicides.

Part IV

Thatchers

10   Phase 1: 1790–1840

In 1790, there were nearly one million thatched buildings in the country. One in five houses were thatched, while in a stronghold like the south-west of England, thatchers were required to service well over half of all the houses in the region. Half a century later, there had been a slight decline in the overall total of thatched buildings, although this masks an increase of 50,000 thatched dwellings. Any gains were concentrated in the southern heartlands. Dramatic losses occurred in the north, but even in 1790 the thatcher was employed on only 3.75% of the region's dwellings. In the Midlands, the numbers remained fairly static in the first half of the nineteenth century, although thatch became proportionately less and less significant as urbanization and industrialization created a new stock of housing roofed in more durable materials. In both regions, therefore, thatching was a minority occupation even in 1790, and by 1840 had become even more so. The 1841 census records a total of only 322 thatchers in the eighteen counties. Devon alone had over twice as many (PP 1843).

The usual caveat must be made when making use of the census data. The thatcher enjoyed a quite different, more embracing status to others engaged in the building trades, causing headaches for the census enumerators. John Farey asked that for the 1821 census, 'the former mode of returning the employ of Persons ... under three well explained Classes of Occupations' be adopted, the first, or Agricultural Class to contain 'Certain Handicrafts, occasionally employed on dwelling-houses, as Thatchers of Ricks and Hovels' (Farey 1811 **3**, 590). There is the insoluble problem of fathoming the relationship between the numbers of individuals who classed themselves or were classified as thatchers and the numbers who actually thatched. In the north, the discrepancy may have been accentuated because of the significance of heather-thatching in the region. This could evidently be carried out on a DIY basis. One of Chapman's informants (born in 1887) described how he had re-thatched a hog house but 'wasn't trained to do it'. He just 'saw the building, so knew how it was done'. (Chapman 1982, 9). The wet-straw method of Lancashire thatching was also probably easier to master than techniques used in the south. Individuals proficient in patching and repairs appear to have multiplied in proportion to the decline of full-time thatchers in these areas.

Conversion to more durable materials also had a particular impact on thatchers in the north and the Midlands. There is good evidence to demonstrate that at the end of the eighteenth century, thatching in these regions was still being practiced in combination with the daubing of stud-built cottages. In 1791, James Wilmer was paid 'for Work Done at a Cottage at Keelby', Lincolnshire, amounting to £1 15s 4d (£1.77) for 17½ rods of thatching, and £1 18s (£1.90) for 19 rods of daubing, both at 2s (10p) a rod (Lincolnshire Record Office 2). Unfortunately, the rod was such a variable measurement historically that it is impossible to be certain what these figures mean in terms of cost per standard unit. As late as 1853, Matthew Halliwell was paid for 'Thatching and Dobing etc at Wm Heskeths Cottage in Mawdsley' (Lancashire Record Office 1/7). With the increasing use of stone or brick as a walling material, the clay and straw link was severed, thus curtailing the thatcher's involvement in the building process.

In the south of the country, where his skills were much more in demand, the occupational status of the thatcher was somewhat more clearly defined at the beginning of the period. Documentary sources such as wills illustrate that thatchers were likely to be typical examples of small independent craftsmen, often accumulating sufficient capital to invest in cottage property or even some land. In 1781, John Ayer, a thatcher of Kettering, Northamptonshire, left to his son John 'all my arable land and also my four Doles in Kilnhouse and Walcotes ... also my two Houses in Northall', and to his son Nathaniel 'my house and cottage wherein I now dwell and also the Stock in the yard and also my house now in the occupation of Samuel Harle' (Northamptonshire Record Office 1).

What united these thatchers was their independent status and consequently a resistance to being shoehorned into conventional categories of class. Their smallholder status allowed them a certain liberty to pick and chose, their thatching work being supplemented by a whole variety of other tasks: hedging, ditching, coppicing, threshing, hay and straw tying and so on. It is this variety, rather than a concentration on the single occupation of thatching, which makes their participation in the local economy decidedly non-specialized. While a knowledge of the techniques and methods of thatching a roof obviously formed the basis of their expertise, this knowledge itself was a key to mastering a whole range of other skills such as spar-making (thus providing a grounding in other underwood trades such as hurdle-making and hedging), tying and knotting techniques, sheep-shearing (commonly undertaken by thatchers in areas where thatch was clipped), and in some cases hook-making. This was quite apart from a necessary knowledge of basic building skills of carpentry to repair or replace roof timbers, brickwork, masonry or cob-walling to repair around wall-plates and gables and leadwork for flashings and valleys.

The thatcher was thus much more than just a thatcher, but a jack of all trades. He had to be flexible, capable of switching from one skill to another according to seasonal demand, and willing to move between different local environments; coppices, fields, farmsteads and villages. What differentiated him from the tied labourer? The agricultural labourer might undertake rick thatching as just one of many tasks in the seasonal round of jobs that had to be undertaken on the farm. But he remained dependent on a master to pay his wages. The stake of the smallholding thatcher, on the other hand, provided him with a source of capital to buy and maintain equipment or functioned as a vital reserve for the lean winter months or periods of unemployment. This allowed him to forge a much wider range of contacts than the tied labourer.

The evidence suggests that in 1790 a substantial core of thatchers in the south of the country enjoyed this kind of independent, smallholding status. By 1840, this pattern of relative homogeneity had been disturbed by three important developments.

First, the commissioning of Picturesque cottage orné and rustic shelters by estate landowners created a new demand for ornamental and patterned work. This re-quired enhanced thatching skills and may thus have been responsible for encouraging the emergence of a distinctive class of estate thatchers. Secondly, the extension of the wheat acreage and the introduction of the threshing-machine encouraged farmers to store crops in ricks rather than barns, thus providing many potential recruits with a basic training in rick-thatching techniques. Finally, the rapid increase in the number of thatched buildings in the south in the first half of the nineteenth century was not, it seems, accompanied by a corresponding rise in the number of practicing full-time thatchers. An examination of the ratio of thatchers recorded in the 1861 census (PP 1863) to the number of thatched buildings (Guildhall Library 3) supports this conclusion. Compared to the south east and south west where the number of thatched buildings declined and the ratios were 1:40 and 1:79 respectively, in the south the ratio was as high as one thatcher to every 212 buildings which suggests that the full-time thatchers in the region might have been unable to cope with this workload. It seems reasonable to assume, therefore, that many of the buildings, particularly ancillary structures and the poorer quality housing, would have been roofed by individuals perhaps with rick-thatching skills or using the more easily applied secondary materials where available, such as gorse or heather.

11 Phase 2: 1840–1890

Against this backdrop, subtle shifts in the composition of the thatching workforce must be seen against the national trend which charts the rise in use of more durable materials. Status distinctions between thatchers became more pronounced as the developments already underway in the first phase affected a greater proportion of those engaged in the craft. This is excluding, to all intents and purposes, the whole of the north of England which could muster only 13 thatchers according to the 1891 census (PP 1893–4), while the Midlands fared little better, with the number declining from a total of 408 thatchers in 1851 (PP 1852–3) to only 169 in 1891. The shift towards dairying and livestock farming reduced both the availability of thatching straw and the demand for rick–thatching skills in these areas. The few full-time thatchers declined largely at the whim of large landowners who were actively reroofing or replacing the small stock of thatched buildings left on their estates.

In the south of England, there was also a substantial decline from 5282 thatchers recorded in the 1851 census to 2986 in that of 1891. The south east experienced a 60% loss, the south west 50%, and the south 35%, rates of decline which reflected the extent to which thatch had been removed or replaced in the respective regions. The scale of the loss clearly had major repercussions for the craft, not least the fact that thatchers became more and more isolated from the building industry, and were instead increasingly confined to rural backwaters (Fig 113).

The relationship between thatchers (and some thatching families) and estates was consolidated, and the category of estate thatcher became more clearly defined in the period. Norman Goodland described the thatched houses on the Manytunes Estate, near Stokingbase

(Basingstoke, Hampshire) as 'old ... but in a far better condition than were most other labourers' houses outside the Estate' (Goodland 1953, 87). This was where Goodland's father, a thatcher, found most of his work in the late nineteenth century:

> The work at Manytunes continued throughout the year, for Colonel Cobb had fresh buildings to attend to as soon as my Father neared the end of any one he had in hand. He was almost the Estate thatcher, and the income form it was paid quarterly. (op cit, 110)

As estate work became proportionately more and more significant, it had the effect of enhancing the status of those thatchers who had access to it, in that it conveyed a measure of prestige and respectability while also guaranteeing a steady income. Estates also tended to own and maintain coppices; these were a vital source of thatching materials and many thatchers managed to negotiate advantageous terms with landowners. Finally, estates were useful cushions, providing alternative employment whenever it was too wet to thatch or no thatching work was available. One particularly common estate combination was that of hedging and thatching, skills which dovetailed nicely together in the seasonal round of estate work. John Williams' grandfather was champion stone hedger in the west of England in the latter part of the nineteenth century and began a family thatching business in 1885 (Brough 1976).

An enhancement of status through this type of work was nevertheless bought at a price, namely a tangible loss of independence. Thatchers themselves liked to play down this aspect, the qualification 'almost' applied by Goodland to his father's position as an estate thatcher is revealing in this respect. The tension caused by a fear of being treated as a faceless estate worker breaks out in many anecdotes told by estate thatchers, always at the expense of those who try to belittle or ignore them. Jack Dodson's father worked on an estate near Huntingdon. He had a special arrangement, which meant that he was not a direct employee of the estate. In 1933 the new estate owner was annoyed to find Dodson Senior not on site at 7.00 am, but after a bit of a set-to, the arrangement stayed the same (Cox 1994 **2**, 6).

Estate opportunities were taken up because thatched buildings in other sectors were declining and because wider socio-economic forces were whittling away the independent status of thatchers. In 1851, for example, George Chambers of Southill, Bedfordshire, was de-

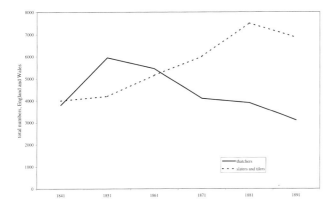

Figure 113 Comparison of total numbers of thatchers and slaters/tilers 1841-91 (James Moir).

Table 15 John Cope's year, 1866 (Bedfordshire Record Office 1).

	on roof	ricking	at home	other
January	12	0	8	7
February	8	0	9	7
March	8	0	4	15
April	8	0	4	13
May	10.5	0	11	5.5
June	11	0	2	13
July	4	19	0	2.5
August	4	16	3	4
September	0	21	3	1
October	14	8.5	2	3
Novermber	12.5	5	4	4.5
December	11	0	7	8
Total	103	69.5	57	83.5

scribed as a thatcher owning two acres (0.8ha) of ground. By 1891, two of his descendants were left in the village, and had clearly experienced a drop in status, one being described as an 'agricultural labourer', the other as a 'thatcher and agricultural labourer' (PP 1852–3). Loss or reduction of the smallholding cushion was compounded by a parallel decline in the secondary occupations on which the smallholder thatcher depended and during the agricultural depression opportunities to find piece-work hedging, ditching, draining and so on all began to drop away.

In one significant area, the situation seems to have improved somewhat. The demand for rick-thatching, particularly in the south, increased as a result of the more widespread adoption of the threshing-machine, and Dutch barns as yet offered no serious competition to this method of crop storage. 'It was accepted throughout the country-side that building thatching had to wait when there were ricks to cover' (Goodland 1953, 92), and the number of thatched buildings that could be worked on at this driest time of the year was reduced. An analysis of the work diary of John Cope of Tempsford, Bed-fordshire for 1866 illustrates the fact that between July and early October, hardly any time was spent on house roofs and that at least one in every five working days in the year was spent on rick-thatching (Bedfordshire Record Office 1; Table 15).

Rick-thatching was built into the house-thatching system because it was in the short term a means of earning money quickly; but opportunities to expand the house-thatching aspect of the business were con-sequently being lost.

The expansion in demand for rick-thatching also undoubtedly encouraged more agricultural labourers to become proficient in it. By the 1890s individuals who undertook thatching could be broadly classified accord-ing to the following categories:

- Agricultural labourers who undertook rick thatching as part of their seasonal work on their employers' farms. In this category, too, can be classed the DIY thatcher who occasionally undertook thatching on buildings. While the first class grew the latter class declined in numbers, as a result in particular of the dramatic loss of thatched ancillary buildings.
- A second tier, again decreasing in numbers, com-prised the earlier core of skilled, independent rural workers who apart from thatching houses, farm build-ings, ancillary structures and ricks, also still undertook a range of secondary tasks.
- At the top of the ladder were the estate thatchers who derived a considerable proportion of their work from a single estate. They did not sever their connections entirely from their smallholding roots. Rick-thatch-ing took up most of the summer months, but apart from this, they were specializing on an increasing scale on house thatching, and work outside the estate reflected this bias.

The decline of the independent smallholding thatcher had a profound effect on the craft not only because it forced thatchers either to move into estate or house thatching work or to explore secondary occupations, but because it knocked out the essential stepping stone whereby labourers with rick-thatching skills could move up into the house thatching market. The eclipse of this intermediate tier may partly explain why the very large numbers of agricultural labourers who gained some experience in rick thatching (this number was probably increasing in fact in the late nineteenth century) rarely passed into the ranks of house thatchers. Indeed, in most cases the slip backwards from thatcher to agricultural. labourer seems more likely.

12 Phase 3: 1890–1940

In the third phase, the three classes of thatcher noted above tended to splinter into further sub-categories, while the divisions between the categories became more blurred.

In the house-thatching group, the top rung of the ladder was being occupied by the new independent firms like Farmans and Cowells, who turned their backs on the agricultural market and forged ahead with their water reed promotion campaigns. These firms attempted to impose building industry-style management, not always with total success. One of Cowells' thatchers simply refused to fill in time sheets: 'I have not put Hours down as I think there is no occasion for me to do that as I work from 7.30 in the morning till dark ½ Hour for dinner' (Cambridgeshire Record Office 1).

The impact of these large water reed firms on the thatching industry was highly significant, despite the fact that there were only a handful in the whole country. That these firms were the exception rather than the rule is illustrated in Thomas Bagshawe's remarkable survey which he undertook 'between May 1948 and October 1949 [when] an effort was made to trace and interview all thatchers in the county of Bedford' (Bagshawe 1951, 1121). Bagshawe's work involved, among other things, establishing the genealogies of the thatchers he interviewed and also taking a very detailed inventory of each of their tool bags.

Bagshawe found that the total number of working thatchers in the county by this date was fifteen; in addition he interviewed five retired thatchers. None were operating Farman-type businesses, although a majority of the twenty thatchers in the county could be classed as estate and house thatchers.

ESTATE AND HOUSE THATCHERS

Robert Henman and John Walker, Maulden and Lidlington (1 and 2)

Robert Henman was 72 years of age when Bagshawe interviewed him but 'still engaged in his craft'. Robert's cousin, John or 'Jack' Walker, had 'retired from work in 1948'. Both could trace their thatching roots back several generations. Jack's great-grandfather, William, born in 1778 at Wootton, Bedfordshire, had settled in Lidlington by 1851, an interesting move as this took him into the orbit of the Woburn Estate. Both Robert and Jack stated that they were mainly concerned with 'building thatching, that is to say the thatching of houses and cottages' (op cit, 1126).

Charles Dunkley, Riseley; John Dunkley, St Neots; Wilfred Haigh, Biggleswade (3, 4, 5)

Charles Dunkley, who had been established in Bedfordshire for over forty years when interviewed, was born at Bythorn in Huntingdonshire in 1869 but very significantly had moved to Riseley in 1904 at the invitation of Lord St John, to attend to the thatched buildings on the Melchbourne estate. Charles' cousin John Dunkley, was based in St Neots in Huntingdonshire (having moved there from Ellington in 1925) but worked mostly in Bedfordshire, and consequently was included in the survey (op cit, 1127). John had also trained his nephew Wilfred Haigh, who 'began independent work at Biggleswade in 1947' (op cit, 1121)

Frank, Albert and Charles Humberstone, Wrestlingworth (6, 7, 8)

Bagshawe just captured the end of an impressive dynasty of thatchers when he interviewed Frank, Albert and Charles Humberstone (two brothers and a cousin) all living in Wrestlingworth and all in their seventies. Only Albert was still engaged in thatching.

> The three ... descend from a grandfather Jehu (pronounced 'Jayhu') who was very much a character in the village. At one time representatives of three generations were at work as thatchers simultaneously. They consisted of grandfather, three sons, and three grandsons. (op cit, 1133)

The 1881 census (Bedfordshire Record Office 2) pushes their ancestry another generation back as we find Jehu's father, John, recorded as a thatcher: he was born in Eyeworth and therefore was probably the representative who brought the family to Wrestlingworth. The reason for the move again appears to have been due to opportunities provided by the local estate at Cockayne Hatley. Frank Humberstone was still obtaining all his coppice for spit-and-rod making from the estate woods in the 1940s. The estate work probably provided the necessary boost to nudge the family up from smallholder status to 'building' thatchers. John Humberstone was plainly described in 1871 as a thatcher but his son Jehu combined this skill with that of jobbing bricklayer and carpenter, while of the three grandsons interviewed by Bagshawe, Frank had been a thatcher, jobbing bricklayer and carpenter as well as a well-digger; Charles Humberstone retained the estate connection having worked also as 'a land drainer' (Bagshawe 1951, 1134).

A further four thatchers interviewed by Bagshawe had received training from one or other of these established estate thatching families.

Albert Church, Biddenham (9)

Church was a general estate labourer who had taken up rick and house thatching some three or four months before Bagshawe interviewed him in March 1949. He had worked for 23 years on the same estate and the demand for thatchers caused him to take up the trade seriously. 'But he is no novice for he acted as server to Robert Henman, the Maulden thatcher, for five years' (op cit, 1121).

Eric Burgoine, Maulden (10)

He was 'of a Maulden family but without a family tradition of thatching. Burgoine started to learn the craft when he was 17 or 18 years old, as a pupil of Robert Henman, the Maulden thatcher' (op cit, 1125) .

Lewis Ben Cooper and Cyril Stonebridge, Eaton Socon and Potton (11, 12)

The remaining two thatchers who had established themselves as independent businesses were also both from a single school of thatching, this time the very well-established Cope and Lewin families of Tempsford. Although this school just missed inclusion in the biographies given above, because Arthur Lewin had died in 1947 and William Cope a year later, their continuing influence on Bedfordshire thatching was in fact perpetuated through their apprentices. William Cope was the last in an unbroken line of Cope thatchers stretching back at least to his grandfather, John Cope, born in 1778. The family operated from Tempsford throughout this period, and carried out extensive work on the properties belonging to the various successive owners of the Tempsford House Estate. William's grandfather (whose account books survive [Bedfordshire Record Office 1] for the latter part of his life) had two sons who went into the thatching business, John (born 1846) and James (born 1849). Their eldest sister, Hannah (born 1839) married William Lewin and their son Edwin trained as a thatcher with the Cope family. Edwin's own son Arthur took over the business but died in 1947 at the age of 50 without an heir to succeed him.

Lewis Ben Cooper 'established as a house and stack thatcher at Eaton Socon in 1918–19 and has lived there since 1921, before which he lived in Tempsford ... He started to learn the craft at the age of 14 years, being apprenticed without indentures, to Cope of Tempsford for 6 years' (op cit, 1124). Cyril Stonebridge 'comes of a Potton family and belongs to the younger generation of Bedfordshire thatchers ... He started to learn the trade at the age of seventeen from Arthur Lewin of Tempsford. Two years ago [ie 1946] he started on his own and works with his brother' (op cit, 1126).

Bagshawe had therefore identified four main schools in the county: Henman/Walker, Dunkley, Humberstone and Cope/Lewin. All of the thatchers trained in these schools worked primarily as house thatchers, and all had their roots in the estate system, although the links with the respective estates of origin had weakened somewhat by the mid twentieth century. But one very interesting clue to the common ancestry of these thatchers is revealed in the inventories of their tools. Bedfordshire was almost exclusively a long straw county in 1948. What is to be made, therefore, of the fact that six thatchers interviewed by Bagshawe possessed a leggat, hardly a tool normally associates with this style of thatching?

The reason becomes clear when the biographies of the thatchers possessing them are analysed. They all belonged to the four main schools, they all possessed leggats, and all had sprung from estate thatching backgrounds; the leggat, then, was a symbol of the long-standing connection between water reed and its use on estate buildings. But only two of these six thatchers, Ben Cooper and John Dunkley, were still using water reed by the time of Bagshawe's survey. Cooper had learned reed thatching from Dick Dunkley, despite also having trained in the Cope and Lewin school (op cit, 1124). John Dunkley drew 'his reeds from the Norfolk Broads and Ramsey Height in Huntingdonshire'. Interestingly, too 'before 1930 he did some thatching with heather' (op cit, 1129). The other four thatchers, however, were lapsed reed thatchers. John's cousin, Charles Dunkley, as we have seen, had:

> moved to Riseley in 1904 to work as a reed thatcher on the Melchbourne estate (Lord St John) ... Charles specialized in thatching cottages, houses and farm buildings in reed and straw, but he also did some 'rickyard work' ... Latterly mostly local straw was used and not much reed thatching had been done for the past 20 years. Reeds came from Colworth. (op cit, 1127)

Another of the principal house thatching firms which had lapsed from reed thatching completely was the Cope and Lewin family: 'Edwin [Lewin] was a reed and straw thatcher, Arthur worked with straw only' (op cit, 1130). Similarly, Albert Humberstone 'works with straw but years ago worked with reed as well' while Charles Humberstone 'thatched houses, barns and ricks in straw and also did a little reed thatching on houses and barns until about 1930 at Waresley Park in Huntingdonshire. The reeds came from Upwell in Huntingdonshire' (op cit, 1137). The attenuation of a reed-thatching tradition in Bedfordshire was thus directly linked to the dwindling economic fortunes of large landed estates in the first half of the twentieth century.

SMALLHOLDERS

The economic status of the independent, smallholding thatcher had been affected badly in the late nineteenth century, as we have seen, but there were still representatives of this tradition at the time of Bagshawe's survey.

Reginald Parrott, Thurleigh (13)

Walter Reginald Parrott was born in 1901: 'My father, Ernest Parrott, was born in the same village, as was his father, George Parrott, both of them being expert thatchers' (Parrott 1974, 3). Walter's autobiography reveals that the family were clearly better off than the average agricultural labourer:

As well as the garden, my father cultivated two roods [0.5 acres, 0.2ha] of allotment ... My father would grow enough potatoes for us ... One rood would be set aside for wheat, and at the harvest time it would be mown with a scythe, stooked and later threshed with a machine or flail. (op cit, 5)

Parrott's father was a typical example of the smallholder thatcher in that he had his finger in many other pies:

In the winter months my father would leave the thatching and do any other jobs that came along such as tree felling, soot sowing, hedge layering, digging, corn setting with dibs, threshing corn with machines and flail, ditching, grave digging, etc. (op cit, 33)

He and his wife also found time to act as caretakers at the local smallpox hospital 'with a small salary, on the understanding that if the hospital were used at any time, they would have to live there in isolation and act as cook and do all the necessary chores' (op cit, 7).

The son evidently inherited his father's eye for the main chance and the smallholding tradition clearly exerted a powerful influence on Parrott throughout his life.

From my youth I always had a desire to do a bit of farming myself and in 1922 I was fortunate enough to become the tenant of five acres of arable land. This was farmed by me as a spare-time activity. Each year the prices farmers received for their produce were getting lower, but I was able to hold my own especially with a crop of wheat, as, in addition to selling the corn, the straw would be used for thatching purposes, and so expenditure on materials was saved. (op cit, 35)

Herbert Kingham, Wingfield (14)

The Kinghams, like the Parrotts, seem to have been house thatchers who retained strong links with a diverse agricultural past, despite being in the business of house thatching for at least four generations. John Kingham had died in 1948, his nephew taking over the business. 'The uncle was a hay and straw tier as well as a house and rick thatcher. The nephew carries on the double trade' (Bagshawe 1951, 1132).

Wilfred Hawkins, Colmworth (15)

Wilfred Hawkins of Colmworth 'comes of a Bolnhurst family and is a rick and house thatcher. His father, Josiah Hawkins (died 1947, aged 80) was a smallholder at Bolnhurst and practiced thatching, and also sheep-shearing' (op cit, 1122).

The smallholder thatcher had not therefore disappeared entirely during this period, and in Parrott's case at least, had somewhat improved his position.

RICK-THATCHING AND DIY

Ricks

The division between house and rick thatching may have been accentuated as a result of the First World War. On the one hand, thatching was classed among the sheltered occupations, and this emphasized the skilled nature of the craft (anon 1923a). On the other, the continuing demand for able-bodied soldiers clearly denuded farms of men with rick-thatching skills. Training centres for the Women's Land Army were therefore set up, and here, thatching, in which women became very skilled, was also taught. Returns relating to 12,657 women (23,000 altogether were trained) taken in August 1918 show that there were 84 thatchers compared to 5,734 milkers (Prothero 1923, 183). The teaching was restricted of course, to rick thatching, and this may have coaxed the public into thinking that this skill was easy to master, whereas house thatching was a closed book. Conversely, many house thatchers were obliged to undertake significantly more rick thatching during the war years. The First World War therefore played up a one-way process which saw house thatchers increasingly undertake rick thatching, but rick thatchers decreasingly breaking through into the house thatching market.

Bagshawe's survey suggests that several thatchers in Bedfordshire could trace their origins to rick thatching roots.

Geoffrey Tompkins, Chalton (16)

Bagshawe records that Geoffrey Tompkins's father and grandfather 'passed on their knowledge of thatching to him' (Bagshawe 1951, 1122). No Tompkins are listed specifically as thatchers in the censuses at the end of the nineteenth century and it must be assumed therefore that thatching was just one of the skills of the father and grandfather.

Harry Cheshire, Eaton Bray (17)

Bagshawe states Harry Cheshire 'is now [in 1949] over 70 years old and has retired. He was a farm-worker, hedger and thatcher, but principally a rick thatcher' (op cit, 1124).

George and Cecil Purser, Westoning (18 and 19)

Although not from a house-thatching family George's grandfather and father thatched ricks and he 'began to learn thatching at the age of 16 by assisting his father on ricks.' George's son Cecil 'who started before 1939 on his own as a thatcher at Woburn' was taught by his father to thatch (op cit, 1131).

This case in fact illustrates that there was seldom an instant transformation from ordinary agricultural labourer undertaking some rick thatching straight to house thatcher. George Purser began to learn thatching at the age of 16 by assisting his father on ricks, 'but he received lessons in house thatching from Fisher a Barton thatcher' (op cit, 1131). His father's and grandfather's knowledge were not sufficient to take George out of rick thatching and into the house thatching ranks, a boost could only be given through an established house thatcher.

Charles Colgrave, Colmworth (20)

Charles Colgrave had no background in thatching and was the only individual in the survey who did not undertake rick thatching. Instead, he also worked as a 'hedger and does all kinds of farm-work'. He was simply 'self-taught' (op cit, 1122). Bagshawe does not explain how this was achieved but his case was not unique. Connie Stranks recalled that her father 'carried on a house thatching business. There was a great deal of thatched property in Warmington [Warwickshire] and the nearby villages and no-one to repair the thatch, so he taught himself the craft. This he worked in with his smallholding' (Stranks 1990, 3).

The Bagshawe survey indicates that of the 20 thatchers interviewed (15 working and five retired) a very high proportion were either from estate/house thatching dynasties or had trained with one or more of them. The four schools of established house thatchers (Henman and Walker; Cope and Lewin; Dunkley; Humberstone) between them accounted for eight out of the fifteen working thatchers in 1948-9 and four out of the five retired thatchers interviewed. Three thatchers were the surviving representatives of the smallholding tradition, while the remaining five formed a more amorphous group which included those thatchers who had entered the trade without a significant house thatching past: all but one, however, had some traceable thatching roots.

By 1948-9, these roots in some cases stretched back several generations, and signify the considerable weight of inheritance borne by most thatchers at that time.

Transmission of tradition

None of the Bedfordshire thatchers could quite match the Farmans' claims to antiquity.

> 'Established many centuries' reads the notepaper used by the firm of Mr R W Farman, reed-thatcher of North Walsham, Norfolk. And this is no exaggeration, for Farmans have been reed-thatchers since the 12th century. So it was quite natural that Farman should take over the business that had been his father's, grandfather's and great-grandfather's before him and which will be his son's after him. (anon 1949)

The Bedfordshire material suggests that the lineage of many of the thatchers at work in the middle of this century could be traced back to the late eighteenth century.

Out of the twenty thatchers interviewed by Bagshawe, the very high proportion of fourteen could claim to be at least second-generation thatchers. In most cases (12 out of 14) descent had been direct from father to son, the other two cases reflecting only a slight lateral shift from uncle to nephew. The four apprentices, Church, Burgoine, Cooper and Stonebridge, had all trained with house-thatching firms who had roots stretching back into at least the eighteenth century, and were in this sense just as much inheritors of long-established techniques and methods.

In the period 1890–1940, dynastic house-thatching families were thus by far the most important route into thatching and would appear to confirm the widely held assumption that one could not become a thatcher without some kind of pedigree. References to lineage begin to appear as guarantees against poor workmanship, although in fact claiming descent through X generations may not in itself confer much in the way of thatching expertise. Nor does claiming a long pedigree imply *per se* that methods and techniques will be passed on from father to son. One of the stories collected from 'Cotswold Characters' and published in 1921 told how the son and heir of Joe Pentifer, the local thatcher, was called Aesop and had from early youth been bred to thatching, and had acquired some proficiency in the job.

> Aesop was not a bungler, but he knew nothing of the secret magic, and his father saw no compensation for middling technique in an increased wage. The difference between the senior partner's handiwork and the junior's was a thing for fine perceptions only. Aesop, for all his father's care, was not aware of it. Sometimes when, sorely against his will, Joe had to relinquish a piece of work to his son, an untrained eye, or even a trained eye of the duller kind, would hardly detect the transition from genius to common talent. (Sutton 1991, 143–4)

Walter Parrott recalled that both his father and grandfather were 'powerfully built and of great physique. The harder they worked, the better they liked it, so much so that they thought everyone else ought to be able to do the same whatever the circumstances' (Parrott 1974, 3). One of the most realistic portrayals of the angst within thatching dynasties can be found in Norman Goodland's *My Father Before Me* which details the progress of the Weston family who thatched near Basingstoke, Hampshire. Unfortunately, the eldest son leaves home clandestinely in the middle of the night too afraid to confront his father, who can only lamely declare when he hears of this 'It ain't exactly the way the head of the house should be treated, is it?' (Goodland 1953, 103) The second son, Tom, then filled the eldest son's place.

> His thatching was good, and although he did not show the mastery Fred had done, or ever took any initiative, he worked well under my Father, and it seemed as if he was not going to bother with anything else. (Goodland 1953, 108)

But Tom eventually plucked up the courage also to declare his interest lay in other quarters, and found a place in service as a trainee butler. Fortunately for the parent, the third son wanted to stay with his father and learn the trade, and this he succeeded in doing without falling out with his father. The autobiography beautifully captures the twin stresses of having to learn the craft under an often overbearing patriarch and being exposed to the temptations of more highly paid work either in the neighbouring towns or estate households.

> At the age of sixteen quite a number of teenagers left the farms to work in the munitions factory in Bedford, the money paid being far in excess of that being paid for farm workers. Some of my pals who had gone there to work tried to entice me to go there so after a while I left my father and went there to work myself. (Parrott 1974, 48)

Parrott himself soon found 'that factory life, with its unhealthy atmosphere and also the restrictions, was not my cup of tea. This made up my mind for me, and in about six months time I was back again working with my father' (op cit, 48). Parrott's brief encounter with industry stands as a reminder that not all sons were destined to step naturally into their father's shoes. Equally, fathers were reluctant to convey responsibilities to sons. In *My Father Before Me*, the son who did succeed his father felt the resentment this engendered.

> I was conscious of my Father's mixed feelings at my progress. At first, he encouraged me and helped me all he could. He still did so; but I felt that he took more pleasure in me when I was learning my work than now I had learned. He warned me constantly about getting a 'sight too big for your boots, boy', and on occasions he sharply reminded me: 'Look here, you young sprig, your Father hasn't given up yet, nor likely to for a good long time'. (Goodland 1953, 179)

Apprenticeship or training meant whatever the father wanted it to mean, but completion of the training did not guarantee independence. 'On leaving school, James [Fosberry of Sussex] was apprenticed to his father for seven years. Later, he acted as his father's labourer, until at 25 he was ready to spread his wings as a fully fledged craftsman' (Nugat 1950, 246).

In thatching families sons were often obliged to assist with the business, even before they had started a formal education. Frank Humberstone learnt the trade of thatching from his father whom he first started to help when only six years of age. His father kept long hours at harvest time, working from 5 am to 9 pm and even midnight in the stack-yard. As a child he would be called in the early hours of the morning to carry breakfast to his father who might be working 3 miles away at Dunton, and at the age of eight or nine he had worked in the stack-yard with his father up to midnight (Bagshawe 1951, 1134).

Frank's cousin Charles learnt the trade of thatching from his father and started rending spits when still at school (aged seven to eight). He also carried spits, straw and beer up the ladder to his father (op cit, 1137).

A thatcher's son could likely to miss out on a proper childhood. John Brown, as a young boy helping his father, remembered a

day in the heat with the odour of wet straw under my nose and worrying insects I retain another lasting impression and pen a few lines that seem appropriate:

> On a lovely summer's day
> When other children are at play
> Their voices trailing oer the shimmering heat
> While weary I, hard pressed and near defeat.
> (Brown 1974, 40–1)

Later he mentions 'Father by now had laid claim to me, on holidays, weekends, and in between school hours' (op cit, 47). Nor was there ever any question of staying on at school to further one's education. The schoolmaster who meets Thatcher Weston in the village says of Weston's son, 'A pity we could not have had him at school a while longer. We might have made more of him'. Weston asks what he means by this: 'By the time I've finished with him *I'll* make more on'n, sir. He'll be the finest thatcher in the district. Aye, and maybe in the South o' the country by the time he's finished, sir'. When told that his son could have been more educated, Weston replies 'I can't help sort of thinkin', sir, as if a lad can't learn to read and write and do his sums by the time he's twelve, sir, he won't do it by the time he's twenty and twelve, sir'. The schoolmaster tries to argue that there is more to education than the three Rs, such as 'how to be a good citizen'. Weston comes back with the argument that craftsmen are the backbone of the country and that none of those he knew 'stayed larnin' until they was twelve, sir. If you don't mind I a-sayin' such a thing, sir, if we'd spent so long a time at book-larnin' we'd never have knowed our crafts like we do' (Goodland 1953, 161–2).

A consequence of growing up in an established house-thatching family was that a formal education could be cut short, and yet expectations would be so much more. Such as having to pay back nearly all one's hard-earned wage into the family purse to pay for one's keep.

> To the best of my recollection I left school at Easter 1914 being just over thirteen years old, and started work with my father ... When first I worked for my father I was not very big or strong and the job proved to be very hard work. My wages for the first two years were board and lodgings and clothes, and 2d a week spending money. (Parrott 1974, 33)

Most sons of course began working as yealmers.

> Father will drive my 'pathetic' row of straw forward into one yelm, dunning it into me to pull it out in 'big bits and thick with both hands'. These hands were very sore, and the insides of my forearms, in the yealming, and great cracks would open up in the joints, sometimes bleeding or a butt of straw would find one, digging into raw flesh. Father leaves me with my misery. (Brown 1974, 44–45)

The advantage of using family labour is also summed up by Brown. 'In the years before the Great War we were sparing Father much paid help. We had learnt the business of thatching and hay-tying' (Brown 1974, 60).

In some cases, the son was destined to remain in the role of server until the death of their parent; for younger sons, the prospects might be even less rosy. Herbert Kingham's father, for example, acted as server to his elder brother John and never graduated beyond this function.

The inherent tendency to treat family labour as cheap labour must have tempted impatient sons to look outside the business for fuller wage packets. In some instances external factors, such as the First World War or the depression, also intervened to prevent a smooth inheritance from father to son. Although Sydney Williams of Cornwall eventually joined his father, the hard times of the depression made it impossible for him to practice his craft immediately. So for several years he worked as a farmer, building up his business until he was able to devote all his time to thatching (Seymour 1956). It is worth noting that Sydney learnt the trade with his two brothers, both of whom moved to Australia, emigration thus creaming off potential family recruits.

Unless these alternative avenues were pursued, one's earning potential was usually delayed by remaining with the family business. The Bagshawe survey suggests that many thatchers remained single and were therefore without sons to take over the business. Conversely, having sons did not guarantee that the business would continue. Of a total of 83 thatchers' sons of all ages listed in Bedfordshire in 1851, only seven were recorded as thatching in the county in 1881 (Bedfordshire Record Office 2 and 3). Bagshawe noted in 1948–9 that 'In only one case, that of the Pursers of Westoning, was a son working with his father' (Bagshawe 1951, 1141).

Compared to the healthy pedigrees of the majority of thatchers interviewed by Bagshawe, the survey suggests that thatching in Bedfordshire was suffering a complete breakdown in family continuity. The drastic decline in number of thatchers (Table 16) in the period 1890–1940 appears to confirm this bleak outlook. The data indicate that the seeds of this decline were being sown in the nineteenth century and the thread of inheritance became more fragile as more and more sons declined to take up their father's trade.

A comparison of the census returns with the Bagshawe material is revealing. Bagshawe found 15 individual working thatchers. The 1881 census (Bedfordshire Record Office 3) recorded 31 thatchers in the county. When located in the returns, in some cases a father and son are both listed as thatchers living in the same household. In other cases several thatching branches of the same family are found living in the same parish. For example, in Henlow parish, George Watts was the head of one household, while two sons Frederick and Arthur had got married and were living nearby with their families. Together these account for three out of the total of 31 thatchers. It is instructive to compare the number of family units recorded in the census and those recorded by Bagshawe (Table 17). In 1948–9, only two of the fifteen thatchers were related (father and son George and Cecil Purser) so the total for this date was 14 separate family units engaged in thatching. In 1881, however, there were eight cases of related thatchers. In addition, one of the entries that was counted as a full thatcher in the overall totals was only a thatcher's labourer, so that we end up with only 20 separate family units. The loss of six family units between 1881 and 1947–8, after two World Wars, does not therefore appear so dramatic, but the difference in terms of the security of inheritance is.

Table 17 charts the fact that whereas in 1851 it was the accepted procedure that several, if not all of the sons in a family should take up thatching, by 1948–9 it was virtually impossible to find a father and son team working together anywhere in the county. This was not due to a general lack of male heirs; in the case of John Walker of Lidlington Bagshawe noted the family's thatching history and commented: 'The tradition might have continued even further for Jack's son took over his father's tools and started as a thatcher but gave it up to work on the railway' (Bagshawe 1951, 1125).

The continuity of tradition in Bedfordshire reflected in the pedigrees of the individual thatchers interviewed in 1948–9 must therefore be seen in a wider context. Fuller analysis of the data demonstrates that inheritance was increasingly failing to provide a smooth, pre-ordained passage of skills from father to son. This breakdown was the result of many different factors, in particular the lure of better opportunities elsewhere. In the final analysis, however, much of the responsibility for driving sons away from the craft must be laid at the feet of the fathers who failed to ensure better pay or working conditions, refused to invest their sons with greater responsibilities at an earlier age, and in some cases stifled talent. Nor can the exertion of patriarchal authority in too overbearing a manner be ignored.

> The tyranny of Father's father was not entirely lifted from his son's brow, and I confess I have much of the 'old block' 'n me. My mirror reflects Father, I am he in many ways. When I plod on my way it is his feet, only improved laws and circumstantial changes put a different label on me. (Brown 1974, 26)

Table 16 Number of thatchers in Bedfordshire: 1841–1948–9 (PP 1844, PP 1852–3, PP 1863, PP 1873, PP 1883; Bagshawe 1951).

Date	thatchers
1841	41
1851	69
1861	58
1871	38
1881	31
1891	43
1948–9	15

Table 17 Ratio of individual thatchers and family units in Bedfordshire: 1851, 1881 and 1948–9 (PP 1852–3, PP 1883; Bagshawe 1951).

Year	Number of thatchers	Number of family units	Ratio
1851	69	40	1.73
1881	31	20	1.55
1948–9	15	14	1.07

The breakdown in family continuity provided some new opportunities for outsiders to move into the craft, but the uptake was likely to be constrained by economic factors, which encouraged the use of family labour rather than apprenticeships.

The secrecy surrounding the craft was identified as a bar to the introduction of any type of apprenticeship scheme. In 1948, a local newspaper praised the Rural Industry Bureau efforts in this field and wagged a finger at the industry.

> If the scheme is to succeed, there will have to be no 'closed shops' among the thatching fraternity. Rightly enough they are 'jealous of their ancient craft and its secrets' but the time is at hand when they will have to render these up to a new generation of thatchers in order that this practical and beautiful craft may live to delight all those who love the England that is truly England. (anon 1948)

Plump order books combined with a penchant for secrecy and an inevitable independence of spirit meant some thatchers turned their backs on any potential assistance: 'we're meant to be the most cussed of all craftsmen, we'd tell anyone to go to hell, we always had that much work in hand' (Watkins 1981, 168).

In Bedfordshire, none of the three Humberstones interviewed by Bagshawe appears to have taken on apprentices, their yealmers having been drawn from the local community on an *ad hoc* basis. Albert used 'Sidney Bonfield, landlord of the Chequers public house, who takes them to work in his car' while Frank had 'employed young men of 21 to 30 years of age as 'yelmers'. But 'for the last 10 years of his working life [he] did his own 'yelming' (Bagshawe 1951, 1132–7).

The decline in the number of sons willing to take up thatching caused some of the estate/house thatchers to look outside their immediate families for assistance. This was how the four apprentices interviewed by Bagshawe had entered the craft.

Potential apprentices were not necessarily easy to find. As early as 1804, having commented on the great advance in thatching prices between 1790 and 1803, the commentator attributed 'its cause from few learning the business; as it does not give constant employment throughout the year, there is not an inducement' (Young 1804b, 518–9). A thatcher from Oakley, Hampshire, in the 1950s grumbled that 'young fellows don't take it on. They can go into these factories, work five days and then have a rest' (North West Sound Archive 1).

There was also the unhappy prospect of long-term physical deterioration: work was 'healthy up to a point – you get rheumatics and fibrositis'. Even if recruits could be found, then the problem was keeping them: 'I haven't got anyone with me now – I've had one or two ... they had a month or two and then that's it ... they've got to like heights, they've got to like the cold and wet' (Centre for Oxfordshire Studies Sound Archive 2). The nature of the work inevitably exposed the thatcher to a good deal of risk. 'Sydney Williams' thatching days have had their moments like the time when he fell over the top of the ridge and rolled down the other side of the roof' (Seymour

1956). Alfred Wright 'thatched part-time until a fall from the roof injured his back' (Nash 1994, 16–19). Frank Humberstone 'retired from work in 1945 after falling off a stack' (Bagshawe 1951, 1133). Reginald Parrott's father was badly injured as a result of a passing 'motor cycle "taxi", the foot rest of which touched the bottom of my father's ladder, dragging it down from the roof with my father clinging to it' (Parrott 1974, 37). Hugh Dunmore Walker 'fell off the roof at fifteen, drunk on parsnip wine' (Watkins 1981, 167).

Despite the poor advancement prospects and the dangers involved, a thatching apprenticeship could nevertheless be a way for boys from poorer, labouring backgrounds to move a few rungs up the social ladder into a trade. Sam Blackburn, born in 1905 at Salhouse, Norfolk, was the youngest boy of a poor family of ten. He joined the Farmans as an apprentice, and the benefits this reaped for his family are reflected in the fact that Sam was able to assist his father in renting a small farm (Blackburn 1982, 6).

The term apprenticeship, it should be stressed, can only be applied loosely in this context for it has formal contractual overtones which do not tally with the *ad hoc* agreements reached between thatcher and trainee. In the case of Albert Church, of Biddenham, Bedfordshire, he had simply worked as a server to Robert Henman for five years, there was really no implied ladder of training involved (Bagshawe 1951, 1121). Lewis Ben Cooper was apprenticed for six years to Cope of Tempsford 'without indentures' (op cit, 1124). The unstructured character of this recruiting system is brought out in Blackburn's own case. He started work at the age of 12 bird-scaring, but in 1918

> a Law was made that men were to get thirty shillings [£1.50] and boys were to get seven shillings [35p]. Farmer told me to find another job as he could not afford me. I got a temporary job in the thatching yard for a Mr Farman, peeling osiers. I asked Mr Farman if he would give me a regular job. He said he would let me know. On the Whit Monday there were the village sports and I won the boys under 15 race. Mr Farman presented me with my prize – a pocket knife. I asked him about the job and he said I could start on Monday. (Blackburn 1982, 8)

Blackburn vividly recalled his first day on a roof.

> I arrived a long time before the 8 am starting time. There were fifteen men and boys working there. Mr Farman told me I could go with Mr [Billy] Chapman and two other men. We went in a pony and cart to the village of Buckingham [Buckenham] near Cantley. When we got there Mr Chapman went up on the roof and took a small ladder, rope and long thatching needles with him. He fixed the ladder to the ridge down the side of the house. Then he called down for a bolt [half a bunch] of reed. I took it up the ladder to the top of this tallest house I had ever seen in my life. I was very frightened when I got to the top. Mr Chapman lifted me off the ladder and sat me across the ridge. He gave me a knife and told me to go along the ridge and trim all the loose bits of thatch off. When I got to the end I dare not turn around so Mr

Chapman walked along the ridge, picked me up and turned me round so I could trim the other side. (op cit, 8)

Becoming an apprentice provided no guarantee that the association with the master thatcher would be a binding one. Nor was there ever a stated period of time after which the apprentice could himself claim to be a master thatcher, a recipe for uncertainty and frustration. There was an in-built hierarchy in thatching which literally translated itself into the physical working relationship between the master up on the roof and servant down on the ground.

Learning the craft really meant watching, observing, and copying. 'Watch, boy, watch. You've got to learn by looking. That way it registers and doesn't drift away' (Dyer 1981, 13). Any indication of inventiveness could be frowned upon. Jack Lumsden of Farndale learned as a boy from an old travelling 'theaker', David Hawnby. Jack often 'stopped off skeeal ti sarve 'im ', and when he first tried himself, the old man said, 'Ah allus tellt tha, Shonnie, 'at that way o' theeakin was neea good. If tha dizzn't theeak seeam waay as ah diz, thi job's good for nowr – it'll blaw up I' i'fost wind ar blaws' (Cowley 1955, 39).

Jack Dyer, of Ruscombe, Berkshire, began his thatching career by joining a local thatcher, Harry Turner (who had no children of his own) during the First World War.

At Dad's suggestion I started helping Mr Turner when his apprentice was called up into the army. I was pleased at the idea for it meant I could earn myself a few shillings each week and pocket money wasn't easily come by in those days. (Dyer 1981, 10)

His frustration grew quickly because of the slowness of the training which comes through strongly in the following passage.

After a few months of apprenticeship I began to wonder if I'd ever get a chance to work on an actual roof itself, for all Mr Turner would let me do, during those early days, was to prepare the straw and heave it up the ladder to him. This wasn't my idea of being a thatcher at all. (op cit, 11)

Dyer's confinement to yealming placed a strain on the relationship between master and apprentice.

I got a bit careless one day and started rushing the job a little. I seemed to be for ever up and down that ladder with the bundles, so I was a bit surprised to hear him call out for yet another load. 'I've just taken you up a bundle'. Mr Turner went on working at the thatch, scarcely turning his head. 'Look beside you, boy.' There at my side was the bundle I'd only recently heaved up the ladder. 'If you call those yealms, young Dyer, you're no good to me. Make me some more.' I was hot, tired and annoyed. 'Well, you'll have to wait while I make them then'. Back came the reply, 'I don't mind waiting, so long as they're done properly'. (op cit, 12)

It appears to have been at least five years before Dyer was let loose even on a rick. And that was only because it was he who took the initiative.

I wish I had a record of the very first job I tackled on my own. It was for a small farmer in Waltham St Lawrence and I was in my late teens. I knew I was capable of thatching a complete roof on my own, but Mr Turner and the farmers were always hesitant about letting me try. The answer was always 'No, your thatch might let in the wet and I wouldn't like to risk it.' Cycling home one lunchtime I noticed a stack that was all ready for thatch and, plucking up courage, I approached the farmer. 'Mr Horwood, I see you need someone to thatch your bean stack.' He stroked his chin thoughtfully. I suppose he must have been amused by my eagerness for he suddenly smiled and clapped me on the back. 'All right, lad you come over and have a go if you want'. I was overjoyed. At last someone had enough faith in me to let me do a job properly on my own. (op cit, 18)

He tackled his first house at the age of twenty. Dyer started work on ten shillings (50p) a week at the age of thirteen, and remained on this wage for five years.

As I grew older and I was given more and more responsibility in my work, I felt the ten shillings [50p] a week for an eighteen-year-old wasn't anything like sufficient and I thought it was high time I spoke up about it. My opportunity came one day when I was working with twenty-two other men building a rick – a hazardous proceeding at the best of times, because it is so easy to get stuck accidently by a fork when so many work together. 'This is a man's job and no mistake' I said to Mr Turner, 'Don't you think it's about time I got a man's pay?' Mr Turner nodded towards Mr Richard Cotterell, who was sitting below, watching the men at work. 'All right, boy, if you think you deserve it, go and ask Mr Cotterell there – he's paying for the job.' I got down slowly and approached the farmer a little hesitantly. 'Look here sir,' I stammered, 'you've been watching us working up there, don't you think I should rate a man's pay?' Mr Cotterell looked up and, to my relief, smiled. 'Tell Turner to remind me on Friday night.' From then on it was a pound a week for me whatever the job, for Mr Turner was a fair man. (op cit, 18)

There is nothing to suggest that Harry Turner deliberately undertrained Dyer, but apprentices did not always acquire their master's full range of skills. The training history of Lewis Ben Cooper, one of Bagshawe's informants, is of particular interest. From the age of 14 to 20 he worked with Cope of Tempsford followed by four years with Edwin Lewin. Cope and Lewin were reed thatchers, but we are told that Cooper later went on to learn 'reed thatching from "Dick" Dunkley in Huntingdonshire. He estimates that it was nearly 10 years after he first started to learn that he became fully proficient' (Bagshawe 1951, 1124).

There is no clear explanation why Cooper needed this extra training, but a significant proportion of his apprenticeship was probably spent on the ground or acting as server to his master. It was always feasible to train up an apprentice to rick thatching standards, so that they could assist, but not challenge the master's role. In the end, the same constraints for sons acting as servers also applied to apprentices in that in many cases only the death of the master would open up the prospect of an independent working life for the trainee.

THE IMPOVERISHMENT OF TRADITION

By 1940 the transmission of skills, methods and techniques in thatching was primarily through the family line or through apprentices who effectively acted as surrogate sons. The lineages of thatchers interviewed by Bagshawe were impressive, but had apparently been truncated for a variety of reasons. Bagshawe's comprehensive survey allows us to move beyond the anecdotal evidence of individual thatchers' fortunes and working methods, and to examine the entire demographic, social, technological and economic context within which traditions evolved and changed.

It is perhaps an axiom that society only perceives a skill as traditional when it is under threat. Bagshawe's study was revealingly titled *Disappearing Rural Industries, Trades, Crafts and Occupations*. The implication was that the tradition as such was running out of steam and that it could only be a remnant of its former self. In numerical terms the drastic decline in the number of thatchers between 1790 and 1940 bears witness to the terrible loss of expertise over one and a half centuries. The sheer number of individuals involved in the craft in the early nineteenth century must have contributed to a rich and varied roofscape. In the north the thread of continuity in terms of inherited thatching skills appears to have been completely severed prior to the Second World War.

In a southern county like Bedfordshire the craft was now largely monopolized by a few dynastic schools. This had clearly influence the development of the craft. It is worth considering the actual nature of the inheritance and how it had changed in the period 1790–1940. An inheritance can encompass many different things such as the passing on of skills and working methods, or a commitment to both rick and house thatching, rather than specialization. It might also be something as tangible as a customer order book, or an established working patch, invaluable in a very territorial trade. If the patch consisted of all the buildings on a single large estate, then a whole bundle of obligations to the estate landlord might come wrapped in the bequest of skills from father to son. Inheritance might also encompass working capital, land, an existing workforce, or simply a tool chest.

Traditions were not transmitted in a vacuum. Relationships between neighbouring thatchers could often be cool and critical and so limit the chances of cross-fertilization of ideas and techniques. However, Lewis Ben Cooper's career was influenced by two of the principal dynastic thatching families in Bedfordshire. Seasonal yealmers could also carry new ideas as they moved from one master to another.

The thatcher's craft was rarely as isolating and secretive as is often suggested. He had to interact with the owners of buildings, farmers, farm labourers, suppliers and employees. His work took him to the heart of the rural economy.

The water reed firms

In the 1900s it was the larger thatching firms, mostly concentrated in East Anglia, which conformed to the capitalist structure found in building trades. Reed thatchers working for the Cowells or the Farmans experienced very different lifestyles and working conditions to the straw thatchers.

Sam Blackburn, a Norfolk reed-thatcher with the Farmans had 'thatched roofs in every county of England, including a summerhouse at Sandringham. He has also thatched lampshades and a dolls' house which he made for an exhibition at Windsor Castle' (Blackburn 1982, 16). Contact with other thatchers would be more frequent. Blackburn lists at least eleven thatchers he had worked with during 51 years in the trade. The reed firms extended the horizons of the thatchers who worked for them.

Reed-thatching firms retained a more formal master/servant relationships when compared to the straw-thatching areas. Comparison of the statistics given in the 1851 census indicates that in only two areas of the country did thatchers employ additional labour (Table 18). Reed might also be supplied over longer distances than straw, and was more likely to be chosen for superior buildings. The successful reed-thatching firms that emerged had strong foundations. Their inheritance was considerable, but this did not stifle inventiveness: the fancy patterning on reedwork reputedly introduced by the Farman Brothers in the 1920s, is a case in point.

Estate/house thatchers

The situation was very different for the estate/house thatcher who emerged during the nineteenth century under the patronage of large landowners. On the estate, the thatcher was partially sheltered from competition and the need to apply thatch profitably. Materials were produced or purchased as required, and delivered to site at the thatcher's request. Quality of work and the appearance of the final product were the prime concerns, and the materials and styles employed were influenced both by the decisions of the landlord and farm manager as well as by local tradition. Sons born into this type of thatching family were cushioned by an inheritance which incorporated a guaranteed stock of thatched buildings and materials, a known clientele and plenty of secondary employment opportunities on the estate.

This apparently secure inheritance suffered a major rupture with the break-up of large estates in the first part of this century. Thatchers had to construct an economically viable patch in the private sector, with new responsibilities for obtaining supplies, transporting them to site,

Table 18 Number of thatching employers by region: 1851 (PP 1852–3).

Number of men employed	East Anglia	south west
1	15	14
2	1	4
3	1	
4	1	

applying them profitably, and charging work at competitive rates. The integrity of estate thatchers could hinder their ability to adapt to the free market.

Mr Webber, thatcher on the Castle Estate, Somerset, was praised by Albino in 1946 for the quality of his work.

> Besides this fine workmanship there is the honesty of purpose and social responsibility which are second nature to the true craftsman. Mr Webber was once given an order for thatching a house, but on examining the roof, as he always does before starting, he found a rafter which was dangerously exposed to the chimney, causing a risk of fire. He would not undertake the thatching of that house. Once, being employed by a speculative builder on some work, he soon found that what was wanted was shoddy, cheap work. That builder had to find someone else to finish the job. (Albino 1946a, 71)

Some estate thatchers did not make the transition with the result that thatched roofs fell into disrepair and the changeover to other roofing materials was swift. Even where the transition was made, as with the Dunkleys, Humberstones and Copes of Bedfordshire, it was bought at a price; in this case the attenuation of reed thatching skills. This was reflected in the generational differences between the twenty thatchers interviewed by Bagshawe, who divided very clearly into two age groups. The first group of ten consisted of all those aged over 60, five of whom were still working. The second group also of ten included all those aged under 50; there were no thatchers at all aged between 50 and 60. Of those in the older age group, six were capable of working in both straw and reed and all were products of the four main Bedfordshire thatching schools.

For most thatchers, but perhaps for estate thatchers in particular, the obtaining of wood for spar making was an inherited aspect of the contractual obligations or *ad hoc* arrangements made with the local landowner. Only Geoffrey Tompkins of all the Bedfordshire thatchers in 1948–9 obtained 'the wood for his staves and spars from a wood merchant at Potton' (Bagshawe 1951, 1122). Even Tompkins made his own fixings, however, and this was true of all of Bagshawe's informants. In Charles Dunkley's garden 'There is a thatched wooden shed with window and earthen floor where he keeps his tools and made "spits" when the weather was too bad for thatching ... In the shed there is a wood block on which the spits could be sharpened' (op cit, 1127). The Cope diaries minutely record the numbers manufactured during the season by members of the family.

Spit making was different from rick-thatching in two respects. On the one hand it could occupy the thatcher or his sons during bad weather and therefore ensured that the preparatory work for house thatching was being carried out at a time when working on a roof was not feasible or desirable. In Bedfordshire the decline in the number of sons willing to take on the father's occupations inevitably meant, however, that the task fell increasingly on the shoulders of the thatcher himself. Similarly, the expansion in rick thatching also in-

creased the demand for spars, tying the thatcher more and more to the rending block.

On the other hand there was no immediate economic return from spar-making, it was simply a task that had to be carried out before thatching could take place. While the house thatcher could do without rick thatching, he could not do without spars. But he need not make them himself. In the coppice counties it remained an established feature that at least a proportion of spars would be bought in. A comparison between a Dorset and a Bedfordshire thatcher would illustrate that the former was spending less time on the ground, and theoretically could release more time for actual work on the roofs.

The extension of rick thatching and spit making helps to explain why the working horizons of the estate/house thatchers remained so limited in Bedfordshire during the first half of the century. These were practices which could tease out the work available without having to look further afield for work. Thus, despite the drastic decline in the number of thatched buildings in the county, few thatchers were working more than twelve miles (19km) from home. Hence techniques spread very slowly. In Cornwall, by contrast, a 'dearth of thatched property meant that their work often took them beyond the borders of Devon and Somerset' (anon 1959a).

The restricted working horizons of Bedfordshire thatchers are surprising given that new technologies should have opened up the possibility of working further afield. The Farmans and Cowells of Soham were busy transporting thatchers and reeds around the country using new forms of transport, while in Bedfordshire one thatcher still used a pony and trap, six a bicycle, four a motorcycle and only four possessed a car. Although a majority had graduated beyond Shank's pony, this does not seem to have drastically extended the thatcher's horizons. Of fifteen thatchers for which modes of transport are mentioned in 1948–9, none possessed the wherewithal to transport their own materials.

This unwillingness to move very far afield on a daily or short-term basis is echoed in the relative geographical immobility of thatching families over a more extended time-scale. Analysis of the 1851 census reveals that 38 of the 59 thatchers were still working in the parishes of their birth. A century later, Bagshawe found the Humberstones of Wrestlingworth a particularly 'interesting family for they have remained in one village' (Bagshawe 1951, 1132). None of the other thatchers interviewed were so rooted to their native parishes, but most had not moved very far. A move may have been prompted through necessity where two sons would otherwise have had to share their father's patch. A simpler motive might be provided through an invitation to thatch on a distant estate.

Short-range mobility may have nudged techniques and styles into adjacent parishes, and over county boundaries, but the minor distances involved suggests techniques would take the course of a lifetime to transfer from one parish to another.

It is also important to stress that working areas were rarely discrete as a map of Bedfordshire working areas in 1948–9 would illustrate. Patches overlapped and thatchers regularly encountered their competitors at work. Tools, yealms and techniques would all be visible at a glance and a competitor's work could be examined in detail whenever an owner changed thatchers. Such constant exposure reinforced the continuity of techniques and materials, but at the same time prevented complete insularity. It also bypassed any need for direct communication with competitors. The thatched roof was, in a sense, an arms' length training medium. No formal associations were required where thatchers could discuss techniques and standards. The blueprint was ever present, on each and every roof.

Smallholders

One of the most significant changes in the whole period 1790–1940 was the decline of the smallholding tradition. In terms of inheritance, the effects were wide-ranging.

The increasing lack of smallholders denuded the thatching industry of an important source of recruits with a solid background in rural skills. The shrinking influence of the smallholding tradition forced established house thatching into greater prominence, a process which dovetailed with the Rural Industry Bureau's policy to invent the house thatcher for the purpose of establishing its training programmes (Cox 1994 **1**, 5–14). Another consequence of the decline was the loss of a workforce that had maintained and repaired the vast range of ancillary buildings, which in the nineteenth century had vastly outnumbered the number of thatched dwellings. Again, with the established families concentrating more and more on house thatching, this huge inheritance of thatched structures was left to decay and almost totally disappear.

It is impossible to quantify the consequent loss of idiosyncratic inventiveness that characterized the smallholders approach to problem-solving. Wilfred Hawkins of Colmworth showed Bagshawe a tool which consisted of 'three tines from an old hand drag set into a piece of wood 30 in [76cm] long, and resembles a large comb'. It was not in fact a hand comb or rake, but rather an idea of his father's used 'to hold thatch tight at the eaves while being cut' (Bagshawe 1951, 1160). Another tool with an individualistic imprint was the needle with an eye at both ends used exclusively, it appears, by Cyril Purser of Westoning. It apparently saved work in threading and transferred the responsibility for tying the knot to the person inside the roof space.

Smallholding thatchers were particularly good at transforming tools and artefacts used in other trades and crafts to suit their own purposes. Spit knives were adapted from old sickle or hook blades, or old files or rasps, or in one case a bayonet blade (Bagshawe 1951, 1146). For carrying bundles of yealms, hurdle shackles might be attached to an ordinary piece of rope to make a noose. Hobnails were driven into blocks for use as leggats. Tompkins of Chalton, the self-taught thatcher, was undoubtedly the most inventive of all those interviewed by Bagshawe. He had 'an old "spar sharpener" made from a sickle blade but prefers a sugar beet knife' (op cit, 1144), used 'a mallet made by his grandfather from a piece of wheel hub' (op

cit, 1154), a side rake 'made from an old barrel stave' (op cit, 1158), and a paring knife 'adapted from a scythe blade' (op cit, 1161). Recycling extended to thatcher's dress: Hawkins had adapted his knee-pads from old horse pads (op cit, 1163).

Established house thatchers were also flexible and adaptive, but were more circumscribed by an expectation to continue using tools which bequeathed from one generation to the next. 'After Arthur [Lewin's] death most of the thatching tools were taken over by Cyril Stonebridge, the Potton thatcher, who had been apprenticed to him' (op cit, 1130).

In Bedfordshire there is some evidence of a trend towards lighter tools. The move away from the heavier hatchets to the use of adapted sickle blades or bill hooks to make spars perhaps reflects changes in coppicing methods, shorter coppice cycles producing thinner and more easily worked shoots. New industrial processes introduced redesigned and lighter thatching tools. By 1948–9 shears were all 'Sheffield-made tools bought by the thatchers from ironmongers' (op cit, 1160).

One must try to distinguish between idiosyncratic practice and determined innovation. Bagshawe's survey makes it quite clear that individual thatchers were chang-

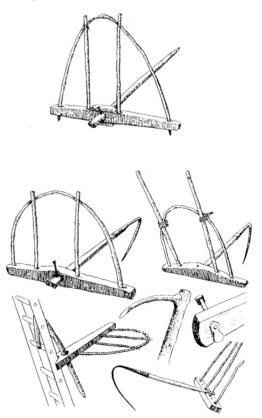

Figure 114 Jacks and naves used by thatchers in Bedfordshire: (clockwise from bottom left) jack with length of arm 2 feet 10.5 inches, Tempsford (Lewin); jack with length of arm 4 feet 2 inches, Wrestlingworth, made about 1900 (Charles Humberstone); nave with length of arm 3 feet, Lidlington, made about 1933 (Walker); nave with length of arm 2 feet 4 inches, Billington; arm of jack with length 3 feet 8 inches, Wrestlingworth (Charles Humberstone); jack, from Chalton, Moggerhanger, from a 1948 photograph (Tompkins); jack with hooked arm, length 3 feet 3 inches, Keysoe Mill (all images reproduced by kind permission of the Bagshawe Collection).

ing and adapting the tools they used throughout their lifetimes. In examining the tools used for rending spits, he recorded that

> among the tools of a retired wheelwright at Stotfold was found a 'thatching hammer' or 'axe' used for rending and cutting thatching spits. It is a local blacksmith-made tool and is reputed to have been made previous to 1848. Frank Humberstone the Wrestlingworth thatcher examined it and called it a 'thatching hatchet for quartering spit wood'. He said 'I remember my grandfather having one and I have used the same type myself. I prefer a straight handle, and for spit making latterly I have used a bill with a beak to cut the wood into lengths before rending. (op cit, 1145–6)

Here at least three different versions of a tool were used for the same function in the lifetime of one thatcher.

Adaptation could occur within a thatching school, but once a tool had been adapted, its inheritors could become dogmatic about retaining it. The special type of jack devised by the Copes of Tempsford had as its characteristic feature the fact that it could be suspended on a ladder using a natural hazelwood hook fixed almost at right angles by the V notch cut into the end of the main bottom rail. This holder is entirely recognisable as still being within the Bedfordshire tradition; it is a modification of, rather than a departure from, the established model. Of more interest is the fact that Copes' nineteenth-century pattern was in use by three other thatchers in the 1940s. Arthur Lewin, Ben Cooper and Cyril Stonebridge were trained by the Copes and their school thus invented and retained the pattern as a distinctive trademark, a symbol perhaps of the constraining effects of inheritance through a family-based tradition (Fig 114).

Despite the fact that tools produced by heavy industrial processes had been around for over a century and a half, there is only scant evidence in 1948–9 of the abandonment of the local blacksmith in favour of the ironmonger. Standard industrially-produced chains were only just beginning to replace wood and rope appliances for carrying yealms up onto the roof. All the needles used for sewing thatch onto the rafters were still blacksmith-made tools in 1948–9, as were the thatching hooks or spikes and even the wire-netting hooks Bagshawe examined. Thatchers still operated within a wood culture, with some input from the blacksmith.

Much of the information that Bagshawe recorded reveals an acceptance of technological change that did not substantially alter fixing techniques or appearances.

Conclusion

Implicit in the study of most rural crafts are three widely held assumptions. First, that they tend to operate within an unbroken, unchanging tradition. Secondly, that this continuity is desirable and the reason why the craft has survived at all. Thirdly, that any changes that occur emanate from the harsh, outside world and ultimately will destroy the craft.

None of these assumptions is particularly valid in the case of thatching. There were very pronounced changes in the composition of the workforce, including the emergence of the estate/house thatching dynasties at the expense of the smallholding tradition. As the number of thatched buildings declined rick and smallholding thatchers had been squeezed out, leaving a handful of thatching dynasties with an impressive, but more restricted inheritance. No-one disputes that a host of extraneous factors such as settlement patterns, farming methods, economic prosperity and the availability of other roofing materials had contributed to the decline of the craft. At the heart of the problem was the nature of the thatcher's inheritance. With the virtual disappearance of the smallholding tradition as a means of entry into the craft, the family had become the controlling unit, and the sole context within which sons or apprentices could be trained. Patriarchal authority usually dispensed with contractual obligations and did not always encourage inventiveness or adaption.

The Bagshawe material makes it very clear that the reed tradition in Bedfordshire slipped away which is surprising given the popularity of water reed at this time and that it took off in areas without a tradition of water reed thatching.

The narrowing of the horizons to long straw was undoubtedly triggered by the fact that local supplies of reed clearly dried up in the period, while the decline of the major estates in the early part of the century also reduced demand. Finally, Bedfordshire did not attract the same kind of suburban Arts and Crafts developments that occurred in neighbouring counties. In the end, a firm like Cowell's of Soham faced with the same problem of supply and demand managed to survive by finding new markets and purchasing reed from further afield.

THE RURAL INDUSTRIES BUREAU AND THE DISCOVERY OF THATCHERS

All the changes described in this chapter took place in the absence of a useful support network for the thatching industry. This took some time to grow up because the various agencies that should have been instrumental in promoting it failed to grasp its idiosyncratic nature. Some initiatives were developed, but their true impact was not felt until the Second World War. These initiatives group into three phases.

Phase 1 1909–20

The Development and Road Improvements Funds Act was passed in 1909 as a response to the whole spectrum of changes outlined in previous chapters, the break up of estates, cheap rapid transport and industrialization, as being contributory factors in the decline of village craft skills. The Act was intended 'to promote the Economic Development of the United Kingdom', and the Commissioners were empowered to make grants or loans to various named bodies for the purpose of 'aiding and developing agriculture and rural industries' (Williams 1958, 5).

Thatching was a potential candidate for financial aid but the implementation of this Act was interrupted by the First World War. Agriculture, which had been relatively prosperous since 1896, benefited from the sharp drop in imports and demand and the crafts which served the farmer flourished (op cit, 4).

Phase 2 1921–26

At the end of the first phase prices of farm products were beginning to fall. Rural industries and crafts faced grave difficulties, and in November 1921 the Development Commission (using the powers granted to it under the 1909 Act) established the first Trustees of the Rural Industries Bureau.

In its early years its principal objective was 'to provide skilled advice to all who are concerned in the promotion and extension of these [rural] industries' based on the premises that village life 'has been stirred by the war and can be looked to for more enterprise and energy' (Public Record Office 2). Because one object was to assist 'the large number of disabled and subnormal ex-service men now receiving treatment and training' the types of 'rural industry' envisaged were cottage industries that produced fancy jewellery, turned woodwork, artificial flowers and ribbon weaving (Public Record Office 2). A Co-Operative Trading Society was established to supply raw materials and sell goods (Public Record Office 2).

Established crafts such as thatching received no attention in the early days of the Rural Industry Bureau but as recession bit deeper into these traditional sectors of rural employment, the Rural Industries Bureau was criticized for ignoring these traditional sectors of rural employment. As early as 1922, the *Birmingham Post* remarked

> If the Treasury can spare money for the promotion of rural industries, let it be by making grants to those who are already engaged on the work rather than by setting up people in an advisory capacity who may, or may not, have the knowledge for dealing with the problem. (anon 1922c)

The Rural Industries Bureau limped through its early years: 'Undoubtedly, its work benefited small numbers of individuals, but as an instrument of any wider reconstruction it was hopelessly inadequate' (Creasey & Ward 1984, 14).

Phase 3 *c* 1925–32

Progress in the development of the Rural Industries Bureau during this period was desperately slow. Rural Community Councils had also been established in 1921 'to act as local representatives of the Bureau in the counties' (Public Record Office 1), but coordination was difficult given their *ad hoc* origins and most soon began to operate largely under their own initiatives. Some employed 'craftsmen organizers', but it was not until 1925 that grants became available to employ them. Only in Kent were different organizers employed for different

crafts. The problem was always that the organizers lacked sufficient expertise, which the Bureau thought it should provide.

The Rural Industries Bureau was slower to focus its attention on strengthening existing traditional crafts rather than seeking to create an entirely new economic base. Blacksmiths, wheelwrights and saddlers attracted much attention in surveys of rural industries in the 1930s, but thatch is rarely mentioned. The smith's position could be improved by providing him with power, welding gear, or cheaper raw materials, in which case the smith could compete with the more highly capitalized implement maker. The wheelwright could turn to cabinet-making or coffin-making and even the saddler, who was sometimes perceived as a hopeless case, could learn how to restring tennis rackets. Major Longden, a member of the Rural Industry Bureau Committee in 1931, 'said that there were many articles which saddlers could make, such as golf bags' (Public Record Office 1).

Thatchers, however, could not shift easily into the production of small craft items and the thatcher's finished article was not a commodity that could be traded. Improving access to the raw materials used by thatchers was not something that the meagre resources of the Rural Industry Bureau could address. In both smithing and saddlery, there was a direct and tangible link between urban and rural aspects. On the other hand the thatcher could not buy his materials from the towns, and he had no urban competitors.

Phase 4 1933–39

In the 1931 review of the Bureau's decade of work it was stated that 'Rural craftsmen have been unearthed, surveyed and catalogued' (Public Record Office 1) although thatching had yet to figure in any survey. A more realistic attitude gradually evolved which recognized that the demand for ancillary agricultural crafts had continued to diminish and it was now necessary to stem the decline.

The thatcher was finally shifted into the limelight as one of the last symbols of disappearing rural craftsmanship and culture.

At the 1931 Inquiry a Mr Baker from the Cambridgeshire Rural Community Council said:

> that during the last 5 or 6 years there had been no drop in the number of craftsmen, except, perhaps, in the number of thatchers. Some were taking up a new type of work, but the decline in agricultural work was only due to the agricultural depression. Mr Baker said something should be done for the thatchers, who were numerous on the edge of the fens. (Public Record Office 1)

Nothing changed until 1937–8 when the Rural Industries Bureau finally carried out the first national survey of thatchers, which revealed that there were about 517 house thatchers in England using straw (Public Record Office 3). Action was delayed, however, by the outbreak of the Second World War.

13   Conclusion

The origins of thatching may well be lost in the mists of antiquity, but there is enough evidence, historical, botanical, technical and *in situ*, to sketch an outline of the changes that influenced the development of the craft between 1790 and 1940. It is the obvious decline of thatching over this period that has attracted the greatest attention from scholars. The evidence clearly indicates that in 1790 thatch was abundant in almost every part of the country and on almost every class of building, and the list of materials used was almost as impressive as the range of techniques employed. By 1940, however, the numbers of thatched buildings and practising thatchers had declined to the point at which the craft teetered on the edge of extinction. The spectrum of materials available was severely attenuated as a result of environmental and agricultural change, and the gamut of techniques once used to apply them had been distilled down to the three basic thatching methods we recognise today, using water reed, combed wheat reed and long straw. The future of long straw thatching in particular appeared doomed as it suffered the disapprobation of its own practitioners and government advocates as well as home owners.

Closer analysis indicates that the path of decline was by no means as straight as it first appears. Even in 1790 thatch was not the predominant roofing material in many parts of the country; stone slates and peg-tiles had been the traditional covering for centuries in some areas, and pantiles had been vigorously displacing thatch for at least a half century. In what could be called the first phase of the process of attrition from 1790 to 1840, thatch was gradually squeezed out of urban areas not because of the fear or reality of fire damage but because of rising prosperity. It also persisted in some urban districts for much longer than is commonly believed. In general, losses occurred most dramatically in the industrialized north, followed by the Midlands, the south west and the south east. Surprisingly, the insurance policy records indicate that the number of thatched buildings actually increased in the south in the first half of the nineteenth century in response to rural population growth and an expanding agricultural sector in this region, but the boom was short-lived and cereal output was to plummet with the collapse of grain prices after 1870.

Industrialization and the population movements it provoked created immense difficulties for a craft whose continuity depended on a well-populated countryside and an abundance of inexpensive straw. Wages in the factories were much higher than on the farms, however, and entire generations of young people abandoned the thatched houses of their parents, and the needles and tarred cord of their grandfathers, for a life in the city. Those who remained behind were forced to widen their patches in order to continue in their profession full-time, which brought them increasingly into contact with other thatchers and began to blur hitherto local distinctions in style and technique. With each passing generation the craft lost more and more of its thatchers, traditions and diversity. At the same time, thatch was being condemned by agricultural improvers and architects who viewed tiles and slates as the roofing material of the new age.

All of the evidence supports the view that English buildings were largely thatched with cereal straw at the beginning of the period under review, and the emphasis on heather in the north and water reed, fen sedge or other wetland species in fenland and coastal districts was not nearly as great as is commonly believed. Straw thatched roofs could be found in the very heart of the Fens and the Broads, although their unexposed base coats and fixings might well be composed of plants that were unfamiliar to thatchers in other regions. Straw was simply the only material that was available cheaply, in sufficient quantity and on a renewable basis to service the country's sizeable stock of vernacular structures, and it could be made to perform adequately even after being threshed if well prepared and applied. In striking contrast to the present day, straw was a carefully managed resource in 1790 and was valued for a variety of purposes other than thatching. Straw was particularly well husbanded in regions where it was less abundant, in general terms in the north, the west and in upland and wetland districts, and in the West Country a reed straw tradition had developed reflecting centuries of experience of thatching shallow-pitched roofs with rye and wheat straw in what is a relatively wet climate. Maximum performance was achieved by using straw that had been as little bruised as possible during threshing, and which was subsequently combed of extraneous leaf and weed tissue that might retain moisture and encourage fungal decay. The combed reed straw produced was fixed securely with spars and sways and dressed into position with a straw leggat to form a tight, but breathable coat.

In arable districts further east, three different types of straw thatch might be used depending on local reaping, threshing and thatching traditions. Halm was a less groomed version of West Country reed. It was flailed or scutched only at its apex to remove the grain without bruising the straw, and was then combed or heaped and drawn from a wetted bed to remove extraneous leaf, weed and short straw. Unlike West Country reed straw, however, it was fixed with spars and sways in the same manner as crushed straw and was not dressed into position with a leggat. Straw crushed over much of its length by the flail could be applied butts-together if the sheaf remained intact, or could be drawn and yealmed from a wetted bed as in modern long straw if it was jumbled either by flailing or mechanical threshing. It was fixed as with reed straw but could not physically be dressed into position with a leggat. A third straw option in many areas was stubble, whose disappearance in the mid to late nineteenth century is perhaps one of the most striking lost traditions in English thatching. Stubble was associated primarily with open-field (champion) country where tall crops were reaped high on the stem leaving the lower 50cm of the stem standing. Tall stubble, in some areas also confusingly called haulm, was scythed after the main crops had been secured, and was commonly used for animal bedding and fuel as well as thatching. It was widely used in base coats and was usually fixed externally with spars and sways when used as a main coat because of its short length.

Changes in the way cereal crops were harvested and processed altered the nature of the straw available for thatching and consequently the relative importance of the different materials used. Most easily overlooked is the gradual replacement of the serrated reaping hook by the cereal scythe (and later by the mechanical reaper) which entirely eliminated stubble thatching as an option in areas where it had formerly been common. The invention of the mechanical thresher was also an obvious milestone in the history of thatching, although its initial impact was quite different from its long-term influence. Straw was probably as crushed by the early machines as it is today by the combine harvester, but it was soon discovered that unbruised haulm could be produced very efficiently by feeding only the ears of a sheaf into the mouth of the threshing drum. The initial impact was thus an increase in the availability of unbruised reed-straw halm beyond the West Country. Only later, when the thresher had acquired wheels and the damage it inflicted on straw had been subdued, was the former preference for halm eschewed in favour of crushed straw akin to modern long straw.

Beyond the wheat fields of eastern and southern England, the period between 1790 and 1840 also witnessed an abandonment of the use of alternative materials that were once gathered in quantity from common heathlands and wetlands, particularly by the rural poor; stands of heather once maintained specifically for thatching were now enclosed and grazed by cattle or grouse and yielded material suitable only for base coats; the tall pasture rushes that once provided four or five years of shelter on a poor cottage or outbuilding were now grazed and trammelled by livestock and suitable only for patching or rick thatching; local bogs that had for centuries provided sufficient black bog rush, reed mace or fen sedge for thin spar coating or ridging were drained and planted to vegetables for the London market; and many of the reed beds beyond Norfolk that had once produced small

but useful amounts of reed for thatching and fleeking became increasingly uneconomic and were either drained or allowed to succeed to impenetrable carr. At the same time, the labour cost of constructing a solid roof of gorse for a cartshed similar to the example recorded at Stanton St John, Oxfordshire, gradually outstripped the cost of purchasing low quality timber and building a standard raftered roof that could be thatched or tiled. Only water reed in the Norfolk Broads region and perhaps parts of the Fens could challenge the supremacy of straw as the principal thatching material in England, due to its long established reputation for neatness and longevity. Norfolk reed may well have been exported to other parts of East Anglia on a regular basis, particularly to inland areas navigable by barge, but the preponderance of reed on roofs decreased rapidly with every mile it moved beyond the Broads due to the high cost of overland transport.

The *in situ* and historical evidence certainly confirms the general supremacy of straw thatching in England prior to 1840, but alternative wetland materials are not uncommon and the evidence represents more than a relict tradition, particularly in fenland districts in Cambridgeshire and Bedfordshire. It is also probable that an entire swathe of poorer cottages and ancillary buildings, the numbers having risen at this time in the south, were thatched with a wider range of materials. Most of these structures have disappeared without a trace, but that they were thatched with alternative materials more frequently than the mainstream buildings which have survived to be analysed is not an unreasonable assumption. The more unusual materials tend to survive in base coats beneath later spar coats of straw, and it is entirely possible that intervening spar coats of alternatives were stripped at previous rethatchings. In any case, materials used only or primarily in base coats are no less important than external materials in the technical history of thatching, and their frequency in base coats is significant even if they occur much less frequently than straw in later levels.

In the period from 1790 to 1840 landowners and their architects were busily advocating the use of water reed, and to a lesser degree West Country reed straw, on new estate buildings constructed in the Picturesque manner, a promotion that helped sow the seeds for more commercially oriented reed thatching firms later in the century. To what degree the demand for reed thatching and highly ornamented eaves and ridges spilt over estate boundaries into the vernacular mainstream is not entirely clear, but the rediscovery of thatch by estate owners did help quell the virulent calls for its banishment by agricultural improvers and social reformers who condemned it as a fire risk, an eyesore and a robber of manure. These new buildings almost always incorporated challenges such as adjacent valleys, steep pitches and dormer windows, particularly when they were designed by architects with little familiarity with thatch, and they undoubtedly helped create a new class of skilled estate thatchers more concerned with ornament and appearance than thatchers in the past. On such estates the choice of material was often imposed leaving the crushed straw thatcher with little control.

The reformer's zeal for light and air to stave off gloom and disease triumphed in the period from 1840 to 1890. Thatching declined in all parts of the country, including the arable south, as the country once again found itself in the throes of an agricultural depression. Thatch attracted a modicum of respect only in the new seaside resorts which transferred the polite interest in Picturesque to a more middle-class clientele. Rural poverty forced many agricultural labourers and smallholder-thatchers to seek a life in the city or abroad, leaving estate thatchers to consolidate their positions and carry the craft into the new century. Labour shortages encouraged mechanization, and the introduction of the reaper in mid-century continued where the scythe left off, consigning stubble to the annals of agricultural history.

The reaper may also have encouraged the development of wheat varieties yielding shorter-stemmed straw. In fact, the actual character of straw changed significantly over the second half of the nineteenth century due to a variety of factors, all of which rested on the increasing success of plant breeding programmes. The genetically diverse $c150cm-180cm$ land races of the medieval and post-medieval periods had been replaced by relatively pure $c110cm-140cm$ commercial varieties by 1890, and these new varieties produced much tougher and coarser straw. More importantly, they also produced crops of even height that also ripened evenly because of their genetic purity and the fact that they were now grown in more homogeneous conditions. If cut while still a little green, the straw of these new varieties was more suitable for thatching than that available a century before. Cereals thresh more easily when they are fully ripe, however, and plant breeders assisted the shift to mechanized cereal production by creating improved varieties that could be left to ripen more fully in the field without shedding their grain. Unfortunately, this delayed harvest also reduced the quality of the straw in terms of thatching. English rivet wheat, which had provided quality thatching straw and well-tasting biscuit flour since at least the medieval period, was entirely abandoned in the pursuit for varieties with superior bread-baking qualities, and a plethora of English and foreign bread wheats flooded the market providing farmers with an unparalleled degree of varietal choice.

Between 1840–90 the distinction between long straw and West Country combed wheat reed was accentuated by improvements in threshing technology that reduced the damage inflicted on the straw, as well as by the invention of the comber attachment which greatly increased the efficiency of reed straw production. The modern type thresher that carried the new technology to the small farmer even in remote areas was simply a transportable version of earlier barn-based machinery, and its development probably saved the craft of straw thatching from extinction, even though brutish machinery is usually cast as the culprit in the story of thatch. The long straw available by 1890 was less crushed and more thoroughly cleaned of residual grain, short straw and cavings than earlier products, but was essentially the same material as was produced in the medieval period when a jumbled crop of lodged wheat was flailed. In contrast, the comber attachment improved the speed at which reed straw was produced but not its quality or nature.

Scientific advances influenced thatching even more forcibly over the final period from 1890 to 1940, most visibly through plant breeding programmes that reduced the height of cereal varieties while drastically increasing their yields and baking qualities. The introduction of semi-dwarf varieties, combined with the rapid adoption of the combine harvester, eventually severed the traditional link between thatching and mainstream cereal production. Traditional English varieties were either abandoned or crossed with foreign varieties to create higher yielding hybrids that are the basis of the modern crop. By 1940 the death knell of thatching, and for long straw in particular, had been rung, but the corpse refused to be buried. By the time the botanical basis of the collapse had been recognised by government bodies such as the Rural Industries Bureau, a new tier of specialist straw producers had emerged to supply the craft with much higher quality long straw and combed wheat reed using traditional varieties better suited to the task.

To some degree, the link between farming and thatching had already been broken by the revival of water reed as a thatching material by the Arts and Crafts movement, in a conscious reaction to the increasing use of hard materials such as corrugated iron and asbestos tiles in rural areas. The few East Anglian firms who had carried the craft through the doldrums quickly expanded their operations and stretched the craft to its technical limits, using imported reed when the production from Norfolk and minor sources was insufficient. The emergence of aggressively commercial thatchers and middlemen reed dealers, as recorded in the private papers of J Cowell, clearly illustrates that at least a part of the profession could be extremely pro-active when required. Water reed thatching was soon being marketed aggressively throughout England, with much of its success being built upon the denigration of straw thatching and exaggerated notions of its own longevity and performance. In fact, the quality of straw thatching had improved drastically from its pre-Second World War position and water reed thatch rarely performed as well in southern or western regions as it did on steeply pitched roofs in East Anglia.

The emergence of the large water reed firms could only have occurred on the back of estate-based reed thatchers. The remarkable Bagshawe archive records how this tradition was lost in Bedfordshire over the early part of this century to the point at which all of the thatchers interviewed in the 1940s thatched exclusively with long straw. Their numbers declined not because of the attrition of thatched roofs and the collapse of estates, but primarily because an overbearing patriarchal craft had created a stifling environment that offered little incentive for younger people to take up the craft. The insularity in Bedfordshire contrasts with the boldness with which the major East Anglian water reed firms exported their tradition to other regions, thus sowing the seeds of the debate over regional traditions that provoked the present study.

The current debate rests on the premise that identifiable thatching traditions can be identified, and presumably preserved, in different parts of the country, but the problems begin as soon as an attempt is made to pinpoint their points of origin. As this report demonstrates, thatching in the period 1790 to 1940 appears always to have been in a state of flux and the data provide limited support for its popular image as the most unchanging of ancient building crafts. In reality, both the main coat materials and fixings employed varied tremendously in response to a multitude of social, economic, environmental and botanical pressures, eventually crystallizing into the three principal traditions which remain: long straw produced by the threshing machine, combed wheat reed by the comber attachment and water reed cut from the Norfolk Broads or imported. Only long straw is now geographically circumscribed in that it is not used in the West Country. A wide spectrum of materials and techniques has also been lost; wet-straw thatching in Lancashire, stapple thatch in Cumberland, heather thatch in the north, Kent and Surrey, broom thatch in Dartmoor, solid gorse thatch in Oxfordshire and stubble and halm thatch in the south. Many of these uniquely English traditions had distinctive regional distributions, and this evidence survives to a considerable degree on roofs that are being stripped of their ancient thatch at a frenetic pace without receiving even basic recording or sampling.

Thatching is a living craft and its history is obviously still being written, and regularly destroyed, by thatchers who continue to adapt their methods and materials to the economic and material realities of the modern age. In this sense, the underlying tradition of thatching had remained unchanged and its freedom to innovate will undoubtedly be essential to its survival in the future. However, the unique, multi-layered record of thatch that survives on many ancient roofs is a national treasure of much greater scientific, technical and historical value. Additional *in situ*, historical and ethnographic studies will be vital in helping to establish an objective and historically valid approach to the conservation of local and regional thatching traditions, and it is only through such studies that the history of thatching in any region will be established with any accuracy. These sources of data survive in unexpected profusion, and the present study will hopefully provide a springboard for the compilation of regional histories that will led to the formulation of conservation policies that will ensure the survival of at least a part of the *in situ* record, without stifling innovations in material and technique that will carry the ancient craft of house thatching into the new millennium.

163

Appendix A

Buildings excavated and sampled (see Fig 92)

Table A1A Buildings visited (Appendix A)

Appendix number	County	Grid reference	Address
1	Bedfordshire	TL 10 48 19	Water End Road, Cople
2	Bedfordshire	TQ 91 29	1 Conger Lane, Toddington
3	Berkshire	SU 53 76	Oak House Farm, Hampstead Norries
4	Buckinghamshire	SP 88 26	Hollingdon Grange, Soulbury
5	Buckinghamshire	SP 92 25	The Cruck Cottage, Clipstone, Eggington
6	Buckinghamshire	SP 64 07	Ickford House, Little Ickford
7	Cambridgeshire	TL 22 74	Great Stukeley
8	Cambridgeshire	TL 36 50	18 High Street, Orwell
9	Cambridgeshire	TL 62 57	Brook End Cottage, Westley Waterless
10	Devon	ST 24 04	Land Farm, Stockland
11	Devon	SS 56 46	Capel Cottage Berrynarbor
12	Devon	–	near Cullompton
13	Dorset	SY 72 83	Jasmine Cottage, Osmington
14	Leicestershire	SK 90 04	9 Post Office Lane, Lyndon
15	Northamptonshire	SP 883 648	Tanglewood Cottage, 24 High Street, Great Doddington
16	Oxfordshire	SU 60 84	Kate's Cottage, High Street, South Stoke
17	Oxfordshire	SP 57 09	cartshed, Stanton St John
18	Suffolk	TM 05 67	The Tavern Barn, Bacton
19	Wiltshire	SU 14 80	Hawkins' Barn, 93 High Street, Wroughton
20	Wiltshire	SU 557 239	Norrie Cottage, Collingbourne Kingston

A1 BEDFORDSHIRE (TABLE A1)

19 Water End Road, *Cople*
Grid reference: TL1048
Date of survey: 21st June 1994
Owner: Mr Bennett
Architect: Bruce Deacon
Thatcher: Keith Quantrill
Locality: on outskirts of Cople village, 5 km east of Bedford. Arable district of heavy clay soils

Building description

Timber-framed, brick infill, two-up/two-down cottage, constructed early eighteenth century as one of two (second now destroyed). Two tall brick chimney stacks

Table A1 19 Water End Road, Cople, Bedfordshire

Main coat	Ridge	Principal components	Fixings	Depth (cm)
L1		BW, LS, butts-together, modern crushed	spars & sways	16
L2		BW, ears/butts evenly mixed, crushed	spars & sways	20
	R3	BW, mostly basal	spars & sways	16
L3		BW, mostly basal, very crushed	spars & sways	14
	R4	BW, mostly basal, occasional (crushed) middle & upper	spars & sways	
L4		BW, basal & (often crushed) upper	spars & sways	15
L5		BW, basal & (ears/butts evenly mixed) upper, all modern crushed	tarred twine	14
L6		BW middle, occasional (base (crushed) basal, many short coat) (with distinct blows)	grass rope	16
L7		WR clamped (fleeking)		5
L8		BW, ears/butts evenly (underlay) mixed, modern crushed	–	4–6

built onto rear (south) face. Rear centre wall without timber framing. Roof reconstructed at eaves on rear face when original timber-framed centre wall was rebuilt in brick. Two semicircular dormers on front face (particular to this region). Orientation: roughly east/west. Rafter pitch c 45°. No internal access. First floor ceilings plastered onto internal laths. Original roof of pole rafters 8–12 cm, with later repair using sawn rafters 8–10 cm x 10–15 cm over lower 3 m from rear eaves. Pole rafters and tie beams pegged to rear wall plate. Sawn rafters nailed to wall plate. New sawn and riven oak plank battens, 3–5 cm x 10 cm, spaced c 35 cm apart, nailed to rafters, forms support base in this lower section. Thinner sawn battens east of sampling area. 2 cm x 6–8 cm riven oak laths, wedged vertically into place with bases resting on second batten from eaves, forming a key for lime and horsehair plaster (applied from inside in this c 1.5 m section from top of wall plate and at base of first floor ceiling wall). External gap also filled with knotted wheat straw. Flared iron hooks (crooks) nailed into lower one or two battens and gable sill to fix lower and gable courses with sways (crook flare stands c 20 cm above rafters). Battening of

Figure A1.

(original) upper section of roof to ridge composed of horizontal water reed fleeking, *c* 1–3 stem layers thick, clamped into place by laths *c* 5 cm diameter nailed to rafters (Fig A1). This water reed very coarse, *c* 2.5 m in length, tied into a mat using twisted grass rope. The mat was stitched on the ground and simply rolled upwards onto rafters as required.

Sampling background

Rescue samples taken during stripping. Stripping order rescinded after inspection of rafters (perfectly sound) and recommendation of thatcher. To be rethatched in September due to shortage of long straw this season. Sampling limited due to limited stripping. Sample series obtained from the south (rear) face between chimneys where water reed fleeking exposed. Limited access to ridge layers. Thatch clearly thicker at the ridge than at eaves. Six distinct main coat layers, but thatch probably truncated in past at point of sampling.

Thatch summary

External coat of mainly butts-together bread wheat long straw. Scalloped block cut ridge. Layer 2 (L2) of bread wheat crushed and with ears/butts evenly mixed. L3–5 of mostly basal specimens with occasional roots but all with some middle or upper specimens. Base coat of bread wheat, mainly of crushed middle but occasional basal

specimens (and many short specimens showing distinct blows) tied to rafters with twisted two-ply grass rope. L5 tied to rafters with tarred twine. Thatch in undisturbed section towards ridge rests on a fleeking of water reed tied into mats with grass rope and clamped to roof by split poles nailed to rafters. Underlay of evenly mixed and moderately crushed bread wheat (beneath base coat) rests on plank battens. Lower courses fixed to wall plate and gable with iron crooks and wooden sways. Pitch of thatch, *c* 55 °, increased by *c* 10 ° over pitch of roof timbers. Ridge consolidated with five-ply tarred twine stitched through thatch and looped around ridge pole. All other layers fixed with usual spars and sways.

Thatch (external):

main: long straw applied in 1953, now very decayed especially on south (rear) face, moss-covered, wired, pitch *c* 55 °

ridge: straw, raised with (simple) scalloping, diamented, very decayed, *c* 140 cm total depth (?)

eaves: liggered, decayed, much slippage and loss around front dormers, *c* 40 cm overhang.

gables: liggered, overhang, very decayed

Samples:

Main coat:

L1: external coat of bread wheat long straw, mostly butts-together but with some mixing, evenly crushed. Ears long and lax, grown locally in 1953. Specimens *c* 80 cm but with occasionally 110 cm (folded). Unexposed straw still golden.

L2: bread wheat straw, ears/butts evenly mixed and stems crushed over full length. Average 45 cm, mostly upper stem segments (butts weathered). Moderate flag and no weed. Unexposed straw well preserved.

L3: bread wheat straw, mostly basal stem specimens, very coarse and very crushed. Specimens *c* 30 cm. Occasional root specimens (raking?). Most specimens cut just above ground level. Distinct cut and flail marks. Moderate flag leaf and weeds (not drawn). Significant dog leg. Specimens mostly butts-together and applied butts-up at sample location.

L4: bread wheat straw, mix of basal and (often crushed) upper stem specimens with few ears. Occasional basal specimens with roots (raked?), *c* 10 cm. Upper stem specimens *c* 35 cm. Spring variety due to upright habit?.

L5: bread wheat straw, mix of basal and upper stem specimens, moderately crushed. Upper stem specimens mixed ears and butts, *c* 25 cm and either crushed/cut or broken/cut. Basal (stubble?) specimens *c* 10 cm with occasional root (raked?) and moderately coarse. One specimen to 42 cm, another to 107 cm, with roots and crushed at apex. Specimens mostly taller than L4 basal specimens. Occasional ear of bread wheat and one specimen of barley. Crop weeds, especially wild oat and thistle (*Cirsium* sp).

L6: base coat of bread wheat straw, mostly middle stem specimens, crushed with few ears. Occasional basal specimens with roots, *c* 30 cm, flailed at cut end. Many short specimens with distinct flail blows.

L7: fleeking of water reed one to three stems thick. Specimens both coarse and fine, flower heads mostly intact, stems very hard and 1.5 – 2.5 m.

L8: underlay of bread wheat straw, modern crushed, mixed ears and butts and applied to battens on rebuilt section south of water reed fleeking from eaves to *c* 3 m up roof. Ears long and lax.

Ridge:

R3: ridge coat above L3. Mostly short basal specimens with very occasional roots (raked?). Bread wheat, spring variety due to upright habit?.

R4: ridge coat above L4. Mostly short basal specimens, *c* 15 cm, occasional with roots (raked?). Also some middle and upper stem segments, very crushed (flailed?). Few ears (one ear of bread wheat).

Fixings

Water reed fleeking (L7) in oldest section clamped to roof with lengths of split pole nailed to rafters. No other battening in this section. Base coat of threshed straw (L6) tied to rafters with two-ply twisted grass rope (cf Gramineae) passing through the fleeking, and plastered into place from within first floor ceilings. L5 of stubble straw tied into place with five-ply homespun (cf tarred sisal) twine which splits into three sections when used to consolidate ridge. L4–1 fixed with (cf willow *Salix* spp and hazel *Corylus avellana*) spars (30 – 45cm) and sways. Binder twine in L2 used to bind sheaf in field rather than as fixing on roof. Ridge coat (R4) fixed with *c* 30 cm spars. Forged metal crooks nailed into rafters used to fix sways on bottom course on eaves and gable. Wooden spars in L4 – 1 longer than usual (according to thatcher). Underlay in rebuilt eaves section held in place beneath base coat tied to rafters and plank battens with two-ply tarred twine.

Interpretation

Oldest thatch in upper section of roof supported on a fleeking of water reed tied into a mat with twisted grass rope and clamped onto rafters. Fleeking in lower section of roof of water reed laid horizontally in bundles and clamped directly onto rafters. Water reed contains a mixture of tall/short and soft/hard stems suggesting it was not cut from a managed bed. Mats probably rolled onto roof in lengths as required. Fleeking not strong enough to support a thatcher, but provides fair support for 1.0 m or more of thatch. Base coat of threshed straw (L6) (perhaps containing drawn stubble) and L5 tied to roof with grass rope and tarred twine. No more tying possible due to plastering of inside ceilings. All subsequent layers sparred and swayed in usual way. Stubble straw, probably scythed, raked, possibly drawn and probably mixed with longer upper-stem specimens, used on ridge, but not all layers available for sampling. Additional tying with tarred twine required to consolidate ridge at L4–5.

A2 BEDFORDSHIRE (TABLE A2)

1 Conger Lane, Toddington
Grid reference: TQ9129
Date of survey: 27th May 1994
Thatcher: Keith Quantrill
Locality: 9km east of Leighton Buzzard

Table A2 1 Conger Lane, Toddington, Bedfordshire

Samples	Principal components	Fixings
L1	BW, evenly mixed, crushed	spars and sways
L2	BW, ears/butts evenly mixed, lightly crushed	spars
L3	BW, butts-together, apex crushed, stem lightly crushed	spars and sways
L4	BW, mostly butts-together and crushed, many basal	spars and sways
L5	BW, middle and upper, mostly butts-together, crushed	spars
L6	BW, mostly basal, very crushed	spars and sways
L7	BW, ears/butts evenly mixed, mostly very crushed with occasional distinct blows	spars and sways
L8	BW, ears/butts mixed, mostly crushed	spars and sways
L9	BW, mostly butts-together, crushed	spars
L10	BW, ears/butts mixed, crushed	spars
L11	BW, ears/butts mixed with distinct blows	tarred twine

Building description

Standard three-room, seventeenth-century, lobby en-try-plan cottage much altered in twentieth century. Roof of idiosyncratic construction, with much reused timber. In first raising the entire roof was lifted by *c* 2.4 m. Rear pitch then flattened when roof extended over added outshot using softwood, probably in first half of nineteenth century. Thatch layers present suggest *c* 1830 if each coat lasted 15 years. Rafters: pole rafters and occasional rough-sawn squared rafters, all 10–12 cm diameter and at *c* 45 cm spacings. Joints pegged. Battens: riven oak laths, nailed to rafters at *c* 25 cm spacings, except where disturbed. Also occasional *c* 2 cm x 8 cm sawn planks inserted for extra support. Orientation: north-west/south-east. External pitch of thatch over rear outshot: *c* 38°, so roof pitch *c* 30°.

Sampling background

Rescue sampling during rethatching and selective strip-ping. Back of roof stripped to sound base coat. Thick *c* 10 cm moss held in place by wire netting. Rethatching in long straw (front) and combed wheat reed (back) due to slack pitch. Sampled by J Letts and J Moir with assistance of thatcher. Vertical series taken from north-east (back) face at joint with later (tiled) extension, *c* 3.0 m from ridge and west of chimney. No other sampling possible. Old base coat surviving on north-west (back) face consolidated with sways and spars prior to rethatching. Thatch a little thicker at ridge, but unlikely that more than one or two layers missed at point of sampling. All samples post-date addition of outshot. Base coat samples more decayed and confused than external ones. No access to ridge layers.

Thatch summary

Eleven layers of bread wheat straw. L1: Long straw, applied *c* 15 years ago, fairly well preserved beneath thick layer of (protective?) moss. Fixed with spars and sways, with usual liggering at eaves and extra liggering fixing rolled gable ends. Block cut ridge of simple scallop design. Sampled only at back where pitch very shallow due to extended outshot roof. L2 similar to L1 but fixed with spars only, as with L5, L9 and L10. L3 butts-together and with apex crushed. L4 and L5 laid butts-together and down on roof. L4 evenly crushed, but L5 shows distinct crushing blows. L9 butts-together and crushed, well preserved and bright yellow in colour. L10 evenly crushed and mixed with occasional distinct blows. L11 ears and butts mixed, with distinct blows, specimens probably not exposed. L3, 4, 6, and 8 fixed with spars and straw bonds (continuous or pulled from adjacent bundle). Base coat tied with tarred twine. Roof pitch *c* 38 °. Total depth at point of sampling *c* 100 cm, but thicker towards ridge and thinner towards eaves.

Thatch (external):

main: bread wheat long straw, well preserved below *c* 10 cm of moss, *c* 15 years old, wired, metal guttering in valleys

ridge: straw, raised and scalloped, decayed but visible, *c* 8 years old, numerous free-standing spars.

eaves: liggered and sparred, *c* 40 cm overhang, horizontal cut

gables: rolled, decayed, liggered, extended overhang at ridge of *c* 40 cm

Samples:

Main coat:

L1: external coat of bread wheat long straw, specimens *c* 60 cm, evenly mixed ears/butts, crushed and most ears either cut or broken. Sample discarded due to decay in laboratory.

L2: bread wheat straw, specimens *c* 65 cm, lightly crushed, evenly mixed ears and butts and well preserved. Occasional distinct crush marks (fixings?). Most specimens with two nodes. Occasional arable weeds (*Papaver* sp.).

L3: bread wheat straw, lightly crushed over stem but with crushed apex and butts intact (and together). Evenly mixed ears and butts. Occasional specimens undamaged or with one distinct blow. Specimens mostly *c* 45 cm (in bundles of *c* 85 cm). Few ears and minimal rubbish.

L4: bread wheat straw, specimens *c* 70 cm, usually of two nodes, mostly crushed along entire length but occasional with specimens undamaged. Mostly butts-together and applied butts-down on roof. Most ears intact. Many basal specimens

L5: bread wheat straw, specimens *c* 75 cm, mostly with two nodes and middle and upper stem specimens. Upper specimens usually crushed over entire length of stem, but some with distinct blow marks and many with missing ears. Mostly butts-together and applied butts-down on roof. One specimen with intact ear of 10 cm plus internode measurements of 38 cm:22 cm:14 cm:13 cm (+ *c* 15 cm for missing basal internodes) = original plant height of *c* 102 cm.

L6: bread wheat straw, specimens *c* 30 cm, mostly basal specimens, very crushed and broken. Moderate flag leaf and weed.

L7: bread wheat straw, specimens *c* 40 cm (in bundle *c* 55 cm) and of one node, mostly very crushed and with occasional distinct blows. Ears and butts evenly mixed. Ears exceptionally long.

L8: bread wheat straw, specimens *c* 40 cm, mostly crushed but with many stems intact. Ears and butts mixed. Moderate flag leaf and rubbish. Poorly preserved.

L9: bread wheat straw, specimens *c* 70 cm, crushed along entire stem and butts-together. Retains yellow colour.

L10: bread wheat straw, specimens *c* 60 cm, evenly crushed and ears and butts mixed. Most specimens two nodes.

L11: bread wheat straw, specimens *c* 35 cm, with distinct blow marks. Ears and butts mixed.

New coat: combed wheat reed, cultivar *Maris Widgeon*, *c* 80 cm, cut below third node, grown locally.

Fixings

L1 fixed with 30 cm spars and sways. L2, L5, L9 and L10 fixed with spars only. All other layers fixed with spars and straw bonds, except L11. Base coat fixed with tarred twine to battens and rafters. No sways used on roof. Many layers use continuous straw bonds or interrupted straw bonds (ie handful of straw from one sparred bundle used as sway to fix adjacent bundle). Occasional individual bunches fixed with spar only.

Interpretation

Roof of unusual construction, and of extremely shallow pitch (*c* 30 °) for thatch due to inclusion of early nineteenth-century rear outshot beneath thatch. This contrasts with the uniform thatch tradition of bread wheat long straw fixed with spars or spars and straw bonds. Only last coat applied (L1) is fixed with spars and sways in usual way. Base coat tied to riven oak laths, with all succeeding layers sparred (Fig A2). Pitch of rear face built up over years by selective stripping of eaves leaving thicker ridge. Top three layers stripped to provide a sound base coat for rethatching. All 11 layers made of bread wheat straw, the last coat preserved beneath thick layer of moss. Several layers (L7, L8, L11) suggest straw was hand-flailed and crushed primarily at apex of sheaf leaving butts uncrushed (but subsequently mixed ears-butts prior to thatching). In other cases straw is crushed over its entire length,

Figure A2.

Table A3 barn at Oak House Farm, Hampstead Norries, Berkshire

Sample	Principal components	Fixings	Depth cm
MC1 (E)	rye 'reed straw', combed, butts-down	spar and sways	30
MC2 (E)	rye straw, crushed, mixed ears and butts	spars and sways	25
MC3 (E)	BW straw, crushed, mostly upper, mixed ears and butts	sways and tarred twine	25
MC4 (W)	BW straw, crushed, mostly upper, mixed ears and butts	sways and tarred twine	
H1N	rye 'reed straw', mostly upper, butts-down	spars	20
H2N	rye straw, mixed but mostly upper, crushed, mixed ears and butts	sways and tarred twine	20
H3N	BW straw, crushed, mixed ears and butts	sways and tarred twine	25
H1 (SE)	BW straw, crushed, mixed ears and butts, decayed	spars and sways	?
H2 (SE)	BW straw, crushed, mixed ears and butts	sways and tarred twine	25
R1N	rye 'reed straw', combed, butts-down	spars and liggers	10
R2N	rye 'reed straw', combed, butts-down, decayed	spars (liggers ?)	15
R3N	BW straw, crushed, mixed ears and butts	spars and liggers	15
R4N	BW straw, crushed, mixed ears and butts	spars	10
R5N	rye straw, crushed	spars, liggers and tarred twine	10
R6N	rye straw, evenly crushed, mixed ears and butts	tied	15
R1 (SE)	bread wheat straw, crushed	spars and liggers	?

either by machine or by flail, and mixed ears butts. L3, L4, L5 and L9 mainly butts-together, threshed either by careful machine processing or by flailing in sheaf to produce an uncombed reed straw that perhaps gave better performance due to slack pitch. New combed wheat reed being applied for same reason. Earlier layers contain more arable weeds (especially grasses). L9 very well preserved and still yellow in colour. L10 perhaps sparred on at same time as base coat (L11), which is composed of short straw that would have provided an inferior external coat. Age estimate: 11 x *c* 15 years/layer = *c* 165 years (ie base coat applied over outshot in *c* 1830).

A3 BERKSHIRE (TABLE A3)

barn at Oak House Farm, Hampstead Norries
Grid reference: SU5376
Date of survey: 5th January 1995
Owner: The Palmer Trust
Manager: C J Pratt
Survey: Dan Miles
Thatcher: Tom Mariner (last repair), Mr Mullins (last main coat thatch).
Locality: Farm on outskirts of Hampstead Norries village, north east of Newbury. Set amidst flat, light arable soil. Mixed farm with significant cereal production (especially barley and wheat) but no rye.

Building description

Late eighteenth-century staddle barn, half-hipped, open-sided with floor, composed in part of stacked wattle and brushwood, resting on staddle stones. Building oriented north/south, originally two buildings: older south section of two double bays joined to similar two double bay north structure creating a small storage bay. Half hips steeply pitched. Structure recorded and dismantled by Dan Miles. Rafters: 8cm–15 cm diameter, of both round and split poles and square-sawn timber (some reused). Rafters coupled, nailed or pegged to ridge pole and resting on a large diameter purlin mid-way. Occasional sawn rafters inserted as repairs. Spacing of rafters variable, some adjacent and others at *c* 40 cm intervals. Rafters of west face less well preserved than east face. Battens: east face battens sawn, *c* 8 cm x 2 cm, relatively wide and solid

Figure A3.

for battens and evenly spaced. First ridge row nailed to rafters just below ridge pole. Battens on north half-hip evenly spaced with 18cm–20 cm between mid-points. Battens occasionally of reused wood. Battens on west face of thinner riven laths, *c* 4 cm x 1.5 cm, often uneven and of reused timber (riven). Occasional evidence of repair. Battens of west face less well preserved. Lower eaves batten on north hip sawn, *c* 12 cm x 2 cm (wider than other 6 cm hip battens), nailed to rafters leaving a 20 cm overhang. Many thinner battens split where nailed (Fig A3).

Sampling background

Barn collapsed in storm *c* 1988. Situated on large estate farm with several other thatched buildings, including large thatched barn with tiled flanking outshots immedi-ately adjacent to west, and thatched stable 15 m to east. Much of internal timberwork decayed, but roof largely intact on first sampling visit. Most of roof collapsed by second visit, especially central section, with large sections of thatch wetted, furrowed and decayed. Extensive patches of white rot mould visible on base coat from within. Sampled in January 1995 and again in June 1996 in advance of full stripping and dismantling. Samples taken from section excavated through ridge and adjacent main coat on east face *c* 5 m from north hip, and also from north-east corner of north hip. Spot samples taken from centre of north hip, west main coat and from base coats.

Thatch summary

Roof last thatched in mid 1970s with combed reed straw of rye by Mr Mullins, a local thatcher, using binder-cut rye grown on nearby farm. Rye formerly grown by tenants on estate and cut green (unthreshed) for use as thatch. Last ridged in early 1980s by Tom Mariner. Late 1950s photograph shows external details very similar to that on current estate buildings, ie a flush, wrapped and patterned ridge with one additional horizontal ligger above simple diamonding. External main coat neatly dressed, now *c* 25 cm thick and without eaves ligger. Half hips very steeply pitched with eaves dressed to a shallow angle. Eaves dressed flat, all with considerable overhang. Heavy coat of lichen/algae on north face where thatch permanently damp, but underlying thatch well preserved (probably due to steep *c* 65 ° pitch). Much decay and vegetation (grass, weeds, lichen) in furrows of collapse between rafters on both east and west faces. External pitch of main coat originally 45 ° – 50 °, but material pitch 35 ° – 40 ° (with base coat pitch of 30 ° – 35 °).

External coat well preserved, but last ridge coat mostly decayed. External main coat of rye on north end (MC1) wrapped over ridge roll (R2) above a previous ridge capping and roll of wheat straw (R3 and R4). These overlie a ridge coat and roll of crushed rye straw (R5 and R6). R5 continues down roof to form a base coat (MC2) that overlapped the start of a new base coat of crushed and jumbled bread wheat straw (MC3) *c* 100 cm away from ridge. MC3 continues towards eaves, but principal eaves section lost to decay. MC3 oldest existing coat, tied to

battens and rafters with lightly tarred twine, perhaps early this century or when roof rebuilt. Base coat straw applied without a fleeking over battens and with butts and ears mixed in bundle and on battens. This base coat replaced on east face by MC2 of crushed and jumbled rye straw, tied and capped by R5/6. R5/6 eventually capped by a new wheat straw ridge R3/4. MC2 and MC3 fixed with spars primarily of split hazel and sways of split or roundwood hazel and willow. East face better preserved than west face. North hip well preserved due to steep pitch. Base coat of crushed and jumbled rye straw (H2N) fixed by sways tied to battens with tarred twine (and occasionally with wire), probably coeval with MC2. External hip coat of combed rye reed straw (H1N) sparred in bundles and with occasional sways used near base of hip to H2N. Base coat of crushed and jumbled bread wheat straw (H3N) on north east corner of hip overlaps H2N and so is probably a later repair, perhaps coeval with R3/4. Existing layers could be accounted by a base coat applied in *c* 1940s (MC3) with subsequent rethatching and re-ridging in mid 1950s (MC2, R5/6), mid 1960s (R3/4) and late 1970s (MC1, R1/2). MC3 probably applied at least early this century and main coat and ridge layers almost certainly removed between MC1 and MC2/3 and before/after R3/4. R3 possibly remains of a main coat left to increase pitch. Evidence suggests local tradition of flush/patterned ridges with main coats of crushed rye or wheat straw mixed ears and butts. Base coat tied unevenly with tarred twine. Sways and spars of earlier layers of both roundwood and split hazel and willow.

Other thatched buildings on farm include a hipped stable 15 m to east, with at least four layers visible at eaves:

1 *c* 35 cm external coat of combed wheat reed, cf *Maris Widgeon* (ex Thatching Advisory Service)
2 *c* 15 cm layer of combed wheat reed
3 *c* 15 cm layer of bread wheat straw, crushed and mixed ears and butts
4 *c* 10 cm layer of mature rye straw, crushed and mixed ears and butts. External pitch *c* 50 °. Thick overhang at eaves, and furrows of decay forming where vertical swathes not well joined. Adjacent large tiled barn thatched with combed wheat reed and with base coat tied to riven laths. A small barn south-west of this also thatched with combed wheat reed, but with water reed repairs on east (front) eaves. This water reed spans five to eight battens and is fixed with iron crooks. Stitches of straw base coat visible every three or four battens.

Thatch (external):
- Main: combed wheat reed applied *c* 1975, now decayed to base in places and covered with lichen and moss. Occasional patches of grass growing in furrows of collapsed thatch (between rafters). Pitch shallow, originally *c* 45 ° – 50 °.
- Ridge: straw, very decayed, hazel liggers at lower depths. Total depth: *c* 80 cm.
- Eaves: west and east eaves cut and dressed flat. No liggers. Two layers visible.

- Hips: steeply-pitched half-hip, *c* 65 ° pitch, eaves cut and flared outwards at *c* 10 ° – 15 °. No liggers. External repair with bread wheat long straw on north east corner at last re-ridging (early 1980s).

Samples:

MAIN COAT (EAST FACE):

MC1: external coat of well combed rye reed straw, specimens *c* 75 cm, mostly of two upper nodes and applied butts-down. No ears and with top of stem cut at angle (pitched?).

MC2: mature rye straw, very crushed, mixed ears and butts, specimens *c* 65 cm and well preserved. MC2 overlies MC3 and is absent beyond *c* 1.8 m from ridge. Sampled 1 m below ridge on east face. Layer of weathering visible between MC2 and MC1.

MC3: base coat of bread wheat straw, specimens *c* 50 cm, mixed ears and butts, mostly upper stem specimens and evenly crushed over stem. Depth *c* 25 cm, extending from eaves to *c* 80 cm below ridge. Much flag leaf, weed and broken straw specimens. Layer of weathering between MC3 and MC1.

MAIN COAT (WEST FACE)

MC4: base coat of bread wheat straw, specimens 50 cm, mostly upper stem specimens, evenly mixed ears and butts and very crushed. Many broken straw specimens and weed. Sampled from west face.

HALF-HIP (NORTH)

H1N: external coat of rye reed straw, no ears (pitched?), specimens *c* 90 cm, mostly upper two nodes. Most specimens cut 10 cm below second node, with butts cut at angle (and occasionally weathered) and top cut also cut at angle.

H2N: base coat of mature rye straw, specimens *c* 75 cm, mixture of upper and lower stem specimens but mostly upper stem specimens cut immediately below second node. Mixed ears and butts and evenly crushed over stem. Stems occasionally folded into two. Drawn into a bundle *c* 90 cm. Wheat long-eared and relatively modern. Layer of weathering between H2N and H1N.

H3/NE: (corner). Base coat of bread wheat straw, specimens *c* 50 cm, mostly upper stem specimens, mostly butts-together and applied butts-down. Sample very dirty, with much flag, weed, threshed rachises and broken straw specimens Weathering between H3 (north east corner) and H1N.

HALF HIP (SOUTH)

H1/SE: (corner). Exterior repair, bread wheat straw, crushed, mixed ears and butts, very decayed.

H2/SE: (corner). Base coat of bread wheat straw, specimens *c* 60 cm, mixed ears and butts and very crushed.

RIDGE SAMPLES:

NORTH SECTION:

R1N: external ridge coat of short, mature rye reed straw, specimens *c* 60 cm, mostly upper stem specimens (but without most of first internode). Butts-together and applied butts-down. No ears. Probably combed. Very decayed. Wrap-over ridge.

R2N: ridge roll of mature rye straw, mostly uncrushed.

R3N: ridge coat of bread wheat straw, specimens *c* 40 cm, mostly upper stem specimens, mixed ears and butts, specimens of uniform length and evenly crushed over stem. Occasionally folded in two. Distinct blow marks. Wrap-over ridge.

R4N: ridge roll of bread wheat straw, specimens *c* 30 cm, mixture of upper and lower stem specimens, lower stem specimens crushed but upper stem specimens less so.

R5N: ridge coat of matured rye straw, specimens *c* 30 cm and very crushed. Very messy with much flag leaf and weed specimens.

R6N: ridge roll of mature rye straw, specimens *c* 70 cm, evenly crushed over stem and mixed heads and butts.

SOUTH SECTION:

R1S: internal layer of bread wheat straw, crushed, very decayed.

Fixings

Main coat (east)

MC1: spars and sways. Sways *c* 60–80 cm of roundwood hazel. Spars U-shaped, *c* 40 cm of split hazel.

MC2: spars and sways. Sways *c* 50–60 cm, of split hazel and willow *c* 3 cm diameter. Spars U-shaped, *c* 30 cm of split hazel with three-faced points. Occasional sway tied to battens with galvanised wire (ie later repair).

MC3: sways *c* 45–75 cm x 2–3 cm diameter, of split and roundwood hazel, mostly tied to rafters and every two or three battens with coarse three-ply binder twine, lightly tarred. Tying pattern variable and ad hoc.

Half-hip (north end)

H1N: spars and sways. Spars of split hazel, *c* 40 cm, with three-face points. Occasional sway *c* 40 cm of split hazel, but most of top coat fixed individually by bundles at *c* 25 cm intervals, using flat-U spars.

H2N: First course bundles folded in two and wedged into position between lowermost and second eaves batten. This course held in place by overlying courses without additional fixings. Upper courses fixed by sways tied to battens and rafters with lightly tarred twine or occasional wire (especially near ridge). Sways both split and roundwood, *c* 60 cm long and 2–3 cm diameter, spaced at *c* 15–20 cm intervals for bottom three courses and 25–30 cm for upper courses.

Lowermost sway overhangs lower batten by *c* 15 cm creating large overhang of thatch. Sways bent around hip corners. Stitches visible every *c* 2–3 battens and occasionally around rafters. Flat-U spars also used to fix individual bundles. Fixings of this base coat well preserved.

H3/NE: (corner). Base coat tied to battens with split hazel sways and binder twine (and occasional wire)

Ridge (north section)

R1N: spars *c* 28 cm of split hazel, with three-faced points. U-section decayed.

R3N: spars *c* 30–40 cm of roundwood and split willow, with three-faced points. Liggers of roundwood willow and hazel, pointed. Consolidated with galvanized wire (repair).

R4N: spars split from large diameter roundwood (into four or five sections). Points four-faced. Only 10 cm sections remaining.

R5N: spars *c* 25–38 cm, of split willow and three-faced points. Liggers of 3 cm diameter roundwood willow, *c* 75 cm, pointed and three-faced. Spars fixing liggers of ridge coat.

R6N: ridge roll fixed to ridge pole with coarse binder twine, three-ply and lightly tarred.

A4 BUCKINGHAMSHIRE (TABLE A4)

Hollingdon Grange, Soulbury
Grid reference: SP 8826
Date of survey: 21ˢᵗ September 1993
Thatcher: Nick Mackay
Locality: 4km north west of Leighton Buzzard. Area of heavy arable fields, with occasional surviving ridge and furrow.

Building description

Two-bay timber-framed lobby entry house, early seventeenth century. Oriented north-east/south-west. Kitchen end (west) much altered this century, tiled. Thatch surviving only on parlour (east) end. Central brick

Table A4 Hollingdon Grange, Soulbury, Buckinghamshire

Samples	Principal components	Fixings
S1	BW LS	spars and sways
S2	BW, occasional rivet, basal and upper, very crushed, mixed ears and butts	spars and sways
S3	BW, occasional rivet, basal and upper, very crushed, mixed ears and butts, distinct blow marks	spars and sways
S4	BW, basal, crushed, distinct blow marks	spars and sways
S5	BW, upper, crushed, occasional basal, occasional rye	spars and sways
S6	BW, mostly basal, crushed and undamaged, mixed ears and butts	spars and sways
S7	BW, crushed, mixed ears and butts	twisted straw, saplings, sways
S8	base coat, bread and rivet wheat straw, basal and upper, crushed, mixed ears and butts	twisted straw, saplings, sways

Figure A4.

chimney stack. Dormer windows on south face. Rafters near stack lightly blackened due to smoke seepage. Ceilings plastered directly onto lath and thatch in stack bay.

Sampling background

Rescue samples obtained during brief visit with J Moir. Entire thatch to be replaced by new long straw (Fig A4). Limited access to roofspace in chimney bay on front (south-east) face of roof at junction of north (thatched) bay and west tiled bay (to be replaced with thatch). Base coat sample removed from within roofspace. Samples very wet due to rain and S3–S7 eventually discarded due to rapid decay in sample bag.

Thatch summary

External long straw thatch of bread wheat straw fixed with spars and sways. Scalloped, block-cut ridge with eaves liggers. Half hip on east gable well preserved due to steep pitch. Base coat (S8), mid nineteenth century, a mixture of (mostly) short basal specimens and upper stem specimens, both crushed. Basal specimens *c* 10 cm, crushed at both ends, without roots, containing much weed and flag leaf and numerous ears of rivet wheat. Six main coat samples between base coat and surface coat (S1), all of crushed straw, mixed ears and butts, mostly of bread wheat (with occasional ears of rivet wheat in S2 and S3), all sparred and swayed. Several early layers (not sampled) almost totally decayed.

Thatch (external):

Main: long straw, very decayed, *c* 15 years old, to be replaced with long straw. More decay on south (rear) than north face. Pitch *c* 46 °.

Ridge: wrapover, raised and scalloped, diamented, very decayed, wired only at ridge. Depth: *c* 65 cm.

Eaves: liggered, very decayed, *c* 40 cm overhang.

Gables: half-hipped on east end, straw here well preserved due to steep pitch.

Samples:

MAIN COAT:

S1: External coat of bread wheat long straw, specimens *c* 50 cm, evenly crushed over stem, mixed heads and butts and very decayed.

S2: bread wheat straw, specimens *c* 25 cm, basal and upper stem specimens, occasional longer upper stem specimens (*c* 60 cm, cut high on stem), all very crushed and evenly mixed heads and butts. Ears both awned and awnless. Occasional tall specimens of rivet wheat. Few weeds.

S3: bread wheat straw, specimens *c* 30 cm, both upper and basal specimens, mostly very crushed, evenly mixed heads/butts and with distinct blow marks. Occasional ear of rivet wheat. Moderate flag leaf and debris. Occasional thorny branch segments of sloe (cf *Prunus spinosa*).

S4: bread wheat straw, specimens *c* 20 cm, mostly basal specimens cut/flailed with little root. Modern crushed with distinct flail blows. Moderate flag leaf and debris.

S5: bread wheat straw, specimens *c* 50 cm, upper stem specimens cut below top node and with very occasional basal specimen. Ears and butts mixed. Most specimens crushed, some over entire stem, but occasionally undamaged.

S6: bread wheat straw, specimens mostly *c* 15–20 cm, basal but with some upper stem specimens. Some (upper) specimens crushed entirely, others over top two thirds and some undamaged. Moderate flag leaf and weeds. Rakings from threshing pile (?).

S7: bread wheat straw, crushed, mixed ears and butts.

S8: Base coat of crushed straw, mixture of basal specimens *c* 10 cm crushed at both ends and without root and upper stem specimens. Mostly small and lax-eared bread wheat but with numerous small and dense-eared (tillers?) of rivet wheat. Moderate debris and weeds.

Fixings

Base coat and overlying layer S7 fixed to rafters and battens with sways tied with twisted straw rope and saplings (cf willow). Most layers sparred and swayed, with occasional use of straw bonds (scuds) in place of sways.

Interpretation

Typical multi-layered straw-thatched roof fixed with spars, sways and straw bond, with two basal coats tied with twisted straw rope. Occasional use of straw rope (consolidation) in upper layers. External coat of typical modern long straw, but other layers unusual in containing mixture of distinctly basal and upper stem specimens. Perhaps stubble deliberately mixed with threshed, high-cut straw for use as thatch. Samples mostly evenly mixed heads and butts. Specimens in some samples with distinct blow (flail?) marks. S6 perhaps rakings from threshing pile. Base coat, S2 and S3 contain small amounts of rivet wheat. Bread wheat in S2 has both awned and awnless ears, implying cultivation of either a varietal mixture or a genetically impure crop (ie a land race). S2 is at least early twentieth century, so post-early 1900 spar coats removed prior to rethatching with S1.

A5 BUCKINGHAMSHIRE (TABLE A5)

The Cruck Cottage, Clipstone, Eggington
Grid reference: SP9225
Date of survey: 21ˢᵗ February 1995
Owner: John Batchelor
Thatcher: Nick Mackay
Locality: Cottage and outbuildings set amidst arable fields on east edge of Leighton Buzzard. Abundant abandoned ridge and furrow field in vicinity.

Building description

Fifteenth-century cruck-framed open hall, much renovated, with smoke-blackened timbers but no smoke blackened thatch. Rethatched by Mr Batchelor (senior) in 1927. Oriented south-east/north-west. Medieval floor and residual open hearth located in south-east room during exploratory excavations. Smoke-blackened rafters, *c* 10 cm x 10 cm, survive above purlin level on northast (back) face. Pitch *c* 45°. Split pole rafters, *c* 8 cm x 12 cm, inserted below purlin on both front (south-east) and rear faces (including sampled area B). These rafters then replaced or supplemented by square-sawn rafters, *c* 8 cm x 8 cm, over south-east end. Pole rafters *c* 10 cm x 12c m (not split) supplementing original smoke-blackened rafters at north-west end. Rafters pegged to wall plate at *c* 50 cm intervals on front face, leaving a *c* 15 cm overhang over front of wall. Occasional long rods, *c* 5 cm diameter, inserted vertically between original rafters but above battens. Roof plastered to purlin height through-

Table A5 The Cruck Cottage, Clipstone, Eggington, Buckinghamshire

Sample	Principal components	Fixings
Main coat	*Series A (front face)*	
L1	BW LS, mixed ears and butts, evenly crushed	roundwood sways and spars, occasional spars only
L2	BW straw, mixed ears and butts, evenly crushed	roundwood sways and spars
L3	BW straw, mixed ears and butts, very crushed evenly, poorly drawn	sways and tarred twine
L4	BW straw, mixed ears and butts, very crushed, evenly, poorly drawn	roundwood sways and mixed ties (twine, saplings, twisted rods, straw)
Main coat	*Series B (SE hip)*	
L1-4b	BW straw, mixed ears and butts, crushed evenly	sways and tarred twine, occasional spars
L5b	BW straw, stubble (?) without roots, rubbish	roundwood sways and tarred twine
L6b	rush (*Juncus* sp.) + grass	stob repair/filler (no fixings)
L7b	bread wheat straw, mixed ears and butts, very crushed	roundwood sways and ties of clematis, saplings and tarred twine
Ridge	*(SE hip)*	
L1r	bread wheat straw, very degraded	
L2r	bread wheat straw, very degraded	

Figure A5.

out (ceilings now removed). Occasional smoke-blackened split-pole battens survive in south-east end above purlin, and occasional below purlin in north-west end (rear face) (Fig A5). These occasionally replaced by later roundwood poles, and more commonly by riven laths of oak, *c* 8 cm x 12 cm, occasionally nailed to rafters but with most nails now degraded resulting in slippage. Battens often missing in south-east sections below purlins. First eaves batten on front face a sawn plank, *c* 2 cm x 14 cm, fixed to rafters *c* 20 cm from rafter foot. North-west (full) hip largely intact. Original timbers pegged to gable end truncated on inside of gable wall. Replacement rafters of hip extended from side walls and corners to ridge, spanned by strong pole battens, creating a sub-vertical hip face held in place with abundant thatch and ample fixings (especially tying). This area thus unavoidably problematic. Some smoke-blackening visible on apex of north-west hip. About 50 cm of thatch survives beneath corrugated iron applied in 1943.

Sampling background

Cottage not inhabited for decades, now being renovated, stripped and rethatched for occupation. Samples taken from beneath corrugated iron with assistance of N German. Series A taken from south west (front) face *c* 3 m from gable end. Series B taken from lower level of hip on south-east end.

Thatch summary

Surface coat (L1), applied in *c* 1927, of bread wheat straw, very crushed evenly over stem and mixed ears and butts. L1 with less rubbish and short straw than basal coats (ie well drawn), fixed with spars and roundwood sways, but occasionally by spars fixing individual bunches. Under-

lying coats fixed to battens with sways and a mixture of ties including tarred twine, straw and saplings. Top four coats on hip of bread wheat straw, crushed, mixed ears and butts, very similar to L1, but with L5b mostly of basal specimens (probably stubble) and L6b of a mixture of coarse grass and pasture rush, all fixed with short sways and tarred twine, and also with spars. L5b stubble contains no rooty material, so that the sample probably reflects a scythed tall stubble and not simply raked gleanings. L6b, a stobbed repair/filler on the hip, contains mostly pasture rush (*Juncus* sp.) and grass and would not have functioned for long as an external coat. L7b was fixed to the (repaired) hip battens and rafters using sways tied with saplings and tarred twine. The two surviving ridge layers of crushed and jumbled bread wheat straw near the apex of the hip very poorly preserved, but were probably wrapped over ridge and fixed flush. The thatch on this cottage was probably left in a state of disrepair for a number of years prior to the application of corrugated iron, and was then much disturbed by rodents and birds. Many coats, including the base coat, have been stripped and replaced over the centuries. The current base coat probably represents thatch applied when the hip was repaired and pole rafters inserted (early nineteenth century?).

Thatch (external):
Main: bread wheat long straw, well-threshed, mixed ears and butts. Pitch: *c* 47 °.
Ridge: straw, wrap-over, flush, simple liggering.
Eaves: cut and liggered (single row).
Gables: full hips, pitch: *c* 65 °.

Samples:
MAIN COAT, SERIES A (SOUTH WEST FACE):
L1a: bread wheat long straw, specimens *c* 45 cm, very crushed, mixed ears and butts and very degraded. Large gulley of decay between L1a and L2a filled with extra L1a straw.
L2a: bread wheat straw, very similar to L1.
L3a: bread wheat straw, specimens *c* 50 cm, very crushed over stem, mixed ears and butts, weathered with much rubbish. (L4 in slides)
L4a: bread wheat straw, specimens 40 cm, very crushed over entire stem, mixed ears and butts with much rubbish. (L5 in slides)

MAIN COAT, SERIES B (SOUTH EAST HIP):
L1–4b: bread wheat straw, crushed, mixed ears and butts, very similar to L2a.
L5b: bread wheat straw, basal specimens, *c* 30 cm, much rubbish, no roots (stubble?). Occasional stripped rachis.
L6b: mixed sample, very grassy, mostly pasture rush (*Juncus* sp) and grass indet, specimens *c* 25 cm, layer *c* 25 cm. Sample looks superficially like flax.
L7b: base coat of bread wheat straw, specimens *c* 30 cm, very crushed and mixed heads and butts.

RIDGE, SOUTH EAST HIP:
L1r: bread wheat straw, crushed, mixed ears and butts.
L2r: rivet wheat straw, crushed, mixed ears and butts.

Fixings:

Main coat, series A (south-west face):

L1: roundwood sways (both quarter sections of 3.5 cm rod, and unsplit specimen 2 cm diameter), spars *c* 45 cm., occasional spars only.

L2: large diameter roundwood sways, spars.

L3: sways and tarred twine (L4 in slides).

L4: long roundwood sways fixed to battens with tarred twine, twisted straw bonds, clematis (cf *Clematis* sp.) stems, multiple and single-stemmed saplings (cf willow), twisted rods (cf hazel). Occasional sway *c* 60 cm. (L5 in slides).

Main coat, series B (south east hip):

L1–4b: short sways, tarred twine, occasional spars.

L5b: tarred twine and roundwood sways.

L6b: stob (ie no fixings, forced up and held in place by compression).

L7b: roundwood sways and ties of clematis, withes and tarred twine.

A6 BUCKINGHAMSHIRE (TABLE A6)

Ickford House, Little Ickford
Grid reference: SP6407
Date of survey: 21st April 1997
Owner: Mr and Mrs Stony
Thatcher: W J Cross
Locality: In thatched village 15 km east of Oxford, 8 km south east of Otmoor. Adjacent to various branches of the river Thames in an area formerly producing bulrush (*Schoenoplectus lacustris*) commercially for the manufacture of chair seats and basketry. Building surrounded by mature trees. Close to a large, mid eighteenth-century brick house on south. Adjacent to a pond.

Building description

Listed, cruck-framed former open hall, said to be early seventeenth century but possibly earlier. Oriented north/

Table A6 Ickford House, Little Ickford, Buckinghamshire

Main	Other	Principal components	Fixings	Depth (cm)
L1		BW straw, crushed, mixed ears and butts	spars and occasional sways	20
L2		BW straw, crushed, mixed ears and butts	spars and occasional sways	5
	L2a	BW straw, crushed, mixed ears and butts, repair	spars	10
L3		BW straw, mixed ears and butts, decayed	spars and sways	5
L4		BW straw, crushed, mixed ears and butts	spars and sways	10
L5		BW straw, crushed, mixed ears and butts	spars	10
	L6 ?	BW straw, crushed, mixed ears and butts, repair	mud, sways, tarred twine	15
L7		BW and oat straw, crushed, mixed ears and butts	sways, tarred twine	15
	dollie	bulrush (*S. schoenoplectus*)	(filler)	

Figure A6.

south. Stone-faced, with interior walls of wattle and daub with chopped straw/threshing waste providing a key for finishing coat. Now three bays running north/south, but originally two bays extended north when chimney and first floor inserted. Floor over hall later removed to allow insertion of a weaving loom (according to local knowledge) and never reinstated. Extended north bay half-hipped, with chimney forming the bulk of a partition wall between bays 1 and 2, but with west half of upper floor still open to hall. Bays 2 and 3 partitioned on first floor by wattle and daub panel with hazel horizontals and timber uprights. Partition plastered on interior face to first floor ceiling level, and not smoke-blackened above this level and so constructed after insertion of chimney. Second chimney on south gable wall, perhaps constructed when hip removed to accommodate construction of adjacent brick building in eighteenth century. Access to first floor room of bay 3 by extending ladder. This room is lit by small dormer window of long-standing insertion *c* 1.0 m from wall-plate just south of partition wall, and by later window inserted into south gable. North bay half-hipped. First floor room in bay 1 lit by small window beneath half-hip. Dormer window inserted at first floor level in front of bay 2 and recessed like rear dormer due to rethatching. Dormers without lead aprons. Ceilings plastered at first floor level. No access to roofspace, but photographs obtained by inserting camera into hole created by sampling. Purlins and some rafters of central hall bay smoke-blackened. Replacement rafters roughly squared, *c* 8 cm x 7 cm, fixed to squared, smoke-blackened ridge piece. Rafters pitched at *c* 55 °+. Purlins extend beyond south hip wall to carry external wall plate supporting hip rafters. Battens of *c* 2–3 cm diameter hazel and willow rods placed at *c* 30–40 cm intervals, with occasional *c* 3 cm split wooden battens, held in place by the tying of the base coat to rafters.

Sampling background

Interior examined briefly in March 1997 and roof sampled during rethatching in April. Roof maintained for past 50+ years by Cross family (thatchers) and regularly patched rather than rethatched. Rescue samples removed from south east (front) face during rethatching. Section opened to right of dormer window 1.3–2.0 m from ridge, above first floor ceiling level of central hall bay 2. Sample of rush dollie (packing) taken from back (north-east) face. Rear thatch also of five or six main coat layers of bread wheat long straw. All samples are of main coats. Ridge layers not accessible.

Thatch summary

Early seventeenth-century thatched cottage. Typical multi-layered straw-thatched roof sampled during rethatching. All layers sampled are of bread wheat straw, usually very crushed and always mixed ears and butts. Many layers undoubtedly stripped during previous rethatchings. Uppermost layers fixed in individual bundles as well as with sways, while L6 and base coat L7 fixed with sways tied to rafters at *c* 30 cm intervals with coarse tarred twine. L6 also sealed by extensive 4 cm thick patch of mud which formed an anchor for spars (possibly fixing an overlying patch of repair). No equivalent layer ever encountered in this district (according to thatcher), but anecdotal evidence exists of mud used in courses and on ridges in this region. Regular evidence of repair using stobs forced up into bird and rodent holes. A dollie of bulrush wrapped into a tight brick-shaped wad used to fill holes at top of rear wall beneath an eaves course. Marshy plants such as bulrush were once commonly used for packing and patching according to thatcher. Front south-west face of roof more exposed to sun and weathers more quickly than rear face. Ridge pole and some rafters smoke-blackened, but no smoke blackened thatch in central bay above ceiling. Wattle and daub partition of first floor between bays 2 and 3 not smoke-blackened and hence post-dating insertion of chimney. Being rethatched with combed wheat reed of *Maris Widgeon* grown in Somerset. South gable stripped back to wall plate, rest of roof stripped back one or two layers to a sound base before application of new coat. Hazel rods cut by thatcher from a local copse in order to obtain spars and sways of differing lengths for use on different areas of a roof. Spars split and sharpened on site, and used in conjunction with roundwood sways (Fig A6). New ridge diamonded and slightly raised but not cut to pattern. Approximately 2.5 tons of combed wheat reed will be used in rethatching this roof, supplied by a grower in bundles of variable size. The thatcher's father used rye for thatching in this area in the 1950s, perhaps only for ridging. Thatch almost always long straw in this area in past with flush ridges, having been replaced by combed wheat reed and water reed with block cut and patterned ridges (due to public demand) in recent decades. This long straw was always threshed by machine and drawn from a heap with a resulting mix of ears and butts. Fleekings and underlays of water reed occasionally encountered in district, as are thick accumulations of straw thatch, but these are rarely stripped completely (by this thatcher) as this is unnecessary and time-consuming.

Thatch (external):

main: combed wheat reed, very patched with visible sways. Weathered with extensive patches of lichen and moss (very dried by drought). Wired. External pitch *c* 50°, with slight dip in pitch at junction of ridge and main coat.

ridge: straw, raised and scalloped, wrapover, diamented, very decayed with hedgehog display of spars.

eaves: dressed and cut to flat pitch and *c* 50 cm overhang on front, rear and hip. Wired. Much repaired (ie stobbed).

gables: north bay half-hipped, steeply pitched, cantilevered over wall by hip rafters resting on beam supported by main purlins. Minimum three layers of thatch and repairs visible on south and north gables. Heavy rodent damage on south gable.

Samples:

MAIN COAT:

L1: Bread wheat long straw, applied in early 1980s, now very decayed. Specimens *c* 35 cm, very crushed and mixed ears and butts. External coat very dry due to drought, with butt ends curled and lichen/moss dead and easily removed in large clumps.

L2: Bread wheat straw, specimens *c* 40 cm, evenly crushed over stem and mixed ears and butts. Layer truncated *c* 2 m from ridge. Much detritus, flag leaf and weeds (especially dock *Rumex* sp.).

L2a: Repair above L3. Bread wheat straw, specimens *c* 50 cm, crushed, mixed ears and butts and well preserved.

L3: Bread wheat straw, mixed ears and butts and now almost entirely decayed.

L4: Bread wheat straw, specimens *c* 45 cm, crushed and mixed ears and butts. Includes a stob bent over at apex.

L5: Bread wheat straw, specimens *c* 40 cm, crushed and mixed ears and butts.

L6: Bread wheat straw, specimens *c* 35 cm, very crushed, mixed ears and butts and stems with severe dogleg. Repair partially filling gulley formed by decay..

L7: Mixed sample of bread wheat and cultivated oat (*Avena sativa*) straw, specimens *c* 40–50 cm, very crushed and mixed ears and butts. Butts cut at an angle indicating hand harvesting. Surface covered by layer of moss and decay.

Dollie of bulrush (*Schoenoplectus lacustris*) tied into a *c* 25 cm x 25 cm x 20 cm rectangular wad for filling a hole near eaves on east face.

Fixings:

L1: Split hazel spars, with three-faced points cut very thin, *c* 35 cm, used to fix individual bundles. Very occasional sways.

L2: Split hazel spars with three-faced points, *c* 25 cm long, used to fix individual bundles and also in combination with split hazel sways.

L2a: Split hazel spars with three-faced points, *c* 30 cm.

L3: Split cf willow spars with three-faced points, *c* 20 cm. Mostly of half or quarter sections. Roundwood sways.

L4: Split hazel spars and roundwood sways.

L5: Split cf willow spars, *c* 40–30 cm.

L6: Large (*c* 5 cm) hazel roundwood sway tied to rafters through base coat with 0.5 cm diameter tarred twine. Portion of this course, probably in area requiring repair prior to rethatching, sealed by *c* 25 cm x 30 cm x 4 cm layer of mud with imprints and imbedded straw on both surfaces. Spars pierced this mud while it was still wet.

L7: 3 cm diameter roundwood sways tied to rafters with tarred twine *c* 0.5 cm diameter.

A7 CAMBRIDGESHIRE (TABLE A7)

Cottage, Great Stukeley
Grid reference: TL2274
Date of survey: 7th September 1993
Owner: Ian Kerr
Thatcher: M Dodson.
Locality: 2 km north west of Huntingdon. Arable district 8 km south of main peat district of Fens.

Building description

Early eighteenth-century stone cottage. Oriented north west/south east. No access to interior, but portion of roofspace visible through area under reconstruction. Roof forms ceiling of first floor, plastered from within (over ties fixing base coat of thatch). Thatch supported on a woven fleeking of water reed. Last coat of thatch (long straw) applied in *c* 1964 (by Mr Dodson senior) and still in moderately good shape.

Sampling background

Contacted by M Dodson, visited in September 1993. Thatch stripped where new rafters inserted to support a new dormer window. Samples taken from exposed section on south (front) face towards east end of house.

Thatch summary

Eighteenth-century cottage with top coat of bread wheat long straw almost 30 years old and with minimum of another five years possible wear. L2 of bread wheat straw, crushed and jumbled. L1 and L2 fixed primarily with spars and sways, but L2 consolidated at ridge with tarred twine. L3 very unusual main coat layer of black bog rush (*Schoenus nigricans*), an aquatic/fen species, not prolific, not known for growing in dense stands, and previously unrecorded as a thatching material. This layer is stitched

Table A7 Cottage, Great Stukeley, Cambridgeshire

Main coat	Principal components	Fixings	Depth cm
L1	BW LS, crushed, mixed ears and butts	spars and sways	30
L2	BW straw, mixed lengths, crushed, mixed ears and butts	spars and sways, occasional sisal (?) cord	20
L3	black bog rush (*S. nigricans*)	sedge and sisal cord, occasional saplings and spars	20
L4	bread wheat straw (stubble) with mud and roots	applied to fleeking roots/mud down, fixed by ties of L3	8
L5	fleeking of water reed	clamped in position with split willow rods nailed to rafters	

to roof with both sedge and sisal cord (and occasional spar). L4 also unusual, a relatively thin layer of residual stubble of bread wheat, specimens *c* 35 cm, pulled with a little mud adhering to roots and applied roots down onto the water reed fleeking (and onto backside of lath and plaster below purlin height). This layer fixed by ties of L3, and could not have functioned as an external coat. Evidence of this material and method hitherto anecdotal. Fleeking of woven water reed, clamped into position to every third rafter with split willow rods nailed to rafters. Inner surface of this water reed formed a key for plastering to first floor ceiling.

Thatch details (external):

main: bread wheat Long straw, in fair shape but with considerable wear and occasional patches of moss. Pitch *c* 48 °.

ridge: straw, wrap-over, raised and scalloped, diamented.

eaves: sparred and liggered. Stripped to rafters during rethatching in *c* 1964.

gables: stripped to rafters during rethatching in *c* 1964.

Samples:

MAIN COAT:

L1: bread wheat long straw, specimens *c* 85 cm, 75% butts-together and applied butts-down on roof. Wheat locally grown. Straw well preserved, yellow in colour, with thick and semi-solid stems ('very strong' according to thatcher). Occasional stobs used to repair/fill L2 prior to rethatching.

L2: bread wheat straw, specimens variable in length, often *c* 60 cm, mixed ears and butts and crushed. Many shorter specimens Straw softer and less well preserved than L1. Applied *c* 1930.

L3: black bog rush (*Schoenus nigricans*), called marsh grass or sedge by thatcher. Specimens *c* 45 cm. Occasional other herbaceous specimens, grass indet, short straw specimens and lumps of rhizomatous root (cf sedge/rush). Layer is well preserved, no evidence of significant weathering and separates cleanly from L2. Applied at same time as base coat L4.

L4: base coat of bread wheat (?) straw (stubble), specimens range from 20–60 cm, usually in bunches of two or three stems attached to roots. Many specimens cut/cut or cut/broken and with very occasional flail marks. Applied roots-up with mud adhering to roots laid against water reed fleeking.

L5: Fleeking of horizontal water reed clamped to roof with split willow rods nailed to every third rafter. Plastered from within to purlin height. Sedge and cf sisal fixings of L4 also visible from within.

Fixings:

L1: sways and hazel spars.

L2: ridge consolidated with sisal cord. Main coat fixed by willow sways and hazel spars.

L3: twisted two-ply sedge rope (eight to nine strands), occasional sisal cord (according thatcher), saplings

Figure A7.

Figure A8.

(cf willow) and spars, all tied to rafters and battens through fleeking (Fig A7).

L4: fixings of L3 fix L4 (applied at same time).

A8 CAMBRIDGESHIRE (TABLE A8)

18 High Street, Orwell
Grid reference: TL3650
Date of survey: 14th March 1994
Owner: Cambridgeshire Cottage Housing Society
Consultant: Peter Brockett
Thatcher: Barney Bardsley
Locality: In village of Orwell, amidst arable fields, 10km north of Royston.

Table A8 18 High Street, Orwell, Cambridgeshire

Main coat	Principal components	Fixings	Depth cm
1	BW CWR	spars and sways, binder twine	20
2	BW LS	peg spar and hempen twine	10
3	BW LS (base coat)	hempen twine	10
4	Bread wheat LS (base coat)	hempen twine	15

Building description

Two-storey, three bay stone cottage, late sixteenth-century, oriented south-west/north-east, with nineteenth-century tiled extension extending south-east from south-west gable and early twentieth-century extension to north-east. No access to interior. Possibly open hall in origin with central chimney stack and first floor inserted in seventeenth century. A second brick stack placed centrally on north-east gable and a third on west corner. Prominent dormers on front (south) face. Roof timbers pitched at 55 °. North east face of external first floor wall around chimney coarsely wattled.

Sampling background

Cottage in process of renovation and rethatching under auspices of the Cottage Improvement Society. Building visited with P Brockett. External coat of combed wheat reed applied in 1983 by Dodson brothers (Cambridgeshire). Thatch already stripped where new rafters inserted on rear face, and older coats of thatch largely inaccessible beneath external coats on remainder of building. Front face re-ridged with no access to samples. No access to inside of building or roofspace. Three samples removed from rear (north-west) face where thatch removed to make way for new roof timbers.

Thatch summary

New coat of bread wheat long straw being applied to rebuilt rear face of roof and junction with existing thatch. Last coat of combed wheat reed (L1) applied in 1983. Two previous coats of bread wheat long straw, L2 fixed with long (60cm) peg spars and hempen twine, and L3 tied to battens and rafters with lightly tarred hempen twine. L3 very decayed. Long straw layers generally well-crushed and containing ample weed and detritus. Combed wheat reed slipping from fixings on ridge and dormers (Fig A8).

Thatch (external):

main: Combed wheat reed applied in 1983. Wired. Material pitch *c* 35 °, roof pitch *c* 55 o.

ridge: Straw, wrap-over, flush, diamented with extra upper horizontal ligger.

eaves: Dressed into position at slight upward angle. Eaves entirely stripped at last rethatching. Overhang *c* 35 cm.

gable: Dressed and wired.

Samples:

MAIN COAT:

L1: Combed wheat reed of bread wheat, applied by Dodson brothers in 1983. Specimens now 35 cm, well combed and with ears well preserved. Variety cf *Aquila* or *Bouquet*.

L2: Long straw of bread wheat. Specimens now *c* 40 cm, very crushed and primarily butts-together and down on roof. Both coarse and upper stem sections present. Much flag, weed and rubbish.

L3: Very decayed sample of bread wheat long straw.

New coat: Bread wheat long straw. Specimens *c* 85 cm, crushed over entire length of stem except apex. Ample weed, flag leaf and detritus. Ears and butts evenly mixed. Variety cf *Squareheads Master*.

Fixings:

L1: Split hazel spars and sways. Pink plastic binder twine fixing eaves course.

L2: Coarse hempen rope twinned around peg spar, *c* 60 cm, sharpened only at one end.

L3: Base coat stitched to battens and rafters with hempen twine.

New coat: Split hazel sways and iron crooks driven into new timber rafters.

A9 CAMBRIDGESHIRE (TABLE A9)

Brook End Cottage, Westley Waterless
Grid reference: TL6257
Date of survey: 12th February 1996
Owner: Philip White
Thatcher: Andrew Neeves
Locality: 6 km south west of Newmarket. House set amidst light-textured arable fields near tributary of the river Cam, east of Wilbraham Fen (a southern extension of the Fens). Large reed-filled pond 0.3 km from building said to be 'very old'.

Building description

Late seventeenth-century two room cottage, with single room extension to west. Ceilings of three upstairs rooms plastered to main purlin 2 m below ridge. Wattle and daub partition (cut through) above first floor ceilings between rooms 1 and 2 inserted before plastered ceilings. Roof steeply pitched, rafters *c* 50 °. Orientation: east/west, residual snow on north side. Stone-tiled dormer into room 2 upstairs. Small clay-tiled outshot on east end.

Table A9 Brook End Cottage, Westley Waterless, Cambridgeshire

Main	Ridge	Other	Principal components	Depth (cm)
	R1a		BW, decayed, not sampled	
L1			BW, basal and upper, crushed, mixed but mostly butts-together	15
	R2b		BW, crushed, decayed	
	R2a		BW, crushed, decayed	
L2			BW, crushed, ears and butts mixed but mostly butts-together	18
L3			fen sedge	20
	R4a		BW, crushed, decayed	
L4			BW, crushed, degraded	13
	R5b		fen sedge, occasional rye and barley	
	R5a		fen sedge, occasional rye	
L5			BW, crushed, ears and butts mixed	15
	R6a		fen sedge and occasional rye and barley	
L6			fen sedge and occasional bread wheat, rye and coarse basal specimens	20
		OS6	BW, crushed, ears and butts mixed, 'stob' repair in L6	N
		OSa	stubble	S face
		OSb	rye straw, crushed, ears and butts mixed, occasional bread wheat	S face
		OSc	BW, crushed, ears and butts mixed, decayed	S face

Two brick chimney stacks, on west end and between rooms 2 and 3, concrete flashing. Ceilings of east and west rooms plastered onto thin split rods nailed to inside face of rafters. Ceiling of central room plastered onto external coarse battens. External render of dormer: daub onto *c* 5–8 cm diameter split rods/poles. Dormer insertion coeval with new squared rafters and replastering of end room ceilings (with new base coat fixings?). Room 2 ceiling predates adjacent rooms, plastered onto coarse battens sealing original fixings. East and west rooms (1 and 3) plastered onto interior laths. Ridge of room 3 (west) 60cm below rooms 1 and 2.

Rafters: rough-sawn pole and square-cut rafters, *c* 7–10 cm diameter, *c* 115 cm spacings, cut flush or maximum 15 cm beyond outer face of wall, pegged or nailed to wall plate. Rafters crossing above ridge pole, not always partnered, and pegged onto ridge pole which is supported on short collar between main rafters at wall partitions and next to chimneys. Rafters coupled above first floor ceiling. Front: one (inserted) square rafter for every three poles. Back: pole rafters only. New rafters lapped and pegged. New rafters inserted early to mid nineteenth century. Occasional 8 cm diameter pole brace, nailed, running at 45 ° from east base of dormer to top east corner of ridge. Battens: lower two thirds of roof: debarked split poles, 3–8 cm diameter, occasional 10 cm near eaves, spaced 3–8 cm at eaves and 10–16 cm towards purlin at height of first floor ceiling. Also occasional 3–5 cm riven laths and roundwood rods. Spiked/nailed to rafters and clamped at top of gable by sawn 10 cm x 3 cm plank pegged into wall. Last lower batten fixed *c* 5–8 cm back from outer face of wall. Upper third of roof (above first floor ceiling to ridge): evenly spaced split poles and riven laths, 3–5 cm. Top batten *c* 30 cm from ridge joint.

Sampling background

Rescue excavation during complete stripping and replacement of rafters and battens. Front of roof stripped prior to visit. Rethatching in Dodson combed wheat reed. Sampled on a very cold day, with snow lingering in shade of north face. Stepped vertical series taken from upper north face, from mid-point to ridge, at *c* 5.0 m from east gable, where thatch better preserved (but thinner than south face). South (front) face stripped and in garden. Samples dried before storage.

Thatch summary

Base coat (L6) of fen sedge, overlain by two layers of crushed bread wheat straw (L5 and L4), mixed ears and butts, another layer of fen sedge (L3) and two further layers of crushed bread wheat straw (L2 and top coat L1), both mostly butts-together, but with some mixing of ears and butts. Ridge layers difficult to sample due to degradation. Several layers probably missed between R2 and R4. Upper layers of bread wheat (R1, R2 and R3), but lower layers of fen sedge (R5 and R6). Repair stob of crushed wheat straw (OS6), ears and butts mixed, thrust

Figure A9.

into L5. Useful samples recovered from straw heap in garden, stripped previous week from south (front) face: immature, crushed and butts-together rye straw (OSb), coarse stubble with roots (OSa) and crushed and jumbled bread wheat straw (OSc). Base coat fixed by split sways tied to battens with twisted rod-rope and saplings. L5 tied to battens with tarred twine (coarsely spun), twisted bulrush rope, saplings and spars. L4 fixed with tarred twine and spars, and L3 with twisted grass rope and spars. Early fixings sealed by plaster of first floor ceilings. Thatch pitch c 8 ° above roof rafter pitch due to buildup at ridge and disproportionate stripping of eaves. Total depth c 120 cm at ridge and c 100 cm at bottom of north section.

Interpretation

Roof of local rough-hewn pole timber and small diameter wood pegged and nailed into place (Fig A9). Coarse battens on lower two thirds (forming key for plaster of room 2 ceiling) and support base for thatch in rooms 1 and 3. Battens of fine split rods on upper third. Base coat and first ridge of fen sedge, not unexpected on edge of the Fens, but the sample also contains some specimens of rye, bread wheat and coarse stubble. Perhaps sedge was mixed with waste straw to provide bulk (filler). The light soils of this area are conducive to rye cultivation. L5 fixed with a variety of fixings including rope of woven bulrush, which implies access to shallow water habitat that would also have been conducive to the growth of water reed. There is no evidence of the use of water reed on the site, however, in spite of the numerous ditches in area and a very large, old reed-filled pond 250 m from house. Verge grass probably used as repair on south face (and definitely as rope).

Thatch (external):

main: north (rear) face of bread wheat long straw, pitch: c 58 °. South (front) face stripped, very decayed.
ridge: straw, wrap-over, raised and scalloped, diamented, depth c 20 cm but now very decayed. Total depth c 120 cm (estimated) eaves: cut flat, c 45 cm overhang, sparred and liggered.
gables: cut at angle, c 60 cm overhang, sparred and liggered.

Samples:

MAIN COAT (NORTH FACE):

L1: bread wheat straw, specimens c 70 cm, basal and fine upper stem specimens, all crushed over entire stem, ears and butts mixed but mostly butts-together and applied butts-down. Moderate flag leaf and few weeds. Applied in tight bundle in c 1984.
L2: bread wheat straw, specimens c 75 cm and occasional to c 90 cm, crushed over entire stem, ears and butts mixed but mostly butts-together and applied butts-down. Moderate flag leaf and weeds (especially grass).
L3: fen sedge *Cladium mariscus*, specimens c 70 cm, layer covered with moss.
L4: bread wheat straw, specimens c 45 cm, crushed along entire stem, very degraded. Moderate flag leaf.
L5: bread wheat straw, specimens c 35 cm, crushed over entire stem, ears and butts mixed, moderate flag leaf, ears lax.
L6: fen sedge *Cladium mariscus*, specimens c 75 cm, with occasional short rye, bread wheat and coarse basal specimens (stubble?).

RIDGE (ABOVE NORTH FACE SERIES):

R1a: bread wheat straw, decayed, not sampled, original depth c 25 cm, spars now standing free 15 cm.
R2a: bread wheat straw, crushed, very decayed
R2b: bread wheat straw, very decayed
R4a: bread wheat straw, very decayed with only c 15 cm surviving. Moderate weed. Wrap-over?
R5a: fen sedge *Cladium mariscus*, specimens c 75 cm, occasional rye. Much moss.
R5b: fen sedge *Cladium mariscus*, specimens c 60 cm, with mixed herbaceous aquatic spp, occasional rye, two-row barley and coarse basal specimens (stubble?). Wrap-over.
R6a: fen sedge *Cladium mariscus*, specimens c 50 cm, with occasional bread wheat and rye.

OTHER SAMPLES:

OS6: bread wheat straw, specimens c 55 cm, crushed, ears and butts mixed, repair stob thrust into sedge base coat north face

Samples taken from straw heap in garden, stripped the previous week from south (front) face:

OSa: coarse straw, basal specimens with roots (ie stubble), c 30–40 cm, no ears.
OSb: immature rye and occasional bread wheat straw, specimens c 30 cm, crushed, mostly butts-together
OSc: bread wheat straw, specimens c 45 cm, crushed, ears and butts mixed, degraded

Village 'elder' mentioned that a former owner named Jack Straw was the village thatcher (1930–50s). Used 'threshed straw', 'rye grass' (ie immature rye, laid butts-down) and 'verge grass' scythed from roadside in 1930s.

Fixings:

Main coat

L3: rope of six–eight strands of twisted grass, spars

L4: four-ply tarred cord, spars

L5: tied to battens with handspun two- to three-ply tarred twine, two- and four-ply rope of twisted bulrush (cf *Schoenoplectus lacustris*) and twisted saplings, occasional roundwood spars *c* 15–25 cm with two or three faceted points.

L6: horizontal *c* 3 cm diameter split rods (several spp) and saplings tied to battens with twisted (hazel) rod-rope and saplings (cf willow withes) at 150 cm intervals (vertical).

Fixings of L1–L4 plastered into first floor ceiling. External main coats L1 and L2 fixed with spars (willow and hazel) and sways (miscellaneous spp including split rods and branches). Spars: occasional spars without sways in L3, L4 and L5. Additional tying with twisted grass rope and tarred twine in L 3 and L 4 (towards ridge).

Ridge:

5a: sway (willow?) tied to uppermost batten with saplings (withe)

5b: handspun tarred twine, two- to three-ply and of uneven thickness, ties ridge coat to top batten on north and south. Numerous spars and roundwood (sapling) sways.

• Occasional miscellaneous sways (willow) and spars (willow and hazel spars), very decayed.

Other fixings

Found in straw heap in garden, stripped from front (south) face previous week:

• *c* 45 cm spars (hazel), associated with rye (OSb)
• *c* 40 cm spars (hazel), associated with bread wheat straw
• twisted grass rope, six- to eight-ply, made from verge or pasture grass.

A10 DEVON (TABLE A10)

Land Farm, Stockland
Grid reference: ST2404
Date of survey: 5th December 1995
Thatcher: Jeff Thame.
Locality: Between Stockland and Furley villages, 14km north east of Honiton. District quite hilly with mixed arable and pasture.

Sampling background

Smoke blackened thatch revealed during roof repair and rethatching. Notified by thatcher. Bulk of smoke blackened thatch left intact with new roof constructed over original sixteenth-century structure to improve pitch for application of imported water reed. Samples taken during rethatching/repair. *c* 2 m x 1 m section revealed on west face of south

Table A10 Land Farm, Stockland, Devon

Layer	Composition	Fixings	Depth (cm)
L1	BW, CWR	spars and sways	15
L2	BW, reed-straw, crushed apex, butts-down	spars	20
L3	BW, reed-straw, crushed apex, butts-down	spars, saplings, cord	7
L4	BW, reed-straw, crushed apex, butts-down	spars	10
L5	BW straw, crushed	spars	5
L6	BW, reed-straw, crushed apex, mostly butts-down	spars	7
L7	BW, reed-straw, combed, lashed ?	spars ?	7
L8	BW, reed-straw, crushed apex, combed	spar, straw bonds ?	10
SBT1	BW and rivet wheat, reed-straw, crushed apex, butts-down, ridge coat ?	spars (+/- wattle)	7
SBT2	BW and rivet wheat, reed-straw, crushed apex, combed, butts-together and applied butts-up, ridge coat ?	spars + wattle	15
SBT3	BW and rivet wheat, reed-straw, crushed apex, combed, butts-together and applied butts-down as underlay	spars + wattle	5
wattle	halved and roundwood rods, mostly hazel, constructed on ground and finished *in situ*	tied to rafter with rods	

extension from ridge and *c* 3.0 m from south gable. Smoke blackened thatch samples removed near ridge.

Building description

Large, two-storey, stone and cob-walled, cruck-framed open hall much renovated in seventeenth century and extended in later centuries. Said to be a yeoman farmer's house constructed in 1620s, but perhaps sixteenth century. Building now T-shaped. Original south core with smoke-blackened rafters and base coat. Eighteenth-century east extension now rethatched with water reed and timbers not visible (actually oriented south-east/north-west). Later west extension tiled. Rafters *c* 12 cm x 12 cm, pegged in adjacent pairs at *c* 60 cm intervals and resting on a *c* 15 cm x 15 cm ridge piece. Thatch supported on a tight wattle structure of *c* 2 cm diameter hazel rods tied to rafters at regular intervals with twisted hazel rods (Fig A10). Wattle

Figure A10.

extends smoothly over crest of ridge (ie constructed in situ). Original pitch *c* 44°. Sharpened *c* 8 cm staves, driven into thatch from eaves between every three rafter pairs to provide additional support for rafters, extend almost to ridge above smoke-blackened base coat.

Thatch summary

Early post-medieval cruck-framed open hall with smoke-blackened thatch supported on a wattle base. Smoke-blackened thatch base coat at Land Farm composed of three layers, all of full length reed straw mixtures of bread wheat and rivet wheat, flailed only at apex (leaving most of stem uncrushed) and combed; L3 a thin back coat or underlay applied butts-down; L2 a layer now *c* 20 cm thick, applied butts-up; and L1 composed of more thoroughly threshed straw (perhaps a wrap-over layer beneath a butts-up ridge coat now removed). All top coats of bread reed straw, mostly apex-flailed or lashed (with more ears surviving intact). L5 perhaps long straw but insufficient length preserved. Some samples crushed a considerable distance away from ears, others mostly within 25 cm of ear. Some samples well combed, others with abundant rubbish (eg L6). All applied butts-down and survive only with top 1.5–2 internodes due to weathering. Smoke-blackened thatch L2 and L3 fixed with spars driven into wattle. Smoke-blackened thatch L1 cf sparred to smoke blackened thatch base coats. Subsequent layers largely fixed with spars, with *c* 30 cm tines, (but with little evidence of sways except towards top coats). Occasional evidence of straw bonds (eg L8) and consolidation using withes and hempen rope (L3) tied to rafters. Earlier spars often of small diameter roundwood or larger diameter split spars. Spars of later layers of usual split hazel or willow.

Thatch (external):
main: combed wheat reed applied *c* 1970, sparred and swayed. Pitch: *c* 42 °.
ridge: straw (combed wheat reed), butts-up, raised, diamented.
eaves: flush, dressed to angle, minimum three coats visible.
gable: flush, dressed into position

Samples:
MAIN COAT:
L1: modern bread wheat combed wheat reed, specimens *c* 75 cm, ears mostly undamaged but some detached, very clean.
L2: bread wheat reed straw, specimens *c* 45 cm, crushed over top half of first internode, crushed apex with *c* 10% of ears attached. Butts uncrushed and mostly weathered, original length *c* 70 cm. Applied butts-down on roof.
L3: very similar to L2, specimens *c* 60 cm.
L4: bread wheat reed straw, specimens *c* 55 cm, very crushed at apex but with most ears intact, butts weathered, applied butts-down on roof.

L5: bread wheat straw, specimens *c* 15 cm, very decayed, very crushed with distinct crush blow, many loose ears and ears +10 cm of upper internode.
L6: bread wheat reed straw, specimens *c* 70 cm, crushed over top half of first internode, *c* 15% of ears still attached, mostly butts-together (but with some mixing) and applied butts-down on roof. Abundant rubbish (poorly combed).
L7: bread wheat reed straw, specimens *c* 70 cm, mostly upper 1.5 internodes, threshed but not very crushed at apex (lashed?), ears mostly intact, butts weathered and straw combed.
L8: bread wheat reed straw, specimens *c* 60 cm, upper internode very crushed but with most ears intact, combed, butts weathered, together and applied butts-down on roof.

Smoke blackened thatch base coat samples:

SBT1: sheaf of bread and rivet wheat reed straw, specimens *c* 50 cm, crushed over much of upper internode, butts-together and applied butts-down onto SBT2. First external layer of smoke blackened thatch. Truncated by L8.
SBT2: full-length sheaf of bread and rivet wheat reed straw, specimens *c* 90 cm, well preserved, mostly with 3 internodes, crushed upper internodes and cut butts still sharp. Butts-together and applied butts-up on roof (possible butts-up ridge). Occasional rye and abundant flag leaf and arable weeds.
SBT3: sheaf of bread and rivet wheat reed straw, specimens *c* 85 cm, crushed over upper half of stems, butts well preserved, together, and applied butts-down as an underlay with upper third of small, slightly twisted, straw bundle folded over apex of ridge wattle. Occasional rye and arable weeds.
Wattle: halved, quartered and roundwood rods, mainly of about five-year-old hazel. Probably constructed on the ground, tied to battens once applied and ridge section finished *in situ*. Structure still very strong although with occasional (inactive) patches of woodworm and decay. Sample also contains smoke-blackened spars, mostly of halved roundwood (cf hazel and willow) with two-faced points once clamped into wattle from overlying coats.

Fixings:

L1: Split (hazel) spars and sways. Spars *c* 40 cm.
L2: Spars (cf hazel)
L3: Spar (hazel and cf willow), *c* 30 cm and three-faced. Occasional ties of saplings (willow) and hempen rope.
L4: Spars (cf hazel), *c* 29 cm, three-faced, blackened near broad (*c* 7 cm) twist.
L5: Roundwood spars (cf willow), *c* 33 cm, degraded at twist

L6: Small diameter roundwood and larger split spars, *c* 25–30 cm, three-faced points, degraded at twist

L7: spars? (not recovered)

L8: Roundwood spars and cf straw bond, *c* 25 cm, three-faced points

SBT: Spars driven into wattle base, mostly of halved roundwood (cf willow and hazel), two-faced points, twist degraded.

A11 DEVON (TABLE A11)

Capel Cottage, Berrynarbor
Grid reference: SS5646
Date of survey: 23rd June 1994
Thatcher: Brian Hummerston.
Locality: 12km south west of Ilfracombe. Near estuary of Taw River in Barnstaple Bay.

Building description

Sixteenth-century cruck-framed open hall of cob, much altered. Oriented east/west. Rear face being entirely rebuilt, but with smoke-blackened thatch left intact on front face. Rafters *c* 15 cm diameter and battens *c* 8–10 x 1.5 cm, all heavily smoke-blackened. Newer battens *c* 6–8 cm x 1.5 cm.

Sampling background

Sample visit organised at short notice during sampling trip to West Country. Thatch on rear face already removed, but continuous sequence obtained from exposed section (including smoke-blackened thatch). Smoke-blackened thatch also taken from three locations. Limited time for recording of building. Fixings not available for all samples. Ridge layers very complex and largely degraded and very difficult to sample in short time available.

Thatch summary

Devon roof of standard shallow pitch, with minimum of nine layers of mostly reed straw (Fig A11). Rafters and

Figure A11.

most battens smoke blackened, overlain by surviving pockets of reed straw fleeking (S4) and a large expanse of original smoke-blackened base coat material (S1–S3), all heavily smoke blackened. Smoke-blackened thatch samples probably derived from the short rakings of the threshing pile, ie the coarsest straw and threshed ears raked out of the pile after threshing was completed. Samples contain ears of bread wheat and rye and abundant specimens of other crops (eg broad beans, cultivated vetch, pea). Arable weeds also abundant (corn cockle, grasses, bindweed, dock). Smoke-blackened thatch fixed to battens and rafters with twisted, de-thorned stems of blackberry. Layers immediately above smoke-blackened thatch of degraded rye (L8) and bread wheat (L7) reed straw, crushed only at the apex and combed. Overlying layers mostly of similar, butts-together reed straw applied butts-down on roof. L2 is an unusual layer of bread wheat straw, crushed evenly over the entire stem but mostly butts-together and applied butts-down on roof. L2 contains too much rubbish and flag leaf to have been combed. This layer was perhaps applied early this century (and later spar coats were removed when existing top coat of Norfolk water reed was applied in early 1980s). L6 and possibly L3 perhaps lashed and combed rather than apex-flailed. Post-smoke-blackened thatch layers mostly sparred using with a variety of horizontal fixings (eg roundwood hazel, split hazel (L1), tarred or homespun twine (L2), straw bonds (L7), dethorned stems of blackberry (L7) or branched saplings (L8). Top coat of water reed fixed with spars, sways and iron crooks driven into added wall plate. Original eaves coat applied (and sparred into) wet mud on top of cob wall (and sealed with additional mud from within). Water reed has been regularly spar-coated to multi-layered straw roofs in this area since the early 1970s according to thatcher, due primarily to a perceived reduction in the quality of combed wheat reed available (ie the phenomenon of premature decay).

Thatch (external):

main: water reed, applied *c* 1983, sparred onto combed wheat reed. Pitch *c* 42 °
ridge: fen sedge, raised and scalloped, diamented
eaves: dressed flat

Table A11 Capel Cottage, Berrynarbor, Devon

Sample	Principal components	Fixings	Depth cm
L1	Norfolk WR	spars, hazel sways, crooks on eaves	25
L2	BW straw, crushed, butts-down	spars, tarred and homespun twine	8
L3	BW reed straw, lashed ?, butts-down	spars and sways	8
L4	BW reed straw, crushed apex, butts-down	spars (?) and straw bonds	10
L5	BW reed straw, crushed apex, butts-down	spars (?) and straw bonds	5
L6	BW reed straw, lashed ?, butts-down	spars and straw bonds	8
L7	BW reed straw, apex crushed, butts-down	spars, straw bonds, blackberry stems	8
L8	rye reed straw, crushed apex, butts-down	spars, withes to consolidate	5
SBT	threshing waste, mixed spp., short specimens	blackberry stems	20

Samples:

MAIN COAT:

L1: spar coat of fine Norfolk reed (water reed) applied *c* 1983, specimens now *c* 115 cm, flowering heads mostly cut off at application.

L2: bread wheat straw, specimens *c* 60 cm, cut low on stem, crushed over entire stem with little rachis surviving, mostly butts together and applied butts-down on roof. Much flag leaf (ie not combed).

L3: bread wheat reed straw, specimens *c* 60 cm, combed, with rachis stripped of chaff and with many ears missing. Straw largely undamaged, butts-together and applied butts-down on roof.

L4: bread wheat reed straw, specimens *c* 85 cm, very crushed at apex, combed, butts-together and applied butts-down on roof. Long last internode with lax ear and distinctive zig-zag rachis.

L5: bread wheat reed straw, crushed and fragmented, mostly butts-together and applied butts-down on roof. Weathered.

L6: bread wheat reed straw, specimens *c* 65 cm, mainly of one node, combed with little flag leaf or weed. Many ears missing but many also intact (lashed?). Mostly butts-together and applied butts-down on roof.

L7: bread wheat reed straw, specimens *c* 70 cm, well preserved, mainly of upper stem specimens, apex-flailed, with distinct blow marks and ears mostly missing. Rachis narrow and lax. Combed with little flag leaf or weed. Occasional specimens of rye. Mostly butts-together and applied butts-down.

L8: rye straw, originally reed straw, specimens *c* 40 cm, cut below second node, now composed mainly of ears due to weathering of stems. Mostly butts-together and applied butts-down on roof. Apex moderately crushed. Occasional ears of bread wheat and abundant weed. Sample lightly blackened by dust and soot.

SMOKE-BLACKENED THATCH:

S1: crushed and broken straw, mostly of *c* 35 cm specimens of straw, mostly bread wheat and two-row hulled barley, little root, abundant arable weed (thistle *Cirsium* sp, black bindweed *Fallopia convolvulus*, grasses, corn cockle *Agrostemma githago*, dock *Rumex* sp) and rubbish. Occasional large-podded broad bean (*Vicia sativa* ssp *major*) and pea (*P. sativum*) with seeds. Rakings of threshing heap?

S2: crushed and broken straw, mostly of very short *c* 15 cm specimens, with ears of rye and bread wheat, ample rubbish and crop weeds (including cultivated vetch *Vicia sativa*). Rakings of threshing heap?

S3: crushed rye straw, specimens *c* 15 cm, with occasional ears of barley, bread wheat and abundant arable weeds. Rakings of threshing heap?

S4: residual pockets of degraded reed straw fleeking, bread wheat, applied butts-up.

RIDGE

(R1) Rye straw, wrap-over ridge?, specimens now *c* 30 cm and very decayed.

OTHER

Bread wheat and rye straw, repair stob, specimens *c* 20 cm, most ears missing, sparred into L8.

Fixings:

Main coat

L1: iron crooks fixed into wall plate on eaves course. Spars and split hazel sways

L2: spars, tarred twine and homespun twine of variable thickness (as sways)

L3: spars and cf hazel sways

L4: cf spars and straw bonds (not recovered in sample area)

L5: cf spars and straw bonds (not recovered in sample area)

L6: spars, straw bonds

L7: spars, strong twisted straw bonds, dethorned and twisted blackberry stems (*Rubus* sp)

L8: spars *c* 25 cm, branched withes (cf willow)

SBT: dethorned and twisted blackberry stems (*Rubus* sp), short spars

A12 DEVON (TABLE A12)

(address withheld by request), near Cullompton
Date of survey: 2nd August 1994
Thatcher: Arthur Hannabus

Building description

Sixteenth-century cottage of cob and stone, two storeys, perhaps an open hall and much altered, with thatched hip to south and thatched hip plus outshot to north. Oriented

Table A12 Devon, near Cullompton

Sample	Principal components	Fixings	Depth cm
1a	WR , Hungarian	spars and sways, tarred twine, crooks	55
1b	BW, CWR, filler/repair, butts-up	spars	–
2a	BW reed straw, crushed apex, combed, butts-down	spars, straw bond	10
2b	BW reed straw, filler/repair, crushed apex, combed, butts-up	cf spars	–
3	BW reed straw, crushed apex, combed, butts-down	spars	10
4	BW reed straw, crushed apex, combed, mostly butts-down	cf spars	8
5	BW reed straw, apex crushed, combed, butts-down	spars, straw bonds	8
6	BW reed straw, lashed (?), combed, butts-down	roundwood peg spars, tarred twine	8
7	BW reed straw, crushed apex, combed, butts-down	spars, tarred twine	5
8	BW reed straw, crushed apex, combed, butts-down	saplings, bark, sway, hempen twine	10
9	BW reed straw fleeking, crushed apex, combed, butts-up	fixed by L 8	3

north/south. No access to interior except to roofspace above first floor ceiling. Dormer to rear (east). Immense purlins with ceiling of lath and plaster to purlin height. Roof timbers lightly smoke-blackened. One central chimney stack (inserted?). Wattle and daub partition north of stack separates roof space into two sections. Front (west) rafters north of stack of quarter section softwood pole with bark *c* 20 cm diameter, replacing original square cut rafters. Front rafters south of stack and on east (rear) face original roughly square-sawn rafters (*c* 15 cm diameter) supplemented by *c* 16 cm diameter roundwood poles notched and spiked. Original square rafters once carried lath and plaster to above purlin height (removed and replaced by existing ceiling). Battening and thatch post-dates this repair. Rafters pegged to ridge piece and wall plate (originals imbedded in top of cob wall) at *c* 50 cm intervals. Hip formed by short rafters running from gable wall to full-length corner rafters, all supported by purlin on a central principal. Pitch of front rafters *c* 42 ° and hip rafters *c* 35 °. Battens, 6–7 cm x 1 cm on hip and *c* 5 cm on west face, of split oak nailed to rafters at *c* 20 cm intervals on hip and *c* 26 cm on west face. First eaves batten over wall plate, sawn and modern. Tilting fillet fixed to wall plate also modern.

Sampling background

Building with a multi-layered straw roof with a top coat of Hungarian water reed applied in *c* 1982 showing signs of rapid decay. Entire roof to be stripped prior to application of new water reed. Samples taken during stripping from front (west) face and south hip.

Thatch summary

Base coats composed of a fleeking of bread wheat reed straw applied butts-up to create a smooth finish, and an overlying layer (8) of well-threshed reed straw applied butts-down. This first main coat layer crushed almost over the entire length of the stem and thus very similar to long straw, except that it appears to have been combed (cf prior to flailing) and is mostly butts-together. Overlying layers similar, either of lashed (chaff intact, many ears broken off) or apex-flailed (chaff largely removed) reed straw, combed and usually applied butts-together and down on roof. Sample 4 with a greater degree of mixing heads and butts, although still reed straw with stem largely undamaged. Top coat of Hungarian water reed, 12 years old, with a decay front of *c* 15 cm rapidly approaching spar fixings (but bundles also tied into bundles with tarred twine). This coat tied to eaves batten with tarred twine and occasional crooked into wall plate. Most reed straw layers fixed with spars and straw bonds, but layer 6 fixed by roundwood peg spars plus tarred twine and base coat sample fixed by sways tied to rafters with twisted withes (cf willow), hempen rope and in at least one case by twisted bark rope (Fig A12). Tied to rafter at every batten joint. Thick twisted straw rope used to consolidate thatch base coats at apex. No spars penetrating roof space. Ridge not fully accessible, but com-

Figure A12.

posed of numerous layers of horizontal ridge rolls and overcoats of knuckled or butts-up ridges. Outshot to north end with thin coat of thatch. Thickness of thatch has built up gradually at ridge increasing the pitch of the roof exterior to *c* 45 ° (but the pitch of the material itself is below this). Stripping of existing thatch very labourious (15 man days) with discarded thatch filling six large truckloads (disposed of offsite).

Thatch (external):

main: Hungarian water reed, applied 1982, tied with tarred twine to lowermost batten at eaves/gables, occasional crooked, double sparred and with individual bundles also tied with tarred twine. Pitch: *c* 45 °. Wired. Surface very damp with *c* 15 cm section of decay up stem.

ridge: straw, butts-up and scalloped, diamented. Depth: *c* 115 cm.

eaves: dressed, *c* 40 cm overhang

gables: dressed, overhanging

Samples:

MAIN COAT:

1a: Hungarian water reed applied *c* 1982. Variable in size and hardness, with *c* 15 cm area of decay visible in section and *c* 20 cm of straw surviving above fixings (three to five years further life expectancy).

1b: Bread wheat combed wheat reed, repair, specimens *c* 75 cm and with two or three nodes, applied butts-up, few ears surviving (trimmed on roof?). Well combed.

2a: Bread wheat reed straw, specimens *c* 70 cm, mostly single node specimens, combed and applied butts-down. Most ears stripped of chaff and remaining ears dense. Well combed with little surviving flag, short straw or weed.

2b: Bread wheat reed straw, repair/filler, specimens *c* 75 cm and mostly three nodes, well preserved, crushed at apex, combed and applied butts-up onto layer 3 prior to rethatching. Ears mostly missing.

3: Bread wheat reed straw, specimens *c* 100 cm and mostly two or three node, apex crushed, butts intact, combed and applied butts down.

4: Bread wheat reed straw, specimens *c* 80 cm and mostly upper specimens with two or three nodes, apex and upper internode crushed (also occasional below), mostly butts-together (*c* 20% ears reversed) and applied butts-down on hip. One specimen with a top internode of 62 cm. Combed with numerous stripped rachises and little flag leaf.

5: Bread wheat reed straw, specimens *c* 95 cm mostly with two nodes surviving, apex crushed beyond top node (about half of specimen), largely butts-together and applied butts-down on roof. Combed with most rachises stripped and with little flag leaf.

6: Bread wheat reed straw, specimens *c* 80 cm, mostly with two nodes, straw wiry, combed, many ears uncrushed (but threshed) and with many ears missing (lashed?).

7: Bread wheat reed straw, specimens *c* 60 cm, mostly with one node, apex crushed to first node (with distinct blow marks), combed, applied butts-down.

8: Base coat of bread wheat reed straw, specimens *c* 90 cm and occasional to 110 cm, mostly with one or two nodes, crushing extends from apex to *c* 30 cm above butt, combed with little flag leaf and most ears stripped of chaff, butts-together and applied butts-down on roof.

9: fleeking of bread wheat reed straw, specimens *c* 80cm and mostly with two nodes, very well preserved, crushed at apex, straw wiry, fine and with distinct blow marks. Ears both awned and awnless. Applied in a layer *c* 5 cm thick, butts-up and overlapping so no ears visible from below. Occasional grass stems (now also combed).

Fixings:

Main coat

1a: Water reed bundles tied with tarred twine to eaves batten, sparred and swayed, crooked on wall plate
1b: spars
2a: spars *c* 45 cm, with occasional straw sway
2b: cf spars
3: spars 60 cm.
4: cf spars (not recovered)
5: spars, cf straw bonds
6: roundwood peg spars, tarred twine
7: spars *c* 38cm, coarse tarred twine
8: split wood sway tied to rafters with withes, occasional tied with twisted bark

A13 DORSET (TABLE A13)

Jasmine Cottage, Osmington
Grid reference: SY7283
Date of survey: 23rd April 1994
Owner: Mrs Sewel
Thatcher: Rod Miller.
Locality: In Osmington village, 8km north east of Weymouth. 1km from shore of Weymouth Bay. Village set amidst rolling fields of chalky arable. Deciduous trees adjacent to house.

Building description

Early eighteenth-century two-storey stone cottage, oriented roughly east/west. Several original 6–10 cm diameter pole rafters collapsed, and occasional rough-sawn rafters pointed and inserted from eaves for extra support. Sawn rafters *c* 6 cm x 15 cm, lapped and pegged at ridge. Small diameter rods also used in place of rafters. Principal rafter spacing *c* 1.5 m. Rough-squared purlin, *c* 15 cm diameter, just above first floor ceiling now collapsed. No ridge pole. Thatch rests on long riven laths, *c* 4 cm x 2 cm nailed to rafters at *c* 20 cm intervals. Last course of thatch course crooked to wall plates on both gables and eaves, but thatch originally fixed to stone wall tops with mud. Rafter pitch: *c* 45 °.

Thatch summary

Classic Dorset roof of high-quality, multi-layered reed straw, earlier layers mostly of pitched reed and top coat of modern combed wheat reed with a (now decayed) block cut and patterned ridge. This overlying a similar layer of very similar reed straw (S1) also sparred and swayed. Layers S2, S5, S6 and underlay (S7) also of pitched reed straw, ie unbruised straw, combed to remove flag and weeds, ears cut off *c* 10 cm below ear and with straw of even length. Specimens ranging from 35 cm to 60 cm (with obvious weathering at butts). S3 similar but with ears lashed and semi-intact rather than pitched. Base coat (S6) applied butts-up, at least in sampling location. A thin underlay (S7) also applied butts-up producing a smooth surface viewed from below. Many layers probably removed during past

Table A13 Jasmine Cottage, Osmington, Dorset

Sample	Principal components	Fixings	Depth cm
S0	BW CWR, applied butts-down	spars and sways, crooks	25
S1	BW 'reed straw', combed, pitched, butts-down	spars and sways, crooks	20
S2	BW 'reed straw', combed, pitched, butts-down	spars and sways	15
S3	BW 'reed straw', combed, lashed, butts-down	spars and sways	10
S4	BW 'reed straw', combed, pitched, butts-down	spars and sways	15
S5	BW 'reed straw', combed, pitched, butts-down	sways and spars	10
S6	BW 'reed straw', combed, pitched, butts-up	sways and tarred twine, cloth	10
S7	underlay, identical to S6	clamped into place by S6	20

Figure A13.

rethatchings (according to thatcher), eg between S1 and S2, but considerable build-up remains (*c* 2.2 m at ridge). Pitch gradually increased by selective stripping of eaves and addition of ridge rolls at rethatching. External layer of modern combed wheat reed very similar in appearance to nearby house thatched with fine Norfolk water reed. All layers dressed into position after sparring in order to tighten the reed straw in its fixings and to create a uniform external finish.

Sampling background

Samples taken during full stripping of roof to replace collapsed pole rafters. Stepped series taken with help of thatcher from front (south) face to left (west) of chimney above upper purlin on east side of roof (Fig A13). Stripping/sampling difficult due to compaction of thatch, dust and weak roof timbers.

Thatch (external):
main: combed wheat reed, applied *c* 1982. Pitch: *c* 55 °.
ridge: block cut, patterned, now very decayed. Depth: *c* 2.2 m +
eaves: dressed to slope inwards, *c* 50 cm overhang, base coat course crooked to sill.
gable: base coat crooked to sill, dressed with *c* 50 cm overhang.

Samples:
MAIN COAT:
S0: external coat of combed wheat reed, specimens *c* 80 cm
S1: bread wheat reed straw, specimens *c* 65 cm, applied butts–down, butts intact but weathered, combed, ears crushed
S2: bread wheat reed straw, specimens *c* 50 cm, applied butts–down, weathered, combed, ears pitched
S3: bread wheat reed straw, specimens *c* 35 cm, applied butts–down, weathered, combed, apex lashed
S4: bread wheat reed straw, specimens *c* 45 cm, applied butts–down, weathered, combed, ears pitched
S5: bread wheat reed straw, specimens *c* 50 cm, applied butts–down, weathered, combed, ears pitched
S6: bread wheat reed straw, specimens *c* 60 cm, applied butts–up (apex weathered), combed
S7: thin underlay of bread wheat reed straw, applied butts–down, ears pitched, combed (identical to S6)

Fixings

Base coat (S6) and thin underlay (S7) fixed with tarred twine tied around battens and rafters, and occasional ties of twisted cloth rope (probably only for repairs). All subsequent layers fixed with spars and sways, mainly of split and occasional roundwood hazel. Bottom eaves and gable courses of last coat fixed to gable and wall plates with iron crooks at *c* 25 cm intervals. Eaves and gable courses fixed with mud prior to addition of wall plates. Spars and sways mostly *c* 60–80 cm.

A14 LEICESTERSHIRE (TABLE A14)

9 Post Office Lane, Lyndon
Grid reference: SK9004
Date of survey: 14th June 1996
Owner: Lyndon Estate, Edward Conant
Thatcher: Dodson brothers
Locality: 12km west of Stamford (and Fens), and immediately south of Rutland Water. An area of heavy soil, with abundant residual ridge and furrow once farmed in open fields but now enclosed and primarily pasture. Tall deciduous trees in vicinity of house.

Building description

Stone cottage built for workers at founding of Lyndon Estate in 1663. Oriented east/west. Two brick chimney stacks, one central and another on east end. Stone gables, coped at east end and outer half raised by *c* 40 cm. Wall raised *c* 1 m above ground floor ceiling height to accommodate first-floor rooms with ceilings plastered onto laths nailed to rafters. No access to roofspace. Rafters paired, coupled and pegged onto ridge beam, notched and pegged onto wooden plate fixed to centre of wall plate, and pegged to purlin at first floor ceiling height. Base coat of thatch supported on reed fleeking. Roof pitch *c* 55 °. Infill on inside of wall between rafters and top of wall of yellow clay, daub and plaster.

Table A14 9 Post Office Lane, Lyndon, Leicestershire

Main	Ridge	Other	Principal components	Fixings	Depth cm
S1			BW LS (discarded)	peg and twine	28
S2			BW straw, basal and upper, evenly crushed, ears and butts mixed	peg and twine	20
S3			BW straw, crushed, jumbled, repair	spars	15
S4			BW straw, basal and upper, crushed, ears and butts mixed	spars	20
S5			BW straw, basal and upper, crushed, ears and butts mixed	spars	15
S9			BW stubble + upper stem specimens, all crushed, jumbled	grass rope	20
S10			WR fleeking (2 forms)	clamped	3
	R1		pasture rush (*Juncus* sp.)	spars and sways	10
		S7a	BW stubble, middle stem, mostly crushed	spars and mud	20
		S7b	see S7a	spars and mud	20
S6			pasture rush (*Juncus* sp.)	grass rope.	15
S8			mix of stubble, middle and upper stem specimens, mostly crushed, jumbled	tarred twine	15

Sampling background

Contacted by M Dodson. Sampled during complete stripping in advance of refurbishment (Fig A14). Stepped series taken from section just west of east end chimney on rear face running from ridge to purlin. Special attention given to mud coursing on eaves and ridge. No access to front of roof. Few samples taken from ridge due to decay. Inside of roof just visible through fleeking. Samples dried in laboratory.

Thatch summary

Fleeking (S10) below purlin height made from small bundles of water reed stitched into a mat with grass rope, rolled onto the rafters and clamped to roof with split laths nailed to rafters. Water reed clamped directly to roof in larger bundles above purlin. Base coat (S9) of stubble straw, specimens *c* 30 cm, with rooty material and occasional taller specimens, stitched to roof through fleeking with braided grass rope. Later spar coats all of crushed and jumbled bread wheat straw. Two layers above the base coat (S4 and S5) are fixed with spars only, as is the repair stob (S3) filling rodent gulley above S4. Top coats are stitched into place with hempen rope (S2) and plastic binder twine (S1) twisted at *c* 40 cm intervals around straight wooden peg-spars, pointed at one end with flat tops. Rush layer (S6) discovered in centre of roof, and continues over ridge above base coat in this section. This layer not present in main sampling area and overlies a base coat of crushed and jumbled bread wheat

Figure A14.

straw (S8) rather than the stubble base coat (S9). Early ridge layers sealed with thick (up to 7 cm) layers clay-mud, but straw between these layers very decayed. Ridge composed of at least six top layers of (mainly pegged) straw, crushed and jumbled, above about six layers of straw/mud (ie straw pegged into mud layer beneath it). Pasture rush noted on at least one lower ridge layer (R1). Total depth of ridge *c* 140 cm, much thicker than at eaves due to disproportionate stripping and regular re-ridging. Eaves very solid and built up of overlapping layers of mud and straw as on ridge: wall top + mud + coarse stubble + mud + stubble fixed with split willow sways nailed to rafters (and with occasional spar). Thatch on gable end bedded into gable gap and covered by mortar flashing to seal joint.

Interpretation

Late seventeenth-century cottage, well-built and well thatched with base coat of stubble straw over water reed fleeking. Stubble also used on eaves and ridge in combination with mud to provide a solid anchor for overlying spar coats. Presence of stubble indicates reaping high on stem, and in many samples is mixed with longer straw. Cottage is surrounded by medieval ridge and furrow open fields (now enclosed pasture). More general straw samples are poorly drawn and contain abundant flag leaf, short fragmented straw and crop weeds. Upper layers were almost certainly threshed by machine, and many other layers have probably been lost through stripping. The base coat of stubble (unweathered) is unlikely to have been used as an external coat and was probably applied at the same time as the crushed and jumbled straw layer applied above it. Top two layers and at least the top six ridge layers were all fixed with twine and flat topped spar-pegs. This method was commonly used in thatching ricks, but was undoubtedly common on house roofs in the past as well. The top coat, pegged with pink plastic binder twine, was applied *c* 1970. The gradual thickening of the thatch on the ridge has gradually raised the effective pitch of the roof by at least *c* 5 °, but houses in this area are already quite steeply pitched at 55 °. A layer of rush (S6) over a base coat of crushed and jumbled bread wheat straw in the centre of roof indicates stripping back to timbers in this section, followed by patching and spar coating other materials (perhaps to bring this area back to level). Presence of elm leaves in S3 implies autumn rethatching.

Thatch (external):

main: bread wheat long straw, very decayed on south (rear) face. Much less worn on front face. Pitch: *c* 60 °.

ridge: straw, raised, diamented, very decayed, spars now standing *c* 20 cm free of surface, total depth: *c* 150 cm

eaves: cut flat, rear (decayed), front with *c* 30 cm and four visible layers, double row of liggers.

gables: thatch slotted into gable gap, with mortar flashing extending over thatch.

Samples:

MAIN COAT:

S1: external coat of modern bread wheat long straw, very evenly crushed, ears and butts mixed, applied *c* 1974. Discarded due to rotting.

S2: bread wheat straw, specimens *c* 50 cm, basal and upper stem, all very crushed over entire stem, ears mostly intact, ears and butts evenly mixed. Wheat variety lax-eared, reddish-chaffed. Much flag leaf and debris but no weed.

S3: bread wheat straw, specimens *c* 30 cm, more crushed than L2 over entire stem and with many broken specimens. Fills gulley leading to rodent's nest in L4, weathered so applied as repair prior to S2. Moderate flag leaf and no weed. Straw congealed with mould and decay. Sample contains abundant leaves of wych elm (*Ulmus glabra*).

S4: bread wheat straw, specimens *c* 30cm, crushed with ears and butts evenly mixed. Layer worn forming a gulley in sample area.

S5: bread wheat straw, specimens *c* 45 cm, well preserved, crushed over entire stem, moderate flag leaf and no weed.

S9: base coat of bread wheat straw, mostly coarse basal specimens (stubble) *c* 30 cm, occasional to 50 cm, very short or with roots, with angled cuts on butts but mixed with finer upper stem material. Basal specimens mostly very crushed, some at both ends, but mostly cut/broken. Few ears and very occasional stripped rachis. Few weeds (occasional thistle (*Cirsium* sp.). Root specimens often *c* 20 cm but to 56 cm (root/cut). Non-root specimens taller (eg 39 cm and 52 cm) and usually cut/cut). Base coat at sampling point overlies 7a/b on eaves.

S10: fleeking of water reed stitched into a mat, specimens *c* 2–2.5 m, plumes intact, stems very hard, sharp butts.

Ridge samples

R1: pasture rush (*Juncus* cf *effusus*), specimens *c* 35 cm, decayed, mixed with bunches of grass (Gramineae indet) and often folded into knuckles due to being the uppermost course at ridge.

Eaves samples

S7a: bread wheat stubble, specimens *c* 45 cm, mostly from middle stem, mostly crushed and with few ears or upper stem specimens. Mostly cut/crushed but occasional cut/cut. Occasional with roots *c* 25 cm,

but ranging from 8–28 cm and many with solid stems. Moderate flag leaf and little weed. Sample also contains leaves of oak. Similar to S9.

S7b: bread wheat stubble (identical to S7a)

S7c: mud sample from eaves

SECOND SERIES (WEST OF SERIES 1)

S6: pasture rush (*Juncus* cf *effusus*), specimens *c* 35 cm (but with many specimens broken), coarse, brown, pithy, with tufted lateral flower heads. Sample relatively pure but with grass (Gramineae) and occasional minor spp. Sample knuckled for use as a repair stob (?). Sample taken from east (right) of central chimney stack, but this layer not present in main section.

S8: bread wheat straw, mixture of short upper, middle and bottom specimens *c* 30 cm with few ears. Occasional fine basal specimens *c* 20–25 cm. Specimens mostly cut/flailed and occasional cut/cut, and many with distinct blow marks. Little weed. S8 overlies base coat S9 and beneath rush layer S6.

Fixings:

Main coat

S1: external coat stitched into place with modern (pink) nylon binder twine twisted around end of straight roundwood pegs, *c* 30 cm, sharpened to three faces on internal point and cut flat externally.

S2: two-ply hempen-type rope twisted twice around a straight peg as in L1. Some pegs of split hazel, very thin and very long, with two or three facet points and flat tops.

S3: repair stob fixed with split hazel spars.

S4: split hazel or willow spars.

S5: long, split hazel spars, *c* 60 cm, with two or three facets.

S9: base coat fixed with twisted, three-ply grass rope.

S10: water reed fleeking. Lower section of roof is formed by bunches of five to six stems stitched horizontally into a mat with grass rope, the mat then clamped to roof with split laths nailed (vertically) to every second rafter. Occasional tying with braided grass rope. On upper section of roof (above purlin) the water reed is clamped to rafters in this same manner but in bunches of 10–15 stems rather than as a stitched mat.

Eaves samples

S7b: layer of stubble straw, *c* 15 cm thick, bedded onto mud on top of wall. This layer then covered by *c* 5–8 cm of mud and then by stubble sample S7a.

S7a: layer of stubble straw identical to S7b above, bedded onto mud overlying S7a at eaves, and fixed with a further layer of mud, occasional split hazel spars, but primarily with split (willow?) sways, *c* 5 cm diameter, shaved flat at their extremities where they are nailed to rafters.

SECOND SERIES

S6: layer of pasture rush tied to rafters with twisted and braided grass rope (identical to fixings of water reed mat fleeking).

S8:　straw, crushed and jumbled, fixed with hempen twine (not tarred).

A15 NORTHAMPTONSHIRE (TABLE A15)

Tanglewood Cottage, 24 High Street, Great Doddington
Grid reference: SP883648
Date of survey: 24ᵗʰ April 1995
Conservation Officer: Michel Kerrou
Thatcher: Roger Scanlon.
Locality: cottage in village of Great Doddington, 4km south of Wellingborough and 0.5km from the River Nene. Soils in area are of modern heavy clay, with pockets of poorly-drained and marshy land common in district. A large conifer overhangs east gable. West gable adjoins Fuschia Cottage. Building oriented south-west/north-east with front facing south-south-east (taken as east/west and south below). Disused nineteenth-century brick pits now filled with water 0.5km south across fields.

Building description

Building recorded by the Royal Commission on the Historical Monuments of England in July 1995. Former open hall, fifteenth-century, with cruck-framed roof of three bays and stone walls. Much altered in seventeenth century with the addition of a north-west extension to rear (perhaps to replace a service wing of the open hall on site of Fuschia Cottage). Front entrance opens to a cross passage, originally with open hall on west and parlour on

east. Hall initially open to thatch, with light provided by a small window in upper wall of east gable. Floor (over parlour and hall), chimney stacks (on west and east gables) and staircase (on west gable) inserted in early seventeenth century. Front and rear walls also raised, east gable window blocked and front dormer windows also inserted at this time to create living space on first floor. Roof of three irregular bays (4.1 m / 3.5 m / 2.2 m west/east) defined by trusses supporting 12 cm x 8 cm sawn purlins. Original rafters both squared and of sawn poles, *c* 12–15 cm², heavily blackened and soot encrusted. Many common rafters replaced by round staves when front and rear walls raised. Reed(?) and plaster ceiling formerly nailed to top of purlin and rafters, but replaced by existing reed and plaster ceiling in nineteenth century. Ridge purlin (and east chimney stack) collapsed *c* 1.0 m from inner face of east gable wall in late nineteenth century. This area is now braced by posts inserted below the area of collapse on both ground and first floors. Broken purlin collapsed onto ceiling joists and thatch was used to bridge the gap and raise this area back to ridge height. Additional softwood support joists in roofspace also inserted in nineteenth century. Feet of rafters rest on inner face of wall plate and top of wall covered with mud which seals base coat of stubble to eaves. Western-most roof truss has a closed collar (blackened on both sides). Main west truss and three pairs of rafters adjacent to it (towards east) have pegs *c* 46 cm below ridge that probably mark the position of a former louvre (also noted by disturbance of smoke-blackened thatch). Smoke-blackened fleeking of woven water reed (used in place of battens) survives above upper purlin in central roof bay on front and rear faces, and on portions of front faces of west and east bays. Mats of horizontal water reed, unblackened and nailed to top of rafters with riven laths, used as repair on front face of west bay and on lower sections of roof below purlin height (over the rafters that were inserted when front and rear walls were raised and dormers inserted in seventeenth century). Fleeking mostly cleared from east roof bay and replaced with split pole battens and laths.

Sampling background

Building noted during Northamptonshire search for potential examples of medieval smoke-blackened thatch. Tanglewood Cottage and Fuschia Cottage listed as early eighteenth century, but identified as medieval by Michel Kerrou. Repair to east section of roof provided opportunity for multi-layer sampling of all existing coats and ridge. Small samples taken of smoke-blackened reed fleeking and base coat from within roof space in middle bay at two locations where thatch previously disturbed and accessible. East bay to be stripped above upper purlin for insertion of new ridge purlin and repair of rafters. External transverse section revealed through ridge *c* 2 m from inside of east gable (above truss defining start of east roof bay. Stepped section also revealed from ridge section down north face of roof to eaves. Samples taken rapidly with the assistance of R Scanlon and Dr D de Moulins.

Table A15 Tanglewood Cottage, 24 High Street, Great Doddington, Northamptonshire

Main	Other	Principal components	Fixings
new		BW 'LS', straw uncrushed, ears and butts mixed	spars and sways
MC1		BW straw, crushed, ears and butts mixed	spars and sways
MC2		BW reed-straw, ears and butts mixed	spars and sways
MC3		BW straw, crushed, ears and butts mixed	spars
MC4		BW straw, crushed, degraded	spars
MC5		BW straw, crushed, degraded	spars
MC6		BW straw, crushed, basal and upper specimens, mixed ears and butts	spars
MC7		BW straw, mostly basal, occasional upper	twisted saplings, dethorned blackberry stems
MC8		fleeking, WR	clamped to rafters with split oak laths
MC9a/b		stubble straw, mostly barley	mud, occasional spars
	MC10	SBT, barley straw, threshing waste	saplings, clamped by overlying layer
	MC11	SBT, fleeking of WR (woven and mats)	clamped, saplings
	MC12	BW LS, ears and butts mixed	saplings
	RBC1	BW stubble, crushed, mixed ears and butts	saplings

Thatch summary

Former open hall, much rebuilt in seventeenth century, with a multi-layered roof of straw and smoke blackened thatch surviving above first floor ceiling. Base coat of heavily smoke-blackened barley straw, reaped, raked and threshed. Most specimens crushed and some with roots. Abundant weeds. Original base coat tied to rafters, over a fleeking of water reed woven in situ, with wooden saplings, stems of blackberry (*Rubus* sp.) and two-ply grass rope. This fleeking repaired at various points with later (seventeenth century?) fleeking stitched horizontally into mats with grass rope prior to use and clamped to rafters with riven oak laths. Reed mats also used as fleeking on lower sections of roof over rafters inserted in seventeenth century when walls raised and dormers inserted. This rebuilding (probably coeval with insertion of a floor over the open hall and parlour and chimney stacks on west gable) reduced the pitch of the rafters on lower roof section from *c* 55 ° to 40 °− 45 °. This significantly reduced the effectiveness of the thatched roof, encouraging regular stripping of eaves and the addition of extra thatch at ridge at rethatching. Most main coat layers are of bread wheat straw, crushed, mixed ears and butts and fixed with spars or spars and sways of split hazel or willow. Several middle ridge layers are fixed with mud which provided an anchor for spars fixing an overlying coat (Fig A15). Mud ridges are not uncommon on older roofs in this area (R Scanlon). Most ridge layers either missing or too

decayed for analysis, and detailed excavation not possible due the rescue nature of this excavation. Ridge purlin and gable chimney stack in east bay collapsed onto ceiling of first floor in nineteenth century. The gap created was filled by thatch (to a depth of *c* 1.6 m) to reestablish previous ridge height. The first course of barley stubble on north eaves is fixed to wall top with mud, followed by a second layer of mud, a second coat of barley stubble, and by a third layer of wheat stubble (MC7) that was sparred into the underlying eaves layers while mud was still wet. MC7 probably forms the base coat over most of the lower section of the roof, and similar material was also revealed as a base coat on ridge of east bay (RBC1). This stubble must have been cut from a crop reaped at *c* 60 cm above ground level, and this tall stubble was subsequently scythed at *c* 15 cm above ground level to produce a *c* 35−40 cm haulm that was raked for use as thatch. Variation in stubble height between samples might suggest the collection of tall stubble from ridges and shorter stubble from the furrows of ridge and furrowed fields.

Thatch (external):

main: top coat of very decayed bread wheat long straw. Pitch: *c* 50 °. Depth variable but *c* 60 cm.

ridge: straw, very decayed, flush, diamented. Depth: *c* 100 cm.

eaves: decayed, shallow overhang (*c* 25 cm), liggered, base coat sealed to wall top with mud and short spars.

gables: decayed, rolled and liggered.

Samples:

Main coat:

New: bread wheat long straw, specimens *c* 85 cm, ears and butts mixed, straw mostly undamaged. Straw grown in Hertfordshire (variety *Squareheads Master*).

MC1:   external coat of bread wheat straw, crushed, mixed ears and butts, very decayed, applied *c* 1974.

MC2:   bread wheat straw, specimens *c* 50 cm and occasionally shorter, mostly uniform, butts and ears mixed and uncrushed. Layer moist and mouldy.

MC3:   bread wheat straw, specimens *c* 25 cm, uniform, very crushed over entire stem, mixed ears and butts and poorly preserved. Abundant weed (especially dock *Rumex* sp.).

MC4:   bread wheat straw, crushed, degraded, fragmented and with few surviving ears.

MC5:   bread wheat straw, very degraded. This layer visibly feathered beginning at *c* 50 cm from eaves by stripping.

MC6:   bread wheat straw, specimens *c* 40 cm and occasional to 60 cm (and then folded), mostly with crushed internodes but intact nodes. Sample contains both upper and lower stem specimens. Wheat variety reddish chaffed. Abundant weeds (especially dock *Rumex* sp, thistle *Cirsium* sp and fine grasses Gramineae) and one stem of broad bean *Viciafaba*. Layer feathered towards eaves.

Figure A15.

MC7: straw, mostly bread wheat with occasional barley, composed mostly of short basal specimens but occasional longer, mostly well preserved but with some weathering. Depth *c* 15–30 cm.

MC8: fleeking of water reed, not smoke-blackened, horizontal bunches of three to four stems stitched into a mat with grass rope prior to use on roof. Fleeking visible from within roofspace and revealed at base of step trench on eaves of north face. Specimens *c* 1.4–1.8 m with occasional flower heads.

MC9: coarse straw of two-row barley, mostly basal specimens *c* 30 cm, but also including ears (some with intact grain and awns). (a/b) Probably threshing waste or rakings. Abundant weeds (especially Brassicaceae and grasses Gramineae). Very occasional ears of rye and bread wheat.

OTHER SAMPLES:

MC10: crushed straw, heavily smoke-blackened, sampled from behind fleeking in central bay. Sample is of pure, long-eared, two-row barley with occasional hulled grains surviving still attached to rachis. Only 5% of sample is of short stubble with roots and adhering mud (ie raked?). Specimens mostly *c* 15–20 cm and crushed. Numerous and diverse range of arable crop weeds (Brassicaceae, dock *Rumex* sp, corn marigold *Chrysanthemum* sp, mayweed *Anthemis* sp, grasses Gramineae, etc). One rachis fragment of bread wheat.

MC11: smoke-blackened fleeking of water reed, woven in situ, mostly of coarse lower stems *c* 1.6 m, but with occasional flower heads.

MC12: base coat of bread wheat straw, crushed, mixed ears and butts, sampled in east roof bay.

RIDGE:

Minimum of 14 layers of straw on ridge at point of sampling, including four layers of ridge rolls (R2, R5, R10 and R12). Several principal and ridge roll layers also undoubtedly stripped during past re-ridging and re-thatching. Surviving samples generally of crushed straw mixed ears and butts. Most ridge layers wrapped over and probably fixed flush. Spars and sways of both split and roundwood hazel and willow. Spar and sway fragments occur throughout main coat and ridge sections. At least three layers of clay-mud (with inclusions of stone and shell) of varying thickness survive beneath R7 and R13, most likely applied under new main coat (or at re-ridging) to provide an anchor for spars fixing new outer ridge coat.

RBC1: base coat of coarse bread wheat stubble on north side *c* 1.5 m below ridge near east chimney stack. Occasional upper stem specimens carrying awnless ears with hairy chaff, but sample mostly of basal stem specimens *c* 35–40 cm, cut at both ends and uncrushed. Many specimens with roots and adhering mud, *c* 15–20 cm and with five to six stems bases/plant. Abundant weeds (especially grass), flag leaf, short broken straws

and mud together forming very congealed bundles *c* 50–55 cm. Sample probably derived from a crop reaped *c* 50–60 cm above ground level that left a tall stubble that was scythed 15–20 cm above ground level and raked for use as thatch.

Fixings:

New: split hazel spars and sways

MC1: spars and sways

MC2: spars and sway, spars cf willow, *c* 40 cm, thinned at centre, with four-faced points.

MC3: spars, *c* 20 cm, roundwood, three-faced, very weathered

MC4: spars, *c* 30 cm, four-faced point

MC5: spars. Split cf hazel.

MC6: spars. Roundwood cf hazel.

MC7: stubble tied with twisted saplings of at least two spp (willow and indet). Occasional ties of twisted, dethorned blackberry (original fixing of stubble base coat).

MC8: original water reed fleeking above upper purlin woven in situ and held in place by base coat of smoke-blackened thatch barley stubble. Fleeking woven in simple cross-plait with vertical bunches of 15–20 stems and horizontal bunches of 8–12 stems. Replacement fleeking below purlin (probably applied in seventeenth century when front and rear walls raised and new rafters inserted) also of reed stitched (horizontally) into mats with grass rope, and clamped to rafters with riven oak laths nailed to rafters. Mats used as repair in smoke-blackened sections of roofspace are tied to rafters with two-ply grass rope. Grass and straw rope (bread wheat) also used for fixing new base coat.

MC9: eaves formed by three layers of stubble straw fixed with mud and spars. First layer (MC9a) is bedded onto *c* 10 cm of grey clay-mud which sits on top outer half of stone wall abutting feet of inserted rafters. This is sealed by a second layer of clay-mud, *c* 10 cm thick, applied so as to overlap feet of rafters and first stubble layer. A second layer of stubble MC9b) is bedded onto this second layer of mud. These base coats are covered by another layer of stubble straw (MC7) which was sparred onto the eaves coats while the underlying mud was still wet. This layer forms the base coat over most of the roof to purlin height. Eaves spars short, *c* 20–25 cm, of split hazel, flattened and mostly with three-faced points. Occasional 15–18 cm metal spikes are nailed through split pole sways to clamp base and first coat to rafters.

Base coat in east section is tied to battens and rafters with twisted saplings (willow?). Unblackened split hazel spars pierce roofspace in areas of smoke-blackening.

A16 OXFORDSHIRE (TABLE A16)

Kate's Cottage, (formerly Dilkush Cottage), High Street, South
 Stoke
Grid reference: SU6084
Date of survey: 16ᵗʰ October 1994
Owner: T and I Haslam
Thatcher: Kit Davis.
Locality: fronting road in village of South Stoke, 10 km north
 west of Reading. House adjacent to lane leading to Little
 House (listed). Formerly in Berkshire. House in village set
 amid light and heavy arable fields, 1 km from River Thames.

Building description

Large eighteenth-century timber-framed cottage, half-
hipped, front wall raised with three inserted dormers.
Oriented east/west. Two brick chimney stacks. Roof
timbers pitched *c* 50 °. Large rafters of sawn, straight,
quality timber, *c* 12–15 cm x 5 cm, nailed to wooden
plate at eaves. Rear rafters evenly spaced at *c* 30 cm
between mid-points, overshooting plate by *c* 30 cm.
Rafters support a lath and plaster ceiling on first floor
below central purlin, both back and front. Front rafters of
rough sawn poles, similar but a little coarser than rear
rafters. Rafters pegged to purlins. Rear battens of riven
laths, *c* 60–70 cm long, 5–8 cm x 1.5–2 cm, spanning two
rafters with *c* 10 cm overhangs and sawn ends. Front
battens of similar riven oak, but with occasional batten
almost 4 cm x 4 cm. Battens staggered horizontally and
nailed. Battens probably split from sawn planks. Battens
on front face similar, but a little longer. Roofspace
penetrated by vines of ivy which must have colonized
thatch on west end.

Sampling background

Contacted by thatcher. Stripping of rear centre to join
roof of new extension to main roof. Bulk of section
removed prior to visit and access to exposed section limited.
Samples taken from section on rear (north) face exposed at
junction of roof and new extension, beneath ridge point
of western-most chimney. No access to ridge layers.

*Table A16 Kate's Cottage, (formerly Dilkush Cottage), High Street,
South Stoke, Oxfordshire*

Samples	Principal components	Fixings
S1	BW CWR	spars and sways
S2	BW CWR	spars and sways
S3	BW straw, short, crushed, ears and butts mixed	spars and sways
S4	BW straw, short, crushed, ears and butts mixed	spars and sways
S5	BW straw, short, cut high, crushed, ears and butts mixed	spars and sways
S6	BW straw, short, crushed, ears and butts mixed	spars and sways
S7	BW straw, short, crushed, butts-down	spars and sways
S8	BW straw, basal and upper (apex crushed), ears and butts mixed	branched saplings

Thatch summary

Multi-layered roof of *c* 10 layers of bread wheat long
straw, with top two coats of modern combed wheat reed.
Present ridge raised, block-cut and diamonded. Main
coat at rear pitched *c* 55 °, but half-hip steeper at *c* 65 °–
70 °. Significant overhang at eaves and gable-eaves. No
external liggering except on ridge. Entire thatch covered
with galvanized wire. Penultimate coat also of modern
combed wheat reed. Minimum seven layers sampled
above base coat, all fixed with spars and sways. Samples
S3–S8 (base coat) of threshed bread wheat long straw,
cleaned to variable degrees and occasional containing
very short and crushed straw, flag leaf and weeds. Ears and
butts evenly mixed in most layers, but S7 with straw
crushed but with butts primarily together and down on
roof. Possible evidence of reaping high on stem (S5). Base
coat (S8) probably apex-threshed. Clear tradition of
threshed, jumbled, fragmented and poorly cleaned bread
wheat long straw, but with occasional evidence of well-
drawn, butts-together long straw in early levels.

Thatch (external):
main: combed wheat reed applied in 1991 by K Davis.
 External pitch: *c* 55 °. Thatch swept down between dormers to top of raised wall flush with
 base of dormers. Depth: *c* 90 cm.
ridge: straw (combed wheat reed?), raised and scalloped, diamented. Total depth: *c* 130 cm. (estimate).
eaves: dressed flat with slight inward slant. Overhang of
 c 70 cm.
gables: half-hipped and steeply pitched, *c* 65 ° no liggers
 at eaves or gable, dressed flat.

Samples:
MAIN COAT:
S1: external coat of combed wheat reed applied by K
 Davis in 1991. Specimens *c* 90–100 cm, cut beneath
 third node, butts slightly weathered. Fixed with
 split hazel spars and sways. Wheat variety *Maris
 Widgeon*.
S2: combed wheat reed applied by Thatching Advisory
 Service in late 1970s. Specimens *c* 60–70 cm,
 weathered, butts cut at angles (sheared on roof?).
S3: bread wheat straw, specimens *c* 55 cm when applied
 (but drawn into a longer bundle), crushed, mixed
 evenly ears and butts evenly mixed.
S4: bread wheat straw, specimens *c*40cm when applied,
 very crushed with occasional distinctive blow marks
 and mixed ears and butts.
S5: bread wheat straw, specimens *c* 30 cm and weathered (but short even when applied), and probably
 cut high on stem, very crushed and broken, ears and
 butts mixed.
S6: bread wheat straw, specimens *c* 35 cm when applied, crushed and broken, ears and butts mixed and
 with much flag leaf and weeds.

Figure A16.

S7:   bread wheat straw, specimens *c* 25 cm and very weathered, crushed, mostly butts-together and applied butts-down.

S8:   base coat of bread wheat straw, specimens *c* 35 cm (weathered), coarse basal and finer upper stem specimens, upper specimens very crushed mostly at apex and sample evenly mixed ears and butts. Much flag leaf and very short broken stem specimens (Fig A16).

Several layers probably missed during sampling (especially between S5 and S7). Ridge layers not accessible.

Fixings:

Main coat

S1–S7: sparred and swayed. Lower levels with occasional roundwood sways. Upper layer sways of split hazel. Spars generally of split hazel (and occasional willow) of variable lengths.

S8:   base coat, front and back, tied with branched saplings (cf willow and other spp) of variable diameter and roundwood sways. Tied around rafters at every second batten. Saplings sealed by plaster of first floor ceiling (rear face).

A17 OXFORDSHIRE (TABLE A17)

cart shed, The Old Manor, Stanton St John, OX33 1HF
Grid reference: SP5709
Date of survey: 2nd February 1996
Owner: Dr N and E Gilmour
Conservation Officer: Nick Dogget, South Oxfordshire District Council
Locality: six-bay cart shed with roof of solid thatch adjacent to Manor House in Stanton St John village, 8 km north east of Oxford city centre. An outbuilding of Manor Farm at the principal road junction in the centre of Stanton village, standing 25 m south-east of Manor House with its east (rear) face forming the boundary wall of the property. Village is 2 km from south edge of Otmoor, a shallow, poorly-drained alluvial basin formed by seasonal flooding of the river Ray. Otmoor was drained (unsuccessfully) by government directive in 1836, and now contains several feet of alluvial deposits over a base of Oxford clay. It carries no peat deposits or large stands of water reed, although the historical evidence suggests that it held a mosaic of wetland habitats including fen in the early nineteenth century. Traditionally, it was managed for hay and osiers (Salix spp), and supported large numbers of sheep, cattle and wildfowl. Stanton village stands on rising

Table A17 cart shed, The Old Manor, Stanton St John, Oxfordshire

Main	Ridge	Principal components	Fixings	Depth cm (c)
	1	BW, CWR	spar and ligger	10
	2	BW straw, crushed, ears and butts mixed	plastictwine /spar	15
	3	BW reed-straw, uncrushed	n.r.	5
4		BW, CWR, uncrushed, butts-down	spar and sway, eaves tied	20
	5	BW reed-straw, uncrushed, ears and butts mixed ?	n.r.	5
	6	BW straw, decayed, crushed ?	n.r.	10
7		BW straw, crushed, mixed but mostly butts-down	spar and sway	15
7a		BW straw, crushed, ears and butts mixed	'stob' repair over 8	–
8		BW straw, crushed, ears and butts mixed	spar and sway	15
	9	BW straw, crushed, ears and butts mixed	spar and ligger	5
10		BW straw, crushed, ears and butts mixed	spar and sway	15
11		faggot of hawthorn brushwood	hazel band	30
12		faggot of gorse	hazel and gorse bands	150

ground at c 90 m ASL, and village lands include large stands of sandy and stony ground that have traditionally been used for rough grazing. Other arable fields and meadow are situated on moderately well-drained Oxford clay suited to wheat production. Common fields were largely enclosed by the fifteenth century and remaining holdings consolidated by Act of Parliament in 1778. Lands of Manor Farm consolidated by 1620 and included a large block of meadow, three fields worked in rotation and at least two large fields used for rough grazing (and as a source of gorse fuel by commoners).

Building description

Grade II★ listed cart shed of simple rectilinear form with three rubble stone walls, an open (west facing) front and a full-hipped thatched roof. It does not appear on the enclosure map of 1777 but is visible on maps of 1851 and 1856. Dendrochronological dating indicates that the building timber was felled in the spring of 1801 (Dan Miles, pers comm). Oriented north-east/south-west (taken here as north/south). Six bays with roof of solid thatch (ie no rafters). East/west cross beams (mostly of oak and elm *Ulmus* sp) notched into top of stone walls and overlain by a wooden plate, *c* 15 cm x 25 cm, mostly decayed, resting on outer half of stone walls (largely decayed on east wall) and overlying similar plate on south wall. Cross-beams rest on five timber posts supporting front beam on open face and five central posts. Timber posts stand on pyramidal staddle bases. Northern bay 6 partitioned from remaining open bays. Base of roof composed of overlapping cross-tiers of wood of increasingly small diameter, equally of oak *Quercus* sp., elm, ash *Fraxinus* sp. and occasional larch *Larix* sp., covered with a primitive roof

Figure A17.

of solid thatch. Description below refers primarily to northernmost bay 6 recorded during dismantling (Fig A17).

First tier of about 10 heavy poles spanning individual bays from cross-beam to cross beam are of *c* 25 cm x 20 cm diameter. Front west spars of roughly squared/sawn split timber, reducing to *c* 15–20 cm diameter round poles towards back east face. First tier of bays 1–5 (collapsed) composed of *c* 15–20 cm diameter roundwood poles, roughly squared. Last spar in bay 6 adjacent to east wall *c* 25 cm x 20 cm diameter Some north/south spars are fluted to fit onto north end plate, and most are covered with nails with occasional dowel holes (ie some are from reused timber). Spars have *c* 40 cm gaps between them, with ends flush with outside face of walls. Second tier of bay 6 smaller diameter spars of debarked roundwood, 10–12 cm diameter, running east/west (front/back) over three to four spars with *c* 20–30 cm gaps towards north end of first bay, but more closely spaced in groups of two or three towards south end. Butt end of spar towards open face, with branched end towards centre of bay. Butts also aligned on back wall with branched ends of spar towards core of roof. First spar of second tier aligned with north wall plate. Second tier spars in collapsed bays 2–6 of small *c* 4–6 cm diameter roundwood or absent. Third tier of bay 6 composed of a mixture of *c* 8–10cm diameter roundwood spars and 4–6 cm branches placed roughly north/south with thicker butt ends mostly aligned with bay cross-beams or north wall (with branched ends clumped towards centre of bay). Occasional heavy branching present on larger spars, but most of these straight, debarked and solid. Butts of branches or spars never overhang outside face of walls. Final appearance after excavation is of a coarse, uneven net pattern with occasional gaps in support. This base coat would have been unstable and unruly until the base coat of gorse faggots was applied. General suggestion is that mature trees were cut to purpose, and that construction began at north end in bay 6, with less wood being used in south bays without loss of support strength.

Sampling background

Structure and thatch long in need of repair. Thatch examined in July 1994 and assessed with Peter Brockett in October 1994. Upgraded to II* status due to its rare thatch type in 1995. Five south bays collapsed and dismantled without recording in November/December 1995. Rescue samples taken from straw overcoats, gorse and brushwood core in February 1996. Structure of bays 1–5 similar to bay 6, although with less heavy support base. Basic recording of bay 6 undertaken with the assistance of Dr A Pydyn, N K German and Dr N Gilmour. Series of straw samples taken from *c* 50 cm west of central axis and *c* 150 cm north of tie beam forming fifth and sixth bays. Most straw layers well preserved, but with significant layers of decay on surface and between L3 and L4 (especially on east face) and L4 and L5. Significant section of long-standing, but consolidated, decay in west corner of gorse core immediately beneath external coat. Other localized patches of decay in south section of cart shed surveyed in 1994 but destroyed before full recording. Bottom layer of gorse moderately mildewed, and core samples very brittle and often with broken bands. Most gorse and brushwood samples discarded due to lack of storage facilities. Faggots not suitable for re-use in new structure due to being very brittle, degraded and difficult to work with. Original thatch now entirely destroyed. Stone walls consolidated in 1996. New timber-framed roof built and thatched with water reed (with traditional local ridge design) in January/February 1997.

Thatch summary

Solid thatch roof of gorse faggots stacked into a flat-topped pyramidal shape, capped by bundles of hawthorn and over-coated with several layers of long straw and an external coat of combed wheat reed. The roof is supported on three tiers of spars and brushwood held in place by large tie beams crossing from the open front (west) face of the cart shed to the rear east face. Gorse dry and largely well preserved, but very brittle, spiny and powdery (mildew) throughout. Composed of about six overlapping layers of faggots, each *c* 140 cm x 70 cm x 30 cm and 10 kg, placed so as to overlay the two faggots beneath it. Each faggot tied with simple twisted stem of hazel or gorse, but many now broken. Stacked faggots interbedded naturally in a solid core without additional fixings or timber. North slope of gorse core pitched at *c* 45 ° on north hip, and *c* 36 ° on east and west faces. Smaller bunches of gorse used as infill to create flat surfaces on west, north and east faces. Gorse core capped by three rows of hawthorn faggots, overlapped and staggered to form a north/south ridge underlying the first layer of straw thatch. Total height of gorse and hawthorn *c* 1.9 m.

Total height of straw thatch above hawthorn *c* 1.4 m. Minimum four main coat layers of straw thatch survive beneath existing main coat of combed wheat reed (L7, L8 and L10), all truncated by rethatching except for sections of L10. Former ridge layers also survive but are usually very decayed and fragmentary. Layers 5–10 probably applied in early nineteenth century as core of straw thatch was required to raise the ridge above the gorse/brushwood to bring the pitch to a (shallow) working level of *c* 40 °. The ridge has crept westwards toward open face of cart shed gradually so that east face (at *c* 37 °) is a little flatter than the west face (*c* 42 °) reducing the efficiency of rainwater runoff. Change to shallower pitch also apparent on N hip at junction of gorse core and straw over-thatch. A higher rate of water infiltration, combined with a greater exposure to sunshine, probably led to faster decay on this east face over recent decades. Large section of inactive decay revealed in north-west corner of bay 6 during dismantling beneath two external layers of straw. This section extended *c* 1.0 m towards gorse core almost completely degraded into dry compost and insect frass, but firm enough to hold spars of external main coat L4. Building hipped at both ends. North eaves originally not far surpassing outer face of wall, but later extended by insertion of wooden stakes and a horizontal cross-pole to form a firm support base for a new lower course of straw thatch. Stakes *c* 12 cm x 8 cm and 1.8 m long, of sawn timber sharpened to long tapered point on south inserted end and cut flat on north tip. North-west stake has dowel hole *c* 15 cm from tip. Stake inserted at shallow angle to *c* 80 cm inside inner face of north wall, with *c* 8 cm diameter cross-pole nailed onto stake from above and standing *c* 20 cm free of north-west corner wall. Three staves in north-east half of *c* 8 cm diameter roundwood inserted more deeply into gorse core and with straw between wall plate and stave. Cross-pole surpasses outer face of wall by *c* 15 cm so that north hip end is rounded, and stands above and beyond the north-west corner but is flush with north-east corner. This stave is underlain by *c* 20 cm of gorse. Three recoats of straw visible above inserted cross-pole of north hip producing a *c* 50 cm overhang at widest point. Underlayers not visible on south hip surveyed in 1994.

Roof in desperate need of rethatching by early 1994 due to general weathering, degraded ridge coat, severe gulleying on east face, patches of subsidence and a long-standing hole in the south-east corner sprouting a small elder tree (*Sambucus nigra*) and a significant weed flora. Gorse core intact, however, as it is very resistant to decay: unlike a normal straw roof, the water penetrating through straw overcoats dripped through the open textured gorse onto earthen floor below. Repair to the thatch required at this time was largely superficial, but further decay to timber sub-structure and straw overcoats continued until early 1996.

Thatch (external):

main:	combed wheat reed applied early 1980s, now very decayed and gulleyed with occasional subsidence. Large *c* 1 m x 2 m hole on south-east face. No external liggering. Pitch: *c* 37 ° (east), *c* 42 ° (west) and *c* 45 ° (north hip). Heavily encrusted with lichen and algae.

ridge:	straw, raised, diamented, knotted twist ridge now degraded.

eaves:	full hips on north and south. Front and back stripped back near to surface of gorse at last rethatching. Change in level of west face due to change in elevation of support sill. Overhang of *c* 40–50 cm on east, south and west eaves, and from 50–60 cm on north hip, with reed dressed into place. Gorse not visible. Hipped ends extended

(above). No external liggering. Eaves course tied to spars of support structure.

Samples:

1:	decayed remains of a knotted ridge, now mostly of butt segments due to decay. Heavily encrusted with matchstick lichen.

2:	ridge roll below L1. Bread wheat straw, crushed, mixed ears and butts, now very decayed.

3:	very decayed ridge layer, bread wheat reed straw, specimens *c* 25 cm and residual butt sections not crushed.

4:	main coat of bread wheat combed wheat reed applied early 1980s. Specimens *c* 65 cm, uncrushed but decayed with two upper nodes surviving. Internodes: *c* 24:40:5 cm (weathered). Very short upper internode.

5:	partially decayed ridge layer. Bread wheat straw, specimens *c* 55 cm, mostly uncrushed, mixed ears and butts.

6:	bread wheat straw, specimens *c* 15 cm, very decayed.

7:	main coat layer of bread wheat straw, specimens *c* 50 cm, very crushed, mixed ears and butts but with mostly butts exposed. Wheat variety reddish-chaffed, lax and variable. Little weed but moderate leaf.

7a:	repair stob above layer 8. Bread wheat straw, specimens *c* 80 cm, crushed, ears and butts mixed. Wheat a reddish-chaffed variety. Abundant weed and dog leg at base of straw.

8:	bread wheat straw, specimens *c* 25 cm, very crushed, mixed ears and butts with abundant weed.

9:	decayed ridge layer of bread wheat straw, specimens now *c* 25 cm and very crushed.

10:	base coat of straw over gorse core. Bread wheat straw, specimens *c* 30–60 cm, derived from a tall crop cut *c* 12 cm below second node. Internodes: 35:22:12 cm cut. Straw relatively fine, very crushed and mixed evenly ears and butts. Sample also contains undamaged coarse basal segments *c* 50 cm. Occasional specimen of pasture rush (*Juncus* sp.).

11:	straw filling depressions on surface of gorse core. Bread wheat straw, specimens *c* 40 cm, crushed, mixed ears and butts, similar to L10. Wheat variety reddish-chaffed. Abundant weed (especially poppy *Papaver rhoes* and grasses). Sample not drawn. Brushwood: small diameter branches of hawthorn (*Crataegus* sp) tied into a coarse faggot, *c* 180 cm x *c* 45 cm diameter, with a twisted hazel bond. Butts of coarsest branches mainly together, not surpassing 5 cm and mostly 2–3 cm diameter. Thorns mostly on older wood. Bundle trimmed into shape after manufacture. Band fixed midway.

GORSE

Faggots of gorse (*Ulex europaeus*), *c* 120–140 cm x 70 cm, composed of four to five bundles of branches cut from main stem, stacked with butt ends of smaller bunches overlapping at centre of faggot. Smaller bundles (=stems) *c* 65 cm. Faggot tied with twisted hazel bond. Stacking and trampling produces compact, flat, oval and tapered faggot *c* 30 cm thick weighing *c* 10 kg. Faggots require no additional fixings when stacked because spiny leaves interlock producing a stable, compact stack. Some gorse still green in colour, generally well preserved but brittle with occasional patches of mildew. Dismantling very difficult due to fragmentation of gorse, needles and soil/fungi dust. Faggots also contain significant quantities of bracken (*Pteridium aquilinum*) and grass (Gramineae), occasional stems of field bean *Vicia faba* ssp. *minor,* oak leaves (*Quercus* sp.), woody saplings in bud and miscellaneous detritus. Probable late autumn harvest.

Fixings:

1:    *c* 28–36 cm three-faced hazel spars split from a 3 cm diameter hazel rod (as one of five–six).

2:    *c* 28 cm spars halves with three-faced tines. Straw tied into rolls (dollies) with pink plastic binder twine.

3:    nr

4:    *c* 35 cm split hazel spars cut to three-faced tines.

5:    nr

6:    nr

7:    roundwood sway of cf blackthorn. Split hazel spars with *c* 65 cm and 40 cm tines cut to three-faced points.

8:    split (hazel and willow?) spars *c* 30–40 cm split thinly and sharpened to three-faced points.

9:    split (hazel?) spars *c* 35 cm with four-faced tines.

10:    bundles tied with hazel bands, occasional gorse bands, both twisted and knotted.

11:    bundles tied with hazel bands, twisted and knotted

A18 SUFFOLK (TABLE A18)

Barn, The Railway Tavern, Bacton, IP14 4HP
Grid reference: TM0567
Date of survey: 5th May 1994
Owner: Folly Ales Brewery
Contact: Andrew Stringer.
Locality: 18 km south east of Diss, 10 km from east extent of Fens. Adjacent to pub and house (abandoned due to flooding). Amid arable, light-textured soils and abundant ditches.

Table A18 barn, *The Railway Tavern*, *Bacton*, *Suffolk*

Samples	Principal components	Fixings	Depth cm
L1	WR, fine and coarse, with flower heads	sways, tarred twine, occasional twisted 'rod' rope, crooks	20
L2	BW, crushed,	spars and sways	25
L3	BW and RW, crushed, mostly butts-together	tarred twine, crooks	30
L4	BW, crushed, mostly butts-together	spars and sways, tarred twine	18
L5	BW, crushed, mixed ears and butts	spars and sways	14
L6	mostly RW, occasional BW, crushed, mixed ears and butts	tarred twine, sways	24

Building description

Abandoned barn, of early to mid nineteenth century, main section north/south with central extension to west (rear face). Walls *c* 11 m x 14 m and 3.3 m in height. Weatherboarded. Large central double doors. Modern brick and tiled extension to north. Recent timber and boarding, clay-tiled extension on north-east (rear right). Orientation: north/south with T-extension to west (rear central). Roof pitch: *c* 55 °. Exposed roof support timbers exposed, very decayed and collapsed in north section of main roof. T-extension well preserved. South-west (front right) section intact, but with very decayed thatch and ridge with numerous spars. Rafters: A-frame with well-sawn, *c* 10 cm x 10 cm coupled rafters, *c* 45 cm spacings, nailed to wall plate, purlin and ridge piece. Battens of south-east (front left): 4–8 cm diameter split poles nailed in section with straw base coat. Rough fleeking of water reed, with very occasional 2–4 cm diameter rods, in section immediately south with base coat of water reed. Straight riven-laths, evenly-spaced, nailed in west T-extension. Battens sawn, *c* 3 cm x 10 cm, on north-west (rear right) face.

Sampling background

Barn not used intensively for about 20 years. Noted from roadside and sampled on very rainy day. Spot samples taken during breaks in rainstorm. Roof very unstable, timbers very decayed, but access to ridge possible via west (back) outshot extension. Samples taken from south west face of central extension (L2–L3), north-west (rear) face of main roof just north-west of joint with (west) central extension (L4–6) and south-east (front left) face (L1).

Thatch summary

Water reed (L1) on south-east (front left) face, applied within last 10 years, over a rough water reed fleeking tied directly to rafters (and to very occasional thin rod battens) with tarred twine and occasional twisted rod rope. Fleeking continues to north on split and thin roundwood battens, with a base coat in this section of crushed bread wheat straw tied to rafters and battens with tarred twine and sways (and crooked to wall plate at eaves course). West extension across from double doors with more even battening of small diameter split rods. Minimum two layers of crushed straw on rear (west) face of this section, including thick base coat of rivet and bread wheat (L3), mostly butts together and with much weed (especially grass). This layer tied to battens with tarred twine and crooked to wall plate on eaves course. L3 overlain by L2, grassy bread wheat straw, crushed, sparred and swayed to base coat. Minimum three layers of crushed straw on west (rear) face of main north/south section immediately north of joint with west extension: base coat of fine crushed straw (L6), mostly rivet wheat but with occasional ear of bread wheat, mixed ears and butts and fixed with tarred twine and roundwood sways to rafters and battens; this layer overlain by L5, crushed bread wheat straw mixed ears and butts, sparred to L6; L5 overlain by another coat of crushed bread wheat straw (L4), also sparred and swayed but mostly butts-together in the bundle and applied butts-down on roof. L4 with additional fixings of six-ply tarred twine stitched through base coats to rafters. External pitch of thatch *c* 55 ° and total depth at ridge *c* 60 cm.

Thatch (external):

main: east (front) primarily bread wheat long straw and very decayed. Water reed on south-east (front left) section and gable courses. Pitch *c* 55 °.

ridge: straw, very decayed, numerous free-standing spars, *c* 45 cm.

eaves: decayed, possible remains of eaves ligger, cut horizontally with a *c* 30 cm overhang.

gables: cut, flared, *c* 30 cm overhang, decayed remains of barge boards.

Samples:

MAIN COAT:

L1: water reed, specimens *c* 130 cm, both fine and coarse specimens all with flower heads. Not dressed into position.

L2: bread wheat, crushed evenly over stem, specimens *c* 45cm, both awned and awnless and grassy. Overlies L3.

L3: base coat of bread wheat and small-eared rivet wheat, specimens *c* 35 cm, crushed evenly over stem, mainly butts-together and very grassy.

L4: bundle of bread wheat, specimens *c* 90 cm, very crushed over stem, mostly butts together and applied butts-down on roof. Overlies L5.

L5: bundle of bread wheat, specimens short, very crushed evenly over stem and ears/butts evenly mixed. Overlies L6.

L6: base coat of rivet wheat and occasional bread wheat, evenly crushed over stem and evenly mixed ears and butts. Rivet wheat very fine (ie grassy).

RIDGE

Several ridges of straw survive, much degraded, with numerous spars standing clear of surface. Not sampled.

Fixings:

L1: water reed tied to battens and rafters with six-ply tarred twine and roundwood sways. Also occasional twisted cf hazel rod rope. Eaves course crooked to wall plate (crooks hand-forged, re-used?).

L2: sparred and swayed, both of roundwood (cf hazel).

L3: tied to battens with tarred twine. Lower courses crooked to wall plate (crooks hand-forged).

L4: mostly sparred and swayed, occasional tied to battens with six-ply tarred twine.

L5: sparred and swayed, both of split cf hazel.

L6: roundwood sways and tarred twine.

Interpretation

Well-built nineteenth-century barn with base coat of crushed straw of rivet wheat, bread wheat and both

Figure A18.

species mixed (representing three different base coat phases). Upper layers also of crushed straw of bread and rivet wheat, but with water reed (cut locally) applied as a repair to front south gable end *c* 1984. This water reed fixed with sways and tarred twine, and occasional with twisted rod rope, an unusual fixing in recent times. Water reed also used as a rough fleeking in place of battens on east face. Early layers fixed with tarred twine and roundwood/split sways and spars (Fig A18). Eaves courses fixed with iron crooks. Thick base coat of grassy and small-eared rivet wheat (L6). Upper layer of this sequence (L4) of crushed bread wheat sparred and swayed, but with occasional tarred twine to consolidate. Upper layer (L3) of crushed rivet and bread wheat, mainly butts-together, sparred and swayed. L2 contains a mixture of awned and awnless bread wheat, ie an impure variety or a varietal mixture. Early layers are also relatively grassy and poorly drawn.

A19 WILTSHIRE (TABLE A19)

Hawkins's Barn, 93 High Street, Wroughton
Grid reference: SU1480
Date of survey: 27th April 1994
Owner: Misses D M and M A Hawkins
Contact: Pam Slocombe, Wiltshire Buildings Record.
Locality: abandoned barn on roadside in village of Wroughton, 5km south west of Swindon. Oriented roughly east/west with front (road) facing south-south-west. Local soils light, on edge of Salisbury Plain. Formerly known as Spencer's Farm.

Table A19 Hawkins's Barn, 93 High Street, Wroughton, Wiltshire

Sample	Principal components	Fixings	Depth cm
L1	BW LS, crushed, butts-together	spars and sways	20
L2	BW straw, crushed, ears and butts mixed	spars (sways ?)	10
L3	BW straw, crushed, ears and butts mixed	spars	10
L4	BW and rivet wheat straw, apex crushed, ears and butts mixed	spars	15
L5	BW and rivet wheat, crushed, ears and butts mixed	sways, hempen and tarred twine	20

Building description

Originally three-bay, timber-framed barn, seventeenth-century, much rebuilt and now five bays. Oriented east/west. Half-hipped on east end. Adjacent house formerly thatched but tiled in 1930. Roof timber much decayed. Rafters sawn and pegged to purlins. Battens mostly 8 cm x 2 cm, sawn, nailed to rafters at *c* 40 cm intervals. Roof timbers pitched at 45 °–50 °.

Sampling background

Barn abandoned for about 15 years and much decayed. Spot samples collected from collapsed rear (north) face in well preserved (dry) section. Front face very decayed (not sampled). Base coat layers wet, decaying, riddled with insects but moderately well preserved.

Thatch summary

Multi-layered roof of straw, now collapsed and much decayed (Fig A19). Surface coat on north rear face (L1) of bread wheat straw crushed and applied butts-down. Front south face much decayed. L2 and L3 of bread wheat straw, crushed and mixed ears and butts. Base coat layers L4 and L5 contain a mixture of bread wheat and rivet wheat straw. L4 crushed only at apex and mixed ears and butts. L5 evenly crushed and mixed ears and butts. Rivet wheat with small, dense ears and fine straw (tillers?). L1 fixed with spars and sways, with L2, L3 and L4 sparred in individual bundles (with straw bonds?). Sways fixing base coat tied to battens and rafters with hempen and tarred

twine. Fragmentary remains of what may be a flush ridge with three simple, horizontal liggers. Battens sawn and nailed to rafters at regular intervals of *c* 40 cm. Pitch of both faces *c* 47 °. Building last thatched in 1974 with bread wheat straw grown in the potato field on hill across from building and threshed by machine. Barn once thatched on a regular basis by father of present owner. Wheat once widely grown in this area and kept for thatch. Straw rope, grass rope and a wire-nail thatch rake rest on a peg on barn wall.

Thatch (external):

main: rear face: bread wheat straw, crushed and applied butts-down in 1974, front face: bread wheat straw, crushed, mixed ears and butts. Both faces very decayed.

ridge: straw, very decayed, horizontal liggers survive at east end.

eaves: very decayed, cut to an angle with large overhang, eaves ligger survives on rear face east end.

gables: west hip intact, eaves ligger decayed.

Samples:

MAIN COAT (REAR):

L1: bread wheat long straw, specimens *c* 90 cm, crushed, applied butts-down (rear face).

L2: bread wheat straw, specimens *c* 60 cm, weathered, crushed and mixed ears and butts.

L3: bread wheat straw, crushed and mixed ears and butts.

L4: bread and rivet wheat straw, crushed on apex with bulk of stem undamaged and mixed ears and butts. Rivet wheat with small, dense ears and fine straw.

L5: bread and rivet wheat straw, evenly crushed and mixed ears and butts.

Fixings

External layer (L1) on rear face sparred and swayed with split hazel. L2, L3 and L4 occasionally sparred in individual bundles, some possibly with straw bonds. L5 base coat fixed with sways tied to rafters and battens with hempen and tarred twine. Twisted straw rope (bread wheat) and grass rope stored in barn for thatching hay bundles (D Hawkins, pers comm).

Figure A19.

A20 WILTSHIRE (TABLE A20)

Norrie Cottage, Collingbourne Kingston, SN8 3SD
Grid reference: SU557239
Date: 19th September 1994
Owner: David Smith
Thatcher: J H Harmon
Conservation Officer: April Waterman, Kennet District Council.
Locality: cottage fronting east side of road in village, 15km north west of Andover. Village on east fringe of Salisbury Down set amid light, chalky arable soils. Prevailing winds from south-west.

English Heritage Research Transactions Volume 5

Table A20 Norrie Cottage, Collingbourne Kingston, Wiltshire

Sample	Principal components	Fixings	Depth cm
1	BW, CWR	spars and straw bonds	20
2	BW straw, crushed, mostly butts down	spars	20
3	BW straw, crushed and uncrushed, ears and butts mixed	spars and straw bonds	15
4	BW straw, very degraded	spars and straw bonds	10
5	BW straw, ears/ butts mixed, very decayed	spars and straw bonds	10
6-9	BW straw, very decayed	spars, straw bonds	?13
10	BW straw, crushed, ears and butts mixed, very decayed	spars and sways	10
11	bread wheat straw, crushed, occasional uncrushed upper specimens, mostly butts down, lightly blackened	occasional tarred twine (rear)	20

Building description

Listed grade II, seventeenth-century timber-framed cottage with wattle and daub infill. Ridge oriented north/south with half-hip at north end partially enveloping a brick chimney stack. Second brick stack piercing ridge north of front entrance and standing above thatch *c* 90 cm. Two bays (main hall and inner room) and narrow (1.5 m) smoke bay surviving on first floor with louvre and timber remains of inserted smoke-hood on south wall shared by adjacent cottage (Mayzells). Smoke bay now walled with concrete blocks, but with surviving, lightly blackened, wattle and daub upper sides from first floor ceiling to ridge. Adjacent cottage single storey with dormers. Norrie Cottage raised to two storeys except for smoke bay which is raised by about 10 brick courses only. Original unraised rafter survives embedded in internal wall of smoke bay. Three eyebrow dormers. Partition wall between bays I and II north of central chimney raised to ridge above first floor ceiling by wattle partition (heavily blackened, no daub). Half-hip visible through broken wattle, with lightly blackened thatch lying on attic floor. Roof smoke-blackened throughout, and especially immediately north of smoke bay, with blackening permeating base coat by *c* 10–15 cm. Smoke bay relatively lightly blackened. Limited access to bulk of roofspace.

Rafters rest on a thick purlin, originally lapped (in smoke bay) to purlin of adjoining Mayzells Cottage (but joint now broken and no longer aligned). Front rafters *c* 10 cm x 12 cm (laying flat), of well-sawn high quality timber and smoke-blackened. Rafters rest on timber sill on front eaves, and pegged to purlin. Rear rafters less robust, of rougher sawn wood, some lightly blackened and with occasional (unblackened) repair with roundwood poles (coeval with bridging of louvre). Pointed pole rafter forced up from eaves below purlin beneath decayed thatch layers 6–9. Rafters with *c* 32 cm midpoint distance. Slanted cross piece running north-south from top to bottom of bay braces rear rafters in smoke bay. Pitch of front rafters *c* 45 ° and rear rafters *c* 55 °. Battens: older battens on front of roof of split oat, 3–5 cm x 1–1.5 cm but variable, spaced evenly to leave 7–12 cm gaps and

Figure A20.

nailed to rafters. New sawn battens, *c* 3 cm x 2 cm, inserted as repair. Battens on rear face above purlin are of wider sawn planks, *c* 12–15 cm x 1.5 cm, with *c* 15 cm gaps, nailed to rafters and blackened. Below purlin rear battens are of riven laths and unblackened. Battening on both sides much repaired with evidence of slippage of thatch. Occasional wide sawn plank battens also in upper front portion of smoke bay. Front battens immediately north of smoke bay heavily blackened. Smoke-blackened riven laths also nailed to pole rafter inserted above thatch layer 10. Many nails rusted and failed causing slippage of battens and thatch. Louvre bridged by insertion of a 15 cm diameter (willow?) pole sections east-west across front and back battens, and with thinner (unblackened) riven laths laid upon these north-south to support the thatch. Blocking of louvre not necessarily coeval with insertion of central chimney stack, as Norrie Cottage reputedly used as village blacksmith shop.

Sampling background

Rethatching in progress noted during sampling visit to Wiltshire. Visit confirmed smoke-blackening, but probably not smoke-blackened thatch. Grant aid for spar-coating front (west) face with combed wheat reed made conditional upon preservation of smoke-blackened thatch and provision of access for sampling. Roof inspected with April Waterman and owner. Local elders believe Norrie

Cottage was a village smithy with hearth in smoke bay at south end. Roof leaking on front face at junction with adjacent cottage (Mayzells). Thatcher not present so sampling restricted to a step trench on front face *c* 2 m from south end junction with Mayzells Cottage (Fig A20). Section revealed from ground floor eaves to *c* 1.5 m below ridge and straddling north portion of smoke bay and adjacent roof (and including area of leak). Ridge clearly thicker than main coat but not sampled. Photographs taken from within north end roofspace but access limited.

Thatch summary

Multi-layered roof with a lichen and moss-covered top coat of combed wheat reed applied in 1976. Base coat (11) of crushed, butts-together bread wheat straw fixed with tarred twine. Succeeding layers of crushed bread wheat straw, mostly mixed ears and butts. Many layers too poorly preserved for analysis (eg 6–9). Layer 10 fixed with spars and sways, but succeeding layers fixed with spars and straw bonds rather than wooden sways. Layer 2 bundles fixed only with spars. Spars mainly of split hazel and occasional roundwood. Base coat originally smoke-blackened, probably by seepage from smoke bay or later smoke hood, but not soot encrusted as with medieval smoke blackened thatch. Louvre perhaps maintained after insertion of central chimney if this south smoke bay was used as a smithy. Thatch descends to top of raised front wall, except in smoke bay where it descends to ground floor ceiling height. Pitch of roof gradually increased by disproportionate stripping of eaves and buildup at ridge (especially over north bay 1). Base coat fixings mostly absent, and slippage of thatch apparent on rear face. Depth below ridge *c* 1.2 m.

Thatch (external):

main: bread wheat combed wheat reed, variety *Maris Widgeon*, applied *c* 1976, now *c* 15–20 cm thick and heavily coated with moss, lichen and algae. Pitch: *c* 52 ° and *c* 40 ° above dormers. Wired. Area of depression and more rapid decay below and to right of central stack.

ridge: straw, flush, diamented (horizontal ligger beneath apex with top and tail diamenting), very decayed. Repair below front and rear of chimney. Ridge of bay 2 *c* 30 cm below ridge of bay 1 but slightly above ridge of adjacent cottage. Depth: 1.5 m.

eaves: eaves front and back dressed and cut to shallow pitch. Overhang *c* 35 cm.

gable: thatch swept down over steep, half-hip on north end wrapping chimney. Front hip carried down over gable wall much further than rear gable section of hip. Gable eaves dressed inwards.

Samples:
MAIN COAT:

New: combed wheat reed, bread wheat variety *Maris Widgeon*, specimens *c* 100 cm, well combed and undamaged.

1: external coat of combed wheat reed bread wheat, applied *c* 1976, specimens *c* 30 cm, stems uncrushed and applied butts down. weathered and heavily coated with algae, lichen and moss.

2: bread wheat straw, specimens *c* 45 cm, moderately crushed with many short specimens *c* 15 cm, mixed but mostly butts-together and applied down on roof.

3: bread wheat straw, specimens mostly *c* 20 cm, very weathered, both crushed and uncrushed, and mixed ears and butts.

4: bread wheat straw, specimens *c* 15 cm, very degraded, identification based on rachis fragments.

5: bread wheat straw, specimens *c* 10 cm and very decayed, ears and butts mixed.

6–9: decayed samples, congealed and compacted with much insect frass. Bread wheat identified by microscope. Minimum four layers present in 3 cm, 2 cm, 3 cm and 5 cm bands.

10: bread wheat straw, specimens *c* 20 cm, crushed and mixed ears and butts. Layer very decayed.

11: base coat of bread wheat straw, specimens *c* 50 cm, very weathered, evenly crushed except for well preserved upper sections. Specimens mostly butts-together and applied down on roof. Layer moderately smoke-blackened but not encrusted as with smoke blackened thatch.

Layer of degraded bread wheat between 4 and 5 not sampled, and further layers probably missed between 5 and 6.

Fixings:

1: spars and horizontal straw bonds (mostly pulled from adjacent bundle). Spars of split hazel, 35–38 cm, sparred at 15–20 cm intervals and with 30–35 cm between courses. Each bond of about 10 straws.

2: spars fixing individual bundles. Spars *c* 40 cm, of split hazel and willow.

3: spars and straw bonds. Spars of split hazel.

4: spars and straw bonds. Spars *c* 35 cm, of roundwood and split hazel and willow.

5: spars and straw bonds. Spars *c* 40 cm of split hazel.

6–9: spars and cf straw bonds (visible within decayed layers).

10: spars and wooden sways. Spars *c* 35 cm, of split willow and hazel. Sways of split hazel.

11: occasional tarred twine on rear face. Occasional sway of split and roundwood hazel. No visible fixings on front face.

Numerous spars of split hazel, unblackened, visible inside roofspace piercing base coat at ridge.

Appendix B

Additional buildings visited (see Fig 92)

Table A1B Buildings visited

No.	county	building visited
1	Bedfordshire	West Farm, Hamwick
2	Berkshire	Rose Tree Farm, 29 Nine Mile Ride, Finchampstead
3	Buckinghamshire	cottage, Milton Keynes Village
4	Buckinghamshire	garden shed, Little Ickford
5	Buckinghamshire	garden shed (across lane from Ickford House), Little Ickford
6	Buckinghamshire	Church End Cottage, 1 Bates Lane, Weston Turville
7	Buckinghamshire	Westcot, 10 Lower Green, Aylesbury
8	Buckinghamshire	April Cottage, 10 High Street, Westcott, West Wycombe
9	Cambridgeshire	Pembrooke Farmhouse
10	Cambridgeshire	cottage, Wennington
11	Cambridgeshire	Bramleys, Main Street, Shudy Camps
12	Cambridgeshire	62 High Street, Orwell
13	Cambridgeshire	Oak Cottage, South Street, Litlington
14	Devon	Mortcombe
15	Devon	cottage, Crediton
16	Devon	Stepps Cottage, Stepps Lane, Axmouth, Seaton
17	Devon	Cottage, Ulverton
18	Devon	Broadway House (Post Office), The Square, Whimple
19	Devon	Homestill Cottage, Copplestone, Coleford
20	Devon	Anchoring Farmhouse, Ottery Street, Otterton
21	Devon	barn, Coleford
22	Dorset	unlocated
23	Dorset	cottage, Lytchett Matravers
24	Dorset	Tanyard, Penny Street, Sturminster Newton
25	Gloucestershire	Primrose Cottage, Upton St Leonard
26	Hertfordshire	cottage, Brent Pelham
27	Leicestershire	derelict cottage, Mowsley
28	Lincolnshire	Old Yeomans House, Church Lane, Horbling
29	London	Queen Charlotte's Cottage, Kew Gardens
30	Norfolk	The 5 Gables, Lingwood, Norwich
31	Norfolk	cottage, The Priory, Ranworth
32	Northamptonshire	Church End, Rushden
33	Northamptonshire	8 & 10 Church Street, Lower Weedon
34	Northamptonshire	Little Thatches, Isham
35	Northamptonshire	Carrey House, Great Brington
36	Northamptonshire	bookshop, High Street, Brixworth
37	Oxfordshire	cottage, North Lane, Weston on the Green, Cherwell
38	Oxfordshire	Pommander House, Harwell
39	Oxfordshire	Ryle's Cottage, 76 Main Road, Long Hampborough
40	Oxfordshire	Charlies Cottage, Epwell
41	Suffolk	cottage, Thornham Magna
42	Surrey	Woods Walnut Tree Farm, Kennel Lane, Windlesham
43	Sussex	barn, Court Farm, Falmer, Brighton
44	Wiltshire	Vine Cottage, Union Street, Ramsbury
45	Wiltshire	barn, Lavington

B1 BEDS

West Farm, Hamwick
Thatcher: Ernie Scholler

Visited with Peter Brockett, James Moir and Jo Cox. Recently thatched. Sample taken of previous external layer of combed wheat reed (L1) and of base coat in roofspace (L2, L3 and L4). Base coat fixings confusing and haphazard with much evidence of repair and consolidation. Thatch tied with tarred twine to rafters and split oak laths, but with later re-stitching with hempen cord, fine (tarred) cord of grass (Gramineae indet) and two and three-ply rush rope (cf bulrush *Schoenoplectus lacustris*). Spars penetrating roof space from external coats, particularly at ridge.

L1: external coat of bread wheat combed wheat reed, specimens *c* 80 cm with two upper nodes present, cut below second internode, generally quite fine-strawed, internodes solid–semi-solid and butts weathered. Ears of 95% of specimens cut off towards top of last internode (ie pitched).

L2: base coat of very crushed bread wheat straw, specimens mostly full length, *c* 50 cm, largely butts-together and with much flag leaf and detritus. Fixed with split willow spars. Sample taken from south west corner of bay 1.

L3: base coat mixture of stubble and crushed straw. Stubble specimens *c* 15–25 cm, coarse, undamaged, cut at both ends and often with roots; longer specimens *c*35cm, fine, crushed unevenly and largely without ears, but with occasional ear of bread wheat. Straight stem in stubble specimens with roots possibly suggests a spring wheat variety. Sample contains much soil detritus, possibly included during raking of stubble.

L4: external repair stob of flax (*Linum usitatissimum*), specimens *c* 40 cm, inserted from exterior bird hole (?) down to base coat. Repair fixed in places with two-ply sedge rope. Flax specimens are of threshing waste without capsules (ie scutched). Sample taken *c* 70 cm beneath ridge in south-west corner of bay 1.

Figure B1.

Figure B2.

B2 BERKSHIRE

Rose Tree Farm, 29 Nine Mile Ride, Finchampstead
Thatcher: Thatching Advisory Service Ltd

Early post medieval, cruck-framed former open hall visited in May, 1994, in advance of stripping and rethatching (Fig B1). No smoke-blackened thatch survives, but timberwork and wattle partitions heavily smoke blackened along with patch of whitewashed plaster. Base coat of bread wheat straw, crushed and mixed ears and butts, tied to rafters and battens with lightly tarred twine. Rafters of squared timber, *c* 14 cm x 12 cm, pegged to ridge piece. Battens not smoke-blackened, of thick riven laths *c* 8 cm, nailed to rafters. Clay pegged tiles survive beneath thatch at ridge over *c* 1.0 m section on back face of building. Last external coat is of modern long straw with patterned eaves ligger and flush ridge. No samples taken.

B3 BUCKINGHAMSHIRE

Cottage, Milton Keynes village

Late medieval smoke-blackened open hall, stripped to timbers. Series of rescue samples of smoke-blackened thatch taken in 1993 (Letts 1996). Post smoke-blackened thatch stob sample 6 collected on ground, consists of clean, but very crushed and wiry stems of a grass (Gramineae indet). Specimens *c* 15–20 cm. Contains occasional plantain (*Platanus* sp.), Compositae, mature grasses, cf reedy stems and leaf (*Phalaris* sp.?). Immature grass from wet pasture used as stob repair (nineteenth century?).

B4 BUCKINGHAMSHIRE

Garden shed, Ickford House, Little Ickford
Owner: Mrs Stoney

Potting shed, constructed 1940s, thatched with three layers of bread wheat combed wheat reed. Wired, with a flush ridge and diamenting, *c* 50 cm overhang on eaves and hip dressed to an angle. Inside of roof boarded.

B5 BUCKINGHAMSHIRE

Garden shed, (across lane from Ickford House), Little Ickford

Ornamental garden shed, early twentieth century, with ornamental rough-hewn exterior. Roof pitch very shallow (*c*30°). Thatched with very fine water reed (Fig B2).

B6 BUCKINGHAMSHIRE

Church End Cottage, 1 Bates Lane, Weston Turville
Owners: R Padbury and S Cartwright
Thatcher: John Badmin

Late medieval open hall building sampled on 23 March 1994 during repair of thatch in chimney area and partial re-ridging. No extensive stripping being undertaken so no full series available for analysis. Samples taken from within roof space. Rafters roughly squared (*c* 15 cm x 15 cm) and thatch supported on split oak laths (8–10 cm x 1–2cm), all heavily smoke-blackened with occasional insertion of similar rafters as repair. Base coat of bread wheat straw, very crushed, mixed ears and butts, not smoke-blackened. Overlying layer also of bread wheat straw, crushed and mixed ears and butts (Fig B3). Last rethatched in 1974 by J Badmin with long straw bread wheat, still performing although worn almost to sways. Last coat liggered on eaves with a double (diamented) row of hazel sways and on barges with a double row of (horizontal) liggers. Block-cut ridge with simple scallop cut and diamenting. New coat of straw, combed wheat reed variety *Maris Widgeon*, being applied long straw style with same eaves and barge liggering and without being dressed into place with a leggat. Combed wheat reed and

Figure B3.

long straw distinction 'not important' according to thatcher.

B7 BUCKINGHAMSHIRE

Westcot, 10 Lower Green, Aylesbury
Owner: Mr Ort

Rescue samples obtained during rethatching of north-west face in August 1994. Large timber-framed, two-storey house, mid seventeenth century, with brick infill, three chimneys, dormers, gable ends and nineteenth-century tiled extension to north-east. Pitch *c* 53 ° on north west and *c* 48 ° on south east (north-east pitch increased by *c* 5 ° by gradual disproportionate stripping of eaves). Ridge now off-centre, having crept to north-west due to more frequent rethatching of (now thinner) south-east face. Rafters squared, *c* 14 cm x 12 cm, pegged to wall plate and surpassing it by *c* 10 cm. Rafters and basal battens lightly blackened. Battens of riven laths, 6–8 cm x 1 cm, nailed to rafters at *c* 40 cm spacings. New battens inserted on eaves. First (original) batten placed *c* 12 cm x 1.5 cm above wall plate. Minimum five layers visible on south-east eaves, but about one layer on north-west face due to stripping at last rethatching. Eaves and gables cut and angled. Exterior coat (L1) of combed wheat reed, bread wheat, weathered, specimens *c* 55 cm, fixed with split hazel sways and spars, applied *c* 1982 by Thatching Advisory Service Ltd. Liggered (double row plus diamenting) on eaves and barges in long straw style. Straw ridge, wrap-over, raised, scalloped and diamented (combed wheat reed). New combed wheat reed with similar detailing. L2 of degraded reed straw of bread wheat, butts weathered but uncrushed and mostly together and down on roof, few ears, specimens now *c* 45 cm, fixed with spars and sways. L3 of a lax-eared bread wheat similar to L2 but with specimens *c* 30 cm and occasional crushed. L4–6 very degraded and compacted straw and insect frass, mostly of bread wheat. Only dock (*Rumex* sp.) specimens survive. L7 of bread wheat straw, very crushed, mixed ears and butts, with abundant rubbish, flag leaf, short stem fragments, with specimens *c* 40 cm, evenly crushed and the layer fixed with straw rope (originally to rafters and battens?). Base coat (L8) of bread wheat cf stubble, specimens variable but often *c* 35 cm, crushed evenly but with many basal sections uncrushed, with abundant rubbish, flag leaf, broken straw and both upper and middle stem segments. Base coat tied to rafters and battens with strong, *c* 1 cm diameter three-ply hempen rope. Base coat layers 7 and 8 probably not drawn.

B8 BUCKINGHAMSHIRE

April Cottage, 10 High Street, Westcott

Sample sent by post by M Dodson in July 1994. Contains probable sway of hazel with attached tarred cord and small sample of crushed and jumbled bread wheat straw, specimens *c* 30 cm.

B9 CAMBRIDGESHIRE

Pembrooke Farmhouse

Rescue samples taken during visit in April 1994 with M Dodson. Timber framed cottage, late eighteenth century. Survival helped by steep roof pitch (*c* 57 °). No access to base coat from within building or from exterior as only top layers stripped prior to rethatching. One or two extra basal layers probably present but not sampled.

L1: main coat of bread wheat straw, crushed and mixed ears and butts, applied in *c* 1955 by Dodson brothers. Specimens now *c* 35 cm, crushed evenly over entire stem, mainly butts-together and applied butts-down on roof. Little weed. Straw remarkably well preserved beneath decayed surface.
L2: main coat of fen sedge (*Cladium mariscus*). Also contains small bunches of grass (Gramineae), herbaceous material, small saplings and occasional fragment of water reed. Occasional sedge specimen in flower. Fixed with two-ply rope of rush (*Schoenoplectus lacustris*) and consolidated with spars and sways at last rethatching. Layer *c* 20 cm deep.
L3: main coat of bread wheat straw beneath sedge. Specimens now *c* 30 cm, mostly coarse, crushed at apex, with few ears and mixed ears and butts. Perhaps with a stubble component. Most specimens with cut butts. Occasional finer material. Much weed.
L4: basal coat of very decayed straw, mainly of bread wheat but with occasional rye, specimens very crushed and jumbled. Tied to rafters with hempen cord.

B10 CAMBRIDGESHIRE

Cottage, Wennington

Cottage, late eighteenth century, visited with M Dodson in June 1994. L1 of water reed, specimens now 110 cm, fine and containing abundant other herbaceous species; L2 of threshed (scutched) flax (*Linum usitatissimum*), without a main stem or seed capsules; L3 of bread wheat straw, specimens *c* 35 cm, crushed, mostly butts-together and applied butts-down on roof; L4 of bread wheat reed straw, *c* 50 cm, fine-stemmed, uncrushed, mostly without ears (lashed?), with cut butts applied butts-up on roof; L5 of fen sedge and grass (Graminea indet); base coat L6 mostly of fen sedge with occasional specimens of black bog rush *(Schoenus nigricans)*. Base coats fixed with hempen rope, (sisal?) cord, a strip of bark and saplings (probably willow).

B11 CAMBRIDGESHIRE

Bramleys, Main Street, Shudy Camps
Owners: Barry Guy and Maya Homburger

Largely fifteenth-century cruck-framed cottage with thirteenth-century core, hipped and with smoke-blackened timbers and residual smoke-blackened thatch. Visited 5 April 1994. Plaster applied to inner face of reed fleeking. Woven fleeking of smoke-blackened water reed supporting a smoke-blackened base coat, *c* 30 cm thick, of two-row hulled barley threshing waste (*Hordeum vulgare* ssp. *distichum*). Sample also contains occasional bread wheat, rivet wheat and rye, pea, broad bean, cultivated vetch and abundant crop weeds. A second sample of smoke-blackened thatch contained mostly rye. Area above bedroom (A) not smoke-blackened (as above adjacent room B) with base coat tied with tarred twine and dethorned stems of blackberry (*Rubus* sp.). This sample largely of rivet wheat, specimens short, very crushed and with few crop weeds. External thatch of long straw applied *c* 1979, now with much moss. A rear section with an original smoke-blackened base coat and fleeking replaced with combed wheat reed by the Dodson brothers in 1991. Patterned block ridge, but photograph *c* 1900 shows flush ridge without eaves liggers.

B12 CAMBRIDGESHIRE

2 High Street, Orwell
Owner: M McCabe

Large, timber-framed, seventeenth-century two-storey cottage visited with Peter Brockett in March 1994. Roof steeply pitched at *c* 60 °. External coat of bread wheat combed wheat reed applied mid-1980s. Roughly squared pole rafters supplemented by inserted pole rafters, all pegged to ridge piece and purlins. Original battens of *c* 3–4 cm diameter pole at *c* 35 cm intervals, plastered from within. In areas without internal plastering the battens are of coarse riven laths and reused timber, 8–10 cm x 2–4 cm, nailed to rafters at regular *c* 15 cm intervals. Three phases of tying visible with hempen twine, double-braided hempen twine and coarse tarred twine. Plastering predates all three phases, which required punching holes through plaster where stitch required. Large sections of plaster lost at this time. Original tying must either have been removed, or perhaps the base coat was fixed onto a fleeking of water reed clamped to the external face of rafters. Last phase of tying probably tarred twine. Base coat of threshed straw dominated by bread wheat but also including some rivet wheat.

B13 CAMBRIDGESHIRE

Oak Cottage, South Street, Litlington
Owner: Colin Sinclair

Located by Chris Stanford, visited early 1995. Cruck-framed late medieval cottage with smoke-blackened timbers and fleeking of water reed (in smoke bay). Base coat of bread wheat straw, crushed, mixed ears and butts with occasional ears of rye (not smoke-blackened). Original base coat a woven fleeking of water reed, repaired with riven laths. Fixings of hempen twine, grass rope, thick double-ply hempen rope and saplings (hazel?).

B14 DEVON

Mortcombe, near Cullompton

Sample of oat (*Avena sativa*) reed straw, lightly smoke-blackened, obtained from A Hannabus in June 1994. Specimens *c* 80 cm, with worn butts, lightly crushed at apex (lashed?), stem largely undamaged and butts-together in sheaf. Removed from a base coat layer of a cottage in 1991 that had an early ridge roll of brushwood and a base coat tied with de-thorned blackberry stems. Bound with a twisted straw rope.

B15 DEVON

Cottage, Crediton. Thatcher: Chris Bovey

Building sampled June 1994, being rethatched with imported Hungarian water reed, replacing a previous water reed thatch (now degraded) applied in *c* 1964. New coat being sparred onto existing coat using hazel sways and spars, but with iron sways and crooks for first two courses (and always with double fixings). Crooks scavenged from other buildings. Water reed applied with less tension than in East Anglia to allow roof to breathe. No good quality combed wheat reed available this season for thatching so imported water reed was unavoidable second choice material.

B16 DEVON

Stepps Cottage, Stepps Lane, Axmouth
Owner: David Tresize

Samples obtained on 21 April 1994 from cottage orné style building constructed in 1930s adjacent to Stepps House. Roof stripped and rethatched with fine Norfolk reed in 1993. Finished roof almost identical to combed wheat reed of adjacent cottage applied in *c* 1965. New reed very similar size and texture to combed wheat reed. Seaton is a holiday resort with abundant thatched cottages in area. Ridge formerly butts-up combed wheat reed and block cut, but now of sedge. Roof pitched *c* 50 °.

L1: newly applied Norfolk water reed
L2: bread wheat combed wheat reed applied in *c* 1965, specimens *c* 100 cm, most with three nodes, ears intact and well combed.
L3: bread wheat reed straw, specimens *c* 70 cm, mostly of very fine upper stem specimens with small ears. Sample applied *c* 1940, and described by thatcher as a 'perfect' wheat reed as it is 'fine, waxy, strong, flexible and has a nice colour'. Sample is mostly butts-together and was applied butts-down on roof. Straw is lightly crushed, has been combed to remove flag leaf, contains abundant grass and occasional crop weeds (including *Melampyrum* sp.).
L4: base coat of bread wheat straw applied *c* 1930. Sample has weathered butts but is well preserved. Specimens *c* 100 cm, well-crushed, largely butts-

together and was applied butts-down on roof. Straw also appears to be combed and has most ears intact.

Fixings: base coat fixed with tarred twine. Succeeding coats sparred. New water reed coat crooked directly to roof.

B17 DEVON

Cottage, Ulverton
Thatcher: Chris Bovey

Roof sampled June 1994, of combed wheat reed applied in 1967 being stripped and rethatched with spar coat of imported Hungarian water reed. Combed wheat reed still in good shape, specimens *c* 100 cm, butts intact, ears worn, mostly cut below second node. Last coat fixed with straw and hazel spars to thick base coat. New water reed applied with double fixings and iron sways with a wrap-over ridge.

B18 DEVON

Broadway House, The Square, Whimple
Owner: Mrs Bette Williams

Early seventeenth-century cob building, half-hipped, with a combed wheat reed thatched roof, a block-cut and patterned ridge and dirty, but not smoke-blackened, timbers. Access difficult, with original roof contained within nineteenth-century reconstruction. Samples obtained on 20 April 1994, from original ridge area within roofspace. Base coat sample of bread wheat reed straw, specimens *c* 40 cm, cut to produce two to three nodes and heavily flailed at apex only which removed most ears. Specimens mostly undamaged towards butts. Numerous hazel (and possibly oak) spars. Early ridge bundle tied with straw rope. Base coat with a thin fleeking of wheat reed straw. Base coats tied to battens with straw rope and tarred twine.

B19 DEVON

Homestill Cottage, Copplestone, Coleford
Tenants: David and Eileen Brassington
Owner: Alf Howard

Extended row of cottages visited June 1994. North half hip last thatched with local combed wheat reed by John Canne (assisted by Alf Howard) in *c* 1936. Front last thatched in 1949. Both sections now in need of repair. This reed was apparently quite fine, but varietal name not recorded. The Cannes have long been known in region for tight thatching of high quality. This hip very steep and north facing. Base coat probably tied with tarred twine as in adjacent cottage.

B20 DEVON

Anchoring Farmhouse, Ottery Street, Otterton
Owner: Mrs Adcock

Late medieval, former open hall of cob, visited 2 April 1994. Roughly sawn timbers and wide battens smoke-blackened, with occasional inserted split-pole battens as repairs. Some original rafters collapsed making access difficult. Rethatched in combed wheat reed *c* 1984 by Mr Cole of Colebrook, near Crediton, son of former estate thatcher. Straw currently on roof was grown in field across the road by local farmer Oliver Carter. Smoke-blackened fleeking of *c* 60 cm segments of water reed, laid in a thin layer from eaves to ridge, each course overlapping top of course below it. Base coat of lightly blackened reed straw, specimens *c* 80 cm, primarily of bread wheat but with *c* 20% rivet wheat and occasional rye. Sample crushed at apex with few ears intact and was applied butts-down on roof. Overlying layer very similar but with more rye. Inscription on chimney of adjacent cottage (1708) perhaps suggests late insertion in Anchoring Farmhouse.

B21 DEVON

Barn, Coleford, Devon
Owner: Alf Howard

Cob barn, seventeenth century, with occasional smoke-blackened and squared rafter but mostly with unblackened pole rafters roughly squared. Visited June 1994. Adjacent to new cob building constructed by Alf Howard. Base coat of combed wheat reed with rye reed straw in one corner, tied to main purlins and battens with hempen cord. Top coats fixed with hazel sways and spars.

B22 DORSET

Sample submitted by J Lowe of Dorset County Council. Base coat L6 of bread wheat reed straw, specimens very fine, *c* 55 cm, pitched (ie ears removed) at very top of first (uppermost) internode and with stems cut below second node.

B23 DORSET

Cottage, Lytchett Matravers

Five samples of thatch submitted by J Lowe, Dorset County Council, in March 1997. No background information provided, aside from stratigraphic relationships of L6, L7, L8 and L9a/b (base coat). Samples L6, L7 and L9a/b are weathered examples of Dorset pitched reed.

L6: bread wheat reed straw, specimens *c* 57 cm (N=80), uniform, fine, mostly single node but with occasional two-node tiller. Upper internodes truncated by pitching of ears. Only one ear recovered, of an awned variety with intact grain. Upper internodes *c* 3 9cm (N=80). Butts weathered. Sample is very well combed and contains few weeds (occasional grass stem), flag leaf or short straws. Sample contains degraded willow and hazel spars, one of which was cut from a *c* 3.5 cm rod split into six. Each spar sharpened to three-faceted points.

L7: reed straw, very similar to L6. Specimens *c* 48 cm, mostly single node but a quarter of specimens with finer two-node with short internodes. Sample very uniform, free of flag leaf, weeds or rubbish (except occasional tall specimens of grass). Sample contains several spar fragments, mostly of hazel and cf willow, *c* 15 cm, cut from 2.5–3.5 cm diameter rods into six. Also occasional roundwood spars *c*1.5cm diameter. All spars three-faceted.

L8: sea rush *Juncus maritimus* Lam. Also occasional specimens of saltmarsh rush *Juncus gerardi* Loisel, and abundant grass (*Agrostis stolonifera*) and herbaceous detritus. Immature state of seed heads suggests cutting in early-mid summer. Sample composed of handful-sized bunches of *c* 50 cm specimens, butts-aligned and applied butts down on roof. No evidence of weathering, so an unexposed base coat. Sample contains one degraded willow spar split (one of four) from a *c* 3 cm diameter rod.

L9a: similar to L6 and L7, but with specimens longer, finer and more wiry, *c* 72 cm with internode measures of 39:25:9 cm (truncated). Most with two internodes intact. Occasional fine tillers. Two specimens with surviving ear fragments (of bread wheat). Sample well combed with little surviving flag leaf. Butts weathered. Sample contains spar fragments, mostly of hazel, with three-faced points, split (one of four) from *c* 2 cm diameter rod. Another is derived from a 1.2 cm diameter rod split into two.

L9b: a coarser equivalent to L9a, but with occasional fragmented specimens of an awned bread wheat. Specimens *c* 74 cm, with internode measures of 35:27:11:2 cm (truncated). Upper internode pitched. Butts weathered. Sample also contains a broken spar fragment split (one of two) from a hazel rod *c* 1.5 cm diameter

B24 DORSET

Tanyard, Penny Street, Sturminster Newton
Owner: Peter Malloy

A former timber-framed open-hall building of four bays with jointed-cruck trusses, the eaves heightened *c* 1600. Base coat seventeenth century, of fine rivet wheat (east end). Specimens *c* 80 cm, longest without ears (pitched?) and with well preserved cut butts. West end with eighteenth-century threshed straw of bread wheat with occasional rivet wheat. Fixings of saplings (willow?) and hempen cord (Royal Commission on the Historical Monuments of England 1970, 279–80).

B25 GLOUCESTERSHIRE

Primrose Cottage, Upton St Leonard

Late medieval timber-framed hall-house, possibly fourteenth century, much altered and extended. Crucks large, crude, very steeply pitched and smoke-blackened along with coarse split oak battens. Occasional residual

Figure B4.

pockets of smoke blackened thatch. Roof pitched *c* 55 ^{0}. Early base coat tied with twisted hazel rods. Small sample of post-medieval base coat composed primarily of rivet wheat straw, crushed and mixed ears and butts. This base coat tied to battens and rafters with saplings (willow?) and straw rope.

B26 HERTFORDSHIRE

Cottage, Brent Pelham
Thatcher: Tim Cox

Sampled on 6 April 1994. Wooden weatherboarded cottage, late seventeenth century, half-hipped, being rethatched on rear face. Sampling and recording cancelled due to rain and wind. Last coat of long straw applied *c* 1964, now very decayed (Fig B4). External coats being stripped to provide a sound base coat (essentially the original base coat) for a new spar-coat of long straw. Base coat (L1) of bread wheat straw, crushed and mixed ears and butts. Repair over base coat (L2), extending *c* 1.5 m from eaves, contains a mixture of very crushed bread and rivet wheat mixed ears and butts. L3 above L2 repair of similar material. Rethatching with modern long straw of variety *Maris Widgeon*, grown locally, grain harvested with a header-stripper and with straw cut with an 'American' reaper and round-baled. Round bales transported to site, heaped, wetted and drawn into yealms. Stripping misses shorter-stemmed ears but strips chaff and grain from tallest stems leaving bare rachis. Straw largely undamaged. Round bales stored in barn for two or three years to let rats and birds eat grain missed by header stripper. Ears and butts mixed but yealms mainly butts-together. Full butts-together 'bottles' used on eaves. Water reed being used to provide a firm base coat for header-stripped straw over dormer windows and on eaves. New thatch being fixed to rafters with metal crooks and sways (hence need to strip down to one or two base coats). Final surface combed with a spiked comber and sheared with sickle and shears, although general practice is to leave it shaggy. Block cut and patterned ridge to be reinstated.

B27 LEICESTERSHIRE

Derelict cottage, Mowsley

Derelict cottage, 2 km north of Grand Union Canal, on isolated lane, partially obscured by undergrowth. Rare survival of a late medieval worker's cottage, one-up, one-down, timber-framed with brick and clay infill. Thatch survives beneath corrugated but access difficult and limited samples taken during visit in April 1994. Roof pitch *c* 55 ° with straight gables and wooden barge boards concealing thatch on gable ends. Brick chimney. Adjacent to large derelict mud wall capped by decayed thatch. Sample taken composed of a straw of a dense-eared bread wheat, specimens *c* 45 cm, crushed over the entire stem but with evidence of single blows. Many ears intact ears. Butts with angular cuts (reaped?) and *c* 75 % butts-together. Ample flag leaf, detritus and weeds (particularly dock *Rumex* sp.).

B28 LINCOLNSHIRE

Old Yeomans House, Church Lane, Horbling
Owner: Carol Harrison

Mixed sample, recovered from one of the oldest (and last) originally thatched buildings in Lincolnshire, received in October 1995. Sample contains sections of straw rope (rye or oat), water reed from a base coat, rye straw and fragments of bread wheat.

B29 LONDON

Queen Charlotte's Cottage, Kew Gardens
Submitted by Jo Thwaites, Historic Royal Palaces Agency

Small specimens submitted by Jo Thwaites in September 1996. Sample 1 contained a fragment of tarred hempen twine, a single ear of rye and a bread wheat specimen with 10 cm of straw attached, all recovered from 'eaves in north-west porch roof'. Sample 2, taken from 'north-west porch under a rafter' contained a fragment of an ear of bread wheat.

B30 NORFOLK

The Five Gables, Lingwood
Owner: Mr Watson
Thatcher: David Farman

Cottage, seventeenth century with early nineteenth-century barn (converted and attached) and *c* 1920 extension. Rethatched with Norfolk Reed. Visited in March 1995. Pole rafters on early sections. Existing water reed being stripped down to a thick woven fleeking of water reed (tied to roof with tarred twine except on early nineteenth-century section, here applied in 'calm weather' according to thatcher as fleeking simply laid onto rafters). Nineteenth-century section last thatched in 1976, using iron rod and crooks. Layer removed in 1976 was tied and spar-coated with a second layer of reed (this last layer crooked). Seventeenth-century section last thatched in *c* 1944 with wooden sways tied to rafters with two-ply hemp rope and roundwood hazel sways *c* 2 cm diameter.

New water reed cut from Hickling Broad of inferior quality to 1976 reed being stripped. Original ridges survive (stripping old ridges not good practice according to D Farman). Nineteenth-century ridge now *c* 70 cm thick, of (1) sedge with underlying ridge roll of water reed, (2) fen sedge plus grass and (3) crushed straw of bread wheat. New raised ridge of fen sedge cut to simple diamented pattern. External layer needs replacing because sways have rotted, not water reed. New coat applied is moulded (drifted) with nail-studded leggat and not simply packed. Tight drifting necessary due to wind and rain in East Anglia. New roof will not need netting.

B31 NORFOLK

Cottage, The Priory, Ranworth
Owner: Charles Cater (British Reed Growers Association)

Cottage thatched with 'shoof', fine, grassy water reed with grass and sedge cut from parts of the broads that never produce high quality water reed. Specimens *c* 1.0 m. Once widely used for ridging when nothing else available. Used on barns and adjacent house with a straight flush ridge.

B32 NORTHAMPTONSHIRE

Church End, Rushden

Cottage visited with Peter Brockett, James Moir and Jo Cox in June 1994. Front of roof of straw in following sequence: L1 of combed wheat reed applied *c* 1979, surviving as *c* 20 cm butt specimens, uncrushed, coarse and apparently applied butts-up (unweathered); L2 of very well preserved bread wheat straw, specimens *c* 75 cm, crushed, ears and butts evenly mixed and in a bundle *c* 115 cm. Specimens crushed only on internodes. Sample contains minimal weed or rubbish. L3 of bread wheat straw, specimens *c* 70 cm (in a bundle *c* 100 cm), mixed but mostly butts-together, applied butts-down on roof, and with specimens crushed over entire stem except on nodes. Sample well-drawn with minimal weed or rubbish. L4 of bread wheat straw, specimens *c* 80 cm (in a bundle 110 cm), crushed, mixed but mostly butts-together and applied butts-down on roof. Abundant flag leaf, occasional weeds (eg *Melampyrum* sp., *Rumex* sp., grasses) and rubbish. Sparred. L5 (base coat) of bread wheat straw, specimens *c* 45 cm, evenly crushed, well-drawn, ears and butts mixed but mostly butts-together and applied butts-down on roof. Fixed with lightly-tarred twine (reddish, with very fine individual strands) and roundwood sways tied to rafters. Rear of roof thatched with water reed.

B33 NORTHAMPTONSHIRE

8 & 10 Church Street, Lower Weedon
Owner: Mrs Kate Hickman
Conservation officer: Michel Kerrou, Northamptonshire County
  Council

Visited on 15 April 1994. Large, high status stone house in village centre constructed in 1540. Mullioned stone windows, wattle and daub partition to ridge in roof space, large finely-dressed stone fireplaces and with high quality timber used in construction. Very light smoke-blackening survives on timbering (carved stone fireplaces original features). Roof re-thatched in 1987 with imported water reed. Ancient thatch stripped and rafters and battens replaced, but small samples of straw survive in crevices, on timbers and in patches along ridge. Large quantities of mixed thatch lies in piles on first floor with remains of ceiling. Small samples taken from eaves corners and along side walls (fallen material). Specimens mostly bread wheat with occasional wild oat, all very threshed. Specimens not weathered but short (*c* 30 cm) for straw thatching. Many of well preserved, long and lax-eared bread wheat. Many broken lower stem specimens and *c* 8 cm stubble (?). Occasional wild oat. Most specimens very threshed and broken due to cf flailing. Specimens generally much shorter than specimens in modern long straw. Base coat originally tied with tarred twine, with overlying layers sparred.

B34 NORTHAMPTONSHIRE

Little Thatches, Isham

Visited with Peter Brockett, James Moir and Jo Cox in July 1994. Seventeenth-century/early eighteenth-century brick cottage with gables and stone barges. Samples taken from within roof space. Roof steeply pitched (*c* 55 °). Thatch supported on a roughly woven fleeking of water reed, with upright bunches placed between each set of rafters (Fig B5). Fleeking tied to rafters with twisted grass rope, but very disturbed and absent in some areas. Occasional coarse battening of *c* 8–10 cm diameter split poles. External coat of recently applied combed wheat reed suffering slippage.

L1: base coat composed of rakings (?) from a flailed mixed crop of rye, rivet wheat (*Triticum turgidum*) and bread wheat. All specimens less than 30 cm, very fragmented and variable in length. Occasional two-row hulled barley rachis (*Hordeum vulgare* ssp. *distichum*). Many weeds. Most specimens cut:threshed. Fixed with lime-rich mud and twisted grass rope.

L1(a): taken from area adjacent to visible first course of mortar. Sample differs from L1: most specimens coarse (stubble?), short (*c* 25 cm) and either crushed: crushed or cut: crushed. Some specimens with distinct blow marks, many with butts undamaged.

L2: overlies base coat L1. Similar to L1 but with finer straw. Most ears very small (tillers?) of awned and awnless rivet wheat, but with occasional specimens of immature rye. Occasional mature field bean (*Vicia faba* ssp. *minor*) with pods and seeds intact. Straw specimens *c* 18 cm. Ample weed and flag leaf. Sample very grassy, threshed but unlikely to have produced much grain. Specimens mixed ears and butts. Sample definitely not drawn before application. Fixed with spars, including small diameter roundwood twigs.

L3: overlies L2. Better preserved than base coat samples. Dominated by short, *c* 25 cm, coarse basal specimens (stubble?) cut at their bases and broken at their apex (by crushing), ie bases of full-length straw separated by flailing? Butts mostly undamaged.

B35 NORTHAMPTONSHIRE

Carrey House, Great Brington
Thatcher: Russel Fox

Sample of base coat removed from eaves of early seventeenth-century stone and mud cottage with gable end and raised stone coping. Sample composed entirely of short, coarse, basal stubble of cf bread wheat, with specimens *c* 20–30 cm, cut at one end, broken at other. Ample leaf, weed and grass. Base coat of stubble applied to wet mud on top of wall and sealed by a second coat of mud. Eaves courses then sparred into this wet mud.

B36 NORTHAMPTONSHIRE

Bookshop, High Street, Brixworth

Large seventeenth-century timber-framed house faced with brick. Ceilings of plaster on a key of water reed. Fleeking of water reed clamped to rafters with nailed

Figure B5.

Figure B6.

Figure B7.

laths. Water reed tied in horizontal bunches between every rafter with three-ply rush (*Schoenoplectus lacustris*) rope (Fig B6). Base coat of bread wheat straw, crushed and mixed ears and butts.

B37 OXFORDSHIRE

Cottage, North Lane, Weston on the Green
Thatchers: Mike Minch and Mike Vickers

Samples received via Sally Straddling. 1) Thin base coat fleeking of water reed, 2) bread wheat straw, crushed and mixed ears and butts and 3) modern combed wheat reed (variety *Maris Huntsman?*). Water reed grows in profusion in ponds and ditches in village of Weston on the Green.

B38 OXFORDSHIRE

Pommander House, Harwell

Large, complex brick and timber-framed house. Main roof is of queen-post construction with neatly squared rafters and very even battening of riven oak laths *c* 8–10 cm x 1 cm. Roof very steeply pitched (*c* 60 °) (Fig B7). Small base coat sample recovered from secondary phase of early seventeenth-century smoke bay during visit in September 1994. Sample composed of bread wheat straw, specimens *c* 35 cm, well crushed, mixed ears and butts and lightly smoke-blackened. Fixed with saplings (willow?) on rear face and hempen cord on front face. Occasional surviving patches of a reed straw fleeking.

B39 OXFORDSHIRE

Ryle's Cottage, 76 Main Road, Long Hampborough
Owner: Mrs Lee
Conservation Officer: Gillian Amos, West Oxfordshire District Council
Thatcher: David Barton

Cottage, listed as fifteenth-/sixteenth-century, being stripped on front face for insertion of dormer window.

Visited on three occasions in January 1997, with G Amos and D Barton. Smoke-blackened thatch survives along ridge, above rear dormer and in patches on front face of building. Limited opportunity for sampling post smoke-blackened thatch. Base coat sample (front face) lightly smoke-blackened, of crushed bread and rivet wheat straw, mixed ears and butts. Minimum of four external layers of crushed bread wheat straw, mixed ears and butts, fixed with spars and hazel sways. Being rethatched with uncrushed, mostly butts-together reed straw combed over upper half of stem and occasional long straw.

B40 OXFORDSHIRE

Charlie's Cottage, Epwell
Owner: Mr and Mrs Binns
Thatcher: Conway Freeman

Samples received from Sally Straddling. Bread wheat combed wheat reed, specimens *c* 85 cm, combed but with ample flag leaf. Samples include tarred twine (tied to a roundwood hazel sway), modern split hazel sways *c* 50 cm and *c* 40 cm spar, a segment of rafter with a wooden peg and a hazel rod with a length of tarred twine used by thatcher to transport yealms of straw onto roof (a yoke).

B41 SUFFOLK

Cottage, Thornham Magna
Thatcher: Steven Letch

Building visited for sampling on 5 April 1994 with S Letch. Cottage, late seventeenth-century, steeply pitched (*c* 55 °), last thatched with long straw *c* 1974. Four small samples of straw removed by thatcher from rear face. L1 of early 1970s long straw, golden in colour, specimens now *c* 40 cm, evenly crushed over entire stem and mixed ears and butts. L2 of bread wheat straw, specimens now *c* 25 cm, coarse, threshed over apex, butts mostly intact and mixed ears and butts. L3 of bread wheat straw, specimens *c* 40 cm, coarse, with cut butts and crushed at apex. Abundant weed (particularly dock *Rumex* sp.). Base coat (L4) of bread wheat straw, specimens *c* 40 cm, crushed over full length of straw and mixed ears and butts. Abundant grass.

B42 HAMPSHIRE

Vinery Cottage, Hollybourne, Hampshire

Sample received by post in December 1994, from Clive Brooks (thatcher). Sample taken from base coat of oldest building in village, originally an open hall, but now without smoke-blackened thatch. Sample is a mixture of rye and bread wheat straw, specimens *c* 60 cm, crushed with distinct blows marks and mixed ears and butts. No date given, but probably mid nineteenth century or earlier.

B43 SURREY

Cottage, Wimbledon, Surrey

Sample received by post in December 1994, from Clive Brooks (thatcher). Composed of bread wheat straw, specimens *c* 40 cm, well crushed, fragmented and mixed ears and butts.

B44 SUSSEX

Barn, Court Farm, Falmer

Large, flint and brick, 14-bay thatched barn, with a steeply pitched roof (*c* 50 °), half-hipped, fourteenth century, much rebuilt this century, situated on Pevensey Levels. Visited with Richard Morrice of English Heritage in January 1995. Farm manager born on estate and very informative. Barn was purchased from the Earls of Sussex by Brighton Council in 1947, there being a 'considerable build-up' of straw thatch on the roof at this time. Assisted with threshing wheat straw (variety *Little Joss*) grown on estate used for repairs to barn roof in mid to late 1940s. This straw was fed into threshing machine so that only ears were crushed (ie apex-threshed reed straw). North outshot now slated. South outshot, now thatched, tiled or slated in 1947. Roof repaired, battens replaced and entire roof rethatched with Norfolk reed by a West Country firm in 1949 (that included a Norfolk reed-trained thatching apprentice). This coat capped with a patterned fen sedge (*Cladium mariscus*) ridge in 1949 and again in 1965 (this last ridge just visible on back-north face). Inserted eyebrow dormers and two sets of barn doors with roof extensions re-ridged with fen sedge in 1965, now very weathered. Roof cleaned in 1987. Main coat now *c* 20–25 cm thick, worn through near dormers, doors and ridge, with *c* 0.9–1.2 m of fine-stemmed reed surviving. Front face netted. North face currently has a heavy buildup of moss and lichen (sloughing off in large pieces) and is better preserved than front (south) face. Trees on north face only recently cut down. Roof not maintained in recent years. Hazel sways now exposed (fixed by crooks).

B45 WILTSHIRE

Vine Cottage, Union Street, Ramsbury

Three flint and brick cottages, seventeenth-/eighteenth-century, now combined into a grade II listed house of one storey and attic. Thatch swept low over outshot. Samples obtained via April Waterman, Kennet District Council in March 1995. Sample L6 (sixth layer below surface), composed of rye straw, specimens *c* 40 cm, crushed and mixed ears and butts. L4 of bread wheat straw, specimens *c* 45 cm, crushed and mixed ears and butts.

Figure B8.

B46 WILTSHIRE

Barn, Lavington

Semi-derelict brick barn, mid eighteenth century, on north edge of Salisbury Plain *c* 8 km south of Devizes. Rapid survey in June 1994. Hipped gables and one brick chimney stack. Thatch extends over outshot. Building facing south-west and rear face less weathered. Outer layer very decayed with heavy recolonization by grass, elder, various weeds and mosses (Fig B8). Base coat (L1) of a lax-eared bread wheat straw, specimens *c* 80–100 cm, mostly with three nodes, ears and butts mixed and with stems crushed only at apex. Little rubbish or flag leaf. L2 of bread wheat straw applied *c* 1945, specimens *c* 70 cm, ears and butts mixed and crushed evenly over entire stem. Little rubbish or flag leaf. Thatch supported on thin *c* 3 cm x 1 cm battens (over outshot) nailed to 14 cm x 14 cm rafters, and on coarser riven laths inside barn. Base coat tied to rafters with tarred twine. All layers sparred.

Glossary

ANAEROBIC Without oxygen.

AWN A stiff bristle growing from the ear of the plant.

BARGE The inclined edge of a roof rising along a gable, as opposed to the eaves.

BROACH [brotch, brawtch etc] An alternative term for *spar*.

CARR Fenland with water of a neutral pH.

COMBED WHEAT REED [combed wheat, wheat reed]
1. A form of thatching straw composed of stems that have been combed mechanically to remove grain and extraneous waste material without crushing the stem. The modern form of *reed straw*.
2. The modern technique of thatching a roof with this material, using the material in bundles which retain a common orientation to the stems. The material is dressed into place and usually secured without external fixings other than at the ridge.

CROOK An iron nail with a hooked head used to secure thatch directly to rafters by clasping the *sway* that holds a course of thatch in place. Formerly used only in difficult positions on a roof, but now used routinely in straw and *water reed* thatching.

CRUSHED STRAW Term used in these volumes to denote straw that has been bruised along its length and towards its lower end by threshing, and which subsumes the modern material known as *long straw*.

DRAWING The technique of pulling stems from a heap of material, thus aligning them for use as thatch and removing short stems, leaves and weeds. Now associated with *long straw*, which is drawn into *yealms*.

FLEEKING The practice, and product, of laying a thin coat of *water reed* (or other materials) beneath the lowest layer of the thatch to provide an even surface.

HAULM [halm, helm] See *stubble*, and also *helm*.

HELM [halm, haulm] A term (now obsolete) for *reed straw* as used in southern England beyond the West Country down to the mid nineteenth century, and composed of stems crushed only at their tops during threshing. The relation of *helm* to *haulm* is not yet entirely clear.

LEGGAT [legget, etc] A bat with one surface treated to catch the ends of the straw or reed (in *reed straw* and *water reed* thatching), with which the bundles may be beaten up under the *sways* to tighten the coat. Not used with *crushed straw* or other flexible materials.

LIGGER A length of roundwood (usually hazel or willow), often split, laid over the upper surface of a thatch to hold it in place, with the help of *spars*, and therefore similar to a *sway* except for its position. Rarely used in modern *water reed* or *combed wheat reed* thatching except on ridges, but used to hold in the eaves and *barges* of a *long straw* roof.

LODGING The flattening or buckling of crops in the field by the action of wind and rain (or other factors).

LONG STRAW [longstraw]
1. One of the two principal forms of thatching straw now used in England (the other being *combed wheat reed*) and the modern version of *crushed straw*. This material was identified by this name in the early nineteenth century, to distinguish it from the shorter straw removed in the course of mechanical threshing.
2. The modern technique of thatching with this material. The straw, which has usually been harvested with a reaper-binder and mechanically threshed, is *drawn* out of a wetted heap into *yealms* before being laid on the roof; the straw therefore usually has a proportion of butts pointing up the roof. The roof is crooked into place or is secured to the pre-existing base coat by *spars* and *sways*, rather than dressed into place as in *water reed* or *combed wheat reed* thatching.

MONOCOT Monocotyledonous; botanically, a flowering plant with one seed leaf that often reproduces by rhizomes as well as seed; in thatching, a member of the grass, rush or sedge families.

REED STRAW Generic term for all thatching straw which, in contrast to *crushed straw*, has had its grain removed without crushing the lower portion of the stem. *Combed wheat reed* is a modern version.

RHIZOME An underground stem of variable thickness that produces buds which can grow into new plants.

SPAR A section of roundwood (usually hazel) split, sharpened, and twisted into a U-shape. Thrust into the thatch the spar holds one layer to another, usually by holding down a *ligger* or a *sway*. See also *broach*.

SPAR COATING The fixing of a new layer of thatch onto an existing layer using *spars* and (usually) *sways*. Persistent spar coating produces stratified accumulations of thatch.

STINGING [stingeing] The practice of inserting new material into a roof requiring repair, by opening a hole and forcing the new material into the gap.

STOB A small plug of new material inserted into a roof in the repair process called stobbing or *stinging*.

STUBBLE The uncrushed residue of the straw left standing in the fields after harvesting, which when tall could be mown and used for thatching. In this form also called *haulm*.

SWAY A section of roundwood, formerly of hazel or willow but now often of iron, used horizontally in combination with *spars* or *crooks* to clamp a new course of thatch into position. Each sway is concealed in the finished roof by the next course of thatch or by the ridge. See also *ligger*.

TILLERING Cereals produce tillers, lateral shoots from the base of the stem, during the winter and spring which eventually elongate and produce ears.

WALE Reed-beds cut annually produce 'single-wale'; beds cut every two years produce 'double-wale'.

WATER REED
1. Wetland plant (today *Phragmites australis*) used for thatching.
2. The technique of thatching with this material, which is carried onto the roof in bundles and secured butts down with *sways* and (today) *crooks*. The reed is driven up under the fixings with a *leggat* to tighten the roof.

YEALM The bundle formed in *long straw* thatching from handfuls of straw which have been *drawn* from the heap of threshed material.

YEALMING The practice in *long straw* thatching of forming the bundles called *yealms*, by *drawing*.

Bibliography

PUBLISHED SOURCES

Airs M, 1981 Hovels or helms: some further evidence from the seventeenth century, in *Vernacular Architecture*, **14**, 50–51.

Albino H H, 1946 House thatching, in *Somerset Countryman*, **15**:4, 68–71.

Allingham H and Dick S, 1991 *The Cottage Homes of England*, London, Bracken Books.

Angold R E, Sadd P A and Sanders M, 1998 *Fire and Thatch. Project report for Partners in Technology Project Number: CI 39/3/2866. Specifications for Materials and Treatment of Thatch* Volume 1, High Wycombe, RHM Technology.

Angold R E and Sanders M, 1998 *Longevity of Thatch in Relation to the Surface Properties of Straw. Final Report for the Partners in Technology Project DoE reference CI 39/3/286* Volume 2, High Wycombe, RHM Technology.

anon, nd Time to remember: 100 years of local history, *Northampton Evening Telegraph* [press cuttings file, Northamptonshire Library].

–, 1804 *Results of the Enquiry (on Labour) being a Recapitulation of the Average Wages of Several Counties 1790–1803*, Board of Agriculture.

–, 1807 5th ed *The Complete Farmer or, General Dictionary of Agriculture and Husbandry: comprehending the most-improved methods of cultivation; the different modes of raising timber, fruit and other tree; and the modern management of livestock: with descriptions of the most approved implements, machinery and farm-buildings*

–, 1909 Thatching, in *The British Architect*, **71**, 145–6.

–, 1916 Thatching, in *Journal of the Bath & West Somerset Counties Society*, 5th ser, **XI**, 274–7.

–, 1922a Straw reed for thatching, in *The Architect*, **107**, 276.

–, 1922b A decaying industry, [unknown newspaper cutting, Northamptonshire Local Studies Library].

–, 1922c, in *Birmingham Post*, 31 August.

–, 1923a, in *Western Morning News*, 13 July 1923.

–, 1923b New cottages at Tetbury, in *The Architectural Association Journal*, **39**, 61.

–, 1926 The revival of thatching, in *The Studio*, **91**, 93–7.

–, 1927a Thatching by reedwork, in *The National Builder*, 34–35.

–, 1927b Modern Practice. I – Fireproofing thatch, in *The Architect & Building News*, **117**, 1066.

–, 1931 The present position of the use of fertilisers, in *Journal of the Royal Agricultural Society* **92**, 162–176

–, 1932 The ancient industry of thatching, in *The Builder*, **143**, 130.

–, 1933 The thatched roof, in *The National Builder*, 236–238.

–, 1948 Secrets of thatching must be saved, in *Northamptonshire Independent*, 18 June 1948.

–, 1949 Portrait of a country craftsman: 3: R W Farman, reed thatcher, in *The Village*, **1**.

–, 1953 *A Report from April 1952 to March 1953 on the Development of Skill in Country Workshops*, London, Rural Industries Bureau.

–, 1959a Porthleven's last thatched house, in *The West Briton*, 23 April.

–, 1959b, in *The South Devon Journal*, 29 April.

–, 1962 Running a Cottage to Earth, in *Ideal Home*, June, 31.

–, 1967 Old cottage is protected, in *The Guardian*, 22 March.

–, 1971 *Ideal Home*, July, 44.

–, 1990 *Het Weke Dak*, Den Haag.

Armstrong A, 1988 *Farmworkers: A Social and Economic History 1770–1980*, London, Batsford.

Bacon R N, 1844 *The Report on the Agriculture of Norfolk*, London, Chapman & Hall.

Bagshawe T W, 1951 *Disappearing Rural Industries, Trades, Crafts and Occupations*, 5 vols, unpublished PhD thesis, Bagshawe Collection.

Bailey C, 1856 *Transcripts from the Municipal Archives of Winchester*, Winchester, Hugh Barclay.

Bailey J, 1810 *General View of the Agriculture of the County of Durham, with Observations on the Means of its Improvement*, London, Board of Agriculture.

– and Culley G, 1794 *General View of the Agriculture of the County of Cumberland with Observations on the Means of Improvement*, London, Board of Agriculture.

– , 1800 *General View of the County of Northumberland*, Newcastle, Board of Agriculture.

Baker A E, 1854 *Glossary of Northamptonshire words and phrases*, 2 vols, London, J R Smith.

Banks J, 1807 On the culture of spring wheat, in *The Repertory of Arts and Manufactures*, 2nd ser, **10**, 42–48.

Batchelor T, 1808 *General View of the Agriculture of the County of Bedford*, London, Board of Agriculture.

Bateman S, Turner R K and Bateman I J, 1990 *Socio-economic impact of changes in the quality of thatching reed on the future of the reed growing and thatching industries, and on the wider rural economy*, Report to the Rural Development Commission, School of Environmental Sciences, University of East Anglia.

Batsford H and Fry C, 1938 *The English Cottage*, London, Batsford.

Baxter J, 1834, *The Library of Agricultural and Horticultural Knowledge*, 3rd ed, Lewes, J Baxter.

Beaven E S, 1909 Pedigree seed corn, in *Journal of the Royal Agricultural Society*, **70**, 119–139.

Bell J and Watson M, 1986 *Irish Farming, Implements and Techniques 1750–1900*, Edinburgh, John Donald.

Bibby C J and Lunn J, 1982 Conservation of reed beds and their avifauna in England and Wales, in *Biological Conservation*, **23**, 167–186.

Biffen R H, 1915 Spring wheats, in *Journal of the Royal Agricultural Society*, **76**, 37–48.

Biffen R H and Engledow F L, 1926 *Wheat Breeding Investigations at the Plant Breeding Institute, Cambridge*, Ministry of Agriculture & Fisheries Research Monograph, **4**, London.

Billett M, 1979 (1988) *Thatching and Thatched Buildings*, London, Robert Hale.

Billett, M, 1984 *Thatched Buildings of Dorset*, London, Robert Hale.

Billingsley J, 1798 *General View of the Agriculture in the County of Somerset with Observations on the Means of its Improvement*, 2nd ed, Bath, Board of Agriculture.

Bingham J, 1979 Wheat breeding objectives and prospects, in *Agricultural Progress*, **54**, 1–17.

–, Law C and Miller T, 1991 *Wheat Yesterday, Today and Tomorrow*, Cambridge, Plant Breeding International & Plant Research Ltd.

Blackburn S, 1982 *The Life of a Norfolk Thatcher*, Salhouse, privately published.

Board of Agriculture & Fisheries, 1910 *Thatching*, Board of Agriculture & Fisheries Leaflet **236**, London, Board of Agriculture & Fisheries.

Boardman H C, 1933 Reed thatching in Norfolk, in *Architects Journal*, **77**, 563-7.

Bolton N and Chalkley B, 1990 The rural population turna-round: a case-study of north Devon, in *Journal of Rural Studies*, **6**, 29–43.

Bowick T, 1883 *The Crops of the Farm*, London, Bradbury Agnew.

Bowley M, 1960 *Innovations in Building Materials. An Economic Study*, London, Gerald Duckworth & Co.

Boys J, 1805 *General View of the Agriculture of the County of Kent; with Observations on the Means of its Improvement*, 2nd ed, London, Richard Phillips.

Bradshaw A, 1912 The thatching of ricks, in *Board of Agriculture Journal*, **19**, 301.

Brereton, C, 1991 *The Repair of Historic Buildings: advice on principles and methods*, London, English Heritage.

Brewer J G, 1972 *Enclosures and the Open Fields: A Bibliography*, London, British Agricultural History Society.

British Batavian Trading Company, 1915 *Thatching and How to Make it Permanently Fire-Proof*, London, The British Batavian Trading Company Limited.

Brockett, P, nd *Straw Thatching: When is Straw not a Straw?* unpublished report, private archive.

Brockett P and Wright A, 1986 *The Care and Repair of Thatched Roofs*, Technical Pamphlet **10**, London, Society for the Protection of Ancient Buildings & the Rural Development Commission

Brough S, 1976 A Cornish tradition: John Williams – Thatcher of Chacewater, in *Cornish Life*, **3**, 11–13.

Brown J, 1974 *A Thatcher's Memories*, typescript, Chelmsford Library.

–, 1978 Thatching with Father, *in* Seager 1978, 76–9.

Brown A G and Bradley C, 1995 Past and present alluvial wetlands and the eco-archaeo resource: implications from research in the East Midlands valleys (UK), in Rowley T (ed), The Evolution of Marshland Landscapes, Oxford, Rewley House, 283–95.

Burke J F, 1834–40 *British Husbandry*, 3 vols, London, Baldwin & Cradock.

Burn R S, 1878 [1889–1904] *Outlines of Modern Farming*, 5th edn, 5 vols, London, Crosby & Lockwood.

Burton A, 1891 *Rush-bearing: An Account of the Old Custom of Strewing Rushes; Carrying Rushes to Church; the Rush-cart; Garlands in Churches; Morris-Dancers; the Wakes; the Rush*, Manchester, Brook & Chrystal.

Caird J, 1851 *English Agriculture in 1850–51*, London, Longman & Co.

Campbell D, 1831 On thatching with fern, *Prize Essays and Transactions of the Highland Society of Scotland*, **2**, New Ser, 184–90.

Champion A G, ed, 1989 *Counterurbanization: The Changing Pace and Nature of Popular Decentralization,* London, Edward Arnold.

Chapman V, 1982 Heather-thatched buildings in the northern Pennines, *Transactions of the Architectural & Archaeological Society of Durham & Northumberland*, **4,** new ser, 9–12.

Chapman W, 1798 Specification of the patent granted ... for a method of laying, twisting, or making ropes or cordages, in *Repertory of Arts and Manufactures*, **1**, 2nd ser, 1–44.

Charlton L, 1779 *The History of Whitby and of Whitby Abbey*, York.

Clapham A R, Tutin T G and Moore D M, 1987, *Flora of the British Isles*, 3rd edn, Cambridge, Cambridge University Press.

Clapp B W, Fischer H E S and Jurica A R J, 1977 *Documents in English Economic History*, 2 vols, London, G Bell.

Clark C, 1947 Thatch, thatchers and thatching, in *Agriculture*, **53**, 444–50.

Clark C, 1948 letter *The Times,* January.

Clifton-Taylor A 1972 *The Pattern of English Building*, London, B T Batsford.

Cohen, nd Roofs of reed, undated newspaper cutting, Ipswich Record Office

Collier J, 1831 On thatching with heath, *Prize Essays and Transactions of the Highland Society of Scotland*, **2**, new ser, 190–5.

Collins E J T, 1969 *Sickle to Combine. A Review of Harvest Techniques from 1800 to the Present Day*, Reading, Museum of English Rural Life.

–, 1970 *Harvest Technology and Labour Supply in Britain 1790–1870*, unpublished PhD thesis, University of Nottingham.

Collins W W, 1866 *Armadale*, 2 vols, London.

Coppock J T, 1964 *An Agricultural Atlas of England and Wales*, Faber, London.

–, 1971 *An Agricultural Geography of Great Britain*, London, Faber & Faber

Council for British Archaeology, 1985 *Making Sense of Buildings*, London, Council for British Archaeology.

Cowell J G, nd *Treatise on Thatching*, Soham, privately published.

Cowley W, 1955 The technique and terminology of stacking and thatching in Cleveland, in *Yorkshire Dialect Society Transactions*, **9**, pt 54, 35–40.

Cox J, 1994 *Thatch and Thatching from 1940*, 2 vols, internal report for English Heritage.

– and Thorp J, 1991 Authentic slating in Devon, in *Transactions of the Association for Studies in the Conservation of Historic Buildings*, **16**, 3–12.

Crampton A H, 1935 *Rushwork*, London, The Studio Ltd.

Crampton C and Mochrie E, 1931 *Rushwork*, 2nd edn, Leicester, Dryad Press.

Creasey J and Ward S, 1984 *The Countryside Between the Wars 1918–1940, A Photographic Record*, London, Batsford.

Crowther R E and Evans J, 1986 *Coppice*, 2nd edn, Forestry Commission Leaflet **83**, London, HMSO.

Darby H C (ed), 1976 *A New Historical Geography of England after 1600*, Cambridge, Cambridge University Press.

Darley G, 1978 *Villages of Vision*, London, Paladin.

Davey B J, 1980 *Ashwell 1830–1914. The Decline of the Village Community*, Occasional Paper **5**, 3rd Series, Leicester, Leicester University Press.

Davis T, 1811 *General View of the Agriculture of Wiltshire*, London, Board of Agriculture.

Deas J H, 1939 *Building in Norfolk*, unpublished thesis, Royal Institute of British Architects.

Department of the Environment, 1987 *Circular 8/87. Historic Buildings and Conservation Areas – Policy and Procedures* London, HMSO

Department of the Environment, 1994 *Planning Policy and Guidance: Planning and the Historic Environment*, **15**, London, HMSO

Dickes W F, 1906 *The Norwich School of Painting*, Norwich, Jarrold & Sons.

Dickson R W and Stevenson W A, 1815 *General View of the Agriculture of Lancashire with Observations on the Means of its Improvement*, London, Board of Agriculture.

Diplock A H, 1929 Sussex roofs, in *Sussex County Magazine*, **3**, 620–621.

Dodds L, 1929 Straw thatch as a building material, in *The National Builder*, October, 86–87.

Donaldson J, 1847 *The Cultivated Plants of the Farm*, London, R Groombridge and Sons.

Duckham, A N, Jewell A J, Fox S, Gibb J A C and Pearce J (eds), 1963 *Farming*, **4**, Caxton, London.

Duncan R, 1947 *Home-Made Home*, London, Faber & Faber

Dundonald Earl of, 1794 Specification of the patent granted ... for his method of extracting or making tar, pitch, essential oils, volatile alkali, mineral acids, salts and cinders from pit-coal, in *Repertory of Arts and Manufactures*, **1**, 2nd ser, 145–8.

Dyer J, 1981 *My Early Days*, Twyford, privately published.

East Anglian Master Thatcher's Association, 1989 2nd ed *Technical Pamphlet*, **1**, East Anglian Master Thatcher's Association, Norwich.

Ellis C W, Eastwick-Field J and Eastwick-Field E, 1947 *Buildings in Cob, Pise and Stabilised Earth*, Country Life, London.

Elson M, 1959 Is the thatched roof doomed?, in *Country Life*, **126**, 526–8.

Emery N, 1985 The heather thatching of buildings, in *Making Sense of Buildings*, Council for British Archaeology, London, Council for British Archaeology, 89–94.

–, 1986 Fell Close Farm and the use of 'Black Thack', in *Durham Archaeological Journal*, **2**, 91-95.

Environmental Appraisal Group,1991 *Socio-Economic Impact of Changes in the Quality of Thatching Reed on the Future of the Reed-Growing and Thatching Industries and on the Wider Rural Economy*, School of Environmental Sciences, University of East Anglia

Evans E E, 1957 *Irish Folk Ways*, London, Routledge & Kegan Paul.

Farey J, 1811 *General View of the Agriculture and Minerals of Derbyshire with Observations on the Means of Their Improvement*, 3 vols, London, Board of Agriculture.

Farman A, 1949 Retirement of reed thatcher, in *The Eastern Daily Press*, 3 January.

Fearn J, 1972 *Thatch and Thatching*, Aylesbury, Shire.

Fenton A, 1978 *The Northern Isles, Orkney and Shetlands*, Edinburgh, Donald.

Fielden M E, 1934 Old-time survivals in Devon, *Report & Transactions of the Devonshire Association*, **66**, 357–373.

Filmer R, 1980 Kentish thatch, *Bygone Kent*, **1**, 324-331.

–, 1981 *Kentish Rural Crafts and Industries*, Rainham, Meresborough.

Fitzrandolph H E and Hay M D, 1926 *The Rural Industries of England & Wales. A Survey Made on behalf of the Agricultural Economics Research Institute Oxford. II. Osier-growing and Basketry and Some Rural Factories*, Oxford, Clarendon Press.

Foot P, 1794 *General View of the Agriculture of the County of Middlesex, with Observations on the Means of their Improvement*, London, Board of Agriculture.

Frankel O H, 1976 Natural variation and its conservation, in *Genetic Diversity in Plants Proceedings of an International Symposium on Genetic Control of Diversity in Plants held at Lahore, Pakistan, March 1–7, 1976*, Muhammed A, Aksel R and Borstal R C von, New York, Plenum Press.

Fyfe W W, 1863 Farm seeds and seeding, in *Journal of the Bath & West of England Society*, **11**, new ser, 296–353.

Gailey A, 1984 *Rural Houses of the North of Ireland*, Edinburgh, John Donald.

Gardiner D, 1949 *Companion into Dorset*, 4th edn, London, Methuen.

Gill N T and Vear K C, 1969 *Agricultural Botany*, 2nd edn, London, Duckworth.

Gooch W, 1811 *General View of the Agriculture of the County of Cambridge*, London, Richard Phillips.

Goodland N, 1953 *My Father Before Me*, London, Hutchinson.

Gratton H, 1936 letter, in *The Western Times*, October [cutting in West Country Studies Library].

Greenacre D W, 1958 Reeds for the thatcher, *The Field*, 24 April.

Grigg D, 1980 *Population Growth and Agrarian Change: An Historical Perspective*, Cambridge, Cambridge University Press.

–, 1989 *English Agriculture: An Historical Perspective*, Oxford, Basil Blackwell.

Grove A T, 1962 Fenland, in *Great Britain: Geographical Essays*, Mitchell J B, Cambridge, Cambridge University Press, 104–122.

Gunn E, 1936 The art of the thatcher, *Somerset Countryman*, **6**:2, 30–31.

Halliwell W, 1905 English wheat and the development of British milling, *Journal of the Royal Agricultural Society*, **66**, 224–229.

Hansard 1948 *Oral Answers*, 15 April 1948.

Harman H, 1929 *Buckinghamshire Dialect*, London, Hazell, Watson & Viney.

Harper C G, 1921 Thatch, in *Journal of the American Institute of Architects*, **9**, 389–96.

Harris E and Savage N, 1990 *British Architectural Books and Writers 1556–1785*, Cambridge, Cambridge University Press.

Harrison J R, 1989 Some clay dabbins in Cumberland: their construction and form. Part I, in *Transactions of the Ancient Monuments Society*, **33**, 97–151.

Hartley D, 1939 *Made in England*, London, Methuen.

Hartley M and Ingilby J, 1968 *Life and Tradition in the Yorkshire Dales*, London, Dent.

–, 1972 *Life in the Moorlands of North-East Yorkshire*, London, Dent.

–, 1978 Roofs gathered from nature. Ling thatches, in *Country Life*, **163**, 1022–4.

–, 1986 *Dales Memories*, London, The Dalesman.

Harvey J H, 1945 Mudtown, Walton-on-Thames, in *Surrey Archaeological Collections*, **49**, 127–9.

Haslam S M, 1972 *The Reed (Norfolk Reed)*, 2nd edn, Norwich, Norfolk Reed Growers Association.

–, Sinker C and Wolseley P, 1975 British water plants, in *Journal of Field Studies*, **4**, 243–351.

Hay A C de P, nd *St Michaels Church, Ingram: The Story*, Alnwick, privately published.

Hennell T B, 1934 *Change in the Farm*, Cambridge, Cambridge University Press.

Hervey-Murray C G, 1980 *The Identification of Cereal Varieties*, Cambridge, RHM Arable Services Ltd.

Hetrick B A D and Wilson G W, 1992 Mycorrhizal dependence of modern wheat vars, land races and ancestors, in *Canadian Journal of Botany*, **70**, 2032–2040.

Hickish J R, 1960 Thatching costs a pretty penny, in *Farm and Country*, 3 August.

Hillman G C, 1983 *Archaeobotanical Criteria Used to Distinguish Tetraploid and Hexaploid Wheat Rachis Remains*, MSc course notes, London, Institute of Archaeology.

Hillyard C, 1837 *Practical Farming and Grazing*, 2nd edn, Northampton, T E Dicey.

Hine R, 1914 *The History of Beaminster*, Taunton, Barnicott & Pearce.

Hodgson J C (ed), 1914 Northern journeys of Bishop Richard Pococke, in *Publications of the Surtees Society*, **124**, 199–252.

Holden T G, 1998 *The Archaeology of Scottish Thatch*, Edinburgh, Historic Scotland Technical Advice Note **13**.

Holland H, 1808 *General View of the Agriculture of Cheshire*, London, Board of Agriculture.

Holt J, 1795 *General View of the Agriculture of the County of Lancaster: With Observations on the Means of its Improvement*, London, Board of Agriculture.

Hoppit D, 1985 Thatching, *Traditional Homes*, January, 36.

Horrox D K, 1953 The folk who live at Ramsgill, *The Dalesman* **14**, 513–515.

Humphries A E, 1911 The milling of wheat in the United Kingdom, in *Journal of the Royal Agricultural Society*, **72**, 24–37.

Hunt T F, 1827 *Designs for Parsonage Houses, Alms Houses, etc*, London, Longman & Co.

Hutchins J, 1861–73 *The History and Antiquities of the County of Dorset*, 3rd edn, 4 vols, London, J B Nichols & Sons.

Innocent C F, 1916 *The Development of English Building Construction*, Cambridge, Cambridge University Press.

Isaac J W P, 1856 On the economical adaptation of existing agricultural dwellings to the health and comfort of the inhabitants, on improved sanitary principles, in *Journal of the Bath & West of England Society*, **4**, new ser, 111–125.

Jarman R J and Pickett A A, 1994 *Botanical Descriptions of Cereal Varieties*, Cambridge, National Institute of Agricultural Botany.

Jekyll G, 1899 *Wood and Garden. Notes and Thoughts, Practical and Critical, of a Working Amateur*, London, Longman & Co.

Jenkins D T, nd *Indexes of the Fire Insurance Policies of the Sun Fire Office and the Royal Exchange Assurance 1775–1787*, typescript, Guildhall Library.

Jenkins J G, 1965 *Traditional Country Craftsmen*, London, Routledge & Kegan Paul.

Jobson A, 1949 The reed-thatcher's tools, *Country Life*, **105**, 1187.

–, 1961 The thatched churches of Suffolk, in *East Anglian Magazine*, **20**, 494–504.

Johnson S, 1827 *Dictionary of the English Language*, London.

Johnston J, 1847 *Lectures on Agricultural Chemistry and Geology*, Edinburgh, William Blackwood & Sons.

Jones A M, 1927 *The Rural Industries of England & Wales. A Survey Made on behalf of the Agricultural Economics Research Institute Oxford. IV. Wales*, Oxford, Oxford University Press.

Jones E L, 1968 The reduction of fire damage in southern England, 1650–1850, in *Post-Medieval Archaeology*, **2**, 140–149.

– and Falkus M E, 1990 Urban improvement and the English economy in the seventeenth and eighteenth centuries, in Borsay P (ed), 1990 *The Eighteenth-Century Town; A Reader in English Urban History 1688–1820*, London, Longman, 119–127.

Juniper B E, 1990 Straw: its structure, chemistry and the possibilities for its further use as a raw material for industry, in *Agricultural Progress*, **65**, 23–38

Katz H R, 1976 *The Decline of Thatch*, unpublished thesis, Architectural Association.

Kennaway L M, nd *To Lovers of English Rural Scenery*, privately published.

Kent N, 1796 *General View of the Agriculture of the County of Norfolk; With Observations For the Means of its Improvement*, London, Board of Agriculture.

Kirby J J, Marigold E A and Ansell M P, 1990 *The Quality of Combed Wheat Reed for Thatching*, unpublished manuscript, private collection.

Kirby J J and Rayner A D, 1986 *The Biodegradation of Thatching Straw*, typescript, project reference CSA 900, School of Biological Sciences, University of Bath.

–, 1988 Disturbance, decomposition and patchiness in thatch, in *Proceedings of the Royal Society Edinburgh*, **94B**, 145–153.

–, 1989 *Aspects of the Decomposition, Mechanical Strength and Anatomy of Water Reed (P. Australis) used in Thatching*, MAFF Report, School of Biological Science, University of Bath.

Lambert J M, Jennings J N, Smith C T, Green C and Hutchinson J N, 1960 *The Making of the Broads. A Reconsideration of Their Origin in the Light of New Evidence*, London, John Murray.

Langton J and Morris R J, 1986 *An Atlas of Industrializing Britain, 1780–1914*, London, Methuen.

Lankester E, 1832 *The Library of Entertaining Knowledge. Vegetable substances used for the food of man*, London, Charles Knight.

Laugier M A, 1755 *An Essay on Architecture*, London, T Osborne & Shipton.

Lawton R and Podley C G, 1992 *Britain 1740–1950: An Historical Geography*, London, Edward Arnold.

Laycock C H, 1920 The old Devon farm-house. Part I. Its exterior aspect and general construction, in *Report & Transactions of the Devonshire Association*, **52**, 158–91.

Le Couteur J, 1836 *On the Varieties, Properties and Classification of Wheat*, Jersey, privately published.

Le Vegetal, 1977 *Les toits dans le paysage*, Strasbourg, Maian Mane Clarne, Imprimirie Istra.

Letts J B, 1999 *Smoke-blackened Thatch (SBT). A Unique Source of Late Medieval Plant Remains from Southern England, London & Reading*, London, English Heritage & the University of Reading.

Lisle E, 1757 *Observations in Husbandry*, Faulkner, Dublin.

Loudon J C, 1831 *An Encyclopedia of Agriculture*, 2nd edn, London, Longman, Rees, Orme, Brown & Green.

Low D, 1843 *Elements of Practical Agriculture*, London, Longman, Brown, Green & Longmans.

Lowe J, 1994 *The Dorset Thatching Report*, typescript, Dorset County Council.

Lucas A T, 1960 *Furze. A Survey and History of its Uses in Ireland*, Dublin, Educational Company of Ireland.

Lucas R, 1995 Some observations on descriptions of parsonage buildings made in Norfolk glebe terriers, in *Transactions of the Ancient Monuments Society*, **39**, 85–98.

Lupton F G H, 1987 The history of wheat breeding, in Lupton F G H, *Wheat Breeding: its Scientific Basis*, London, Chapman & Hall, 52–71.

Lyall S, 1988 *Dream Cottages. From Cottage Orné to Stockbroker Tudor. Two Hundred Years of the Cult of the Vernacular*, London, Robert Hale.

Machin R, 1994 *Rural Housing: An Historical Approach*, London, The Historical Association.

Mackenzie E, 1825 *An Historical, Topographical, and Descriptive View of the County of Northumberland*, 2nd edn, 2 vols, Newcastle upon Tyne.

McGlue, nd Separate staircases and thatch over all, *Traditional Homes*, 5.

McLaren G, 1991 *The Conservation of Thatched Buildings in Great Britain*, unpublished diploma thesis, the Architectural Association.

Malcolm W, Malcolm James and Malcolm Jacob, 1794 *General View of the Agriculture of the County of Surrey, with Observations on the Means of its Improvement*, London, Board of Agriculture.

Manners J E, 1979 Roofs for a poor man. Thatching in Ireland, in *Country Life*, **166**, 271–2.

Marshall W, 1790 *The Rural Economy of the West of England: including Devonshire; and Parts of Somersetshire, Dorsetshire, and Cornwall*, 2 vols, London, Nicol.

–, 1818 The Midlands, *Review and Abstracts of the County Records of the Board of Agriculture*, **4**, London, David & Charles.

Martin D and Martin B, 1978 *Historic Buildings in Eastern Sussex Rape of Hastings Architectural Survey*, **2**.

–, 1979 *Historic Buildings in Eastern Sussex Rape of Hastings Architectural Survey*, **4**.

Massingham H J, 1943 *Men of Earth*, London, Chapman & Hall.

Mathias P, 1969 *The First Industrial Nation: An Economic History of Britain, 1700–1914*, London, Methuen.

Maufe E, 1946 *The Architectural use of Building Materials*. Post-War Building Studies **18**, London, HMSO.

Mavor W, 1809 *General View of the Agriculture of Berkshire*, London, Richard Phillips.

McDonnell J (ed), 1963 *A History of Helmsley, Rievaulx and District*, York, Stonegate Press.

McDougall D S, 1958 Harvesting the Norfolk reed, in *The Field*, 21 March, 493–4.

Meeson R A and Welch C M, 1993 Earthfast posts: The persistence of alternative building techniques, in *Vernacular Architecture*, **24**, 1–17.

Meirion-Jones G I, 1976 Some early and primitive building forms in Brittany, in *Folk Life*, **14**, 46–64.

Metcalfe A, 1953 It's warm under the thatch, in *The Dalesman*, **15**, 296–7.

Middleton J, 1798 *View of the Agriculture of Middlesex; With Observations on the Means of its Improvement and Several Essays on Agriculture in General*, London, Board of Agriculture.

–, 1800 *Experiments and Observations on Various Kinds of Manure*, Lambeth, privately published.

Ministry of Agriculture ('John Fallowfield'), 1941 *Harvesting Problems and the Modern Combine: Does the Modern Combine Save Money? An Official Enquirers Report*, London, HMSO.

Mitchell B R and Deane P, 1962 *Abstract of British Historical Statistics*, Cambridge, Cambridge University Press.

Mitchell T J, 1961a Yorkshire thatch, in *The Dalesman*, **22**, 783–788.

–, 1961b Yorkshire thatch, in *The Dalesman*, **23**, 134–135.

Moir J, 1990 *A World unto Themselves? Squatter Settlement in Herefordshire 1780–1880*, unpublished PhD thesis, University of Leicester.

Moore A W, 1982 *John Sell Cotman, 1782–1842*, Norwich, Norfolk Museum Service.

Morgan W E and Cooper F W, 1960 *The Thatcher's Craft*, Salisbury, Rural Industries Bureau.

Morris G L, 1909 The home – III. A thatched cottage, in *The British Architect*, **71**, 149–150.

Morrison J (ed), 1898 *The Diaries of Jeffrey Whitaker 1739–1741*, Wiltshire Record Society **44**, Salisbury.

Morrison J, 1993 *Corn Varieties Grown in the Nineteenth Century At Grants Farm, Bratton, Wiltshire*, typescript, private collection.

Morton J, 1862 *The Farmer's Calendar*, 21st edn, London, Routledge, Warne & Routledge.

Murray J, 1895 *Handbook for Hertfordshire, Bedfordshire and Huntingdonshire*, London, John Murray.

Nash, J, 1991, *Thatchers and Thatching* London, B T Batsford

Nash J, 1994 Harold Wright, in *Somerset Magazine*, **4**, 16–19.

Neve R, 1726 [1969] *The City and Country Purchaser and Builder's Dictionary*, London, David and Charles.

Nightingale F W, 1939 Must a beautiful rural craft die?, in *Northampton Independent*, 24 March, Supplement, iv.

Northamptonshire County Council, 1935 Rural housing, in *Annual Report*, Northampton, Northamptonshire County Council.

Nugat P, 1950 James Fosberry – thatcher, in *The Sussex County Magazine*, **24**, 245–247.

Oldershaw A W, 1944 *Good Farm Crops*, London, Hodder & Stoughton.

– and Porter J, 1929 *British Farm Crops*, London, Ernest Benn.

Oxford English Dictionary, 1989, Oxford, Oxford University Press.

Palmer J, 1978 Craftsmen then and now: the thatcher, in *Northamptonshire Life*, January 1978, 40–43.

Palmer J D, 1970 Plant breeding today, in *Journal of the Royal Agricultural Society*, **131**, 7–17.

Parkinson R, 1808 *General View of the Agriculture of the County of Rutland, with Observations on the Means of its Improvement*, London, Board of Agriculture.

–, 1811 *General View of the Agriculture of the County of Huntingdon*, London, Richard Phillips.

Parrott W R, 1974 *Sixty Years a Thatcher*, Clapham, Beds, privately published.

Partridge M, 1973 *Farm Tools through the Ages*, Reading, Osprey Publishing.

Patterson W G R (ed), 1925 *Farm Crops*, 4 vols, London, Gresham Publishing.

Peachey R A, 1951 *Cereal Varieties in Great Britain*, London, Crosby Lockwood & Son.

Peate I C, 1944 *The Welsh House. A Study in Folk Culture*, 2nd edn, Liverpool, H Evans & Sons.

Percival J, 1921 *The Wheat Plant: A Monograph*, London, Duckworth & Co.

–, 1942, *Agricultural Botany*, 8th edn, London, Duckworth.

–, 1943 *Wheat in Great Britain*, Shinfield, London, Duckworth.

Peters J E C, 1977 The solid thatch roof, in *Vernacular Architecture*, **8**, 825.

Phillips A D M, 1989 *The Underdraining of Farmland in England During the Nineteenth Century*, Cambridge, Cambridge University Press.

Phillips N J A, 1975 *Dykes of Romney Marsh*, Hawkhurst, privately published.

Pitt W, 1809a *General View of the Agriculture of the County of Northampton*, London, Board of Agriculture.

–, 1809b *A General View of the Agriculture of the County of Leicester; with Observations on the Means of its Improvement; to which is annexed a survey of the county of Rutland*, London, Board of Agriculture.

–, 1810 (1969) *General View of the Agriculture of the County of Worcester*, David & Charles

–, 1813 *General View of the Agriculture of the County of Stafford; with Observations on the Means of its Improvement*, London, Board of Agriculture.

Plaw J, 1800 *Sketches for Country Houses, Villas, and Rural Dwellings*, London, J Taylor.

Plymley J, 1803 *General View of the Agriculture of Shropshire: With Observations*, London, Board of Agriculture.

Pocock W F, 1807 *Architectural Designs for Rustic Cottages, Picturesque Dwellings, Villas*, London, J Taylor.

Porter S, 1986 Thatching in early-modern Norwich, in *Norfolk Archaeology*, **39**, 310–312.

Potter T, 1914 Roof coverings – thatch, in *Journal of the Society of Estate Clerks of Works*, **27**, 41–49.

Powell A H, 1923 Modern craftsmanship. 5 – Thatching, in *The Architects Journal*, **58**, 859–862.

Price U, 1794 [1871] *Essays on the Picturesque*, Farnborough.

Priest St J, 1810 *General View of the Agriculture of Buckinghamshire*, London, Richard Phillips.

Prothero R E, 1901 English agriculture in the reign of Queen Victoria, in *Journal of the Royal Agricultural Society*, **62**, 1–39.

–, 1923 *The Land and its People; Chapters in Rural Life and History*, London, Hutchinson & Co.

Prufrock, 1971 Since when were thatchers a Whitehall pressure group?, in *The Sunday Times*, 14 November.

Pullen J H, 1979 *The Production of Wheat Reed for Thatching*, unpublished ms, MAFF (ADAS) Cullompton, Devon.

Purseglove J, 1988 *Taming the Flood, A History and Natural History of Rivers and Wetlands*, Oxford, Oxford University Press with Channel Four.

Rackham O, 1980 *Ancient Woodland, its History, Vegetation and Uses in England*, London, Arnold.

–, 1986a *The History of the Countryside*, London, Dent.

–, 1986b *Marshes, Fens, Rivers and Sea* London, Dent

Ransome J A, 1843 *The Implements of Agriculture*, London, J Ridgway.

Raynes H E, 1964 *A History of British Insurance*, 2nd edn, London, Isaac Pitman & Sons.

Rea J T, 1941 *How to Estimate, being the Analysis of Builders' Prices*, 6th edn, London, Batsford.

Report of the Committee on Land Utilisation in Rural Areas, 1942 London, HMSO.

Rham W L, 1845 *The Dictionary of the Farm*, 2nd edn, London, Charles Knight & Co.

Ricauti T, 1848 *Sketches for Rustic Work*, London, Henry G Bohn.

Ridsdale F J, 1946 Thatched houses, in *The Dalesman*, **8**, 138.

Robertson A J, 1938 *A History of Alresford, Derived from Manuscript Notes by Robert Boys*, Winchester, Warren & Son.

Robinson M, & Lambrick G, 1989 Holocene alluviation and hydrology in the Upper Thames Basin, in *Nature* **308**, 809–814.

Roffey M and Cross C, 1933 *Rush-Work*, London, Pitman.

Rogers J, 1976 *In the Life of a Country Thatcher*, Modbury, Modbury Local History Society.

Rowley T (ed), 1981 *The Evolution of Marshland Landscapes, Papers Presented to A Conference Held in Oxford in December 1979*, Oxford, Oxford University Department for Extramural Studies.

Royal Commission on the Historical Monuments of England, 1987 *Houses of the North York Moors*, London, HMSO.

Royal Society for the Protection of Birds, 1994 *Reedbed management for bitterns* Sandy, RSPB.

Rudge T, 1813 *General View of the Agriculture of the County of Gloucester*, London, Richard Phillips.

Rural Industries Bureau, 1939–47, 1947–1968, 1951–62 *Annual Reports*, Salisbury, Rural Industries Bureau.

Rural Industries Bureau, 1965 *Thatching. A Report on a Survey conducted to Assess the Value of Thatching as a National Asset, on the Present State of the Craft and Factors Affecting it*, Salisbury, Rural Industries Bureau.

Salmon S C, 1964 *The Principles and Practice of Agricultural Research*, London, Leonard Hill.

Salzman L F, 1952 *Building in England Down to 1540. A Documentary History*, London, Oxford University Press

Sandon E, 1977 *Suffolk Houses. A Study of Domestic Architecture*, Woodbridge, Baron Publishing.

Seager E (ed), 1978 *The Countryman Book of Village Trades and Crafts*, Burford, The Countryman.

Seddon Q, 1989 *The Silent Revolution*, London, BBC Books.

Seymour J, 1956 St Day man carrying on almost a lost art, *West Briton*, 4 December.

Seymour J, 1984 *The Forgotten Arts*, London, Dorling Kindersley.

Smedley N, 1976 *Life and Tradition in Suffolk & North-East Essex*, London, Dent.

Snell K D M, 1985 *Annals of the Labouring Poor: Social Change and Agrarian England, 1660–1900*, Cambridge, Cambridge University Press.

Souness J R, 1992 Taighean tugha tirisdeach: The thatched houses of Tiree, in Riches A and Stell G (eds), 1992 *Materials and Traditions in Scottish Building, Essays in Memory of Sonia Hackett*, Regional & Thematic Studies **2** Edinburgh, Scottish Vernacular Buildings Working Group, 81–96.

Stanford C, 1994 *Results of Questionnaire on Thatching*, unpublished manuscript, private collection.

Staniforth A R, 1979 *Cereal Straw*, Oxford, Oxford University Press.

Stedman A R, 1960 *Marlborough and the Upper Kennet Country*, Marlborough, privately published.

Stephens W B, 1908 *Book of the Farm*, 5th edn, 3 vols, Edinburgh, William Blackwood & Sons.

Stevenson W, 1809 *General View of the Agriculture of the County of Surrey*, London, Board of Agriculture.

–, 1812 *General View of the Agriculture of the County of Dorset: with Observations on the Means of its Improvement*, London, Board of Agriculture.

Storer B, 1985 *The Natural History of the Somerset Levels* Wimborne, The Dovecote Press

Stranks C, 1990 *Warmington Remembered: A Warwickshire Village and its People, 1915–1990*, Warmington, Fir Tree.

Street A G, 1933 Thatching and thatchers, in *The Listener*, **9**, 753–4.

Strickland H E, 1812 *A General View of the Agriculture of the East Riding of Yorkshire*, York, Board of Agriculture.

Sutton A (ed), 1991 *Cotswold Tales*, Stroud, Sutton.

Sykes J D, 1981 Agriculture and science, in Mingay G E (ed), 1981 *The Victorian Countryside*, **1**, London, Routledge & Kegan Paul, 260–72.

Thacker F S, 1932 *Kennet Country*, Oxford, Basil Blackwell.

Thomas W E, 1940 Thatching in Dorset, in *Journal of the Ministry of Agriculture*, **46**, 468–472.

Tuke J, 1800 *General View of the Agriculture of the North Riding of Yorkshire*, London, Board of Agriculture.

University of East Anglia, 1991 *Socio–Economic Impact of Changes in the Quality of Thatching Reed on the Future of the Reed-Growing and Thatching Industries and on the Wider Rural Economy*, University of East Anglia, Norwich.

Vancouver C, 1808 *General View of the Agriculture of the County of Devon; with Observations on the means of its Improvement*, London, Board of Agriculture.

–, 1813 *General View of the Agriculture of Hampshire, including the Isle of Wight*, London, Board of Agriculture.

Vilmorin-Andrieux et Cie, [1880] *Les meilleurs blés. Description et culture des principales variétés de froments d'hiver et de printemps*, Paris, Vilmorin-Andrieux et Cie.

Vincent J, 1941 Harvesting the reeds, in *Country Life*, **90**, 1119.

Walker B, McGregor C and Stark G, 1996 *Thatches and Thatching Techniques. A Guide to Conserving Scottish Thatching Traditions*, Edinburgh, Historic Scotland.

Walton J, 1975 The English stone-slaters' craft, in *Folk Life*, **13**, 38–53.

Ward & Lock, 1880 *Ward & Lock's Book of Farm Management and Country Life*, London, Ward, Lock & Co.

Ward J D U, 1939 Some thatched roofs, in *Country Life*, **86**, 431.

–, 1946 The future of thatch, in *Country Life*, 20 September, 529.

–, 1960 Thatched churches of East Anglia, in *Country Life*, **128**, 1508–11.

–, 1963 Thatched churches, in *Town and Country Planning*, **31**, 226–9.

Watkins M, 1981 *The English, the Countryside and its People*, London, Elm Tree.

Watson R C and McClintock M E, 1979 *Traditional Houses of the Fylde*, Centre for North-West Regional Studies, University of Lancaster Occasional Paper **6**, Lancaster, University of Lancaster.

Wedge T, 1794 *General View of the Agriculture of the County Palatine of Chester. With Observations on the Means of its Improvement*, London, Board of Agriculture.

West R C, 1987 *Thatch: A Manual for Owners, Surveyors, Architects and Builders*, Newton Abbot, David & Charles.

Whitlock J, 1960 Thatch as thatch can, in *The Field*, 2 June, 1073.

Williams W M, 1958, *The Country Craftsman. A Study of Some Rural Crafts and the Rural Industries*, London, Routledge & Kegan Paul.

Wilson J, 1862 *British Farming. A Description of The Mixed Husbandry of Great Britain*, Adam & Charles Black, Edinburgh.

Wilson J M, 1871 *The Farmer's Dictionary; or, A Cyclopedia of Agriculture*, 2 vols, Fullarton, Edinburgh.

Wood M P, 1921 Sussex thatch, in *The Builder*, **121**, 544.

Woodforde J 1969 (1979) *The Truth About Cottages*, Routledge Kegan Paul, London.

Wood-Jones R B, 1963 *Traditional Domestic Architecture of the Banbury Region*, Manchester, Manchester University Press.

Woods S H, 1988 *Dartmoor Stone*, Exeter, Devon Books.

Woodward D (ed) 1984 *The Farming and Memorandum Books of Henry Best, of Elmswell, 1642* London, Oxford University Press.

Worgan G B, 1811 *General View of the Agriculture of the County of Cornwall*, London, Board of Agriculture.

Worlidge J, 1694 *Mr Worlidges Two Treatises: the first, of improvement of husbandry … the second, a treatise of cyder*, London.

Wright J (ed), 1905 *The English Dialect Dictionary*, 8 vols, Oxford, Henry Frowde.

Wright R P (ed), 1891 *Principles of Agriculture*, London, W G Blackie & Son.

Wrigley E A, 1988 *Continuity, Chance and Change. The Character of the Industrial Revolution in England*, Cambridge, Cambridge University Press.

Wymer N, 1946 *English Country Crafts*, London, B T Batsford

Young A, 1804a *General View of the Agriculture of Hertfordshire*, London, Macmillan.

–, 1804b *General View of the Agriculture of the County of Norfolk*, London, Macmillan.

–, 1807 *General View of the Agriculture of the County of Essex*, 2 vols, London, Macmillan.

–, 1813a *General View of the Agriculture of the County of Suffolk*, London, Macmillan.

–, 1813b *General View of the Agriculture of the County of Lincolnshire*, 2nd edn, London, Macmillan.

Young A W, & Davies D, 1990 Anatomical investigations of Common Reed Phragmites Australis (CAV) Trin. ex Steudel and Flote grass Glyceria fluitans (L.) R. Br. found in different habitats in the British Isles, in *Agricultural Progress* **65**, 12–22.

Zohary D and Hopf M, 1988 *Domestication of Plants in the Old World, the Origin and Spread of Cultivated Plants in West Asia, Europe and the Nile Valley*, Oxford, Clarendon Press.

MANUSCRIPT SOURCES

Bedfordshire Record Office
1: X362 Ledgers of John Cope
2: Microfilm of 1881 Census Enumerator's Books
3: Microfilm of 1851 Census Enumerator's Books
4: R3 2114/51 Thatching Statement, Woburn Estate, 1805

Centre for Oxfordshire Studies Sound Archive
1: Hello Ambrosden. J Simpson talks to Ted May. TX 5.L.1972.
2: Hodges, Eddie. Woodcote TX 28.4.197. Countrywise.

Cambridgeshire Record Office
1: Cowell Collection (uncatalogued)

Dorset Record Office
1: D200/2

Gloucestershire Record Office
1: D149/A9

Guildhall Library, London
Sun Life and Royal Exchange insurance policies
Insurance policies are a crucial source of data for examining the relative importance of different roofing materials in the nineteenth century. London policies were omitted for this study, the remaining policies giving a good countrywide coverage. As Jenkins remarks, 'some primarily rural counties were … well accustomed to the idea of fire insurance by the 1770s' (nd 13). There is, nevertheless, some geographical bias in the coverage. 'A brief analysis of the place index for the Sun and Royal Exchange county by county, suggests that the southern and south-eastern counties dominated the provincial business activities of both offices' (op cit, 13). The sample study thus exaggerates the prevalence of thatch as a roofing material, for it inevitably included a disproportionate number of thatched buildings from the south where thatch was much more common. The data becomes statistically less reliable as the distance from London increases, and policies from the north relate primarily to large industrial or urban buildings.

Although the polices may not accurately reflect the picture for the whole of the building stock in each county, the breadth of coverage is remarkable. 'One estimate for 1802 suggests that one third of all property in Britain, by value, was covered by fire insurance' (op cit, 11). The nature of the policies themselves ensured that most types of property are covered, for landlords insured both their own freehold properties and their tenanted buildings. Even in cases where only goods or stock were insured, the type of building in which they were housed is also recorded along with the materials used in its construction. So a single policy of, say, a local gentleman farmer might include his dwelling house, offices, stables and his tenanted farms and farm buildings, along with any urban property which could include domestic, retail, trade, and industrial buildings. A single policy might therefore cover up to 50 or 100 structures.

The 1800 sample yielded information on 4299 different buildings, while the 1862–3 policies provide details for 3585 structures.

The 1800 sample was calculated from (1) and (2); the 1862/63 sample was calculated from (3). The numbering system adopted by the offices obscures the fact that the sample is drawn from policies entered consecutively in a single volume. All examples quoted of types of thatched buildings are taken from these policies unless otherwise stated.

1: Sun Life Insurance Policies MS 11937/31 (425 sampled); Policies 699201-300; 699401-500; 699601-700; 699801-900; 701001-701100
2: Royal Exchange Series (RES) 7253, vol 38, (378 policies sampled) Policies 173558-173587, 173633-173799, 173850-173949, 174000-174099, 174130-174185.
3: Sun Life Insurance Policies MS 11937, vol 527, 1999301-1999400, 2001501-2001600, 2003701-2003800, 2004901-200500, 2008101-2008199, 2009301-2009400, 2012501-2012600, 2014701-2014800, 2016901-201700, 2020101-2020200.

Lancashire Record Office
1: DD He 62
2: DD He 110/43
3: DD He 62/710, 7/7, PO 96 PA 1751; 7/7 PO113 PA 1752

Lincolnshire Record Office
1: 2 ANC 7/15/9, G C Scott to J L Kennedy, Grimsthorpe 5 September 1847
2: YARB 5/2/17/1
3: 2 RED 4/1A/1

Local Studies Library, Wakefield
1: *Survey of the Farmhouses and Buildings belonging to Sir Edward Smith, Bart, 1819 and 1823.* John Goodchild Collection.

Northamptonshire Local Studies Library
1: box of newspaper cuttings

Northamptonshire Record Office
1: Wills of John Ayer 1781; James Hobbs 1783; William Pack 1817
2: FHT61: notes of repairs to properties at Kingsthorpe, etc, belonging to William Thornton, 1862-77
3: X4192.10
4: G4244
5: IL2413
6: G4092

North West Sound Archive
1: HA2 [no name] Oakley, Hampshire

Public Record Office
1: D4/421 Rural Industries Inquiry, 1930/1
2: MAFF 33/768
3: MAFF 33/770 6510 Executive Committee Meetings of the Rural Industries Bureau 1941–44
4: MAFF 33/770 6510 'D Straw Thatchers'
5: MAFF 33/772 6510 Thatching Instruction, Rural Industries Bureau
6: MAFF 33/772 6510 Training Arrangements
7: MAFF 113/523 Society for the Protection of Ancient Buildings Conference on housing, 1958
8: MAFF 113/522 Rural Industries Bureau Council Minutes and Papers, 1957–8
9: MAFF 113/99 XC6552
10: D1231 7 December 1966
11: MAFF 113/522 Draft of 1957–8 Rural Industries Bureau Annual Report
12: MAFF 113/98 XC6552 Minutes of Thatchers' Conference
13: D4/903 1953 survey of reed cutting
14: MAFF 113/103 Draft of 1954–5 Rural Industries Bureau Annual Report
15: D4/1200
16: MAFF 113/99 XC6552 Letter from Ruth Pollock, 26 October 1950
17: MAFF 113/523 Analysis of returns received by January 1960, to the Rural Industries Bureau's questionnaire on thatched properties
18: D4/12 7 3

Wakefield Library
1: J Goodchild Collection B/53/2

Yorkshire Archaeological Society archives
1: Bradfer-Lawrence, M335

OFFICIAL PUBLICATIONS

Parliamentary Papers (PP)

PP 1852–3, **87**. Census of Great Britain, Population Tables, II, Ages, Civil Condition, Occupations and Birth Places, vol. I.
PP 1863, **52**. Census of England and Wales, 1861, II (Pt 1), Ages, Civil Condition, Occupations and Birth Places
PP 1873, **81**. Census of England and Wales, 1871, III, Ages, Civil Condition, Occupations and Birth Places

Personal communications
Brockett, P; thatcher, instructor (Bedfordshire)
Cater, C; reed producer (Norfolk)
Cleeve, S; thatcher (Hampshire)
Cousins, J; thatcher (Suffolk)
Davis, K; thatcher (Oxfordshire)
Death, B and M J; thatchers (Suffolk)
Dodson, M and A; thatchers (Huntingdonshire)
Dodson, J; thatcher (Huntingdonshire & Devon)
Dray, M; thatcher (Devon)
Dunkley, G; thatcher (Northamptonshire)
Elston, G; thatcher (Devon & Cornwall)
Farman, D; thatcher (Norfolk)
Fuchs, A; thatcher (Dorset)
Ganly, M; farmer (Oxfordshire)
Gendall, R; Cornish linguist, (Devon)
Glover, G; historian of agricultural machinery (devon)
Godfrey, M; straw grower (Berkshire)
Goodacre, J; historian (Leicestershire)
Greenhill, G; curator (Lincolnshire)
Hall, A; archaeobotanist (Yorkshire)
Handley, T & A; rush chair makers (Oxfordshire)
Hannabuss, A; thatcher (Devon)
Haslam, S; botanist (Cambridgeshire)
Howard, A, cob builder (Devon)
Johnson, T; thatcher (Devon)
Kerrou, M; conservation officer (Northamptonshire)
Lewis, A; thatcher (Wiltshire)
Lowe, J; conservation officer (Dorset)
Miller, R, thatcher, reed dealer (Dorset)
Mustiere, N; thatcher (Brittany, France)
Norman, P; thatcher, instructor (Somerset)
Pearce, S; thatcher (Wiltshire)
Pitt-Rivers; estate owner (Dorset)
Punce, A; thatcher (Devon)
Pydyn, A; archaeologist (Oxfordshire)
Slocombe, P; building historian (Wiltshire)
Snowdon, H; farmer (Devon)
Thomas, B; art historian (Oxfordshire)
White, C; thatcher (Buckinghamshire)
White, I; straw grower (Devon)
Whiteley, T; thatcher (Dorset)
Wisbey, D; thatcher, instructor
Wright, H; thatcher (Somerset)
Wright, R; straw grower, thatcher (Somerset)